THE HOOPS

A History of Shamrock Rovers

THE
HOOPS

A History of Shamrock Rovers

PAUL DOOLAN AND ROBERT GOGGINS

GILL & MACMILLAN

Published in Ireland by
Gill & Macmillan Ltd
Goldenbridge
Dublin 8
with associated companies throughout the world

© *Paul Doolan and Robert Goggins 1993*
0 7171 2121 6
Print origination by Identikit Design Consultants
Printed by ColourBooks Ltd, Dublin

A catalogue record is available for this book
from the British Library.

1 3 5 4 2

CONTENTS

ACKNOWLEDGMENTS

We wish to acknowledge the help of the following people in the research of this book: Eddie Bailham; the late Billy Behan; Gino Brazil; George Briggs; Liam Buckley; Pat Byrne; Alan Campbell; Eamonn Carroll; John Cleary; the late Paddy Coad; Jim Conroy; Sean Creedon; Arthur Cunningham; Pat Dunne; Tommy Dunne; Peter Eccles; Tommy Eglington; Christy Fenlon; Johnny Fullam Snr; Johnny Fullam; Jimmy Gaynor; George Gregg; Podge Gregg; Liam Hennessy; Jimmy Keane; Dermot Keely; John Keogh; Louis Kilcoyne; Noel King; Mick Leech; John McCarthy; John McNamara; Tom McRann; Gerry Mackey; Tom Manning; Mick Meagan; Paddy 'Sonny' Molloy; Jackie Mooney; Ronnie Nolan; Fr Fergus O'Donoghue S.J.; Frank O'Neill; Leo O'Reilly; Sonny O'Reilly; Terry O'Rourke; Larry Palmer; Liam Power; William Reid; 'Emo' Sheeran; Martin Sheridan; Niall Scully; Liam Tuohy.

We also wish to thank the staffs of the National Library of Ireland, the *Irish Independent*, the *Irish Press*, the *Irish Times*, the *Evening Herald*, and *Sport* magazine. The old *Evening Mail* archives proved invaluable.

We also wish to thank the authors of the following books, which we found most useful: *The Gillette Book of the F.A.I. Cup* by Sean Ryan and Terry O'Rourke; *The Bass Book of Irish Soccer* by Sean Ryan and Noel Dunne; *The Book of Irish Goalscorers* by Sean Ryan and Stephen Bourke; *A Record of League of Ireland Football, 1921/22 - 1984/85* by Niall McSweeney; *The Irish Football Handbook 1992/93* by Gerry Desmond and Dave Galvin.

RINGSEND

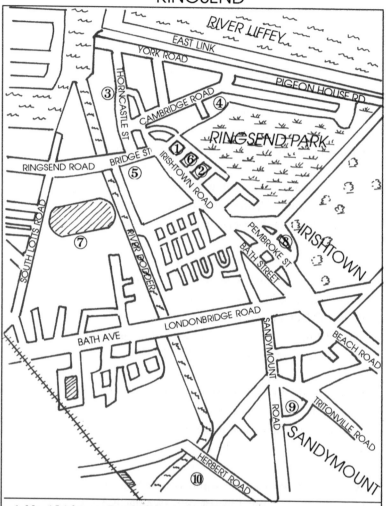

1. No. 4 Irishtown Road—home of 'Lar' Byrne. *
2. The Square, formerly Shamrock Avenue.
3. 'The Bandroom' where the clubhouse stood.
4. Ringsend Park—Rovers' first ground.
5. Beatty's Barber Shop, where Rovers were revived in 1914.
6. St Patrick's Villas—many of the players lived along here.
7. Shelbourne Park.
8. Cunninghams lived at 'Glenmalure House'.
9. Jimmy Dunne lived at Tritonville Road.
10. The Cunninghams moved to a large house.
* *First club secretary—not to be confused with Lar O'Byrne—player in later years.*

Chapter One

'A Star is Born'

(1 9 0 1 - 2 1)

The popular belief has always been that Shamrock Rovers Football Club was formed in 1899 by a Ringsend fisherman called Larry Fitzpatrick. However, it is much more likely that the club was not formed until the summer of 1901, a date generally supported by three sons of founder-members to whom we spoke.

George Gregg, whose father and uncle were founder members, maintains that he can clearly remember his father telling him that the year was indeed 1901. This view was also held by the late Billy Behan, former player, referee, football manager and long time scout for Manchester United, whose father, William Snr, was very active in the club during those early years.

'I am going on what my father told me. It is through word of mouth. I could not have proof otherwise', was Billy's comment.

Martin Sheridan, whose father John was active on the committee and later became chairman of the club, also says that Rovers were definitely formed in 1901 and not 1899. There were claims that Rovers originated when the Isle of the Sea Gaelic club disbanded in 1901. Such claims are not accurate: Rovers had already been established by the time the Gaelic club won the All-Ireland football final of 1903.

It is true, though, that several of their players later turned out for Shamrock Rovers and these included T. Doyle, L. Kelly, J. Whelan and P. Lawless.

Shamrock Rovers first registered with the Leinster Football Association at the start of the 1901/02 season and the original records, which are still intact at the LFA offices in Parnell Square, show that the first secretary of the club was Mr Lar Byrne of no. 4 Irishtown Road.

In 1903/04 the secretary was listed as Mr J. Byrne of no. 14 Thomas Street, Ringsend. He was a brother of Lar who took up the position again the following season. After that another of the Byrnes became secretary. A quarter of a century later, in 1929/30, the secretary was listed as Mr 'Ando' Byrne of no. 21 South Lotts Road, who held the position for many years.

Further proof regarding the foundation date is given in the following extract which was written by 'an old supporter' and which appeared in the programme for the Rovers versus Cork United League game which took place at Milltown on Sunday, 28 December 1941:

'It was in the year 1901 that Shamrock Rovers were first formed. The first meeting was held at no. 4 Irishtown Road, when it was decided to form a football club, but so many names were suggested that it was decided to hold this very important matter over until the next meeting. While awaiting the call of this meeting, club rooms were secured in a spot known as Shamrock Avenue, now The Square, Irishtown Road, and it was this fact that carried the motion that the club be called Shamrock Rovers Football Club.'

It was the Gregg brothers, John and Michael James, who first came up with the idea of forming the club that became known as Shamrock Rovers. These two men, along with William Saunders, William Maguire, 'Mikey' Caulfield, 'Granda' Gaffney, Archie Murphy, John Fullam and others unknown, formed the first committee.

Larry Fitzpatrick was also actively involved in the formation of the club and sat on the early committees. He was employed at the local bottle company as a glass blower but supplemented his income as a fisherman. Larry Fitzpatrick and his family lived in Pembroke Street, Irishtown. His daughter, Mary Jane, later married into the Cunningham family and made her own unique contribution to the club in later years.

The Cunningham family themselves resided in Herbert Place, off Bath Street, at that time. They remained at this house until the early 'forties when they moved to Herbert Road in Sandymount where the Sandymount High School now stands. The house which was owned by the Cunninghams at Herbert Place was later occupied by Luke Burke, a brother of Mickey Burke of 'fifties fame and a son of John Burke who came to Shamrock Rovers in the late 'twenties from Tipperary.

There was also a junior club by the name of Shamrock Celtic at the turn of the century but there was no connection between them and Shamrock Rovers.

By 1906 Shamrock Rovers had gone out of business but re-emerged in 1914 following a meeting in Sam Beatty's barber shop in Bridge Street, Ringsend. Among those present at that important meeting were: John Fullam, William Saunders, Jem Gregg, Archie Murphy (all original founder members), John Sheridan, Sam Beatty and A. E. Alpin. The same set of jerseys which had been used in 1901 were used again when they came back into existence in 1914.

Back in 1903, Shamrock Rovers' very first ground was at Ringsend Park at a spot which was known locally as 'The Clinkers'. Their pitch was close to Shamrock Avenue. Much of the park still remains but the area where Rovers trained, known as 'the short grass', has since been built over. When Rovers re-entered the Leinster Junior League in 1914/15 they also played at Ringsend Park but upon entry into the Leinster Senior League the following season they were forced to seek the use of a private ground. Shelbourne Park was engaged for the entire season with the exception of one game which was played at Ulster Park (Sandymount Road). Ringsend Park was used once more when Rovers came back into football for a third time in 1920/21 as members of the Leinster Junior League.

Rovers secured the use of a private ground at Windy Arbour in 1921/22 when they were again promoted to the Leinster Senior League. Beech Hill (Beaver Row) which was the home of Dublin United, was engaged for several major games and Rutland Avenue (Crumlin) along with Angelsea Road were used on one occasion each.

Rovers first played competitive football when they entered the Leinster Junior Cup competition for 1902/03 and got as far as the semi-finals, having disposed of Abbey and St Matthew's along the way. It took three games before St Patrick's of Inchicore defeated Rovers in the semi-final. Otherwise the club only played friendlies in its first two years but, perhaps encouraged by the cup results, entered a team into the County Dublin League for the 1903/04 season. In their first season of competitive league football they did not do particularly well but at least they held their own against more established clubs. The Rovers team which defeated Kilworth 2-1 at The Strand, Ringsend in February 1904 lined out as follows: Geoghegan, R. Donnelly, J. Keogh, W. Penston, J. Dunne, E. Keogh, Cox, Lawless, Moore, Keefe and W. Byrne. Right half Willie Penston was one of the club's earliest stars, along with his brother, 'Polo', who was a forward.

Again, as in the previous season, Rovers made it as far as the semi-final of the Leinster Junior Cup competition but were beaten 3-2 by Drogheda away.

Shamrock Rovers achieved their first major success in 1904/05 as members of the County Dublin League. The League was sponsored by the Dublin *Evening Mail* and the winners were awarded the *Evening Mail* Cup. Rovers sailed unbeaten through their League campaign to win the title. The major step to the title was taken when they beat their nearest rivals, Cabra, by 3-0 at Ringsend.

On Saturday, 3 December 1904, Rovers met Reginald II in the second round of the Leinster Junior Cup. When the sides had met in the League a month earlier Rovers had won by the odd goal in five. The previous season, 1903/04, Shamrock Rovers had beaten Reginald I in the Leinster Junior Cup. On this occasion the newspaper correspondent criticised Rovers for ungentlemanly conduct because one of their players had said 'put the boot in, Rovers' and he felt that the referee should have sent this player off! The game ended in a thrilling 4-4 draw. Rovers won the replay and having disposed of Richmond Wanderers in the next round they went on to meet Botanic in the semi-final which was held on Saturday, 18 March 1905.

'Shamrock Rovers draw with Botanic', read the headline in the *Evening Mail*, which by now was devoting three columns to association football each Monday. The report also stated:

'There was great excitement in Ringsend when Shamrock Rovers met Botanic to decide which should go into the final of the Leinster Junior Cup. The playing pitch was laid out in great style, well roped in goal nets, even a table and seats for the press representatives. They may be a bit rough down Ringsend way but whenever they take a thing to hand they can carry it out right well.

With a free gate and a crowd of about 3,000 people present the way they managed to keep everything in good order was a credit to the club and an example to many other clubs that are better circumstanced.

The only drawback was the hardness of the ground and the absence of games on it - matters that the committee, of course, were powerless to remedy.

The result of the match, a draw with two goals each, was just as it should be. Further to preserve the equality, both sides scored from a penalty. With a little luck Rovers might have won. They began well but finished weakly, the pace evidently was too much for them. Botanic felt a bit strange on the hard ground, especially the forwards. They began to find their feet near the finish of the game.

For the home team Geoghegan in goal was very safe and did everything he was called upon to do in an able manner. The full backs, J. Keogh and Cleary, completely upset all the efforts of the opposing forwards, seldom letting them get within shooting distance of goal. Of the halves, W. Penston was easily the best, playing a grand game all through, both in defence and attack. The other two halves, Cox and E. Keogh, played well but suffered in comparison with Penston. The great fault of the forwards was that in their anxiety to score they were continually getting offside, especially Dunne and this lost several chances. They all played a hard game but the best effort of the match was the centre by Keefe from the corner which led up the scoring of the second goal.'

It spoke very highly for Rovers that, as a junior club, they were able to make such a fine fight of it with a team that was lying second in the second division of the Leinster Junior League. Not only that, they went on to win the tie, but not without a struggle. It took three games more to settle the issue, Rovers winning the fourth game 3-1. Fullam gave Rovers a 1-0 lead at half-time, Veldon put Botanic back on level terms after the interval but goals from M. Penston and Keefe secured a place for Rovers in the final. Dundalk beat Trojans in the other semi-final.

A record crowd for a junior game attended Dalymount Park on 22 April for the final, a game that effectively brought the curtain down on the junior soccer season. At the start of the season Shamrock Rovers had been virtually unheard of; by now, in late April, they had made their mark.

Willie Penston captained the Rovers team who had an early let off after Dundalk missed a penalty. The game was evenly balanced although at times Dundalk applied some heavy pressure. But they could not get behind a sound Rovers defence. It was scoreless at half-time; after the restart it was Rovers who put their opponents under pressure. Then Dundalk should have scored before the deadlock was finally broken when Sheridan scored from a corner to give Rovers the lead. Then with ten minutes to go, heavy pressure by Rovers saw the Dundalk 'keeper, Hall, put his side further behind when he fisted the ball into the back of his own net. Rovers looked home and dry but from a breakaway Thomas got one back for Dundalk. Too late. Shamrock Rovers had done enough to capture the Leinster Junior Cup in their first real competitive season. The Rovers team on that historic occasion was: Geoghegan, Cleary, Keogh, (J), W. Penston, Cox, Keogh (E), Keefe, Sheridan, Moore, 'Polo' Penston, Whelan.

Later that week the committee of Shamrock Rovers lodged a claim for expenses of two pounds to the Leinster Football Association for the trouble of having to bring players from various places for the final. They also claimed for a bottle of brandy which they bought for the players after the match but were laughed out of the chamber. Their letter stood as having been read.

After that triumphant end to the 1904/05 season the club went from strength to strength and entered the Leinster Junior League the following season winning the title in their first season of membership. The Leinster Junior Cup came to Ringsend for the second successive season when Rovers beat the Royal Irish Fusiliers by 4-3 in the final at Dalymount Park. The report for the game noted that it was 'an excellent game' and 'Polo' Penston, playing as a half back, scored a penalty and came in for particular mention. John Sheridan, father of Martin, played in this game. Martin still has the medal which his father won that day.

The Shamrock Rovers players received the first gold medals struck by the Leinster Football Association for winning the Junior Cup. Other players whose worthy contribution was noted in that game were: Val Fullam (brother of Bob), Tommy Whelan, 'Kit' Moore (a half back), Charlie Cox in the centre, Tommy 'Baller' Lawless on the right wing and a player by the surname of Oliver.

That season Rovers made it into the semi-final of the Irish Junior Cup and drew 1-1 with Sligo St Mary's. They were beaten 1-0 in the replay, though, which took place at Serpentine Avenue which was then the home ground of Shelbourne AFC.

On 26 August 1906, Shamrock Rovers were admitted to the senior ranks of what is known today as the Leinster Senior League. The first League tie was given as a home game against Reginald and this was due to take place on 15 September. Before that, a number of friendlies were arranged including one against Shelbourne's 'B' side. Rovers had great difficulty in getting a team out and had to take to the field without Keogh, Oliver, the Penston brothers and Phil Cleary. Their popular secretary, Lar Byrne, went into goal and they began the game with only nine men, only later managing to bring the number up to eleven. The exercise was proof, however, that Rovers were going to struggle that season despite the fact that they now had a second team which had been entered in the Leinster Junior League. And sure enough, before the season got under way, Shamrock Rovers were forced to inform the Leinster League that they would be unable to participate in the senior ranks as they could not find a suitable ground.

Rovers always had problems in fielding a full team for away fixtures. To travel to the Phoenix Park from Ringsend at that time was in itself a major journey with transport consisting of cycling or a lift on a horse and cart. It was not long before problems began to arise with the Junior League team too. After Rovers failed to send out a team for four weeks in a row they were replaced by the Army Service Corps.

Rovers remained dormant until 1914 when they re-entered the Leinster Junior League once more. After they had gone out of business in 1906, many of the players and club members kept together by associating with a club called St Patrick's which played in the Sunday Leagues, which were not officially recognised by the Leinster Football Association.

Their first competitive game of the 1914/15 season was against Avonmore on 16 September in the Phoenix Park. As before, the home ground of Shamrock Rovers was listed as Ringsend Park. From an early stage in the season Rovers looked good. They drew 1-1 with Avonmore and defeated Jacobs 3-1 in their second game at Ringsend Park. By the end of the season they had brought the Leinster Junior League title to Ringsend for the second time in the history of the club, without a single defeat in the process. The other teams in the League then were: Avonmore, Bohemians 'D', Jacobs, Clarence II, SPD, Kilworth, Richmond Asylum, Marlboro, Adare and Seaview United.

In the Leinster Junior Cup the club received a bye in the first round, beat Adare in the second round, beat Portarlington in the third round and qualified to meet Orwell in the semi-final at the 'Thatch'. It was reported that 'a procession of cars brought nearly all of Ringsend to the "Thatch".' Both teams started the game with an unbeaten record that season but it ended in a 3-0 victory for Rovers. Peter Lawless was in his best form and scored two of the goals; George Lamond got the other. Lar Kelly had a great game at full back and Billy Nagle was very safe in goal.

The final of the Leinster Junior Cup was played at Shelbourne Park and ended scoreless. Meathville provided the opposition and they won the replay by 2-1. A newspaper report noted at the time that 'the familiar name of Penston is still sometimes seen on the Rovers team while Lar Kelly and Lawless still remain. But Cleary, Geoghegan, Doyle, Cox, Sheridan, Whelan and Oliver are all retired. They did their part by winning the Mail Cup and Junior Cup in 1904/05 and Junior League and Junior Cup in 1905/06.'

As finalists of the Leinster Junior Cup Shamrock Rovers qualified for the first round of the Leinster Senior Cup and were drawn against Bohs. The game took place at Dalymount Park on Saturday, 9 January 1915. Bohs won 3-0, Ned Brooks snatching a hat trick and although Rovers did not do too well in this, the very first meeting between the sides, there were to be many more exciting encounters between them in the years to follow. The Rovers team that day was: W. Nagle, W. Smith, P. O'Hagan, L. Bissett, C. Dunne, L. Kelly, P. Lawless, L. Brazil, G. Lamond, Bradley and B. Nolan.

There was success in the All Ireland Irish Junior Cup, however. The first round was an away tie to Avonmore on 28 November which ended 1-1 with Rovers winning the replay 1-0 the following Saturday at Ringsend Park. The second round on 12 December saw Rovers record an impressive 8-1 victory against Jacobs at Rutland Avenue. In the next round a scoreless draw was played with Orwell at Shelbourne Park but the tie did not go to a replay as Rovers lodged a protest and were successful. Victories against Dundalk Great Northern Railway at Ulster Park in Sandymount and the Great Southern & Western Railway at Inchicore saw Shamrock Rovers through to the semi-final where a win against Cliftonville Strollers brought them to the final against Derry Swifts.

The final was staged at Ulster Park and as there was a clash of colours Rovers agreed to change and appeared in the unusual colours of green shirts and red collars. Ben Nolan scored the only goal of the game to give Shamrock Rovers victory and their first national trophy. In winning this game Rovers became only the third side south of the Boyne to win this cup, the others being Reginald and Chapelizod.

In 1915/16 Shamrock Rovers entered the Leinster Senior

9

League and their first game took place at Shelbourne Park against Strandville on Saturday, 17 September 1915, almost nine years to the day since their first abortive entry. Strandville won 3-2. All the scoring was done in the first half, Sullivan and Stafford (2) scoring for Strandville and A. Byrne and Gannon for Shamrock Rovers. 'The winners were rather lucky to take away the points', stated the *Evening Mail*. The Rovers team that day was: Nagle, O'Hagan, Darling, L. Bissett, O. Bissett, Kelly, Lawless, Murphy, J. Byrne, Nolan and A. Byrne.

The first meeting between Rovers and St James's Gate took place on Saturday, 9 October at Dolphins Barn with the 'Gate' winning 2-0. After eight games in the league Rovers had won only two, drawn one and lost five, a pattern which was to continue for the rest of the season. When Rovers and Bohs met on 11 December at Shelbourne Park victory went to Bohs by 2-0. The game was very badly attended as most Rovers supporters thought the result a foregone conclusion: Bohs were leading the League table at the time. The following week Shelbourne were hosts to Rovers at Shelbourne Park in a game which finished 1-1. Only a few dozen supporters attended a game in which Rovers failed to field a full team, starting with only seven men and eventually mustering ten. By the end of the season Shamrock Rovers finished near the bottom of the League table.

There was to be no success in cup competitions either. Having disposed of Ulster and then Frankfurt in the Leinster Senior Cup, Rovers lost to Shelbourne in the semi-final at Shelbourne Park. In the Irish Intermediate Cup they beat St James's Gate 'B' in the first round and then eliminated Strandville in the next round but lost out to Frankfurt in the third round, missing out on a place in the semi-final in the process.

As the 1916/17 season got under way Shamrock Rovers delivered a shock to the Leinster Senior League when they informed the League in writing that they were disbanding the club due to the fact that they could not secure a ground. Trojans were elected to the First Division in their place.

The club did however remain in existence but played only

exhibition and friendly games until 1920/21 when they rejoined the Leinster Junior League.

In August 1921, a meeting was held at which the Football League of Ireland was established and a number of vacancies became available in the Leinster Senior League. Rovers, a much better organised outfit now, were one of the successful applicants. A complete re-organisation of the club took place. For the first time a private ground was secured by the committee, a matter which had proved to be a huge stumbling block for Rovers in the past. Club rooms were secured in Thorncastle Street, Bob Fullam joined from Shelbourne and under his captaincy success soon followed.

On 24 September 1921, Rovers played their first League game of the season against Richmond at Grangegorman and enjoyed a comfortable win with John Joe Flood scoring five goals.

The other teams in the Leinster League Division One that season were: St James's Gate 'B', Bohemians 'B', Bray Unknowns, Midland Athletic, Brooklyn, Shelbourne United, Merrion, Glasnevin, CYMS, Pioneers and Richmond.

After seven games Rovers led the table with seven wins, thirty-one goals for and only five against. The club had not yet played in the hooped jerseys and therefore the nickname 'Hoops' did not apply. Sometimes they were referred to as 'Rock' for short. Although they now had their own ground in Windy Arbour it was not always available to them or was unplayable. Often they had to concede home advantage. One such case was on 11 February 1922 when Rovers played Merrion at Angelsea Road (where the tennis club is now). Playing their home games away from home did not affect the team, though, and on this occasion they won 5-0 with the goals coming from Flood (2), Bob Cowzer, Bob Fullam and Charlie Campbell.

It proved the most successful season for Shamrock Rovers so far. The Leinster Senior League title was won and a run in the FAI Cup which brought the club all the way to the final (this episode is dealt with in detail in the section entitled 'The Path of the Cup', page 31).

In the first round of the Cup, which was confined to non-League of Ireland clubs, Rovers beat UCD by six goals to two at Windy Arbour. Victories against Tipperary Wanderers, St James's Gate 'B' and Shelbourne United saw Rovers through to the first round proper where they disposed of League of Ireland side, Olympia. Victory against another senior side, Dublin United, was recorded in the next round before Rovers caused the shock of the season by defeating Bohemians in the semi-final at Dalymount Park.

Considering the association which Shamrock Rovers were to establish with the FAI Cup in the coming decades it was probably fitting that, even as a non-League side, they should have competed in the inaugural FAI Cup final. Only League of Ireland champions, St James's Gate, stood between Rovers and a famous achievement but after a replay the 'Gate' won the Cup. It was enough, though, to convince the committee of Shamrock Rovers that the time was right to enter into the Football League of Ireland. The wisdom of that decision has been proved correct over and over again: Rovers quickly established themselves as Ireland's top club, bringing the League title to Milltown on a record fourteen occasions and the FAI Cup a record twenty-four times. In addition to that there have been many many other honours; every trophy that was ever competed for in the League of Ireland came to Milltown at some stage or other.

That it was only a matter of time before Shamrock Rovers entered the big time became more evident from the way Rovers organised their game against St James's Gate in the second round of the Leinster Senior Cup. In 1921/22 Rovers had earned a place in the second round by eliminating Chapelizod in the previous round.

Although they were beaten 5-2 by the 'Gate' Rovers earned themselves praise for the arrangements they had made for the game which was staged at Beech Hill, Donnybrook. A crowd in excess of 6,000 was accommodated in a comfortable manner, no mean achievement for a junior club.

By 1921/22 the club had come a long way from the early days

of Shamrock Avenue. Committee meetings were now held in a Corporation owned property called the Bandroom which was situated in Thorncastle Street (a block of flats now stands on the site where the Bandroom was situated). It was so called because first a brass band and then a fife and drum band, used to practise there. The players used the hall to change their gear on Tuesdays and Thursdays, as it was only a short distance from Ringsend Park where they trained in the winter time under gaslight.

It was in the Bandroom that the committee ran fundraising events including the illegal card game 'house'. On one occasion they were surprised by the Dublin Metropolitan Police and the committee members were hauled off to jail. However, they received only a small fine each and the business of the club continued.

Billy Behan, who was born in 1911 and died after a brief illness in 1991, had great memories of Shamrock Rovers.

'My own earliest memories of Rovers go back to the early 'twenties when I used to go to the matches with Bob Fullam who was my cousin. I was only about twelve at that time. I can remember before that when Bob was playing for Shelbourne and he used to go up to the North every second week. Bob then left Shels to join Rovers when they came into the Leinster Senior League. I can remember very well when they got into the final of the FAI Cup and played St James's Gate when they were beaten 1-0 in the replay.'

When Shamrock Rovers were elected to the Leinster Senior League in 1921/22 it was necessary to acquire a private ground. This they managed to do when they secured the use of a field in the Windy Arbour area of Dublin.

The land belonged to a local farmer by the name of Bernard Rogan. It was previously used by Mr Rogan for farming purposes but he had since given up farming and confined his business to his grocery. This ground was known locally as 'Rogan's Field'.

Of course, Dundrum was quite some distance from Ringsend/Irishtown, especially with no public transport available at that time, and the club was forced to look for a ground nearer to the city. Milltown was an acceptable location as it was not too great a distance from where the majority of Rovers supporters were based.

On 7 September 1923, a rental agreement was drawn up between the Jesuit Community and Shamrock Rovers FC. For the Jesuits the signatories were Rev. Fr Finlay and Rev. Fr O'Dwyer. For the club secretary Lawrence (Lar) Byrne and Andrew Byrne signed. Committee member 'Mikey' Dunne, brother of Jimmy who became famous in later years, was also influential in acquiring this ground. It was agreed that Rovers would pay £75 a year for the use of this field which was known as 'Elm Park'. The landlords kept the right to 'graze horses, cattle and sheep' while the tenants agreed to 'ensure that there was no damage to trees, hedges or gates'.

This ground was not the famous Milltown, however, but was adjacent to it. Billy Behan remembered it well:

'They moved to Milltown to a pitch which was at the back of the last ground which they had there. You actually walked over that last ground to get to the original pitch, you went up a laneway which was located along the wall where the garage is now and the pitch was just up at the back of that. Then they got the second ground and all the Ringsend men went up and helped to build it up. It was a real Ringsend club.'

It was in 1926 that Rovers moved to a new ground in the same vicinity, the ground later known as 'Glenmalure Park'. This was also leased from the Jesuits. Initially, a nine-year lease was agreed at an annual rent of £130.

When this lease came up for renewal it emerged that Rovers were in financial difficulties and were £145 in arrears. It was proposed that the old Shamrock Rovers company be taken over by Mr Joe Cunningham and that a new company be set up.

Mr Cunningham asked that time be given for this to come about and Rev. Fr Hannon suggested that this should be accepted as he knew Mr Cunningham well and considered him to be of good character. That was not to be the end of the matter, though, and further developments were to follow within a short time.

In August, 1935, the Jesuits were advised by their solicitors, John J. McDonald and Co., that Rovers were not strong financially and that Mr Cunningham and the trustees of the club should personally guarantee the rent. The Hoops agreed to this.

By 1936 the club were still experiencing deep financial difficulties. They owed £136. 3. 4 on the old lease and £398. 13. 4 on the new one. The Jesuits agreed to accept the arrears in instalments whenever Rovers could pay and also reduced the annual rent from £155 to £100.

In the meantime Rovers managed to pay off most of their debts as matters improved in the League of Ireland and a letter was sent by Andrew Byrne, Secretary, to the Rector, Fr C. J. Power to the effect that: 'I am asked by the Directors of Shamrock Rovers to convey their deep appreciation for the very generous treatment given to them in connection with the above matter.' All correspondence between the two organisations was conducted through their respective solicitors.

Before the Cunninghams acquired complete control of Shamrock Rovers the club was partly financed by the committee members and general members who owned shares. At one stage in the 'twenties when Shamrock Rovers experienced a severe cash flow crisis they were helped out by several locals including Maggie Dunne. She was the daughter of a founder member, 'Mikey' Caulfield, and was a fruit and vegetable stallholder who was also allowed to operate a sweet stall at Milltown for many years in return for her financial assistance.

When looking back at those early years of Shamrock Rovers the contribution of certain families in the Ringsend district to the development of the club was outstanding. These included the Greggs (of which the present Eamonn and Jimmy are descendants), the Fullams and the Caulfields (to which referee Michael Caulfield is related).

There have been other family connections too through the

years. Mick and Jim Maguire who played in the late 'twenties were sons of founder member William Maguire. Brothers Jimmy and Eamonn Gregg played for Rovers in the 'seventies: their great uncles, 'Jemmer' and John were original founder members.

There were other Greggs too who played for the Hoops. 'Oden' Gregg was on the 1924/25 team and Podge, an uncle of Eamonn and Jimmy (and a brother of George Gregg) was with Rovers in the 'forties.

Billy Behan had two spells with Rovers during the 'thirties and his brothers John and Paddy also played. Billy's son, William jnr, kept goal for Rovers reserve side for a spell.

Tommy 'Netler' Doyle, a centre-forward in the 'thirties, was a younger brother of Dinny Doyle and an uncle of Jackie Mooney of 'sixties fame. Tommy's great grandson, Jason, appeared for Rovers during the 1991/92 season. Tommy and Dinny's father, Tommy 'Nettle', was a member of the Rovers team which won the Leinster Junior League in 1905/06.

Fathers and sons at the club over the years include Jimmy Dunne and son Tommy, Paddy Henderson and his son Dave both of whom kept goal for the Hoops, John 'Tipp' Burke and his son Mickey, Mick and Mark Meagan, Mattie Clarke and son Jackie, John Giles and his sons Michael and Christopher, John 'Kit' Lawlor and sons Mick, Martin and Robbie and Gerry Mackey whose son, Dave, played with the Hoops' reserves during the early 'eighties.

By the mid 'thirties Rovers had a very strong social club which involved activities such as tennis, croquet, billiards and cards. When the club applied for a Sports Club Licence there were protests from the Pioneer Total Abstinence Association objecting to the possibility of a bar being opened at Milltown. Later on, other activities such as professional boxing and wrestling were considered by the committee at Glenmalure Park in order to ease the financial difficulties.

While Shamrock Rovers enjoyed a friendly relationship with the Jesuit Community not all of their proposals to put Glenmalure Park to better use were acceptable to the landlords. Yet, matters were always sorted out in an amicable fashion even if it meant that Rovers would lose financially as a result.

In 1941, the club then proposed a plan which involved the acquiring of a sizeable bank loan on the condition that they could acquire a long-term lease. This presented problems as the matter would no longer be dealt with on a local basis alone. The Jesuit Community would have to seek permission from a higher authority in Rome. As it turned out Rovers accepted a new lease of six years at £155 rent per year. By 1955 the annual rent on the lease was running at £300 and rates due to Dublin Corporation amounted to £270.

By 1956 Rovers proposed installing floodlights at Glenmalure Park but the Jesuits voiced their disapproval and the matter was dropped. However, when the issue was raised again in 1960 the Rector, Fr Corboy S.J. agreed to the proposal on the conditions that the number of games played under lights would be limited to twelve per season and that music would not be played at evening games. The plan to install floodlights never came to anything further during the Cunninghams' reign at the club.

When the ground was revalued in 1963 it was suggested by Thos. Dockrell & Sons, Auctioneers, that separate rent should be charged on the pitch and on the buildings which were contained on the site. A rental of £525 per year was suggested but in a letter to their solicitors the Jesuit Community settled for £450 on the basis that 'relations between Milltown Park [the Jesuit house] and Shamrock Rovers have always been good' and that 'the Jesuits did not want to appear to be too exigent in the matter of rent.'

By 1969 the rent had increased to £750, due mainly to the much higher rates which the Jesuits had to pay to Dublin Corporation on their own lands.

In a letter from Brian Kirby, Solicitors, on behalf of SRFC which was sent to John J. McDonald & Co. in 1972 the Cunninghams stated that 'the older members of the family are now unable to attend to the business of running the club and the younger members find that through ill-health and preoccupation with their own business they likewise cannot give it sufficient attention.'

It was stated that another family, namely the Kilcoynes, would take over the running of the club and that some of the Cunningham family would remain as shareholders. The reply from Rev. Fr Patrick Doyle S.J. stated that Rovers 'should act as suggested'.

When the Kilcoyne family pulled Rovers out of Glenmalure Park in 1987 the Hoops were in the fourth year of a sixteen-year lease. Ironically, that was the longest ever agreed between the Jesuit Community and Shamrock Rovers FC.

After 1936 the Cunningham family gradually began to gain full control of Shamrock Rovers. Joe Cunningham Snr originally came from Clonmel in Co. Tipperary while his wife, Mary Jane, came from Ringsend. Mary Jane was the daughter of Larry Fitzpatrick, so her connection with Rovers went back to the very start.

Joe Cunningham was associated with Glenmalure, Co. Wicklow, where his mother once lived and the family home in Irishtown was named 'Glenmalure' in honour of this fact. That house, which was located in Herbert Place off Bath Street, had been built by the Cunninghams themselves.

Originally Rovers' second ground at Milltown was known as Milltown Park but this did not please the Jesuits as this was the name given by them to their own property and they did not wish it to be thought that they were responsible for organising the sports fixtures which took place at Rovers' ground.

After discussions between the parties it was decided to establish a separate identity for Rovers' ground and eventually the name 'Glenmalure Park' was decided upon, the 'Glenmalure' coming from the Cunninghams' Irishtown residence.

Joe Cunningham worked as a clerk in the well-known Dublin department store, Lee's, but later became one of Ireland's better-known turf accountants. Mary Jane was as active in the club as her husband and took on such duties as signing on players. In fact, Mary Jane's role was unique then and even now would still be so regarded.

The couple married in 1915 and had three sons and four

daughters. All three sons, Joe Jnr, Des and Arthur later became directors of the club as did one daughter, Margaret. Joe Jnr, became involved in the running of the club in 1957. Des and Margaret began their involvement in 1961 while Arthur became involved in 1967.

In 1972 the Cunningham family sold out their interests to the Kilcoynes who, in turn, retained control of the club up to July 1988.

SPOTLIGHT ON DINNY DOYLE

Denis 'Dinny' Doyle was a member of the very first Shamrock Rovers side to win the League of Ireland title in the 1922/23 season. A native of Ringsend, he was a son of Tommy 'Nettle' Doyle who himself had played for Shamrock Rovers in the very early years.

Dinny started out as a left-half with a junior side called Queen's Park but played at outside left for Rovers in the FAI Cup final of 1922 when they lost to St James's Gate after a replay. After the 1922/23 season Dinny reverted from a place in the forward line to the defence and occupied the centre-half berth until he left Rovers in 1927.

With Shamrock Rovers Dinny Doyle won three League medals having assisted them to the title in 1922/23, 1924/25 and 1926/27. He also won one FAI Cup medal as a member of the team which beat Shelbourne in the final of 1925. Dinny was on the teams which were FAI Cup runners-up in 1922 and 1926 (against Fordsons).

He won one cap with the Irish senior international team. That was on the occasion of Ireland's first international game which was against Italy in Turin in March 1926.

His younger brother, Tommy 'Netler' Doyle also played for Shamrock Rovers after Dinny had left the club. A nephew of theirs, Jackie Mooney, was a member of the successful Rovers' side of the 'sixties.

In 1927 Dinny went to the United States along with Bob Fullam to pursue a career in soccer there. When Bob came home a year later Dinny decided to stay on and he had spells with clubs there such as Philadelphia Irish, Fall River, New York and Brooklyn St Mary's Celtic.

In September 1990, a live link-up between Philip Green of RTE Radio in Donnybrook and Dinny Doyle at his home in St Catherine's, near Niagara Falls in Canada was arranged to coincide with Shamrock Rovers' inaugural game at the RDS, which was against St Patrick's Athletic. Dinny, the oldest surviving former Rovers player at the age of ninety, spoke fondly of the Hoops and departed with the following words: 'I wish them all the luck in the world because they were very good to me.'

CHAPTER TWO

THE FOUR FS

(1 9 2 2 - 2 8)

In the early years Shamrock Rovers enjoyed massive support as the game of Association Football grew throughout the country.

Around that time players appearing for Shamrock Rovers received around one pound (twenty shillings) per game or thirty shillings for a cup game.

Johnny Fullam, a lifelong Rovers supporter and a first cousin of Bob Fullam, attended his first game in the 1922/23 season when he went to Milltown to watch Rovers against Athlone Town. He recalled that the Rovers' team that day was as follows: Billy Nagle (in goal), Peter 'Wheaser' Warren, Jim Kelly, 'Sacky' Glen, Dinny Doyle, Joe 'Buller' Byrne, Charlie Campbell, Bob Fullam, Harry Birdthistle, Bob Cowzer and John Joe Flood. Sacky Glen had come into the team the season before having previously been with Shelbourne. Jim Kelly was the All-Ireland handball champion. Rovers began their first ever League of Ireland campaign with a 1-0 defeat at home by Shelbourne United on Saturday, 16 September 1922. The following week they recorded a 5-1 victory against Pioneers at Strand Road, Clontarf. They did not look back after that and were to complete a twenty-one-game unbeaten run which brought the League title to Milltown in only their very first season in the League. They scored 77 goals in the process, a record which still stands.

For the first couple of seasons Rovers had to play all their home games involving Shelbourne and Bohemians on their opponents' grounds. The first such 'home' game was against Bohemians on 14 October 1922 when Rovers travelled across the city and recorded a 2-0 victory at Dalymount Park.

The following report appeared in the *Irish Independent*:

'The League of Ireland competition has provided no greater surprise than Saturday's defeat of Bohemians by Shamrock Rovers which took place by arrangement at Dalymount Park. A good company proved what witnessed to be a disappointing exhibition in so much as the game was spoiled by the tactics adopted by the winners who paid little attention to the rules of the game and relied on getting goals by the quickest route.

Shamrock Rovers won by two clear goals but this result does not give any idea of the run of the game. For three-quarters of the ninety minutes they were outplayed and were on the defensive. The light inside forwards of Bohemians however could make heavier opponents [sic] and their shooting left much to be desired, being for the most part weak and wild.'

A couple of vigorous rushes led to Rovers' goals. Fullam opened the scoring early in the game with Fagan getting a second after the interval.

After thirteen games of the Championship had been played Rovers and Shels were neck and neck at the top of the table. Bohs were in third place while the champions of the previous season, St James's Gate, had declined considerably.

The biggest win for Rovers that season was the defeat of Midland Athletic at Milltown on 3 March. Rovers won 9-1; their scorers were John Joe Flood (4), Willie Egan (2), Bob Fullam, Bob Cowzer and Ned Marlowe. At the end of the season Rovers had five points to spare over their nearest rivals, Shelbourne, whom they beat 7-2 in the last game.

The Leinster Senior Cup was won for the first time too when Rovers beat Bohs 3-1 in the final at Dalymount Park on 7 April.

The following season, 1923/24, Rovers slumped and finished seventh in the League. They were beaten by Bohs in the first round of the FAI Cup but did make it to the semi-final of the Leinster Senior Cup against Shelbourne. This was the first Leinster Cup semi-final to be staged at Dalymount Park. Although the game ended in a 2-2 draw it was poor fare for the crowd of 7,000. Shelbourne won the replay by 3-1 with only a small crowd present due to heavy snow. Willie O'Shea, the Rovers centre-forward, got their only goal.

Saturday, 15 March 1924, saw Rovers beat St James's Gate 8-0 in a Shield game at Dolphin's Barn but despite this and some other good results the Shield did not come to Milltown that season. (The Shield was the then equivalent of today's League Cup and was played for on a League basis.)

The following season saw the return of Bob Fullam from Leeds, John Joe Flood from Shelbourne and John 'Kruger' Fagan who had won a League medal with Rovers in 1922/23. Thus emerged the 'Four Fs' in the Rovers forward line completed by Billy 'Juicy' Farrell who had joined the previous season. The new-look forward line also included Charlie 'Spid' Jordan and it was to be instrumental in bringing glory to the club on a scale not previously witnessed.

Rovers went through that 1924/25 championship undefeated and thus became the first side in the brief history of the Free State League to win the title twice. They beat Shelbourne in the FAI Cup final at Dalymount Park and succeeded in bringing the Shield to Milltown for the first time. The League clubs did not participate in the Leinster Senior Cup that season so Rovers went through the whole season unbeaten. They proved that they were the best side in the whole country when they beat Glentoran 2-0 in Belfast for the unofficial title of 'Champions of All Ireland'.

After five games of the League, Rovers and Shels were tied at the top of the table with nine points each, and Bohemians, Champions from the previous season, had six points. Bohs and Rovers met in the League game on 11 October at Dalymount Park where Fullam scored for Rovers in a 1-1 draw.

Their next League game was at home to Fordsons and the old Milltown ground was uncomfortably crowded for the visit of the Corkmen. If Rovers were to continue to be successful and attract huge crowds then a more suitable ground would have to be found. Already the city of Dublin had two excellent grounds in Shelbourne Park and Dalymount Park and Shamrock Rovers would have to follow suit.

The return game between Bohs and Rovers was at Dalymount Park on 13 December where a crowd of 7,000 witnessed a dull 1-1 draw. Murray scored for Bohs before Farrell equalised for Rovers. The Rovers team that day was: P. M. O'Reilly, P. Malone, A. Kirkland, W. Glen, D. Doyle, E. Marlowe, C. Jordan, J. J. Flood, W. Farrell, R. Fullam and J. Fagan. In those days teams played a regular 2-3-5 formation. The title race remained very close right up the end with Rovers and Shels in joint second place with 27 points and Bohs in front with a point more. However, Rovers had a game in hand and a 3-0 victory away to Bray Unknowns secured the title for the Milltown outfit.

The second-last League game against Shelbourne on St Stephen's Day was staged at Shelbourne Park despite it being a home game for Rovers. The Milltown ground would never have been able to hold the crowd of over 17,000 which was a new record for a Free State League game, as were gate receipts of £500. With the title within their grasp Rovers put in a determined fight and the game ended 1-1. Doran scored for Shels shortly after the interval and the equaliser was secured for Rovers by their tiny forward John 'Kruger' Fagan. Fagan, who hailed from the Markets area of Dublin, was only 5' 1¾" tall but yet struck fear into opposing defences.

Rovers looked as though they might retain the title in 1925/26. In the League game away to Shelbourne on 10 October a crowd of 15,000 packed Shelbourne Park and saw Shels win a match that launched them on the way to that season's League title.

Bob Cowzer, who had left Rovers to join Shels, returned to the club in October 1925, and scored twice in the 10-2 win against Pioneers at Milltown, playing on the right wing in the absence of Jordan. When Rovers beat Bohs by 4-1 at Dalymount Park the following week a crowd of over 6,000 attended the fixture.

In the meantime, the Cork side, Fordsons, had hopes themselves of taking the title that season and so great was the interest in the southern capital for the game against Rovers that the tie had to be switched from Ballinlough to the Mardyke rugby ground. A crowd of over 15,000 turned up for the game which saw victory go to Rovers with a goal each from Farrell and Cowzer. Only a defeat by Bohs at Milltown on St Stephen's Day prevented Rovers of at least a play-off for the title and the chance to win the League for the third time.

Shelbourne also won the Shield that season while Rovers were joint runners-up along with Bohs. The Ringsend rivalry between Shels and Rovers was at its best around this time with Rovers inflicting the only defeat on their rivals in the Shield and Shels knocking Rovers out of the Leinster Senior Cup at the semi-final stage. So great was the rivalry between Shels and Rovers that members of the same families were known to fall out with each other.

The 1926/27 season saw Rovers equal their own record of two years beforehand by going through the League campaign undefeated. This was the season in which they moved to Glenmalure Park and in which they appeared in the green and white hoops for the first time.

That season saw the emergence of local boy David 'Babby' Byrne who scored seventeen goals on the way to the League title and the arrival of Joseph 'Lye' Golding, an outside right from Brideville.

The season began well with a 3-0 victory against rivals Shelbourne followed up by a 3-2 win against St James's Gate at Richmond Road (Tolka Park). This was, in fact, a Rovers home game but was played at the northside venue as the new ground at Milltown was not yet ready for use. Perhaps the huge following and enthusiasm generated by the Rovers' supporters could only have been matched by those of Fordsons. The League game between the two sides on 5 September attracted a crowd of over 10,000.

Like the corresponding fixture the season before, the game was held at the Mardyke. The visit by Rovers to Cork was long awaited as a keen rivalry between the two sides existed, particularly so after Fordsons had defeated Rovers in the FAI Cup final of 1926.

Rovers were without the services of Willie Farrell who had

suffered a broken thigh following a motor cycle accident during the summer months. The seriousness of that injury was to be realised only the following season when the career of this great forward was to come to a tragic end.

So great was the interest amongst the Rovers' supporters for the League game against Fordsons that the club placed an advert in the newspapers advising that a fast excursion train would leave Kingsbridge on Sunday for a return fare of ten shillings. A thousand Rovers supporters made the journey south. At that time there were no televisions, few telephones and even fewer radios and the national radio station, 2RN, was yet to be established. Supporters depended on word of mouth or the newspapers for the results.

When the *Evening Herald* announced that they would pin the result of the Fordsons-Rovers game up in the window of their Carlisle Buildings office as soon as possible after the final whistle, thousands converged on D'Olier Street. When the result was announced (a scoreless draw) it was greeted by the cheering of thousands for it was generally accepted that Rovers had done well. So great was the crowd that it overflowed onto O'Connell Street and brought the normal Sunday evening traffic to a standstill!

The Rovers team that season consisted of: Paddy O'Reilly, Mick Maguire, Alec Kirkland, 'Sacky' Glen, Dinny Doyle (who had since returned from London), Ned Marlowe, 'Lye' Golding, Willie Egan, 'Babby' Byrne, Bob Fullam, 'Kruger' Fagan, 'Doc' Malone, Charlie Jordan, Mick McCloskey and a reserve goalkeeper by the name of O'Callaghan who returned to Brideville during the course of the season. John Joe Flood was now with Leeds United. Charlie Jordan left the club about mid way through the season to join Brooklyn and went from there to Athlone Town.

After twelve games had been played Rovers and Bohs were locked together on twelve points each. On Saturday, 20 November 1926, the long awaited meeting between the two sides took place at Milltown and proved to be a most disappointing game for the crowd of 13,000. It was a very one sided affair. Rovers won 4-0 thanks to a hat-trick from 'Babby' Byrne and a goal from Leonard.

The following week Rovers beat Athlone 6-0 to maintain their place at the top of the table. The Rovers front line consisted of Joe Leonard, 'Lye' Golding, 'Babby' Byrne, Bob Fullam and John 'Kruger' Fagan, all of whom, except Golding, contributed to the scoring.

With three games to go Rovers had a one point lead over Shels. Bohs had slipped after a defeat by Bray Unknowns but could still have had a say in the destination of the title as they were due to play both of the other two teams in their last two games. When Shels and Bohs played a 3-3 draw at Shelbourne Park on 18 December and Rovers beat Brideville by 2-1 at St James's Park the following day it left the Milltown side needing only one point from their last game which was against Bohs. When the sides met at Dalymount Park on 1 January 1927, it brought out the biggest crowd of the season. The home side gave Rovers a shock by taking a lead through Jimmy Bermingham and probably should have wrapped up the game when Mick O'Kane hit the base of the upright. But in the second half Rovers scored twice through 'Babby' Byrne to win the game and claim the title. Amongst those to send a telegram of congratulations was Belfast Celtic.

After the League campaign had ended the Shield began and Rovers got off to a good start when they beat Shelbourne 1-0. By mid April the Shield had joined the League trophy at Milltown. The Leinster Senior Cup was added also when Rovers beat Bohemians in the final replay at Shelbourne Park on 27 April.

In 1927/28 Rovers finished third in the League behind the winners Bohemians and runners-up Shelbourne. This was to be Bohs' season and they finished in style by winning not only the League title but also the FAI Cup, Shield and Leinster Senior Cup.

Dinny Doyle and Bob Fullam departed from Dublin for the United States. 'Babby' Byrne was to join Bradford City during the season. A number of good players came to Milltown, though. Included were Paul O'Brien, an inside left from Brideville and John 'Tipp' Burke, a defender from Munster junior side Cahir Park who made his debut against Fordsons in November 1927, as an inside-left. Although Billy 'Juicy' Farrell made a brave attempt to come back to the game he was unable to take his place on the team and he was given a free transfer at his own request. During his time he was probably the best centre forward in the Free State League. There was good news, however, with the return of Charlie Campbell to the forward line. Campbell had been on the Rovers' team that played against St James's Gate in the 1922 Cup final and had since had spells with Reading and Bristol Rovers before returning to the Hoops. He was still an effective player and scored twice against Bray Unknowns in his first game back.

Rovers effectively lost the title in the space of seven days when first they were held to a 2-2 draw by Fordsons in Cork and then beaten by the eventual champions Bohemians at Dalymount Park. The two Dublin sides met on 12 November. Both were unbeaten up to then but in a fast and exciting game the Hoops lost their unbeaten run of League games which extended to thirty in all. Rovers led at half time with goals from Golding and Fagan but Bohs came back to win 3-2, their goals coming from White and Whelan (2). The match report from the *Evening Herald* of 14 November stated that: 'Whether the shouts of jubilation were evidence of delight for a victory won and a definite step taken towards the Championship or of glee for the defeat of Rovers, it is difficult to diagnose.'

There were to be no trophies for Rovers that season or for anybody else, apart from Bohs who had won all the honours, but the Hoops did finish up as runners-up in the Shield competition just one point behind the winners.

Shamrock Rovers were well represented in the Irish international team during the 'twenties. The first game involving the Free State was against Italy in Turin in March 1926. The side was made up exclusively from players on duty with Free State League clubs and included Dinny Doyle, John Joe Flood, Bob Fullam and John Fagan.

The first inter-League meeting between North and South since partition was staged on 13 March 1926, when a crowd of 20,000 paid gate receipts of £1,000 at Dalymount Park. The Rovers players on the team that day were Kirkland, Flood, Farrell, Fullam and Fagan. The Free State won 3-1 with Flood setting up Charlie Dowdall (St James's Gate) for the first goal, Mahood getting an equaliser for the visitors and then Farrell getting the second after he was set up by Fullam. Dowdall got his second and the Free State's third later on.

Saturday, 11 September 1926 was a very important day in the history of Shamrock Rovers playing their very first game at Glenmalure Park. It was history in the making in every sense because the visitors Dundalk were making their first appearance in Dublin. It was not surprising, therefore, that a crowd numbering several thousand made their way, by whatever means possible, to Milltown to witness the occasion. They were not disappointed with the football for they were treated to a 3-3 draw. Both sides had good chances to score before the visitors took the lead after just eight minutes. Dundalk were playing with a strong breeze in their favour and when Swindle swung the ball towards the Rovers' goal the home 'keeper, O'Callaghan, appeared to have it covered but the strong breeze carried it beyond him and into the goal. So the first goal at the new venue did not take long to come about.

This goal encouraged the Dundalk players and they shocked Rovers shortly after that with another score, this time from Frank Rushe's thirty-yard blast. Rovers opened their scoring account not long after that when Willie Egan was fouled by Farrelly and Bob Fullam converted the penalty. Just one minute later it was Egan himself who obtained the equaliser for the home side. It was a fast and exciting first half with Dundalk again taking the lead after O'Callaghan had failed to hold a shot from McMahon and the latter, following up, managed to head the ball into the net. Dundalk were denied victory, though, when Fullam put Rovers back on level terms again in the second half and the game ended 3-3.

The following is a brief account of a journalist's first glimpse of the new ground at Milltown as given in the *Evening Herald* of Wednesday 17 September 1926: 'I first saw the enclosure last

Saturday, and though fairly well acquainted, through hearsay, with the improvements made, I was astonished at the extent and advanced state of the transformation wrought. The pitch is strongly railed, a roomy pavilion is erected, side line seats are provided and some banking is being done. The scheme has not yet reached the state of perfection in which it will eventually emerge but the amount of work accomplished in such a short space of time is marvellous.'

At this time the main stand had not yet been built. That was to follow a couple of years later, and there was still no terracing in place.

The official opening of the ground took place on Sunday, 19 September 1926 when Belfast Celtic provided the opposition and in doing so caused upset to certain groups in the Six Counties who did not approve of them playing a football match on a Sunday. Such was the interest in West Belfast for this game that special trains organised by the Celtic committee were arranged to bring four thousand supporters to Dublin. The crowd was the biggest gathering of people ever seen in the Milltown area of Co. Dublin.

Rovers provided a thousand sideline seats and a refreshment pavilion for the occasion. The gate receipts of £456 represented a crowd of 18,000, the maximum the ground would hold. The crowd included a small group from Newry where Rovers had recently played in an exhibition game. A party of eighty travelled from Athlone for the occasion and the quiet sleepy village of Milltown, hitherto unknown amongst the masses, was never to be the same again.

This game marked the first appearance of 'Lye' Golding, an outside right whom Rovers had signed from Brideville. The full Rovers team was: O'Callaghan, Malone, Kirkland, Doyle, Marlowe, Glen, Golding, Leonard, Egan, Fullam and Fagan.

Rovers began the game well and outshone Celtic in every sector. There was a lot at stake as the unofficial title of All-Ireland champions was being contested. Celtic got the first goal, despite the fact that Rovers had enjoyed most of the play up to then. O'Callaghan failed to control a shot by Hanna and when 'Doc'

Malone failed to clear S. Mahood stepped in and sent the ball into the unguarded net.

Rovers were back on level terms ten minutes later, though when the Celtic right half, Pollock, controlled a shot by Golding with his fist and Bob Fullam beat Diffin with the resultant penalty. After that it was Rovers who maintained the bulk of the pressure.

Celtic improved on their performance in the second half and got the winning goal mid way through this period. It was centre forward Hanna who secured the winner with a low shot past O'Callaghan following good work by Stanley and Jack.

It was a great day in the history of Rovers, no matter the result. It was the beginning of a new era at a ground which was to witness many great games and many great players in the decades to come. This was a pattern which was to continue until it all ended in sadness and bitterness on a Sunday afternoon in April 1987.

In an interview with W. P. M. of the *Irish Independent* prior to the 1940 FAI Cup final Jimmy Dunne recalled what the Elm Park ground looked like where he played before he went to England. The pitch was humpbacked; a railing kept the crowd out - sometimes; there was no serious attempt at banking and the pavilion was an improvised army hut. On his return to Shamrock Rovers, however, all had been transformed. Now, Milltown was like 'a miniature Highbury'.

THE PATH OF THE CUP

Shamrock Rovers began their glorious association with the FAI Cup in fitting fashion with a 6-2 win against University College Dublin. The game took place at Rovers' home ground in Windy Arbour on Saturday 19 November, 1921. The Rovers panel for the game was: Nagle, Murphy, Gregg, Birdthistle, Penston, Byrne, Quinlan, Campbell, Cowzer, Flood, Doyle and Fullam. Rovers played well as a team unit and they proved to be a fitter outfit than their opponents. The result was never in doubt as Rovers had remained unbeaten at that stage of the season.

Tipperary Wanderers beat Cahir in the first round and were

subsequently drawn at home in the next round to Rovers. The tie was listed for 3 December but was postponed to the following Saturday when Rovers travelled down to the garrison town. On that day the home side won the game 1-0. Maloney scored for them early in the second half and in general Rovers never seemed to match their opponents. However, the Dublin side had lodged a protest with the referee before the game on the basis that the pitch was unsuitable. The FAI duly decided that the game should be replayed at the same venue a week later and this time Rovers were the winners. They were then drawn against St James's Gate 'B' at St James's Park, Dolphin's Barn, in the third round.

Included in the Rovers' team were Bob Fullam and John Joe Flood, both forwards who had previously played senior football with Shelbourne. After twenty minutes Fullam opened the scoring from the penalty spot. Then Flood, Byrne and Fullam each got onto the score sheet before half time and that's how it stood at the final whistle.

For the fourth Saturday in a row Rovers were involved in Cup action when the final tie involving the non-League teams took place on Saturday, 31 December. Rovers earned themselves a place in the first round proper which involved the big guns of the newly formed Football League of Ireland. This they achieved by beating Shelbourne United (no association with Shelbourne AFC) 2-1 in a very close affair which was open right up to the final whistle. The game, which was played at Beech Hill, Donnybrook, brought a large crowd up from Ringsend and the rivalry was intense as both sides were based in that district. Rovers made only one change from the side that had defeated St James's Gate 'B' the previous week when C. Kelly stood in for McKendrick in the half back line.

After only five minutes Charlie Campbell scored the opening goal for Rovers after 'keeper Keegan had fisted away a Fullam free. With seven minutes of the first half to go Flood scored number two for Rovers. With a minute to half time remaining Quigley got one back for 'The Reds' but the same result stood at full time after a keenly fought second half.

Rovers included Johnny Murphy in their forward line in that

game. Murphy was a former Shelbourne AFC player who had had spells with Bradford City and Luton Town in the English League. He returned to Dublin some years earlier but had not played any senior football until Rovers coaxed him out of retirement. Also included was Bob Cowzer, whose nephew, Eddie lined out with Rovers in the early 'sixties.

The draw for the first round proper paired Shamrock Rovers with Olympia who were amongst the founder members of the Football League of Ireland some months earlier. It turned out to be a fine game at Shelbourne Park before the biggest crowd of the season at that venue. Rovers performed at their best and won the tie by 3-1. C. Pemberton scored first for Olympia but then Rovers got the equaliser through Fullam and Cowzer got the other two goals.

Next on the list was a quarter-final date with Dublin United at Beech Hill. A crowd of 3,000 turned out to watch the game and while the opposition again scored first Fullam once more secured the equaliser. This time Rovers went on to exert complete authority, running out 5-1 winners with Fullam adding a second to complement two from Cowzer and one from Flood.

A record crowd at Dalymount Park paid £282 (a huge sum in those days) to witness the semi-final between Rovers and Bohemians. Bohs were a long-established club with no fewer than four teams operating in various Leagues each week and boasting many fine players. They were previously members of the Irish League and had won the IFA Cup in 1908 when they beat fellow Dubliners, Shelbourne, in the final.

In the first meeting between Rovers and Bohemians in the FAI Cup the Milltown club pulled off a surprise when Flood gave them the only goal of the game after 35 minutes. Although Bohs tried hard after that to equalise the Rovers' defence was outstanding, in particular Jim Kelly, Peter Warren and Harry Birdthistle.

That victory set them up for a place in the final against St James's Gate first team who had themselves knocked out Shelbourne in the other semi-final. The final was to be an interesting affair between the League of Ireland champions and the champions-elect of the Leinster Senior League.

The first ever FAI Cup final took place on St Patrick's Day 1922, and was graced by fine weather. A crowd of 15,000 converged on Dalymount Park before the appointed 3.30 p.m. kick-off time.

As it happened the Milltown side could have won the game but had to settle for a 1-1 draw. The 'Gate' defence performed wonders. Although Rovers had their opponents on the racks in the opening stages, it was the Crumlin side which took the lead just three minutes before half time when Jack Kelly headed in a clean effort from Johnny Gargan's corner kick. Dinny Doyle and Bob Fullam (with a 35-yard shot) went close for Rovers who deserved to be on level terms at least.

After the break Rovers were again strong with Fullam, Doyle and Flood all causing problems for their opponents. The Milltown side were rewarded for their earlier endeavours a minute into the second half when they forced a corner and from this Charlie Campbell got the equaliser.

The Replay was fixed for 8 April, the same day that Ireland played France in a rugby international at Lansdowne Road. That game attracted a crowd of 18,000 and as a result the attendance at the soccer match was reduced to 10,000. This time there was only one goal in the game and it was the 'Gate' who were victorious. It was Jack Kelly again who got their goal just before half time.

Rovers tried hard to get back on level terms as their opponents were happy to defend, but all their efforts were in vain and their gallant march to glory in the first ever FAI Cup competition came to an unsuccessful end at the final hurdle.

Although they did not get to lift the Cup it was a success in a way for the Hoops were encouraged to enter the League of Ireland which they duly did in the following 1922/23 season. They won the title in their first season but did not progress far in the Cup. Rovers were drawn away to Athlone in the first round and began promisingly when they beat the 'Town' by the odd goal in three before a crowd of 1,200. 'Kruger' Fagan gave Rovers the lead in the first half and he could have probably added to the score before Athlone equalised through McNulty 15 minutes into the second half. Fagan later got a second for Rovers to see them through to the next round against Jacobs at Milltown.

Watched by a crowd of 2,000, Hueston gave the lead to the visitors and then they got a second before Bob Fullam pulled one back for Rovers from the penalty spot but it was not enough and Jacobs went through to the semi-final. There was to be no joy for the Hoops in 1923/24 either, this time going out in the first round by losing to Bohs 1-0.

There was to be success the following season, though, when Rovers met their Ringsend rivals, Shelbourne, in the 1925 final. There was some controversy before the big game, though, when the FAI appointed Mr W. J. Howcroft from England to officiate. The Irish Referees' Association issued a declaration to strike as a result of this appointment although in the end matters were brought to a satisfactory conclusion and the game went ahead as planned.

At 3.15 p.m. a quarter of an hour before the kick off, the gates into Dalymount Park had to be closed, so great were the crowds. Every possible viewing point had been occupied. The football was of the highest standard with both sides performing to the best of their abilities. Rovers had the first opportunity to open the scoring when Farrell headed the ball onto Flood's foot but the latter failed to control it. After 23 minutes they did go ahead. Following a throw-in close to the Shelbourne goal, Flood got a header in to which Fullam managed to get his foot; he duly planted it into the back of the net.

After sixteen minutes of the second half, Rovers went further ahead when Fullam crossed in from the left and, following some confusion in the Shelbourne defence, Flood nipped in to beat Walsh in goal. Later on, under pressure from a Shels attack, 'Sacky' Glen scored an own goal when he put the ball past Paddy O'Reilly. The score remained 2-1 to Rovers up to the final whistle and another chapter in the history of the fast growing club was recorded with the FAI Cup being added to the League title which had also been won in the same season.

In 1926 the Milltown club won its way through to the final again, this time against the Cork side Fordsons. The game, however, was not without drama.

An hour before the start the spectators were entertained by the St James's Band. The gate receipts amounted to £1,500 which was £1,000 more than the 'gate' for the IFA Cup final the same day at Windsor Park between Belfast Celtic and Cliftonville.

There was a sensational opening to the game with each side scoring in the opening three minutes. Fordsons won the game 3-2, the first time they had beaten Shamrock Rovers since their entry into the League of Ireland the previous season. It was Rovers who opened the scoring after Farrell had taken a long-footed shot at goal which the Fordsons' 'keeper, Bill O'Hagan, failed to hold. Then almost immediately Fordsons were awarded a free near the Rovers' goal area which was well taken by James Connolly and Dave Roberts was on hand to put it into the back of the Rovers' net. It was the Dublin side, though, who persevered in the first half and the score stood 2-1 in their favour at the interval after Fagan had got their second after 28 minutes.

It was 'as you were' after the interval and the fast pace of the game was maintained. Fordsons gained an equaliser after Malachy McKinney seized on slack play by Alec Kirkland in an attempted clearance and it was Paddy Barry who made most of the chance, beating O'Reilly in the Rovers' goal. Fordsons were doing most of the attacking but then came the drama. Rovers were awarded a penalty which was taken by Bob Fullam. O'Hagan was unable to hold it and in his attempt to divert the ball he could only succeed in pushing it back out to the path of Fullam. The Rovers man hesitated as he tried to switch it from his right foot to his left but as he was about to shoot he noticed that O'Hagan had advanced and had he taken the shot with that deadly left foot, for which he was renowned, he would almost certainly have killed O'Hagan. Instead Fullam dropped out of the challenge and allowed O'Hagan to safely gather the ball. Afterwards O'Hagan came to the Rovers' dressing-room to thank Fullam for his unselfish action.

'Spid' Jordan missed another chance for Rovers before Fordsons got the winning goal. O'Reilly had tried to clear amid a crowded goal mouth and Barry was ideally placed to tap the ball into the net.

The following season, 1926/27, there was to be no joy for Rovers in the Cup when they were knocked out in the first round by Bray Unknowns at Shelbourne Park. Bray had been in membership of the League for three seasons beforehand and had hardly set the scene alight but on that day they beat Rovers 3-0. Rovers had their chances but Leonard, in goal for Unknowns, was outstanding and time and time again denied the Rovers' forwards. It was a home draw for Bray but so great was the expected crowd that the tie had to be switched to Shelbourne's ground. The referee was Mr J. Stark of Belfast.

Shamrock Rovers wore the green and white hooped jerseys for the very first time in this game. Some supporters felt that the change from the more traditional vertical stripes to the new style was unlucky and that perhaps another occasion should have been chosen to introduce the change! The suggestion to change to the hooped jerseys came from committee member John Sheridan. A very close relationship existed between Rovers and Belfast Celtic and it was on account of this that the idea came about.

The first round of the 1928 Cup competition also brought disappointment for Rovers. They drew 3-3 with Dundalk at Milltown and lost the replay 4-1.

The programme for the Rovers versus Bohemians League game on Sunday, 31 December 1944 noted that the death of Charles 'Spid' Jordan had occurred following a brief illness. He was the first of the 1924/25 team to pass away.

SPOTLIGHT ON BOB FULLAM

Bob Fullam began his footballing days with junior side St Brendans at 16 years of age.

After a year he joined North End and in 1918 he joined Shelbourne and established himself as an outside left on the team.

He won an IFA Cup medal in 1920 but had not played in the final. In fact, the final was not played that year as persistent crowd difficulties in the other semi-final between Glentoran and Belfast Celtic meant that this tie could not be settled and the Cup was awarded to Shelbourne. Bob was also involved in the very last game in which a club from the 'South' took part in the IFA Cup. After Shels had drawn with Glenavon in Belfast the Northern side refused to travel to Dublin on account of the civil disturbances there and the replay was fixed for Belfast also but Shelbourne refused to travel back to the North and the tie was awarded to Glenavon.

In 1921/22 Bob began his association with Shamrock Rovers who were then a Leinster League side. He played in the very first FAI Cup final for Rovers against St James's Gate and only narrowly lost out when the 'Gate' won the replay by 1-0.

When Rovers joined the League of Ireland in 1922/23 Bob was the top scorer that season with twenty-seven League goals. In all he scored a total of ninety-two League goals with Rovers. During his time at the club he won four league medals when he was on the Hoops teams which won the League in 1922/23, 1924/25, 1926/27 and 1930/31. He appeared for Rovers in the Cup finals of 1922, 1925, 1926, 1929, 1930 and 1931 and won four winners medals.

He joined Leeds in 1923/24 but returned to Rovers after one season. The 1925 FAI Cup final saw Bob playing against his old club, Shelbourne. He scored the first goal in a 3-2 win for Rovers and collected the first of his winner's medals.

Bob was well known for his outspokenness but always had time for those in the game. He was a native of Ringsend and lived in Whelan House in Thorncastle Street before he went to London along with his family. In 1927/28 he went to the United States along with Dinny Doyle and several other players from both North and South. The idea was that upon arriving in America they would link up with a group of businessmen who had intended setting up a football club in Philadelphia. However, when they arrived there was no sign of anybody representing their potential employers and when the plans fell through they formed their own club which was known as Irish Philadelphia Celtic. After a year Bob returned to Dublin where he renewed his association with Shamrock Rovers.

He remained actively involved with the team but after they won the League and Cup double in 1931/32 his involvement became less and less. After his playing days Bob continued with the Hoops as a coach, a capacity he held until his departure to London in 1945.

He was capped twice by Ireland and represented the Inter League team six times. Just how deadly a left-footed shot he possessed was seen to its full effect against Italy at Lansdowne Road on 23 April 1927. After Ireland were awarded a free near the visitors' goal area Bob stepped up to hit the ball. The Italian full back, Zarillo, tried to head it out and ended up on the ground unconscious! 'That was the last ball he stopped in that game', said Bob some years later.

'Give it to Bob' was a popular line at the time, originating from supporters who felt that Bob could always do something good with it.

Many players have worn the green and white of Shamrock Rovers and there will always be arguments as to who was the greatest. There can be no doubt, however, that Bob Fullam was one of the best.

Born in 1897, Bob passed away in London in 1974.

SPOTLIGHT ON JOHN JOE FLOOD

John Joe Flood was another of the famous 'Four Fs'. He started his footballing life in Gaelic football with a club called The O'Reilly's but it was in association football that he was to make his mark. In 1919 he joined the Windsor Rangers soccer club and then went to St Patrick's, Ringsend, before joining Shamrock Rovers in the 1922/23 season.

He had a brief spell with Shels before coming back to Rovers for a while and after that he joined up with Leeds United. After a year he returned to Rovers again but his time in the English

League had not come to an end for he had a spell with Crystal Palace before linking up with Shamrock Rovers once more.

As an outside right, first, and then an inside right he won many honours while at Milltown. He was on the League winning teams of 1922/23, 1924/25 and 1931/32. He scored a total of sixty-one League goals for Rovers. John Joe played in eight FAI Cup finals with Rovers, finishing on the winning side on six occasions.

He was one of the players to win five FAI Cup winners medals in a row from 1929 to 1933, the others being John Burke and William 'Sacky' Glen. That record was not broken until 1969 when another Rovers player, Pat Courtney, won his sixth medal in a row.

Pen pictures for the 1933 FAI Cup final said of Flood: 'He may not be able to do all the hard work he used to but he is capable of rising to the occasion.' His benefit game involved a Shamrock Rovers team against a Free State Selection and the gate of £361 was a record for such a game. John Joe Flood became the first player to score a hat-trick for Ireland at international level in the 4-0 win against Belgium in Dublin in April 1929. In total, he was capped five times for Ireland and eight times for the League of Ireland at inter-league level.

In 1935/36 John Joe Flood left Shamrock Rovers to join Reds United, a club from the south side of Dublin who were members of the League of Ireland for just one season.

CHAPTER THREE

PADDY MOORE AND THE NEW GENERATION

(1 9 2 8 - 4 0)

The summer months of 1928 saw a flurry of activity at Milltown with the building of the main grandstand and some embankments around the pitch. The man responsible for the building of the stand was Mr John Calton, a local builder in Ringsend and a new member of the committee. The official blessing of the stand took place on Thursday, 30 August and was performed by Rev. Fr Union and Rev. Fr Hannon S.J.

The first League game of the 1928/29 season was against the newly elected Drumcondra, who, as a Leinster Senior League side, had won the FAI Cup in 1927. The first meeting between Rovers and Drums ended in a 1-1 draw. Fullam gave Rovers the lead and Swan equalised for Drums.

The first home game in the League was against Shelbourne. Special trains from Harcourt Street and special buses from D'Olier Street operated before the game. A big crowd witnessed Rovers suffer a reverse with Shels winning 4-2. The Rovers panel for that occasion was: Cleary, Kirkland, Burke, Glen, Caulfield, Leonard, Golding, Campbell, Luke, Fullam, Sherwin. *Reserve*: Flood.

Fran Watters, the former Shelbourne, Brideville and Drumcondra player signed for Rovers and the return of Bob Fullam from the States was a big boost.

Rovers recorded their all-time record win when they defeated Bray Unknowns 11-0 in a League game at Milltown on Sunday, 28 October. Paddy O'Reilly was in goal for the Hoops and apart from a few early movements he had virtually nothing to do. The scorers were John Joe Flood (3), Fran Watters (3), Bob Fullam (2), Alfred

'Emmer' Sherwin (from a penalty), Ned Marlowe and Johnny Fox.

The Hoops had managed to stay in touch with the leaders, Shels and Bohs, up to the closing stages of the League but they dropped five points in their last three games, including a 2-1 defeat by Bohs, who along with Shels, garnered full points from their last three games.

The season was not to be without success, though, the FAI Cup was won for the second time when Rovers beat Bohs in the final replay at Shelbourne Park. The Leinster Senior Cup came to Milltown for the third time when Rovers beat Dundalk in the final replay on 13 April at Dalymount Park.

The semi-final against Shels took two games to settle with the first game ending in a 3-3 draw. There was drama in the replay at Shelbourne Park before a very large crowd. Rovers took an early lead through Sherwin and not long after that added to their score when Flood set up Golding for a fine goal. In the second half Shels got one back through McMillan following a mistake by O'Reilly in the Rovers goal and then with twelve minutes to go the Hoops' custodian was forced to leave the pitch after he clashed with one of his own players. The Hoops held on to win the game by 2-1 and advanced to the final.

The final itself against Dundalk ended in a scoreless draw. In the replay John Joe Flood, who had returned to Rovers earlier in the season from Crystal Palace, scored in the very last second to give Rovers a 1-0 win.

The Hoops were unbeaten in the shield competition as were Bohs and both sides finished level. A play-off was held on 24 May at Shelbourne Park when Bohs were victorious by 2-0. The 1929/30 season saw the return to the club of David 'Babby' Byrne who had been with Rovers in 1926/27 and 1927/28. 'Babby' was the club's top scorer in both of those seasons, a feat he was to repeat in 1929/30 and 1930/31. In between he had spells with Bradford City and Shelbourne.

As in 1928/29 Rovers lifted the FAI Cup and Leinster Senior Cup, in the Shield they finished runners-up and were third in the League behind the winners Bohemians and Shels. Rovers had kept to within one or two points of Bohs for most of the season and with just three games remaining the Dalymount Park outfit had a one point lead on both the Hoops and Shels. Again, like the previous season, Bohs and Shels collected full points from their final games while Rovers could only manage one point from their last two. There was some satisfaction, though, when the Hoops beat first Bohs in the semi-final of the Leinster Cup and then Shels 2-1 in the final at Dalymount Park.

During the season several players arrived at the club including Paddy Owens, a forward from Jacobs, Jack Sloan, also a forward from Bray Unknowns and Francis Cervi, a full back.

Sadly, long-serving John 'Kruger' Fagan had suffered a serious illness during the summer months of 1929 and was unable to return to the Rovers first team. He departed from Milltown in December but was not long out of football as he appeared shortly afterwards playing as a left half for Kingswood in the Leinster Senior League, second division. 'Emmer' Sherwin, who first came to Rovers in 1926/27, had suffered severe damage to an ankle and his senior football career had also come to an end. Paddy Moore returned from Cardiff in 1930/31 having played previously for the Hoops where he made several appearances in the 1928/29 season.

There was no joy in the League or Shield in 1930/31 as seventh position in both of these competitions was the best the team could manage.

A number of significant signings were made for the 1931/32 season, including Mick McCarthy, the former Fordsons and Cork Bohs 'keeper. This was to be the start of an association between player and club that was to stretch over a ten-year period. Also arriving that season were Vincent Matthews, a centre half who had previously played with Sheffield United and who was also a former English international player; John 'Jock' McMillan who was an impressive outside right and who came to Rovers from Shels; and Jim Smith, a left winger who had played with Rangers and Aberdeen in Scotland.

The Shamrock Rovers committee that season comprised: J. Fox, M. J. Garnett (Vice-President), C. Fitzsimons (Vice-

President), J. McNevin, J. Gregg, A. Byrne (Secretary), T. Scully, G. Lamond, W. Saunders (Treasurer) and Joseph Cunningham (President). The team trainer and physio was John Dundon who had been with the club since its entry into senior football and he held that position until the mid 'thirties. Former player, Joe 'Buller' Byrne took over Dundon's role for a short period before the arrival of Billy Lord who was to give almost fifty years' service to the club. Byrne was responsible for the Leinster Senior League team during the 'thirties and also looked after the gear. He used to wash the jerseys and knicks in a large bath at the ground and hang them out on the pailings to dry.

1931/32 was a very successful season for the Hoops when they captured the League title for the fourth time, won the Shield for the third time without losing a match and beat Dolphin in the FAI Cup final to win the Cup for the fourth successive season.

With sixteen games of the championship played Rovers were a point behind Cork and Waterford but had a game in hand on both. They could have been a point ahead at this stage but had suffered a 5-2 defeat at the hands of Dundalk at the Athletic Grounds. The biggest crowd of the season was recorded in Dundalk that day and included a sizeable contingent from North of the Border and a full train load of Rovers' supporters from Dublin.

Not to be disheartened by that set-back, the Hoops caused a major surprise the following week when they beat title contenders Waterford 8-2 at Milltown. The scorers were Paddy Moore (2), David 'Babby' Byrne (2), Jim Smith (2), John Joe Flood and Bob Fullam. There was a record crowd present at Milltown that day, so much so that a section of the wooden pailings which surrounded the pitch collapsed but the crowd were well behaved and did not encroach onto the pitch. Rovers lined out that day as follows: in goal was Mick McCarthy; the full backs were Jim Daly and John Burke; the halves were William 'Sacky' Glen, Vincent Matthews and Owen Kinsella; while the front line consisted of 'Babby' Byrne, John Joe Flood, Paddy Moore, Bob Fullam and Jim Smith.

The Hoops failed to retain the title in 1932/33 when Dundalk were crowned League champions for the first time. The season started badly for Rovers when they were defeated by Dundalk in the first game. During the season they missed the services of Paddy Moore who had signed for Aberdeen during the summer of 1932.

This season Rovers acquired the services of Peader Gaskins (full back), Jimmy 'Scot' Buchannon (outside left), Tommy 'Netler' Doyle - a centre forward who had previously been with Walsall and Southport - and Frank 'Battler' Molloy, an inside right who had played for Shelbourne and Drumcondra in the past but who had signed for Rovers from junior club Bendigo.

Rovers were due to play Dolphin at Harold's Cross on 6 November in a game from which they had to take both points especially as Dundalk had dropped a point the previous day when they drew 1-1 with Shelbourne.

As it turned out, Dolphin, who had been lying second from the bottom of the League table, enjoyed a good win against the Hoops. They gave what was described as a delightful game of football and their goals came from five different players: Jimmy Somers, Jimmy Bermingham, Charlie Reid, Owen McCarney and Willie Fallon. The Rovers team for the game was: McCarthy, Gaskins, Burke, Glen, Matthews, Kinsella, Buchannon, Flood, Doyle, Graham, and Smith. George Graham was a Scottish forward signed from Waterford. The reserves were Mooney, Molloy and Snowe.

On Saturday, 12 November, Rovers assisted Dundalk in their quest for the title when they beat Shelbourne 3-2 at Milltown. One of the Rovers scorers that day was outside left Jim Smith who was often referred to as the 'Flying Scotsman' and was noted for his speed along the wing and his ability to travel fast with the ball at his feet. Having spent six years at Aberdeen where he played as a full back he had a great advantage as he read the game from a defender's point of view too.

When the champions-elect visited Milltown on 27 November they left in a disappointed mood for the Hoops snatched both points in a 2-1 victory, 'Netler' Doyle getting both goals for Rovers.

The Hoops were boosted by the return of 'Babby' Byrne who

had been with Sheffield United since early in the season. Despite having impressed during his time with the English club Byrne was released due to economic pressures. He lined out as outside right against Dundalk at the expense of Frank Molloy but his return to Milltown was short lived as an offer to join Manchester United was not far away. Even then, though, 'Babby's' association with the Hoops was not to end and he returned once more to the club after that. Dundalk had a three-point lead over second-placed Rovers and five points from their remaining three games was enough for them to finish the season on top of the table with 29 points.

The League of Ireland Shield was won by Rovers, however, as was the Leinster Cup final which was played on St Stephen's Day at Dalymount Park before a crowd of 13,000. Rovers beat Dolphin 2-1. The Hoops' scorers were 'Netler' Doyle and Jim Smith while Owen McCarney scored for Dolphin.

The two sides met in the Shield at Milltown on 5 March when Dolphin were 2-0 victors and this result was made all the more significant by the fact that these two clubs were to meet in the FAI Cup final just two weeks later. But the final ended in a 3-3 draw and Rovers won the replay 3-0.

Bohemians were League champions for the fourth time in the history of the club when they won the title in 1933/34 with only a point to spare over second placed Cork. Rovers came in third, five points behind Bohs.

A single goal settled the crucial Bohs-Rovers match on 3 March when a victory for Rovers would have put them on top of the table, but Bohs won which meant that victory in their last game against Cork, Bohs would ensure the title. As it happened they lost 4-3 but Rovers did them a big favour by beating Cork F.C. 3-0 in their last game.

Jim Daly, the Rovers outside right, missed a great chance in the game against Bohs when the home side were leading. He allowed the Bohs 'keeper, Harry Cannon, to narrow his angle and hit the woodwork instead. Daly, who had been with Rovers previously, had departed for Aberdeen the season before but due to domestic problems he returned to Milltown at the end of the

1932/33 season. Bohs had taken the lead in that game after Fred Horlacher sent in a magnificent thirty-five-yard shot which McCarthy was unable to hold and top scorer Ray Rogers tapped it over the line.

Later in the season Rovers travelled to Sheffield to play Sheffield United in the Duggan Cup, an annual challenge match between the two sides which had been inaugurated the previous season. The result was a 2-2 draw. The first game involving the two sides had taken place at Dalymount Park on 28 April 1933, when the crowd were rewarded with a thrilling encounter which the visitors won by 5-4. Jimmy Dunne was on the United team that day and scored two goals for them.

In the Shield competition of 1933/34 Rovers and Bohs finished level on 28 points each. A play-off was necessary to decide the winners and this was held over until the following season when Bohs beat Rovers 5-2 on 22 August.

The 1934/35 season saw the introduction of the Dublin City Cup competition which was rather strangely named considering that it was competed for by all the clubs in the Free State League. It was initially contested on a League basis. Rovers did not do too well, winning only four out of nine games and finishing in sixth place. Dolphin were the first winners.

The Hoops did not do well in the League that season either and finished in sixth place. They lost both their games to eventual champions Dolphin. The first defeat came on 2 December at Milltown when the visitors won 2-0 and in the return game the champions-elect beat Rovers 2-1 at Dalymount Park to take the title.

The Hoops did better in the Shield and won the competition for the fifth time. That season saw the arrival at the club of Joe Williams from Bray Unknowns. Around this time too came Edward Ryan from St James's Gate, James 'Hooky' Leonard from Shels and Bob Grimes from Bohs.

The following season saw the arrival of Charlie Reid, an inside left from Dolphin, and Joe Ward who came from the Leinster League side Distillery. The return from Aberdeen of Paddy Moore was greeted with joy by the Hoops' faithful as Moore had always been one of the favourites at Milltown. Paul Scully, a forward from Bohs, also signed for Rovers that season and was the top scorer at the club with 18 goals in the League.

The season began well with a 1-0 win against Brideville in the Shield. This was followed a week later with a 2-2 draw with Bohs at Milltown in the same competition. The newspaper report for that game stated that 'the good old days are here again' and that there were 'many thrills and a lot of good football in a keen struggle'. It was also stated that 'Rovers were more clever in attack in which the skills of Moore were clear.'

'Babby' Byrne was back with Rovers once more and lined out in the side that beat Bray Unknowns 4-1 at Milltown on 8 September 1935. That team was: Billy Behan; Joe Williams, John Burke; 'Sacky' Glen, Jim Blake, Owen Kinsella; Joe Ward, Charlie Reid; 'Babby' Byrne, Paddy Moore, Fred Snowe.

The long serving John Joe Flood had since departed for Reds United. The first time that Rovers and Reds United met was in the Shield on 14 September when the Hoops won 3-2. Reds were using Milltown as their home base but played their home games against Rovers at Dalymount Park. The Rovers scorers that day were Paddy Moore, 'Lye' Golding and David 'Babby' Byrne. The Reds goals came from former Rovers player Tommy 'Netler' Doyle and a Joe Williams own goal.

Rovers did not achieve success in either the League or Shield that season and finished sixth in both competitions. The season was marked, however, by the capture of the FAI Cup for the seventh time. The following season, 1936/37, was a bleak year at Milltown with the Hoops out of the running for all trophies. They went close in the Shield, finishing third, two points behind the leaders Waterford and Bohemians.

On Saturday, 12 February, Rovers and Bohs met in a League game at Milltown. Bohs took an early lead through Paddy O'Kane after he had been fed by Fred Horlacher but just three minutes later the referee was forced to abandon the game due to a severe snowstorm which covered the entire pitch. The game was refixed for Tuesday, 13 April, when Rovers won 3-0 before the smallest crowd ever to attend a Shamrock Rovers - Bohemians fixture. The Rovers scorers were Peader Gaskins, Thomas Murphy and Tommy Foy. The team lined out that evening as follows: McCarthy; Williams, Cullen; Glen, Blake, Kinsella; Gaskins, Kiernan, Murphy, Ward and Foy.

The start of the 1937/38 season saw the departure of William 'Sacky' Glen from Milltown and with that the end of an association that went back almost twenty years. 'Sacky' was not finished with football, however, for he was to win FAI Cup honours with Shelbourne the following season.

When Rovers played Shelbourne in a pre season friendly at Shelbourne Park half the crowd stayed outside in protest at a 100 per cent increase in admission prices to Free State League games.

The big talk at the start of the season was the return of Jimmy Dunne to Shamrock Rovers. Dunne had departed in 1925 when he joined New Brighton in the English Third Division. He also had spells with Arsenal, Southampton and Sheffield United. In fact, he turned down the offer of a new contract with Southampton in order to return home and take up the dual post of coach and player with the Hoops. Other signings that season included Joe Creevy - a left half - from junior side Greenmount and Willie Fallon, an outside left who came on loan to Rovers from Sheffield Wednesday. Fallon was originally a Gaelic footballer before he took up soccer with Brideville. It was from Brideville that he was later transferred to Notts County before going from there to Sheffield Wednesday. He was also with Dolphin for a while and was on the side which was beaten by Rovers in the FAI Cup final in 1933.

Patrick 'Sonny' Molloy also made his return to Rovers in 1937/38 after a spell with Dolphin. Sonny had his first spell with Rovers when he came to the club towards the end of 1933/34 and in the total time he spent at Milltown he won a League medal and a Leinster Senior Cup medal. He was presented with an FAI Cup medal by the club after the 1940 final against Sligo Rovers although he did not play in that game due to an injury.

He missed out on a Cup medal in 1936 due to pressures of work and shortly after left the club before returning in 1937/38. It was as a result of his performances in a junior international game against Scotland that Sonny first came to notice.

'I was in demand after that junior game', recalled Sonny. 'At that time I was playing intermediate football with Hospitals' Trust. When there was no place for us in the Intermediate League I decided to sign for Bohemians but "Flash" Bolger, our manager with the Hospitals Trust, got us a place in the Leinster Senior League which was a joke really because it was way above us. That was the place they offered us, though, and "Flash" accepted it so I went back and played for them but I had a row so I went from there to Distillery and then on to Rovers.'

Sonny was most unlucky not to have earned at least one Irish cap. 'I went to Germany and Hungary with the Irish team in 1939. In those days Ireland went by the English rules rather than those of FIFA and that meant that you could not bring on a substitute for an injured player. In the game against Germany, Charlie Harris, the trainer, took Jimmy Dunne off before half time and he came back on for the second half but collapsed after five minutes and at that stage I was not able to come on.'

Sonny was only eighteen years of age when he first joined Rovers. 'I went up as an inside right to replace John Joe Flood. I left the club at the wrong time. I went back to Hospitals' Trust and then to Dolphin before going back to Rovers in 1937/38 as a right half to replace "Sacky" Glen.'

The influence of Jimmy Dunne had an immediate effect on Shamrock Rovers as he brought a new standard of coaching to the club. The League title returned to Milltown and along with it the Shield and the Leinster Senior Cup. At this stage the League was no longer known as the Free State League but had reverted to its original title of the Football League of Ireland.

As the season drew to an end several clubs were in contention for the title with Rovers and Waterford neck and neck on 25 points each at the beginning of April. Rovers had a game in hand, though. The Rovers team which drew with Brideville on 3 April was: McCarthy; Williams, Meek; Molloy, Blake, Kinsella; Donnelly, Dunne, Carroll, Ward, Foy. The following Sunday Rovers beat Cork 3-2 and before that they had beaten Limerick by 1-0 in a midweek game. Shamrock Rovers were now on top on their own with 30 points while Waterford and Brideville were in joint second place on 27 points each, all three having played 20 games and with just two more games to go.

Waterford were then surprisingly beaten by Bray Unknowns while Brideville could only earn a point against Dundalk at home. This meant that if Rovers won at Milltown the following Saturday they would be the new champions.

This they did in style before their own supporters when they beat Bohs 6-1. After eight minutes the Hoops took the lead after Maguire handled and Foy successfully converted from the spot. Six minutes later Ward increased the lead and the title looked to be wrapped up. However, with thirty minutes of the game gone Bohs got one back through Fullam and it was not until eleven minutes of the second half that the Hoops restored their two-goal lead, Joe Ward getting his second. Willie Carroll scored two minutes later and then Ward completed his hat trick before Carroll got the final goal. It was just as well for Rovers that they won the title that day for they gave a terrible display in their final League game against Dundalk when they flopped to the tune of 4-0, Joey Donnelly getting a hat trick in that game with the other goal coming from Harry Johnston.

Rovers won the Shield having lost only one game to Shelbourne on September 11th. There was no success in the Cup, for having beaten non-League Terenure Athletic after a first-round replay and then Bray Unknowns in the quarter-final, which took three games to settle, the Hoops were beaten 2-1 by Dundalk in the semi-final. The Leinster Senior Cup was won, however, for the sixth time when Rovers beat Brideville in the final on St Stephen's Day at Dalymount Park.

The Dublin City Cup avoided them once more and the opening game of the season on 22 August in this competition proved to be a set back for the Hoops. The newly elected Limerick

AFC were playing in their very first game in senior football and celebrated their elevation to the top flight with a shock 1-0 win against Rovers at Dalymount Park. It was to be the first of many meetings between the sides over the years to come.

In 1938/39 the League title came to Milltown once again, Rovers making history as they became the first club in the League of Ireland to retain the title. That was their sole success that season as they won only two of their Shield games and in the Dublin City Cup they were knocked out in the semi-final by Cork City. They failed in the first round of the FAI Cup against Bohemians and had no success in the Leinster Senior Cup either.

The League campaign started off well with a 2-0 defeat of Dundalk at Oriel Park; the scorers were Owen McNally and Michael Crowley. The team line out for that game was: Spain; Healy, Meek; Finnegan, Williams, Creevy; Foy, Molloy, McNally, Sheeran, Crowley. Centre forward Owen McNally had been signed from Bray Unknowns and scored fourteen League goals that season. Shay Healy, the left full, had been with the reserves the previous season and made his big breakthrough this season. Harry Finnegan joined Rovers that season as a right half having previously played junior football with LMS and Hospitals Trust.

Sligo Rovers were the other main contenders for the title that season but the Hoops beat the Westerners 1-0 at the Showgrounds on Sunday, 1 January 1939 to open a five point gap over their nearest rivals and maintain both their unbeaten record in the League and their 100 per cent away record. That result left three teams level in second place for along with Sligo were Bohemians, who had lost to Cork City that weekend, and Dundalk who had drawn 1-1 away to Drumcondra. Missing from the Hoops side that day were Jimmy Dunne and 'Sonny' Molloy, both out for some time due to injury.

Rovers' next engagement was at home to Cork City the following week. Cork had hammered them 7-0 in the Dublin City Cup at the Mardyke in August and again beat the Hoops in the Shield at the same venue by 4-1 in October.

The reappearance of Jimmy Dunne at outside right in the

League game was a great boost to the Hoops and the Rovers' supporters were treated to a 3-1 win by their side. Dunne scored one of the goals with Edmund 'Emo' Sheeran and Joe Ward getting the others.

That result left Rovers with 19 points from ten games. Dundalk and Bohs were in second place with 12 points each and Sligo were in fourth position on 11 points. When Rovers and Dundalk met again on Sunday, 29 January the Hoops won 3-2 having led throughout the game and with Dundalk staging a late rally to come back from 3-0 down. The highlight of the game was the opening goal which was scored by 'Sonny' Molloy direct from a corner.

At this stage Rovers were playing all their home games on a Sunday.

In 1939/40 Rovers made a disastrous start in the League and lost too much ground to challenge for the title. The FAI Cup came to Milltown once again with victory against Sligo Rovers in the final but in the Leinster Senior Cup Rovers lost in the final to Bohs. Again in the Shield Rovers finished at the half way mark although two points behind the eventual winners Bohemians.

It was a good season for Dublin side St James's Gate who captured the League title for only the second time, having won the very first League of Ireland Championship back in 1921/22. Although Rovers finished as runners-up they never came close to winning, finishing six points behind the 'Gate'.

All routes led to Crumlin for the vital League fixture between the 'Gate' and Rovers on Sunday, 11 February 1940. In defeating the 'Gate' by 2-1 Rovers briefly re-opened their own narrow prospects of retaining the title but eventually their challenge fizzled out.

Mick McCarthy was back in goal for Rovers late in the season after a very promising Larry Palmer had kept him out of the team.

Bob Bryson came to Milltown during the course of that season. A Scot, Bryson had spent three seasons as a centre half with Newry Town before joining Rovers.

THE PATH OF THE CUP

The fifth of January 1929 was an historic day for Shamrock Rovers. They beat Shelbourne at Milltown 3-2 in the first round of the FAI Cup and in doing so took the first step on a long unbeaten journey which was to bring the Cup to Milltown for a record five years in a row.

Having eliminated Richmond United in the quarter-finals Rovers then got revenge on Dundalk for the first round defeat the season before, this time beating the Northerners 3-0 in the semi-final. Bohemians, meantime, had beaten Drumcondra 2-0 in the other semi-final and the scene was set for the first FAI Cup final between these two great Dublin clubs. Bohs had won the Cup for the first time the previous season when they beat Drumcondra (who were then a non-League side) 2-1 in the final. Rovers had won the Cup once also when they beat Shelbourne in 1925. Whichever side won this time would become the first club to win it twice. After a replay that honour was bestowed on Shamrock Rovers.

In the drawn game, which took place at Dalymount Park on 18 March, the honours belonged to the respective defences and the game finished scoreless. The replay was held at Shelbourne Park and Shamrock Rovers won 3-0. Alec Morton fouled Flood in the penalty box after just five minutes and the latter scored himself after Glen's penalty kick had rebounded. Bohs had most of the opening play but could not get past a stern Rovers' defence. As the game progressed Rovers came more into it and were rewarded with two more goals, first from a powerful free kick by Fullam and then from Flood.

The following year, Rovers disposed of Shelbourne in the first round, following two replays, then St James's Gate in the quarter-finals and Fordsons in the semi-final before meeting Brideville in the final. The Cup was won again, thanks to local hero David 'Babby' Byrne. He scored the only goal of the game with less than a minute remaining. Although he was credited with heading the ball into the net he admitted some years later that he had controlled it with his hand first. Brideville had the better chances to score but only had themselves to blame for not making the most of them.

The 1931 Cup final between Rovers and Dundalk finished 1-1 and victory again went to Rovers in the replay. Dundalk had already beaten Rovers twice during the season and looked likely to win again after they took the lead in the final with a goal scored by Gerry McCourt and which had stood right up to six minutes from the end when Rovers were lucky to equalise. Rovers settled down better in the second half after 'Babby' Byrne had switched from centre forward to outside left and Paddy Moore moved into the centre. It was Moore who saved the day for the Hoops when he scored the late equaliser.

The replay was held on Saturday, 9 April, also at Dalymount Park. There was only one goal in a fairly evenly contested game. It came a few minutes before the interval and followed a hefty clearance by O'Reilly which was taken down by 'Lye' Golding along the right and sent into Flood who proceeded to set Moore up for the goal. Sam McMullen, in goal for Dundalk, had no chance with Moore's low hard drive but the Border side had played well and were unlucky to lose.

The Cup was won for the fourth year in succession when Dolphin provided the opposition in 1932. Dolphin had almost as much of the play as Rovers and they kept Mick McCarthy busy in the Rovers' goal. He played his part in that victory with some brilliant saves. Fifteen minutes from the end came the only goal of the game. Flood lifted the ball up in front of the goal and Moore was ideally placed to head it into the net. The Cup was now added to the League championship and the Shield.

The two sides met again in the final of 1933. By now, Paddy Moore was no longer with the Hoops, having departed for greener pastures with Aberdeen. A Crowd of 32,000 witnessed the game which lacked quality football but had plenty in the way of thrills and excitement with six goals included, three of which came from the penalty spot. The scorers for Dolphin were George Lennox (with two penalties) and Willie Fallon. 'Babby' Byrne, Jimmy Buchanan and Matthews (from the spot) scored for Rovers.

Dolphin did not rise to the occasion in the replay. From a throw in by Flood, in the first minute of the game, 'Babby' Byrne met the ball and steered it past Slater. There was more pressure from Rovers after that and then it was Dolphin's turn to put Rovers under siege. In the 38th minute Rovers scored again when Jimmy Daly headed in the first of his two goals. The second half was disappointing. After 24 minutes Slater pushed the ball out but only as far as Owen Kinsella and he set up Daly for the third goal. Rovers were clear winners this time with a 3-0 margin in their favour.

That great unbeaten run in the Cup came to an end when Rovers lost 2-1 to St James's Gate in the first round replay of 1934. The sides had drawn 1-1 in the first game which meant that the Hoops had not been defeated in 28 outings. The following year, 1935, Rovers were again beaten in the first round, this time 1-0 by Dundalk at Milltown.

It was back to winning ways in 1936 when the Hoops went all the way to the final and beat Cork by 2-1 to record their seventh success in the competition. Rovers halves and backs gave their finest display in a Cup final to date. Jimmy Turnbull, the Cork dangerman, was controlled well by Jim Blake who closed him down except for the one goal. Paddy Moore had returned to Dublin from Aberdeen and was, without a doubt, the most talented individual on the pitch.

Two minutes after half time Rovers opened the scoring. 'Sacky' Glen, playing in his ninth FAI Cup final with Rovers, sent the ball across to Kinsella who kicked it high in front of goal, Charlie Reid succeeded in heading it out to Moore who went on to score with a low shot. Seven minutes later, Reid increased Rovers' lead when he headed in from Glen's free before Turnbull evaded the Rovers' defenders and beat 'keeper Billy Behan for a consolation goal.

In 1937, the Hoops beat Dolphin in the first round but lost 2-0 to Waterford in the quarter-final. The following year it took two games to dispose of non-League Terenure Athletic, then three to overcome Bray Unknowns in the quarter-final before Dundalk put them out on a score of 2-1 in the semi-final. In 1939 Rovers and Bohs drew 2-2 at Dalymount Park in the first round with Bohs winning the replay at Milltown when Paddy O'Kane scored the only goal before a crowd of 22,000.

The road to the 1940 final began on 4 February when Rovers travelled to the Markets Field where they beat Limerick by 3-1. Joe Ward, Jimmy Dunne and Paddy Reynolds were the scorers for Rovers. In the quarter-final Rovers defeated Drumcondra when Ward scored the only goal of the game. The meeting of Rovers and Bray Unknowns in the semi-final at Shelbourne Park attracted a crowd of 12,915 with victory going to the Hoops. They won by 2-0 with goals from Jimmy Clarke and Willie Fallon.

A record crowd of 38,509 spectators who paid record gate receipts of £2,200 attended the Cup final between Rovers and Sligo Rovers. Full backs Mattie Clarke and Shay Healy along with centre half Bobby Bryson proved to be resourceful defenders and denied Sligo the opportunity to take the initiative. Sligo were unable to convert their early possession into a solid lead. Centre forward Joe McAleer had a wonderful opportunity to open the scoring but he was denied by a superb save by Mick McCarthy in the Rovers' goal. McCarthy then prevented an almost certain goal by throwing himself down at McAleer's feet and putting the ball out of danger.

Before half time the Hoops went ahead with a goal by Joe Ward. The second goal came in the 78th minute after Fallon headed in the ball from Ward's cross. Just on full-time Dunne scored the third with a volley which gave Jimmy Twomey no chance in the Sligo goal.

After the final whistle the Hoops' supporters carried the players shoulder high to the dressing room. Their chief hero was Jimmy Dunne, the blond forward who had played for Rovers in the early 'twenties before he went to England.

William 'Sacky' Glen played in a record ten FAI Cup finals plus four replays. His first was in 1922 when Rovers lost to St James's Gate and his last was in the 1939 final replay when he scored the only goal of the game for Shelbourne against Sligo Rovers.

SPOTLIGHT ON PADDY MOORE

Wherever Paddy Moore played people spoke of his skills, his sheer wizardry on the ball and of his tremendous football brain.

'Paddy Moore, who for all around equipment, goal getting and unselfishness, is the best of the bunch and the leader of my forward line', wrote a Scottish correspondent in November 1932.

The man who brought Moore on in football was Alex Rock of Clonliffe Celtic for whom he played in the late 'twenties. Moore had a brief spell with Bendigo, a well-known junior side in Dublin at that time. He was with another junior side, Richmond Rovers, before he came to Shamrock Rovers. After a brief spell with Cardiff City Paddy came home to Dublin and linked up with the Hoops again. Although originally an inside right Paddy appeared as a centre forward for the Hoops second time around. Bohemians once had the chance of signing this football genius when he was playing junior football in the 'twenties but somehow slipped up in not doing so.

At the beginning of the 1932/33 season Moore joined Scottish club Aberdeen where he continued to entertain the crowds with his superb finishing touch. At the age of twenty-five Paddy came home to Dublin where he linked up once more with the Hoops. Rovers supporter Sonny O'Reilly from Killester has many fond memories of the Hoops and considers himself privileged to have seen Paddy Moore play: 'I would describe him as having been a genius. He would carry the ball and send a player the wrong way and the way he did it was fantastic. Although he had not got great height he could get himself up high for the ball; that was never any problem for him.'

For a short while, during the 1937/38 season, Paddy played for Brideville. He was capped for Ireland six times and scored seven goals including all four in a 4-4 draw with Belgium at Dalymount Park in February 1934. He was also capped by the Irish Football

Association in Belfast when he was selected to play against England in 1932.

Johnny Fullam, a native of Ringsend and a cousin of Bob, was a personal friend of Paddy Moore and recalled one occasion when himself and Moore were standing on the embankment at Milltown watching Rovers: 'It was the day that Twomey and Cochrane came to Rovers. Both of these players had been with Leeds United but when the war broke out they came over here. The game had been held up for fifteen minutes as they were delayed coming down from the North. I was standing on the hill with Paddy Moore, who, I suppose, was no more than 36 years of age. I asked Paddy if he would get out on to the pitch for ten bob and I nearly cried when he said to me that he would get out and play for nothing. It was a terrible tragedy. He was one of the best footballers ever in this country. I think that Paddy Moore was the greatest. He had nothing really except a football brain.'

It was no secret that Paddy Moore was an alcoholic. He died at the age of 41.

For those Rovers' supporters alive today who saw Paddy Moore play his image lives on in their memories as though it was all only yesterday. Had he lived longer he might have been a good scout. When he attended a junior international at Dalymount Park in 1937 Paddy was heard to comment after the game that 'the little fella from Waterford is the only footballer that I could see out there'.

That 'little fella' was none other than the young Paddy Coad.

SPOTLIGHT ON MICK McCARTHY

Mick McCarthy was a goalkeeper of distinction. He was renowned for his bravery, especially when diving at the feet of opposing forwards.

It was on 6 November 1931 that McCarthy signed for the Hoops. He came from Blackrock in Co. Cork, a GAA stronghold, and he was a fine hurler. When he was forced to make a choice between the two codes Mick chose soccer. Tim O'Keefe, the well-known Waterford forward who played in the League of Ireland around the same time as Mick McCarthy, also came from Blackrock.

When he signed for Rovers in 1931 Mick was paid £4 per week plus bonuses. Before joining Rovers he had played with Fordsons and Cork Bohs. A number of Scottish clubs plus Birmingham City made enquiries for him after he had played for the Free State juniors in a representative match in Falkirk but these faded when he opted to sign for the Hoops.

The *Irish Press* correspondent 'Socaro', previewing the 1932 FAI Cup final between Rovers and Dolphin, wrote of the Corkman: 'Under pressure Rovers can rely on McCarthy, their goalkeeper. When all seems lost this player enters the breach and is capable of defying all and sundry to get the ball past him.'

He never ducked out of a challenge and he took some risks but as he said himself in later years, 'at that time goalkeepers carried their lives in their hands.'

Mick McCarthy was with Rovers for three years before he went over to Sheffield United. He was signed by the English club following an impressive display in a 2-2 Duggan Cup draw between the Hoops and United in Sheffield in 1934. He made his debut for them against Manchester United at Bramall Lane in a League game which Sheffield won 3-2.

They loved McCarthy over there but after he incurred a serious thigh injury he was forced to return home. Although told he would never play again he defied the odds and once again linked up with Rovers in 1936/37 following a very brief spell with Brideville.

With Rovers he won three League medals and three FAI Cup medals. He earned one international cap with Ireland when he was on the team that beat Holland by 2-0 in Amsterdam in May 1932. All told, he won every honour in the game.

A greyhound enthusiast, Mick always wore a cap. For many years Rovers' supporters were baffled by this and some never found out why. The reason was simply superstition: he felt that he was not fully equipped without one and that he might be unlucky without it. Long time Shamrock Rovers' supporter, John 'Danny' Cleary of Sandymount attended his first game in Milltown in 1927 and remembers Mick McCarthy well:

'He always wore a cap, we never knew exactly why, and many a time he would dive for the ball and lose his cap but he would always go for the cap first although I don't ever remember him losing the ball in doing so.

He reminds me of Gordon Banks. He was fearless; he was a very good 'keeper and a real favourite with the crowd. There was no messing with Mick McCarthy, he just got in there and did the business. He was definitely one of the best goalkeepers I have seen play for Rovers and we have had some good 'keepers like Collins or Kiernan but McCarthy was a brilliant goalkeeper, no doubt about that.'

John stated that, in his opinion, McCarthy's best game for Rovers was the second replay of the FAI Cup semi-final against Waterford at Dalymount Park in 1941. Although Rovers were beaten 3-2 McCarthy had an outstanding game.

Mick McCarthy died suddenly at his home in Clonskeagh in May 1973.

CHAPTER FOUR

THE EMERGENCY AND THE INFLUX OF PLAYERS

(1 9 4 0 - 4 8)

The war years were good times for League of Ireland football with crowds flocking to grounds up and down the country. Several Irish players who had been carving a career in Britain were forced to return home, amongst them Willie Fallon (mentioned in the previous chapter), a forward who signed for Rovers upon his return from Sheffield Wednesday. A number of Scots along with players from the North of Ireland also came to the League of Ireland around this time including Billy Cameron, an inside left who signed for the Hoops from Limerick in January 1940.

Billy Lord was coach at Limerick then. He was a tremendous athlete in his time and when he retired from active competition he turned his hand to the medical side of sport and became renowned throughout Europe as a physiotherapist. Reared in York Street, Billy was associated with Shamrock Rovers for over fifty years.

In 1985 Billy Lord died at the age of 94. The image of him running on to the pitch to treat injured players at a Rovers' game or an Ireland game with the proverbial cigarette dangling from the side of his mouth will not be forgotten by the many who played the game and the many who looked on.

The 'forties belonged to Cork teams. In 1940/41 Cork United (successors of the club once known as Fordsons) won the first of three League titles in a row. This Southern outfit were the first to win the title three times in succession, matched after that only by Waterford in the 'sixties and Shamrock Rovers in the 'eighties (when the Hoops established a new record by winning the League four times in a row).

In 1940/41 only the President's Cup came to Milltown, after Rovers beat St James's Gate. Rovers beat Cork Bohs by 8-3 in the first round of the FAI Cup and then overcame Brideville in the quarter-final. The semi-final developed into a marathon affair in which three games were necessary to find a winner between themselves and Waterford. The replay at Dalymount Park on Wednesday, 9 April was said to have been one of the best games seen in many years. The sides were required to return to the Phibsboro' venue the following evening to play again when Waterford were victorious by 3-2. Tim O'Keefe scored twice and Johnny Johnstone once for the Blues while Jimmy Dunne scored both goals for Rovers.

Jackie Carey, that great Irish international, who had gone to Manchester United from St James's Gate in 1937, played two games after that for Shamrock Rovers. As a United player, Carey first sought permission from his club to play for Rovers in a League game against Limerick on Sunday, 6 April 1941. He gave a good performance at inside left where he scored one goal in a 5-0 victory. The other Rovers scorers that day were Jimmy Clarke (2), Paddy Leeney and Joe Ward. Also on the Rovers team that day were Billy Black, a half back formerly with Larne. The right half was Niall McIvor, a Scot who spent just one season at Milltown before his untimely death at the age of thirty. Carey returned to Milltown in April of 1942 where he scored twice in a 7-1 rout of Shelbourne.

In 1941/42 Rovers won the Shield for a record seventh time and the runners-up spot in the League was secured. Amongst those to arrive at Milltown that season were Matt Doherty, ex-Belfast Celtic and Derry City right half; Davy Cochrane, a winger from Linfield who, it is said, 'could zig zag along the wing Stanley Matthews style'; and Kevin Harris, son of Shelbourne centre half Val Harris. Peter Farrell emerged with the Hoops this season as an inside left and Paddy Coad, the ex-Waterford inside right, made his debut against Brideville in the FAI Cup first round.

The Shield competition saw a race for honours between Rovers and Dundalk. Rovers needed only one point out of their final game and a scoreless draw against Bohs did the trick.

Sunday, 15 March 1942 saw a crucial League game at the Mardyke involving League leaders Cork United, the champions of 1940/41, and Shamrock Rovers. The sides had met at Milltown on 28 December when the biggest crowd of the season saw a thrilling 4-4 draw. Cork were leading 4-3 with just three minutes remaining when Rovers were awarded a penalty which Bobby Bryson successfully converted.

At the Mardyke a win for Rovers was essential if they wished to win the title. At half-time Rovers were leading 2-1 with goals from Dessie Westby, the reserve centre forward and Jimmy Kelly, the former Derry City and Northern Ireland international outside left. Cork had been taken aback with the start which Rovers made in the game but got back in half way through the first half when Owen Madden beat Twomey in the Rovers goal. The second half had only just begun when Cork got the equaliser with a superb header from Liam O'Neill. With just seven minutes remaining Westby ran through a rather hesitant defence to score the winner for Rovers. The Hoops team that day was: Twomey; Clarke, Healy; Doherty, Bryson, Harris; Cochrane, Dunne, Westby, Farrell, Kelly.

That win at the Mardyke left Rovers just one point behind Cork United but the Southerners had a better chance of retaining the title as only two games remained. Rovers beat Shels 7-1 in their second last game with Westby scoring four times and their final game was a 1-1 draw with Bohs. But Cork won their final two games against Bohs and Brideville to retain the title.

The inaugural Inter-City Cup competition which involved clubs from both sides of the Border was won by Dundalk after they beat Rovers by 1-0 in the final at Dalymount Park on 31 May.

When Rovers won the Inter-City Cup the following season, 1942/43, it was in rather unusual circumstances. The first leg of the final was staged at Windsor Park, Belfast, and there was to be an historic meeting between Rovers and the other finalists,

Bohemians, at the Linfield venue. That game took place on Saturday, 29 May 1943, where a crowd of 5,000 paid gate receipts of £305 to witness the two Dublin sides in action. This was double the gate that had been recorded at the Linfield/Rovers tie in the competition on 8 May.

Bohemians won the first leg 2-0 with Kevin O'Flanagan scoring twice even though Rovers were on top throughout and at the final whistle led 13-5 on corners. Their superiority in forcing corners in that game stood to their advantage at the end of the second leg, however.

That second leg took place at Dalymount Park the following day, on Sunday, 30 May, where a crowd of 10,000 paid gate receipts of £613. The Hoops won 2-0. Terry Clarke, a centre forward on loan from Brideville and signed later on by Rovers, scored the first after seven minutes with Paddy Coad getting the second twelve minutes into the second half. Rovers won the Cup, then, with the total number of corners over the two legs in their favour being 19-9.

Other players to come to the Hoops that season included Liam Crowe, a centre forward signed from Bohs and Mickey Delaney, the former Shelbourne outside right.

Larry Palmer was now the established goalkeeper at Milltown. The regular team that season would have been made up of the following players in typical positions shown: Larry Palmer ('keeper); Mattie Clarke (right full), Shay Healy (left full); Matt Doherty (right half), Charlie Byrne (centre half), Peter Farrell (left half); Paddy Coad (inside right), Kevin Harris (inside left), Mickey Delaney (outside right), Liam Crowe (centre forward), Tommy Eglington (outside left).

Rovers prevented Shelbourne from pulling off the League and Cup 'double' by defeating their long-standing rivals in the Cup final by 3-2. The Hoops' team that day showed two changes to that of above with Bobby Rogers, signed from St James's Gate during the season, in place of Kevin Harris and Joe Nolan in place of Shay Healy.

Jimmy Dunne went to Bohemians at the end of 1941/42 and

responsibility for coaching the teams fell to ex-player Bob Fullam assisted by 'Buller' Byrne. The number of clubs in membership of the League now stood at just eight: Rovers, Cork United, Dundalk, Drumcondra, St James's Gate, Limerick, Bohemians and Shels. Bray Unknowns and Brideville were missing from the previous season but the latter were re-elected to the League in 1944/45 with the resignation of St James's Gate.

The Shield almost came to Milltown in 1943/44 when Rovers narrowly lost out to winners Shelbourne and finished joint second with Drums. The campaign had started badly for Rovers when they were beaten 3-1 by Shelbourne at Milltown in the first game on 10 October. They did, however, go on a winning run and, going into the final series on the weekend beginning 20 November, they held the top spot along with Shels. Disaster struck in the final game when the Hoops went down by 3-1 to Bohs and when Shels beat the 'Gate' 3-1 Rovers knew that they had lost it.

The League campaign got off to a good start and included the defeat of St James's Gate by 7-0, Rogers and Coad each scoring a hat trick with Delaney getting the other goal. Remarkably, Rovers failed to win any of their games in the second half of the championship. The final game was against Shelbourne on 18 March. Shels had to win to take the title, for going into the game they were a point behind Limerick who had by now completed their League programme.

Shels did indeed come out on top in this high scoring encounter, winning 5-3. Their scorers were Tommy Ryan, Billy Kennedy, ex-Hoop Willie Fallon, Syl Walsh and Tommy Kinsella. Delaney (2) and Coad were the scorers for Rovers.

A month later, the Hoops extracted revenge on the 'Reds' when they beat them in the FAI Cup final.

Throughout the season two of the younger players at Milltown showed great promise. Peter Farrell and Tommy Eglington did not go unnoticed and after the war both were signed up by English First Division side Everton.

Eglington never played in Rovers reserves but had come straight into the first team. 'At the time I was playing with

Distillery "B" in the Athletic Union League. At the end of 1942/43 "Buller" Byrne came up to my house and he asked me if I wanted to sign for Shamrock Rovers. I was around nineteen at the time and I did not know what to think but I jumped at the chance anyway', recalled Tommy. 'That happened on a Friday night and the last League game of the season was coming up on the following Sunday when Rovers were due to play against Bray Unknowns at the Carlisle Grounds. The season went on for another month after that when we won the Inter-City Cup. I had come straight into the first team and I kept my place after that.'

Tommy recalled that at that time Rovers had a schoolboy team which played their games at Glenmalure Park on match days prior to a senior game. It was from that team that Fionan Fagan, later with Manchester City, came out of. Fionan was the son of former Rovers star John 'Kruger' Fagan. Eglington and Fionan Fagan were to share the same pitch as Irish international players when the latter made his debut for Ireland against Norway in 1954.

At the time Tommy was playing for Rovers he was working in a butcher's shop in Killester. He says that he 'sliced by' a few opponents in his time but he never 'chopped' any of them up! Training sessions at Milltown were basic and consisted of a couple of runs. 'Buller Byrne would stand at one end of the ground and Bob Fullam at the other to make sure that the players did their laps.'

Travelling long distances to away games was different then to what one would expect now. 'We travelled to Cork by taxis. It was not easy having to get out and play after such a journey but it was something that was done then.' (There were no trains then due to the Emergency and, in general, there was a shortage of materials and fuel.) There were some great players at the club during Tommy's time there and of these he selects the ex-Portadown and Linfield player Davy Cochrane as one of the best. 'He was an outside right who captained the Northern Ireland team and he had superb skills', he said.

Tommy spent just three full seasons at Milltown before he left at the end of 1945/46 along with team mate Peter Farrell to join Everton who were trying to rebuild after the war. It was when the team were returning to Dublin from Belfast on the train that he and Farrell learned from the newspapers that they had been included in the Irish team to play against Spain and Portugal in the first post-war internationals.

'When we returned from Europe with the Irish team we were informed by Mr Joe Cunningham that Everton were interested in signing us and it all happened so quickly from there.' The former Rovers outside left went on to win a total of 24 international caps and on his return from England signed up with Cork Hibernians. 'I don't understand the game nowadays, it has changed so much that it is completely different. For instance they don't play wingers so someone like me would be made redundant', he says.

Three trophies came to Milltown in 1944/45, the FAI Cup, the Dublin City Cup and the President's Cup. For only the second time Rovers and Bohs met in the final of the FAI Cup with victory going to Rovers.

The Dublin City Cup was won outright by the Hoops who collected maximum points from their seven games but in the Shield Rovers collected three points in seven games and finished last in the table amid a serious injury crisis at the club.

The first game of the season saw Rovers beat Drumcondra 2-0 on 20 August to win the President's Cup for the third time in succession. With six games of the League played Rovers shared the top of the table with Cork United on ten points each. A classic encounter was in store at the Mardyke on 21 January when the two leading sides were due to meet.

In that game Rovers were overrun by a Cork side which slammed in six goals without reply. The rout began after 15 minutes following a mistake by centre half Gerry Breen which allowed the Cork inside right, Tommy Moroney, the chance to score. Fifteen minutes after that Owen Madden added the second with Connie Forde getting the first of his two goals not long afterwards. In the second half Moroney got a second, Sean McCarthy made it five and then Forde got his second. It was a superb performance by Cork whose full backs, Hayes and Duffy, along with centre half McGowan, destroyed the Rovers' front line.

When the sides met again in the second last League game of the season the Hoops won 3-2 but Cork had already won the title by then. Liam Crowe scored twice for Rovers whose other goal was scored by Podge Gregg.

1945/46 was a quiet season for Rovers although they did win the Inter-City Cup when they overcame Belfast Celtic in the two-legged final. The President's Cup was won when Rovers beat Shels by 3-2 at Milltown but in the Leinster Senior Cup final the Reds achieved revenge with a 4-0 win. There was no success in the FAI Cup either with Drumcondra beating the Hoops in the final. Davy Cochrane made a return to the club for one season but with the war now over he was set to resume his career in the English League with Leeds United. Jimmy McAlinden, an inside forward from Belfast Celtic, arrived at Rovers during 1945/46. He too, like Cochrane, had been playing in England before the war and he went straight from Milltown back to Portsmouth with the cessation of hostilities. Had Rovers been lucky enough to have had the services of McAlinden some years earlier they might have been able to break the domination of Cork United for the native of West Belfast was instrumental in making Belfast Celtic probably the strongest outfit north of the Border during this time.

As Rovers began the 1946/47 season the departure of Peter Farrell and Tommy Eglington to Everton was a major loss to the League of Ireland in general. Also gone from the club were Davy Cochrane, Jimmy McAlinden and Noel Kelly.

Tom Breen, the former Manchester United and Eire international 'keeper, had signed for the Hoops from Linfield. Around this time too came the former Bohs right half Ossie Nash and Joe Murray from the 'Gate'. A number of young players were introduced to the team including John Behan, a younger brother of Billy, Lar O'Byrne and A. Dunne, all of whom came from CYMS Ringsend. Des Treacy from Home Farm was added to the side while 'keeper Larry Palmer left the club to join Drumcondra.

Eight of the players from the previous season were re-signed: Jimmy Collins ('keeper), Mattie Clarke, Frank Glennon, Charlie Byrne, Bobby Rogers, John Staines, Paddy Coad and Podge Gregg.

Admission prices to grounds had gone up and it now cost 1/6d to the reserved terrace; the unreserved terrace had gone up from 9d to 1/- and the price for schoolboys had doubled from 3d to 6d. Rovers players were earning around £2 per week at this time.

The situation whereby players from another League were free to come and go in the League of Ireland and vice versa was popularly known as 'The Open Door'. The League of Ireland had for many years been trying to get the other 'Home' Associations to recognise its retention lists but to no avail. However, when Rovers signed Jack Dodds, the former Sheffield United and Blackpool centre forward, this stirred up a controversy as Blackpool claimed that he was one of their players.

It was Mary Jane Cunningham who was responsible for bringing Dodds to Milltown. Dodds (29) was a Scottish international who had been transferred from Huddersfield to Sheffield for nothing and later commanded a fee of £10,000 when he moved to Blackpool. In five seasons at Blackpool he scored 255 goals and the English First Division side were seeking the sum of £8,000 for his transfer to another club. The fact that he had decided to pursue his career in the League of Ireland without compensation to Blackpool was too much to take and a major row developed at home and in England.

Dodds arrived in Dublin on the Wednesday prior to the Dublin City Cup game against Drumcondra which was due to take place at Milltown on Sunday, February 8th. He turned out in that game and his presence in the Rovers' team swelled the gate to almost 20,000. The Rovers' team lined out as follows: Breen; Clarke, Glennon; Nash, Staines, Rogers; Coad, Gregg, Delaney, Dodds, O'Byrne.

Dodds opened the scoring for Rovers, 'Kit' Lawlor equalised for Drums from the penalty spot then Dodds again gave Rovers the lead only for that to be cancelled out by Dermot Delaney - and that's how it ended.

Rovers lost their next game to Shelbourne and this effectively meant that they were out of the running for the City Cup. The gate of £718 at Shelbourne Park for that game was the biggest at the venue for fifteen years.

The whole Dodds affair proved to be useful to the League of Ireland for shortly after that the other Home Associations agreed that in future they would recognise the registrations of players who were retained by League of Ireland clubs.

The Inter-City Cup came to Milltown for the third occasion when Rovers beat Drumcondra 4-1 on aggregate to lift the cup. In the League it was a case of so near and yet so far. With Drums having finished their League programme on 18 points, Rovers and Shels shared second place on 17 points but had a game each to play and as luck would have it this final League game was between the two sides. The winners of this game would automatically be declared champions but if a draw was to be the outcome then the three top teams would finish level and a three-way play off would be necessary.

Shels set out in the game to upset Rovers' plans. Brennan started as centre forward but alternated with Hansen and Laing and this often left Rovers centre half John Staines with the task of trying to handle two players at the same time. Shels used the ball very well, their wing halves and forwards were outstanding, especially compared to the Rovers front line. Shelbourne won the game 2-1 and were declared champions for the fifth time.

The late 'forties and early 'fifties were lean times for Shamrock Rovers even though Jimmy Dunne had returned to the club in 1946/47 from Bohs. There was some success during 1947/48 with the Dublin City Cup and FAI Cup coming to Milltown. Cork United won the Shield with a point to spare over Rovers. In the League the Hoops finished in fourth place, Drumcondra were champions with Dundalk and Shels running to a close second. The season was not over yet, though, and it was after the first round, first leg game of the Inter-City Cup against Distillery that some bad feeling began to descend at Milltown. The game was staged four days before the FAI Cup final between Rovers and Drums. The sides drew 2-2 and with a 1-1 draw being recorded for the second leg both sides went through to the second round.

When the Rovers' players opened their pay packets in the week in which the first leg game was played they were surprised to learn that although they had been paid a bonus for drawing with Distillery they had not been paid the customary match fee for playing in an Inter-City Cup game. The arrangement in previous seasons was that the City Cup games would be played at the end of the season when the players were no longer receiving a weekly pay packet and any player who played in an Inter-City Cup game would be paid a fee.

A chain of events was to take place arising out of the failure by Shamrock Rovers to pay the players for that first leg game against Distillery and as a result a number of players were never to play League of Ireland football again. Podge Gregg, who had scored the only goal of the 1945 FAI Cup final was one of those players. 'I would say that the Cunningham family were entitled to do what they did in one sense', he recalled.

'We were playing Drumcondra in the Cup final and Rovers brought an Inter-City Cup game forward by a week to the previous Wednesday. When we got our pay packets we discovered that we had not received our match fee. Tom Dunne was the first to go in and collect his wages; he came back to the pavilion and said that we had been paid only our bonus. Owen Coyle and myself then went in and we had a few words with the club directors about it but we never got anything out of it. The players played on for a couple of more games to try and resolve the matter but when the game against Belfast Celtic came around we decided not to travel to Belfast for the first leg.

Jimmy Collins, Jim Gilbert, Des Treacy and Tom Dunne were not involved but they said that they would not go to Belfast either, we did not want to involve them and told them that but they insisted on it. The whole thing sickened me but it did not stop me from keeping an interest in Rovers after that.'

As the records now show, Rovers honoured their fixture with Celtic in the semi-final when Paddy Coad took a makeshift team up North but the Hoops were beaten 2-1 and lost the tie by 4-2 on aggregate. During his time with Rovers, Podge suffered a serious knee injury and he could not settle down upon his return to the team. 'I was out for eighteen months and after several operations I came back into the first team but I was not happy with the set up so I went to Scotland to work.' When he returned to Dublin Rovers did not want him for they had since signed Bobby Rogers from St James's Gate. He went to Glentoran for a full season before returning to the Hoops and helped them to win the FAI Cup in 1945.

THE PATH OF THE CUP

In 1941 Rovers beat Cork Hibs 8-3 in the first round and then beat Brideville 3-1 in the quarter-final. Joe Ward scored four times in the game against Cork. The semi-final required three games before Waterford were victorious in the final game winning by 3-2.

Paddy Coad made his debut with Rovers in the first round game against Brideville on 8 February 1942. Brideville took the lead with a goal from Sammy Smyth mid way through the second half. Rovers made some positional changes with centre forward Jimmy Dunne switching to inside right and Coad, who had been inside right, moving into the centre. Dunne put Rovers back on level terms with Coad and Davy Cochrane getting two more after that to ensure victory.

The quarter-finals saw the Hoops overcome Bray Unknowns and advance into the semi-finals where they were beaten 2-1 by Dundalk. In 1943 they lost to Brideville in the quarter-final and that was considered to be a surprise defeat. Rovers had taken the lead when Mickey Delaney scored but Byrne got an equaliser for Brideville midway through the second half. They kept up the pressure after that and Smyth made no mistake with his penalty kick after a handball in the box.

In the first leg of the first round (due to the war the first round was held over two legs) Rovers had a decisive win against Bohemians at Dalymount Park winning 2-0. Bohs came back to Milltown the following week in fighting spirit. Kevin O'Flanagan had a shot which hit the upright but the Rovers defence put in a flawless display and the game ended scoreless.

Rovers and Limerick were drawn together in the first round in 1944 with Rovers winning the tie 7-3 on aggregate. The semi-final was also staged over two legs and Rovers and Drumcondra were drawn together. A crowd of 12,069 witnessed the first leg on 25 March which the Hoops won 2-0 thanks to goals from Eglington and Coad. In the second leg a week later Drumcondra took the lead after just three minutes through Tommy McNamara. Just one minute after the restart they got a second from Leo Ward. Then the Hoops showed their true Cup fighting spirit when they scored an unbelievable five times in the final fourteen minutes. The first of these came when Liam Crowe set Coad up and after that the Drums rearguard seemed to collapse as Coad got another and Bobby Rogers got a hat trick. A crowd of 16,892 paid gate receipts of £870 to watch this game which, like the first leg, was staged at Dalymount Park.

The final against Shelbourne which took place at Dalymount Park on 16 April saw Rovers open the scoring after just eight minutes when Liam Crowe paved the way for Rogers to shoot into the net. Ten minutes after that, Larry Palmer was hesitant in going for a lob and Sid Walsh was quick to challenge, the loose ball went to Willie Fallon and he was in the right position to score the equaliser. Eddie Gannon had the misfortune of scoring an own goal to give Rovers the lead again and then five minutes before half-time Fred Kiernan only managed to palm a shot by Coad which went to Crowe who proceeded to loft the ball back over the head of the 'keeper.

Shelbourne had a wonderful chance in the second half but team captain Paddy Kinsella failed to convert a penalty kick after Mattie Clarke handled in the box. With ten minutes to go Mick McCluskey scored a second goal for Shelbourne and Fallon then missed out on a chance to give Shels a replay when his shot went inches wide. The final result, then, was 3-2 to Rovers.

In 1945, Limerick recorded their first ever win at Milltown when they beat Rovers 3-2 in the first round of the Cup. The Hoops redeemed the tie by winning the second leg 3-1 the following week at the Markets Field. When they were beaten 3-0 by Dundalk in the first leg of the semi-final at Dalymount Park it looked all over for the Hoops but, remarkably, Rovers won the second leg 5-0 at Dalymount a week later before a crowd of 24,000. The Rovers' goals came from Coad, an own goal by Matthews and a hat trick from Podge Gregg.

The final between Rovers and Bohs on 22 April 1945 attracted an all-time record attendance of 41,238. Rovers won the game 1-0 and although the Bohs' defence had played well they appeared to lose heart after Podge Gregg had scored in the 56th minute.

The following year the Hoops made it into the final with Drumcondra. It turned out to be an unlucky Cup final number thirteen for Rovers. After just a minute Coad scored for the Hoops and then after 12 minutes Drumcondra equalised through Tommy McCormack. A draw looked likely but five minutes from the end Peter Farrell attempted to clear over the head of Dermot Delaney but it hit the Drums man on the chest and he sent it to Benny 'Rosie' Henderson who then scored the winning goal.

In 1947 Rovers went out to Shelbourne in the first round but were back into the final the following year. Before that, though, Podge Gregg scored four goals in the semi-final against St Pats when Rovers won 8-2.

A chance to avenge the Cup final defeat of 1946 was set up when Rovers and Drums met in the final at Dalymount Park. Coad was in top form and he was the main driving force behind a fine victory. Early in the game Rovers 'keeper Jimmy Collins was forced to make a good save with his fingertips when he managed to divert a low dipping shot by Paddy Daly. Shortly after that the Northsiders took the lead in the 18th minute when 'Rosie' Henderson caught the Rovers defenders by surprise and scored with a hard drive. Both 'keepers were kept busy before Ossie Nash dribbled upfield and slipped the ball to Coad whose first-time shot went in for the equaliser.

After 30 minutes of the second half, a misunderstanding between 'keeper Keogh and Kevin Clarke let Eugene Kirby in to score the second for Rovers. Drums were thrown a late lifeline when Bobby Rogers handled the ball in the box but Henderson had his spot kick saved by Collins. It was Henderson who had scored the winner with a late strike in the final two years before. A close rivalry had developed between Rovers and Drumcondra and the two sides were destined to meet again in the FAI Cup finals of 1955 and 1957.

Jimmy Collins was the regular Rovers' goalkeeper by the time the 1948 final was played but it was his predecessor, Larry Palmer, who had played in the finals of 1944 and 1945.

'The best memory I have about it all is the year that we beat Bohemians in the final when the Cup was run on a home and away basis in the early rounds', recalled Larry Palmer. 'Limerick beat us 3-2 up in Milltown and we went back to Limerick and beat them 3-1. We were travelling from six o'clock on the Saturday evening until seven o'clock the following morning and we were still on time to get Mass in the Augustinian Church in Limerick. The trains were run on turf at that time and it took that long to get from Dublin to Limerick. The frost was beating down at three o'clock in the morning when we were waiting for the train to come from Limerick to Limerick Junction and the only way we had of keeping ourselves warm was to have a game of soccer on the station platform!'

Larry was seven years with the Hoops, having joined in 1939, and it was he who kept Mick McCarthy out of the side. He has many other memories of travelling down the country during the war years.

'At that time you could not go beyond fifty miles and on the journey to Cork by taxi you would have to wait at Portlaoise for another taxi to take you on to Cahir and after you had your poached egg and toast at Cahir House you would then travel on to Cork in another taxi and after the match the journey back to Dublin would have to be made in the same way.

We were coming over The Curragh one Monday morning and it was just gone five o'clock. Mattie Clarke was with us and he had to be in his job in the brewery at six o'clock but that was the way we had to do it then.'

Larry is credited with probably having made the best ever save at Dalymount Park when he denied the late Joey Donnelly in the Inter-City Cup final between Rovers and Dundalk in 1942. Larry was said to have been running back into the goal with his back to Donnelly when he saw the ball heading into the net and somehow managed to turn it away.

'It was just the way a game goes', he recalls, 'I had kicked the ball out to the late Jimmy Dunne but Joey Donnelly got in before Jimmy and whipped it back in; it was heading towards the top corner of the net and I jumped up and grabbed it. I would say that was my best save ever.'

'I enjoyed my years with Rovers', says Larry who went on to Drumcondra after the Hoops but was not happy there and later went on to St Pat's. Today, Larry lives with his family in Mangerton Road, Drimnagh.

'They called him "The Cat" because he could pounce on the ball from about eight or nine feet away', recalled Edmund 'Emo' Sheeran who played at inside left for Rovers during the late 'thirties and early 'forties. 'I saw him stop so many penalties that it was incredible. If a goalkeeper is supposed to stay stationary in the middle of the goal for a penalty, and that's all the time that Larry Palmer had, he could move in that half second real fast by pouncing like a cat.'

It was a tradition for Rovers' supporters to walk behind a white horse from Ringsend on Cup final day. William Reid from Crumlin recalled one such occasion when his father, Stephen, rode the white horse to Dalymount. On that particular occasion the horse belonged to a local coal merchant, a Mr O'Keefe of South Lotts Road. 'Nibby' Warren provided a white horse on another occasion, so there were several white horses over the years.

Spotlight on Paddy Coad

Paddy Coad was born in Waterford City on 14 April 1920. He was sixteen years of age when he started out in minor football with Corinthians.

In 1937/38 he first appeared with Waterford and impressed to such a degree that he was taken on with Irish League side Glenavon with the aim of introducing him to the English League. However, war had broken out in Europe in the meantime and Paddy returned to Kilcohan Park.

During his career, which spanned twenty-three years, Paddy performed at inside left, inside right and on the odd occasion at outside left. In later years he also appeared for Rovers as a wing half, either right or left.

When he first appeared for Waterford in the League of Ireland the Kilcohan Park ground was not new to him for he had attended many a game there in the early 'thirties when he was a schoolboy.

'The trainer then was Davy Christie who was a professional runner', recalled Paddy. 'All of our training then consisted of running long distances, say to Tramore and back, a ten or twelve miles run. We saw the ball only about twice in a week when we had a five-a-side. At Rovers it was similar, only five or six players trained in the morning time, Jimmy Dunne and myself were the only full-time professionals and the rest trained twice a week, on Tuesday and Thursday nights.'

Waterford and Rovers were drawn in the FAI Cup semi-final in 1941 when it took three games to settle the issue. 'The first replay should have been played in the Iveagh Grounds', said Paddy, 'but when we got to Kingsbridge (Heuston station) we were told that the match had been called off as the ground was waterlogged. We never got off the train and we went straight back home! The following Wednesday the game was staged at Dalymount Park and it ended up as a draw again after extra time. The Waterford chairman came into the dressing-room after the game and said that he wanted us to play again the following night but that Shamrock Rovers did not want to play two matches in two days because they had some older players. In any case the FAI wanted to play the game again the following night and we said that we would play. It turned out to be another great game, we were leading Rovers by 3-0 at one stage but it ended up 3-2 after we had to battle like hell to hold on.'

Waterford and Cork United finished level at the top of the League table as the 1940/41 season came to an end. When the Waterford players sought a bonus from the club in the event of their winning the title the club refused to concede the demand and the players responded by refusing to travel to Cork to play in the proposed play-off. As a result, Waterford were dismissed from senior football by the League whose property the players now became.

Waterford's loss was Shamrock Rovers' gain as the young Paddy Coad was signed by the Milltown club but was eligible to play in Cup competitions only. There was a long-held belief that when Paddy came into the team for the first time in the FAI Cup first round game against Brideville in 1942 he did so at the expense of Jimmy Dunne, a favourite of the Milltown faithful. In fact this was not the case, as Paddy himself explained: 'Jimmy Dunne was dropped for the semi-final against Dundalk. People said that it was for me but it was for Dessie Westby. Looking back on it now, it was a mistake because Jimmy had so much experience and Dessie Westby was really a full back whom they used to stick up front now and again.' Rovers were beaten by Dundalk after a replay.

Jimmy Dunne left the Hoops in 1943 to join Bohemians but later on came back to the club. By then Paddy Coad was a well-established player at Milltown and the skills which he displayed on the pitch earned him respect throughout the League. Paddy was well respected off the pitch too and was well valued by the Cunningham family at Milltown.

'I was offered the job of coach when Jimmy Dunne died', recalled Paddy. 'I was reluctant to take it because I thought it was a bit of a daunting task but they told me that I was good enough to do the job. Going back before that, even before I was offered the job of team captain, I thought it was a big job to be captain of Shamrock Rovers having only been there for a few years. I was a quiet sort of player but I learned as I went on. I never spoke a lot on the pitch because Jimmy Dunne used to say that you should not talk to guys on the pitch but as you get hold of the job and get to know the guys around you it is then that you know that you have to get on to some of them and talk them through a game.'

It was generally recognised that Paddy Coad was one of the all-time greats. He added to his knowledge by attending FA coaching courses at Rhyl and Lillishall. Before Paddy became coach at Milltown the team was selected by a committee which comprised of Joe Cunningham Snr, his wife Mary Jane, Captain Tom Scully, Mattie McNevin and Charlie Fitzsimons. When Paddy Coad became coach he used to select the team himself although he always consulted Joe Cunningham Snr.

'On the odd occasion that he did not travel down the country with the team I would always have to ring him when I got back to Dublin, no matter what time, and let him know how the game went and how the team played or what happened if we were beaten. But he would never interfere; he was a great man', said Paddy.

Paddy Coad and his assistants spent much of their time searching for suitable talent and eventually a team was to come together which virtually dominated Irish soccer for the best part of a decade. 'We missed out on some players too', said Paddy, 'for instance, Alan Kelly, the great goalkeeper. I went twice to see him and he did not impress me.'

Rovers won the League of Ireland title in 1953/54 and success just seemed to flow after that. They were rarely out of the running in any competition. During the period that Paddy Coad was in charge at Milltown the League title was won three times, the FAI Cup twice, the Leinster Senior Cup four times, the Dublin City Cup four times and the Top Four competition twice.

The players themselves all became household names and it was not difficult for supporters to memorise the team. O'Callaghan, Burke, Mackey, Nolan, Keogh, Hennessy, McCann, Hamilton, Coad, Ambrose, Peyton and Tuohy were the principal players who brought success to the club on an unprecedented level.

'One thing that stood to that team was that they believed in what they were doing and nothing would put them off. That is why I believe they were so good at the time', recalled Paddy. 'Money never entered into it. When we played the first leg of our European Cup tie against Manchester United we got £25 a man for playing and we got £20 each for the second leg. In later years, after I left Rovers, I listened to other people talking, I mean players were looking for appearance money, £50 just to get out onto the pitch! I think this is what is killing the game a little nowadays.'

Those two games against Manchester United represented the high point of his entire career. The Rovers' team did not prepare any differently for this encounter with the mighty Man. United. As it was, they trained that little bit more than the other clubs in the League of Ireland. Even when they played on a Wednesday they trained at Milltown the following night. Before the tie at Dalymount Park the team met in the Gresham Hotel for a meal.

'We gave them a good game for most of it and it was only a lack of fitness that let us down in the end. It was not through a lack of football ability or that we were not good enough. It was their superior fitness that won it for them'.

The second leg at Old Trafford saw the Hoops restore their pride with a battling performance which took the home side by surprise although United held out for a 3-2 victory.

'We really played well that night. It was one of the best games which the side ever played and as a matter of fact it was that game which more or less decided for me that it was time to stop playing. I felt tired after that game, the first time that I really felt jaded because it was a fast game; there was no let up.

One thing really pleased me afterwards. The Boss Joe Cunningham Snr would not normally say anything but that evening he came into the dressing-room and said that I was outstanding and that I was probably the best player out on the pitch. He had never said anything like that to anybody before and he had just gone out when Peter Farrell came in and shook hands with me and said that he had always sung my praises to the players in England. He had been with some of them that night and they said to him that he had been right "about that boy".'

Gradually Paddy played less and less and, in January 1960, he departed from Milltown to take up the position of coach at Waterford. He played for the 'Blues' on occasion and in all played senior football up to the age of forty-two.

While at Milltown Paddy scored many great goals. He scored over one hundred goals in League games alone but it was one in a Cup game which he considers to have been among the best: 'One of the better goals was in a Cup replay against Evergreen at Milltown in 1953. The ball came across from the right hand side and I happened to be facing with my back towards their goal. When the ball arrived in front of me I knocked it down and stepped over it facing into the goal I was playing into now and I just smacked it straight away with my left foot and it went in like a rocket from about fifteen yards out. Mickey Burke ran the whole length of the pitch and he said to me that he had never seen a goal like it. It was the best goal he had ever seen, he said.'

In total, Paddy Coad won 11 caps with the Irish senior team and also made 26 appearances for the League of Ireland inter-League team from 1943 to 1955. He won three League medals and was also on the winning side in the FAI Cup finals of 1944, 1945, 1948 and 1956. He won runners-up medals from the finals of 1941 (with Waterford), 1946, 1957 and 1958. He was with Rovers when they won the Dublin City Cup four times and he also won four Leinster Senior Cup medals. He led the Hoops twice to victory in the Top Four Competition.

Following a long battle against cancer Paddy Coad died in his native Waterford on 8 March 1992.

SPOTLIGHT ON JIMMY DUNNE

Jimmy Dunne began his career in soccer with local Ringsend sides, Parkview and Riverside Athletic. Having played a number of games with the Rovers senior side, 'Snowy', as his friends called him, was signed by English League side New Brighton.

During the 1925/26 season when Dunne, a centre forward, was signed by New Brighton, he was twenty-one years old. Not long after that he went from New Brighton to Sheffield United where he soon came to fame. It was with Arsenal, though, that he won an English League medal after he had left Sheffield at the start of the 1933/34 season. After three seasons at Highbury Jimmy went to Southampton where he spent just one season before returning to Dublin to take up a position as player/coach with Shamrock Rovers.

Those who remember seeing Dunne play will testify to his undoubted skills. He was as powerful with his head as he was with his foot. Although he scored 230 League goals and when he returned to Milltown for the 1937/38 season he brought a wealth of knowledge with him which was to benefit many players who were to pass through the club in the years to come.

As leader both on and off the field Dunne led Rovers to the League of Ireland title in 1937/38, their first since 1931/32. The following season the Hoops retained the title, Dunne occupying the outside right berth for most of this season, a position he had played in before. His leadership on the pitch was a major factor in Rovers' successes around this period.

Dunne did not always see eye to eye with the Cunningham family and in the 1942/43 season he moved across the city to manage Bohemians. After four years at Dalymount he re-joined Rovers after the club had gone through a lean period. He laid the foundations to revitalise the club but sadly he was not to live to see the results.

His two sons, Tommy and Jimmy, were also to play in the League of Ireland, Tommy for Rovers and St Pat's and Jimmy for St Pat's alone. 'Football was bred through us', recalled Tommy. 'My father never really said a lot. He used to bring us out into the back garden and show us the little things in the game.'

While Jimmy Senior was deadly with his feet those same feet had suffered a lot over the years and he had his own form of medicine to ease the pain. 'He used to send myself and my brother, Jimmy, down to Sandymount Strand to collect buckets of saltwater and put a bit of seaweed in so that he could bathe his feet in it.' In fact, Jimmy, who originally lived in Thorncastle street, played in his bare feet in his younger days as indeed all the young men had to do then. They simply could not afford to buy football boots.

Before he joined Shamrock Rovers Jimmy had been interned by the newly formed government of the Irish Free State because of his active support for the republican movement but according to Tommy he never really held such strong views; in fact, he had been mistaken for his brother Christy ('Crongy') who was the active republican in the family.

'My father was a terrible man for worrying but he was a very quiet man', said Tommy.

During his career Jimmy Dunne was capped by the FAI fifteen times and by the IFA a further seven times. In addition he made six inter-League appearances for the League of Ireland.

It was in November 1949, that Jimmy Dunne died suddenly at his home in Tritonville Road, Sandymount, as a result of a heart attack. Rovers' fans everywhere were stunned. The news immediately spread and crowds soon gathered at the house. Although the morning of the funeral saw heavy rainfall many thousands lined the route of the procession which went through Ringsend and on out to Deansgrange Cemetery.

Many supporters who saw the Rovers sides of the 'thirties, 'forties and 'fifties agree that the three greatest players ever to play for the Hoops were Paddy Moore, Jimmy Dunne and Paddy Coad. All three played on the same Rovers' team which played against Belfast Celtic in Dunne's benefit game on 31 August 1942.

Rovers and Celtic drew 2-2 at Dalymount Park and the following is an extract from the match report of 'Socaro' in the *Irish Press*:

'The attendance was a well merited appreciation of Jimmy Dunne's service to the game and it was equally fitting that Paddy Moore, another Shamrock Rovers product, should enthrall the crowd during the early stages of the game with all his former artistry.

His deft flicks, his headwork and positional play recalled vividly to mind his prowess in his heyday and tumultuous applause greeted his scoring of Rovers first goal. It was a masterly effort.'

Moore's contribution in that game was a fitting tribute from one great star to another.

CHAPTER FIVE

A DRAMATIC NEW ERA

(1 9 4 8 - 5 9)

I n 1948/49 Rovers were never in the running for the League title which went to Drums for the second season in succession but they did win the last Inter-City Cup competition when they beat Dundalk 3-0 in the final at Dalymount Park.

Following the demise of Cork United their place in the League was taken by Cork Athletic and the first meeting between the new club and Shamrock Rovers took place at Milltown on 12 December when the Hoops won 3-1. In the return game at the Mardyke on 13 February 1949, the Hoops squeezed a 4-3 victory; one of their best performances for a long time. Their scorers were Paddy Mullen (2), Frank Glennon and Jimmy Gaynor. The Rovers line-out that day was: Godwin; T. Dunne, O'Byrne; Daly, Coad, Nash; Duffy, Gaynor, Little, Glennon, Mullen. Mattie Clarke, Eugene Kirby and Tommy O'Connor were all absent through injury. Ossie Higgins was also missing.

The following season, 1949/50, Rovers won the Shield for the eighth time but it was their only success that season and they finished well down the League and City Cup tables. Liam Hennessy signed for Rovers after a brief spell with Wolverhampton Wanderers. Frank Radford signed from Shelbourne and slotted in at either half back or in the forward line. Freddie Kiernan, the former Shels and Sligo 'keeper, had been playing in the Leinster Senior League with Drums when Paddy Coad coaxed him out of retirement to play for Rovers. Also arriving at Milltown at that time was Paddy Daly, a centre half who came out of junior football and later went to Aston Villa along with Ossie Higgins. Paddy Ambrose made his debut for Rovers against Transport on 28 August 1949 in a Dublin City Cup game at the Carlisle Grounds when the Hoops lost by 1-0.

1950/51 was one of the few seasons that Rovers were hardly in the running for any trophy, the Shield being the only exception. At the end of the Shield competition Rovers, Drums and Transport all finished level on 13 points each. The two Dublin giants were drawn against each other in the play-off while Transport were given a bye into the final. When the sides met on 18 April a 1-1 draw was recorded which meant that they had to meet again. However, Rovers protested against the appointment of Mr E. Boland as referee and appealed to the Emergency Committee of the FAI. The protest was turned down; the Hoops did not accept the decision and they were put out of the Shield. Drumcondra went on to beat Transport 3-1 in the final play-off. Cork Athletic won the League with Rovers finishing in sixth place, nine points behind the leaders.

That season the Hoops welcomed Jim McGuire, a left full from Glasgow Celtic who had impressed when he lined out for Rovers in a pre-season friendly against Aston Villa. Also arriving in Milltown that season was Brian O'Kelly, an inside left from Bohemians; Freddie Doyle, a former centre forward with Shels; Liam Galvin, a left full or inside left from Drums; Pat Lynch, a centre forward from Dundalk; and Christy Boggan from Home Farm who played up front or in the middle. Robert Ryan, a half back and John Duffy, a goalkeeper, both came from junior football and Christy Bergin, who had played at outside left with Waterford, appeared with the first team that season. Eugene Kirby and Ossie Nash were released by the club around this time.

Mattie Clarke was awarded a benefit game that season for his eleven years' service at the club. A good crowd turned out to witness Rovers defeat Shelbourne 2-0 at Tolka Park.

Rovers may not have set the League of Ireland alight that season but they were represented on the League team which was beaten by the English League at Dalymount Park on 4 April 1951. 'Keeper Freddie Kiernan and Paddy Coad were the two Rovers' players on the side that day.

It was in December 1951 that Liam Hennessy played his first game for Rovers senior team and he never looked back after that.

'The first game I played was quite a milestone because Rovers had not won a game for nine matches and there were three of us brought in from the "B" team to play a League game in Limerick, one of the worst places you could ever play in. Myself, Peter Williams and Con Archbold were the three who were brought in that day. I scored a goal from about 35 yards out and that was a great thrill for me on my debut', Liam recalled.

He appeared as an inside left that day but it was as an outside left and then as a left half that he made his greater contribution. For a period he also played as left full. 'I had a good penalty conversion rate. In 1958 I had scored eleven consecutive penalties but unfortunately I missed one in the Cup final that year against Dundalk. I think I was a little bit over-confident.'

Two years before that he had made certain from the spot when he scored the equaliser in the eightieth minute of that famous Cup final against Cork Athletic. He says that game was one of the highlights of those years while another moment that stands out is the goal which he scored against Nice at Dalymount Park in the European Cup. That goal was a piledriver which was scored from 40 yards out.

'I got a few of those in my day', recalls Liam. He also recalls the size of the crowds then and laughs when he thinks about crowds of 20,000 or more turning up for Rovers games that today would be lucky to attract a thousand.

Quite a few players came to the club in the 1951/52 season including Albie Murphy, a left half from Clyde, Gerry Mackey and Mickey Burke from Johnville, Liam Tuohy from St Mary's, East Wall and Con Archbold, a forward from YMCA. Also signed by the Hoops that season were Liam 'Mousey' Munroe, an outside right; Danny Jordan, a centre forward from Bohemians; and Billy Burns, a centre forward who scored fifteen League goals during the 1951/52 season.

Christy O'Callaghan established himself as the regular 'keeper in the first team while his brother Danny was playing in the forward line. The Rovers' team which lined out against Dundalk in the League on 7 January 1952 was as follows: C. O'Callaghan;

Burke, McGuire; Coad, Daly, Murphy; Gaynor, Williams, Archbold, Hennessy, D. O'Callaghan.

That game ended 1-1 with Peter Williams scoring for Rovers and Fergus Moloney for Dundalk. A remarkable event occurred during this game when a shot by Paddy Coad appeared to have entered the Dundalk net. With the crowd applauding Coad for his 'goal' and referee Barrington running to the centre spot Coad surprised everyone by running up to the match official and pointing out that the ball had entered through the side netting. He requested that Mr Barrington disallow the effort. Coad was not rewarded for his honesty, though, for he missed a penalty later on in the game.

When Rovers and St Pat's met in a crucial League game at Milltown on 20 January the Hoops came out on top with a 3-1 win. Paddy Daly's brilliant marking of the St Pat's dangerman Shay Gibbons restricted the visitors to a single goal. Rovers finished third in the League and again there was no success in the other competitions.

Shamrock Rovers Football Club has had many fine hours in its glorious past but the 'fifties were especially kind to the Hoops and to League of Ireland football in general with crowds flocking to venues all around the country.

The Coad's Colts, so nicknamed by W. P. Murphy of the *Irish Independent* because the players were so much younger than player/coach Paddy Coad himself, won every possible honour in domestic football during this period.

One player who could quite possibly have been a part of this team, but who missed out, was Jimmy Gaynor. He came to Rovers in 1946/47 and he broke into the first team later on that season. Gaynor, an outside right although originally an inside right until Jimmy Dunne converted him into a winger, was transferred to Ipswich Town in the English League Third Division during the 1951/52 season. He returned home in 1962 and had spells in the League of Ireland with Dundalk and Drogheda.

'I could have been one of the Coad's Colts. I missed out on that all right', said Jimmy. 'When I was with Rovers there was a strike on at one time. Some of the players were looking for more money and a good few of them left after that. There always seemed to be a lot of transfers going on, they never really had a settled side, there was always two or three players going away each season.'

Jimmy Gaynor came from a background which was steeped in football tradition. He was a Shelbourne supporter as was his father. 'He nearly went mad when I signed for Rovers', said Jimmy, 'it was not so much what he said, though, it was what his mates said, but he became a Rovers fanatic after that.'

It was actually a change of fortune for the late Jimmy Dunne that brought Gaynor to Milltown in the first instance. 'Jimmy Dunne was manager of Bohs and he asked me up for a trial. I went up one evening full of the joys but he brought me back out and told me to go home saying that he would be in touch with me. I went home very disappointed but the next morning I read in the paper that Jimmy Dunne had resigned from Bohs and was taking over at Milltown, then I realised why he had sent me home. A couple of days later he signed me up for Rovers. He was absolutely brilliant as a coach. He was his own man', said Jimmy.

The sudden death of Jimmy Dunne in November 1949 came as a great shock to everybody connected with the game. 'I will never forget the day that he died', said Jimmy, 'I was going up Westland Row to get a bus to Milltown. I was working in the Docks at that time and if I wasn't working I would go up to the ground in the mornings to train. The newspaper seller held the *Independent* up to show me and called me over to have a look. The headline said; "Jimmy Dunne Dies". He was one of the greatest ever.'

1952/53 saw the arrival at the club of Ronnie Nolan. He was to establish himself first as a half back and later as centre half. Dixie Hale signed from Waterford but stayed for a short while only. Anthony Guildea came from junior side Glebe North and played in the forward line.

The Dublin City Cup came to Milltown in 1952/53 having been converted into a knockout competition the previous season. Rovers defeated Drumcondra by 1-0 in the final at Dalymount

Park before a crowd of 10,000. The only goal of the game was an own goal by Tim Coffey. The Leinster Cup was captured by Rovers when they defeated Bohs in the final replay at Dalymount Park on 31 December. Rovers won 2-0 with Liam Hennessy scoring twice.

The Hoops finished ninth in the Shield table along with Cork Athletic and Limerick but they came fairly close in the League finishing in third place to Shelbourne and Drums.

In 1953/54 the League title came to Milltown for the first time since 1938/39. Rovers finished joint second in the Shield with Drums while Limerick were the winners. There was no luck in the Dublin City Cup or Leinster Senior Cup while a 2-1 defeat at the hands of Drumcondra in the semi-final of the FAI Cup brought their best Cup run in six seasons to an end.

That Cup game between Rovers and Drums took place on 4 April but the season was not yet over for Rovers. The League title had still to be won. When Cork side Evergreen beat second-placed Drums by 2-1 on 14 April at Turner's Cross it put them into joint first place level with Rovers on 28 points. Only one game was needed to settle the issue as the two sides met in the last League game of the season at Milltown on Sunday, 18 April before a crowd of 15,000 which paid gate receipts of £1,060. That deciding game was a poor one under the circumstances. It was, however, a lucky day for young Liam Tuohy who had until now found it hard to break into the first team. In recent weeks he had laid a legitimate claim for a permanent place in the seniors. He had previously been dropped from the side and his place taken by Christy Warren from Pearse Rovers. But now Tuohy came back onto the first team and he was never again dropped while at Shamrock Rovers.

It was outside left Tuohy who scored the only goal after 20 minutes. Evergreen's right wing half, Seamus Madden, made a backpass to 'keeper Derry Barrett who should have gathered safely but let the ball roll out of his hands to where Tuohy was positioned and the Rovers man had the easy task of putting it into the back of the net. That was enough to bring the League title to Milltown for the seventh time.

That season saw the arrival at the club of Noel Peyton and Jimmy 'Maxie' McCann, both of whom came from St Mary's of East Wall, and Johnny Byrne, an inside forward who played mostly with the reserves.

The League title was the only honour to come to Milltown in 1953/54. In 1954/55 it was the only honour which did *not* come to the club! The Hoops made an otherwise clean sweep capturing the FAI Cup, the League of Ireland Shield, the Leinster Senior Cup, the Dublin City Cup and the LFA President's Cup.

Drumcondra had a great side then with players such as Paddy Neville, Johnny Robinson, Benny 'Rosie' Henderson and Tommy Rowe. The first game of the season was the President's Cup when Rovers beat Drums 2-1. The opening round of the Dublin City Cup saw Rovers beat Shelbourne 6-3 at Tolka Park before a crowd of 13,000. The semi-final paired the Hoops and Limerick at Tolka Park where a crowd of around 7,000 saw the Dublin side win comfortably through to the final. All round, the Hoops were impressive and won the game 3-0 with goals from Coad, Tuohy and Hennessy (penalty).

The final of the City Cup took place on Wednesday, 9 September at Dalymount Park where Rovers and Drums attracted a crowd of 11,000. For Rovers, Nolan and Hennessy were magnificent wing halves and won for them by completely controlling the wings. The Hoops won 2-0 with goals from Ambrose and Peyton.

In the Shield Rovers were beaten only once, at Kilcohan Park where a good Waterford side put in a brilliant performance to win by 6-1. Rovers bounced back the following week to beat Shels by 5-0 at Milltown. This win consolidated them at the top of the table on nine points along with St Patrick's Athletic.

These two sides met at St Pat's new ground at Chapelizod when a crowd of 12,300 paid £915. The ground could barely hold this crowd and many hundreds swarmed onto the sidelines. Paddy Coad was one of the few players to remain composed under the circumstances and it was he who set up Noel Peyton ten minutes into the second half for the only goal of the game. Only one point was dropped on the run in to the Shield title, to Sligo Rovers, and at the end the Hoops had three points to spare over the next placed side, Evergreen.

St Pat's won their second League title that season but the experience of that Shield game prompted the legislators to transfer their home League game against Rovers on 21 March to Dalymount Park. It turned out to be a wise decision as a crowd of 22,789 turned up. Rovers surprisingly cruised to a 5-0 win. Paddy Ambrose had a most memorable game scoring four times. His goals came in the 30th, 32nd, 78th and 86th minute. Paddy Coad got Rovers' fourth goal after 83 minutes.

Not many players score a hat trick on their debut but Leo O'Reilly did just that and went one better by scoring four goals altogether when he made his first appearance for Rovers against Dundalk in February 1955. Rovers won that game at Milltown by 7-3 with the other goals coming from Coad, Burke and Tuohy.

Players to come to Rovers that season were Hughie Gannon, an inside right from Johnville, and Tommy Mooney, a left winger from Hammond Lane.

Paddy Coad was rewarded with a benefit game that season and Chelsea provided quality opposition for the event. Chelsea were celebrating their centenary year and this they did in style by winning the English First Division title for the first time in their history. A crowd of 19,000 witnessed a fiery start in which Chelsea were shocked to find themselves 3-0 down after 23 minutes. Amazingly, Leo O'Reilly, a centre forward in the reserves, was called into the side late in the game when Paddy Ambrose was forced to withdraw and he gave a fabulous display. O'Reilly scored twice in the 7th and 23rd minutes with Tuohy getting Rovers' second in the 11th minute. The Hoops got a tremendous ovation from the crowd at half-time .

After the interval Chelsea made a spirited fightback and through Parsons and McNicholl came back to 3-2 with 15 minutes remaining. A great finish was witnessed with Gerry Mackey clearing off the goal line with minutes remaining. The crowd certainly got value for their money and the game was a fitting tribute to a man who had entertained so many for so long. The Rovers team that night was: O'Callaghan; Burke, Mackey; Nolan, Keogh, Hennessy; McCann, Peyton, O'Reilly, Coad, Tuohy.

Many players come and go in any club during a particular era but it is generally accepted that the following named players formed the team at Milltown which became known as the 'Coad's Colts': Christy O'Callaghan (goalkeeper); Mickey Burke (right full), Gerry Mackey (originally a centre half and later on a left full); Ronnie Nolan (right half and later on a centre half), Shay Keogh (centre half), Liam Hennessy (left half); Jimmy 'Maxie' McCann (outside right), Tommy Hamilton (inside left), Paddy Coad (inside forward or left half), Paddy Ambrose (centre forward), Noel Peyton (inside right), Liam Tuohy (outside left). 'Keeper Eamonn Darcy came in later on. Clem Dillon and Liam Munroe were in the forward line in 1953/54.

Gerry Mackey was just seventeen years of age when he was signed for the Hoops from a well-known South Dublin junior side called Johnville. 'I went into the first team in my second season', recalls Gerry. 'I got in as a left full although originally I was a right full. It was after Shay Keogh picked up an injury in a Cup match against Transport at Harold's Cross in March, 1954 that I went in as centre half. We won that game 2-1. I had a particularly good game myself and I was kept centre half after that.'

The general atmosphere among team members was good then and the enthusiasm was second to none. 'It was fantastic. We used to train three nights a week. Most of us used to go straight from work. We used to train on Tuesdays, Wednesdays and Thursdays. We trained very hard from 6.30 or 7 o'clock until 10 o'clock, they would have to pull us in. There were a few old lights about the place and even when it got dark we had sufficient light to train and when it was raining we went in underneath the stand, into what latterly became the "Hoops Bar". We used to call it a gymnasium but in fact there was nothing in it', recalled Gerry.

Gerry Mackey was capped three times by the Republic between 1956 and 1957 and also made ten inter-league appearances for the League of Ireland.

Travelling to away games in the League had not changed much since the 'forties but now the club travelled by train when necessary and like the 'twenties very often filled a train of their own. 'We travelled to away games in taxis, we went in big hired cars to Sligo etc. If it was a particularly important game occasionally we would stay overnight but generally speaking we travelled by car. We would meet at the Ballast Office or McBirney's on the morning of the game. When we really caught on, say if we were playing in Cork, Sligo, Limerick or Waterford, then the club would run an excursion train and we had fantastic crowds travelling with us.'

Each and every player on that team had a dedication to the game that was probably unmatched. There were so many great moments for this team from the time the League title came to Milltown in 1953/54. That honour came to the club again in 1956/57 and 1958/59. For four years on the trot the Hoops competed in the FAI Cup final, winning twice. The Leinster Senior Cup, the Dublin City Cup, the League of Ireland Shield and the Top Four (Independent Cup) all came to Milltown several times during that era. Nine of the team were capped by Ireland at full international level while nearly all of them appeared on the inter-League team.

'The highlight of it all', says Gerry Mackey, 'was the famous FAI Cup final in 1956 against Cork Athletic. I can remember the final goal because when the corner came over I was going for it and Ronnie Nolan came in behind me and I can remember to this day Ronnie saying "leave it" and when I looked up there he was heading it into the corner of the net and that must literally have been in the last seconds of the match. You never had Rovers beaten until the final whistle.'

This Rovers team was the first to represent the League of Ireland in a European competition when they played against Manchester United in 1957. The first leg of the European Cup tie (preliminary round) was played at Dalymount Park. It was a memorable occasion. Everyone knew then that United was probably one of the greatest teams that Britain had ever seen.

'We did particularly well against them and the records show that it was not really until late in the game when we had ourselves run to a standstill that they stuck in three goals against us but then we did particularly well in the return game at Old Trafford. That was a hell of a match', said Gerry Mackey.

When the Munich disaster took place six months later everyone was shocked at the death of so many fine players; but for Shamrock Rovers, who had played against them so recently, it was particularly hard. 'They were nearly all English international players and they were tremendously skilful. I will never forget the day of the disaster. At that time I worked with Irish Shell & BP and our offices were located in Fleet Street. I remember we were going home from work, I was coming down the stairs at about five o'clock and someone came dashing in with the news that they had crashed. It was terrible news.'

In 1955/56 Shamrock Rovers experienced mixed fortunes. The new season got off to a bad start with a 3-1 defeat by St Pat's in the President's Cup and in the Dublin City Cup they got no further than the semi-final when beaten 3-2 by Waterford. The most notable signing was Tommy Hamilton, a forward who had had a brief spell with Manchester United.

The Shield was won again, the Leinster Senior Cup too and it was the year of the famous FAI Cup final when Rovers defeated Cork Athletic 3-2. In the Shield the Hoops went through their eleven-game programme unbeaten and in the Leinster Senior Cup final at Dalymount Park on St Stephen's Day goals from McCann, Coad (pen) and Tuohy saw Rovers beat St Pat's 3-1. A new trophy was to come to Milltown this season with Rovers being the winners of the inaugural Top Four competition for which the Independent (Newspapers) Cup was put up.

Rovers had won nine out of their first ten League games but a 2-1 defeat by Waterford at Milltown on 27 January knocked them out of their stride. Rovers beat St Pat's 4-2 on 13 April in a 'thrilling struggle' which left the top of the table looking like this:

	P	W	D	L	F	A	Pts.
St Pat's	21	15	2	4	58	33	32
Rovers	20	15	1	4	51	24	31

The Rovers' scorers were Ambrose (2) and McCann (2) while Paddy O'Rourke and Shay Gibbons netted for St Pat's.

Rovers then lost 3-1 away to Waterford while in Sligo St Pat's, who were losing 1-0 at half time turned in a brilliant second-half performance to win 3-1 and clinch the title. Rovers then lost their last League game 3-2 to Bohs.

St Pat's and Rovers were drawn together in the semi-final of the Top Four. The game was played at Dalymount Park on Sunday, 22 April before a crowd of 17,500. After extra time the score stood at 3-3 with Rovers winning the game on corners by 9-8. Tuohy, Peyton and Hamilton scored for the Hoops; a Ronnie Nolan own goal gave St Pat's their first, followed by goals from Shay Gibbons and Jimmy Dunne.

Even extra time failed to separate the teams and with five minutes to go they were level on corners with eight apiece. Although Tuohy failed to score in front of an open goal that particular chance had come from Rovers' ninth corner which had been won by Noel Peyton and that extra corner was enough to give the Hoops victory.

Waterford provided the opposition in the final at Dalymount Park on 4 May. The Hoops gained sweet revenge for the League defeats when they beat the Blues through a solitary Maxie McCann goal.

Between the semi-final and final of the Top Four was the matter of the FAI Cup final, an occasion that anyone who was present at Dalymount Park on 29 April 1956 is ever likely to forget (see 'The Path of the Cup', page 104).

Coad's Colts were back again the next season and continued

where they had left off. 1956/57 was to be another tremendous success for this fabulous team. The squad was strengthened by the inclusion of Eugene Hoey, a left winger from the reserves, Hugh Geoghegan from Home Farm, and Eamonn Darcy, the former Dundalk 'keeper who had previously played in the English League with Oldham Athletic. Hughie Gannon was transferred to Shelbourne and was later to go to Dundalk.

In addition to the League title Rovers also won the League of Ireland Shield, the Leinster Senior Cup, the Dublin City Cup and the President's Cup. They made it into the final of the FAI Cup but were beaten by their old rivals Drumcondra.

The rivalry between these two sides was at its best around this period. Rovers pipped Drums to the League and Shield titles, beat them in the final of the Leinster Senior Cup, won on corners in the final of the Dublin City Cup but were beaten by their Northside rivals in the semi-final of the Top Four competition and, as mentioned above, in the FAI Cup final.

The opening game of the League was an away fixture against Drums at Tolka Park which ended 1-1. The Richmond Road venue was bursting at the seams with a crowd of 15,000 present. Drums right full 'Bunny' Fullam hardly gave Liam Tuohy a kick of the ball. In the opening Shield game at Milltown it was Tuohy who gave Fullam the run around.

When the sides met in the return League game at Milltown on 27 January Rovers were clear victors by 5-0. The scorers were Hamilton (2), McCann, Tuohy and Fullam o.g.

The final of the Leinster Senior Cup was played on its traditional date, 26 December. A crowd of 20,000 turned up at Dalymount Park to witness another duel between the top two of the League of Ireland. Rovers lined out as follows: Darcy; Burke, Mackey; Nolan, Keogh, Hennessy; McCann, Peyton, Ambrose, Hamilton, Tuohy. The Drums team was: Kelly; Fullam, McDonnell; Healy, O'Neill, Rowe; Lawlor, Cross, Coleman, McCourt, Campbell.

Alan Kelly in goal for Drums was much more in the action than his opposite number, Eamonn Darcy. Kelly pulled off a good save from Peyton but shortly before half time the latter gave Rovers the lead when he rounded Kelly to shoot into an empty net. Rovers went further ahead two minutes into the second half when Peyton set up Tuohy to run on and beat Kelly with a good shot and give the Hoops victory.

When the sides met in the semi-final of the Top Four competition at Dalymount Park on 1 May a crowd of 16,845 witnessed Drums repeat their FAI Cup final success of a week previously when they defeated Rovers 3-0. 'Kit' Lawlor, Johnny Campbell and Jackie McCourt were the scorers in a very convincing win for the Tolka Park side.

The League was won for the eighth time, though, and there were several big scores with Tommy Hamilton scoring a hat trick in the 6-0 defeat of Bohs at Milltown on 7 December. The only defeat in the League that season came in the final game against Cork Athletic when the home side won by 4-3, but Rovers had the title well wrapped up by then. The rivalry between the Hoops and Drumcondra continued unabated throughout 1957/58. The sides met in the final of the Leinster Senior Cup, the Top Four, the Dublin City Cup and the President's Cup with victory going to Rovers in all cases.

Drums won the League on 33 points with the Hoops coming in second with 31. Rovers again won the Shield this season for the fourth consecutive time. In the FAI Cup they were beaten by Dundalk in the final.

The 1957/58 season began with a 3-3 draw between the Hoops and Drums in the President's Cup. The replay was won by Rovers at Dalymount Park on 11 September with a lone goal from Tommy Hamilton. The final of the Dublin City Cup between the sides had taken place a week before that when a crowd of 14,000 went along to Dalymount Park to see the fierce rivals in action. They were not to be disappointed. Six goals were scored; unfortunately for Drums, Rovers scored four of them.

The meeting of Shamrock Rovers and Matt Busby's Manchester United in the European Cup, preliminary round, first leg tie at Dalymount Park on 25 September 1957, attracted a crowd of 46,000. The crowd witnessed an exciting and eventful first half in which the Hoops played well against a strong wind in the first half but yet trailed by a single goal at the interval.

The opening stages saw the Rovers defence of Burke, Mackey, Nolan, Keogh and Hennessy all play well with 'keeper Darcy pulling off some good saves from Liam Whelan and David Pegg. Later in the game Ray Wood cleared a Liam Tuohy chance off the line. Paddy Coad missed a golden opportunity and Noel Peyton had a shot rebound off the crossbar. United had more control of the play and Rovers were forced to do a lot of running, the result of which was to take its toll later on as the game progressed. Dennis Violett had a long shot rebound off the bar for the visitors and Darcy was forced into quick action in order to deflect a piledriver of a shot by Johnny Berry. Violett then successfully made a pass to Tommy Taylor which enabled the latter to beat Darcy and give the visitors the lead.

Just six minutes into the second half Whelan scored United's second goal after a cross from Violett had been headed on by Berry. Six minutes later, Whelan was on the scoresheet again when he headed in past Darcy from Pegg's centre. At the other end, Wood deflected a Coad shot out for a corner. Then for the Hoops Shay Keogh was in action at his end of the field when he put a Pegg cross out of danger when Darcy was beaten.

The score stood at 3-0 in favour of the 'Red Devils' with just 11 minutes remaining. The going was too tough for the Irish part-timers and by the time Belgium referee, Mr Van Nuffel, had blown the final whistle, Rovers had conceded a further three goals. Taylor got his second from a Violett cross and then Berry from a return pass by Taylor. With just four minutes remaining Pegg rubbed salt into the wounds when he brought United's lead up to six goals without reply.

The Rovers team that evening was: Darcy; Burke, Mackey; Nolan, Keogh, Hennessy; Peyton, Ambrose, Hamilton, Coad, Tuohy. The United team was: Wood; Foulkes, Byrne; Godwin, Blanchflower, Edwards; Berry, Whelan, Taylor, Violett, Pegg.

In the return leg at Old Trafford the Hoops set out to restore their dented pride. Making better use of the ball this time around Rovers improved as the game progressed. It looked as if the 'Busby Babes' were going to cruise to another easy victory as Dennis Violett (6 mins) and David Pegg (22 mins) gave the home team an early 2-0 lead. However, Rovers had not come to Manchester for another thrashing and after ten minutes into the second half Maxie McCann became the first League of Ireland player to score in European competition after he latched onto a cross by Noel Peyton which had 'keeper Ray Wood beaten.

United restored their two goal lead five minutes later when Violett got his second. Tommy Hamilton then got the second for Rovers mid way through the second half and the result stood at 3-2 in favour of the home team. That was the way it ended and as they left the pitch Shamrock Rovers received a marvellous ovation from the crowd.

No one who saw the European Cup games between Rovers and United could have foreseen the terrible tragedy which was to befall the Old Trafford club just four months later and which was to claim so many lives.

At home, the Leinster Senior Cup final between Rovers and Drums on St Stephen's Day 1957, ended in a 1-1 draw and when the sides met in the replay at Tolka Park on 5 February a lone goal from Liam Tuohy saw the Cup go to Milltown for the fourth successive season.

The sides met in the first League game of the 1957/58 season at Glenmalure Park on 10 November when Rovers took both points in a 3-0 win, the goals coming from Tuohy (2) and Ambrose. The Hoops certainly had the Indian sign over their Northside rivals with Drums failing to beat Rovers in any of the nine games in which they met that season, although they had the last laugh by pipping Rovers for the League title.

The return game at Tolka Park on 6 January saw no lack of action on or off the pitch. Drums were sitting on top of the table followed by Shels; Rovers were in fifth place. There was fantastic interest in the city for the meeting of the big two at Tolka Park. It was the first time a League game was made an all-ticket affair.

The attendance was 12,053 but many thousands more climbed over the fencing at the ground and the entire sidelines around the pitch were packed with spectators. After 35 minutes of the first half the Hoops took the lead when Ronnie Nolan took a throw in by Maxie McCann and hit a left footed shot into the net. Just before half time Paddy Coad took a pass from Tommy Hamilton and ran on to score Rovers' second.

Drumcondra, reduced to ten men in the second half following 'Kit' Lawlor's departure due to injury, fought back well with Pownall scoring from the penalty spot following Keogh's foul on Coleman. Five minutes after that, Hamilton was put clean through by Noel Peyton only to be upended by Alan Kelly in the Drumcondra goal and he went hurtling into the crowd standing on the end of the line. The referee blew for a free of some kind or other but no sooner had he done so when the crowd came swarming onto the pitch. The small force of Gardai on duty attempted to clear the pitch but it proved to be too big a task for them. The Drums' chairman, Roy Prole, attempted to push a few youngsters back to the fence but was then set upon by another youngster. A lone Garda ran to his aid and referee Cannon, taking advantage of the diversion, made a run for it and shortly afterwards announced that he had abandoned the game. The League of Ireland later awarded the points to Rovers. As we saw, Drumcondra eventually won the League with 33 points, Rovers were runners-up on 31, while Evergreen were third.

That game was Noel Peyton's last for Rovers. He was heading off to Leeds United the following day having been signed by manager Raich Carter. Peyton was made captain for the day with the usual captain, Paddy Coad, coming out last onto the pitch.

Rovers and Drums met again in the final of the Top Four when two goals from Paddy Ambrose brought the Independent Cup to Milltown for the second time.

Many players have gone through the books of Shamrock Rovers over the decades. Some only made it into the first team on a handful of occasions and some never got beyond the reserve team. It would be impossible to name all of them here but one player who appeared with the first team on several occasions was left full Liam Power who was on this Top Four winning team, which was: Darcy; Burke, Power; Nolan, Keogh, Hennessy; McCann, Hamilton, Ambrose, Coad and Tuohy. Amongst those to appear for Rovers this season were Sean Carroll, a centre forward, and centre half Tommy Farrell, both from Home Farm, Eamonn Grumley and Danny Bennett.

Leeds came to Dublin on 5 May to provide the opposition to Rovers in an exhibition game with the Hoops winning by 3-0. The scorers were Ambrose, Hamilton and McCann.

One of the best-known soccer administrators during this period was Captain Tom Scully of Shamrock Rovers. A former Irish Army captain, Tom Scully was Secretary/Director with the Hoops up to the early 'seventies having taken over from 'Ando' Byrne who himself had served Rovers as Secretary for many years. Tom Scully lived at Leeson Park, Donnybrook, although originally he came from Dun Laoghaire. At one stage he held the position of chairman of the Football Association of Ireland and was chairman of the committee which selected players for international duty. His wife, Mary, assisted him in his administrative and book-keeping duties. Tom Scully passed away in January 1977 at the age of 82.

In 1958/59 Shamrock Rovers once again brought the League title to Milltown but had no success in any of the other competitions.

Waterford pipped the Hoops to the Shield title but the League seldom looked in doubt. After nine games the Hoops had only dropped one point and had opened a five-point lead at the top of the table. After thirteen games the top of the League table looked like this:

	P	W	D	L	F	A	Pts.
Shamrock Rovers	13	10	2	1	35	15	22
Waterford	13	10	0	3	36	18	20
Limerick	13	6	4	3	25	14	16

A remarkable League game took place at Kilcohan Park on 1 March 1959 between Rovers and Waterford. It was a day for the forwards and every move seemed to pose danger. Waterford scored first in the third minute through Alfie Hale. A minute later Liam Tuohy equalised for the Hoops. Another three minutes later Hamilton put Rovers ahead and then Mick Lynch made it 3-1. In the twelfth minute of the second half Tuohy scored again to make it 4-1 but then an explosion from the Waterford forward line saw high drama in a nine-minute spell during which Alfie Hale scored Waterford's second goal with Peter Fitzgerald and Denny Fitzgerald both scoring twice to make it 6-4 before Paddy Turner got one for Rovers to finish the scoring at 6-5 in Waterford's favour.

The Hoops were beaten at home the following week by Evergreen but won three of their remaining five games and drew the other two which enabled them to finish at the top of the table and claim their ninth League title. Waterford's challenge slipped when they were beaten by Shels and then by Evergreen in their remaining games.

In 1958/59 a season ticket for Shamrock Rovers cost the following: *Gentlemen - £2*; *Ladies and Juveniles - £1.5.0*.

THE PATH OF THE CUP

In 1949 non-League side St Patrick's Athletic knocked the Hoops out of the FAI Cup when they won a first-round replay 2-1 at Milltown after the sides had drawn 1-1 previously. The first game took place at Glenmalure Park on Saturday, 19 February. The gate receipts of £520 were the biggest of the first round and were double those of the next biggest gate which was taken at the Dundalk-Cork Athletic tie at Oriel Park.

Rovers had not been doing well this season and a crippling injury list did not help. Regular inside right Paddy Coad was playing at left half while left full Frank Glennon was appearing at centre forward.

The team that played against St Pat's was: Godwin; Clarke, O'Byrne; Nash, Daly, Coad; Gaynor, Little, F. Glennon, Mullen,

Duffy. The St Pat's team was: Kinahan; Balfe, Staines; Reddick, Cummins, Shields; Rogers, Cassidy, Gregg, Noble, Donnelly.

Rovers took the lead in the first few minutes through Paddy Mullen but in general they were poor and St Pat's were all over them. When Lar O'Byrne fouled Bobby Rogers, Jimmy Shields sent his penalty shot wide but after 26 minutes St Pat's were back on level terms when John Cassidy got a well-deserved goal.

The replay also took place at Milltown at the request of the St Pat's committee as their own ground at Inchicore was not passed by the FAI. After seven minutes Rovers took the lead when the St Pat's 'keeper, Kinahan, failed to hold a shot from Gaynor and Higgins was there to put the ball into the net.

It was a keenly fought game and the Leinster League side equalised 16 minutes into the second half through Podge Gregg. Not long after that the winning goal came for St Pat's when Bobby Rogers was successful with a header. What an irony this was for the Hoops with two of the players who had left the club over the Inter-City Cup dispute getting the St Pat's goals.

Rovers went out in the second round (or quarter-final) for three successive years beginning in 1950. They were knocked out by Cork Athletic that year, by Shelbourne the following year and by Cork Athletic again in 1952. Worse was to follow in 1953 when another Cork side, Evergreen, were 4-2 winners in the first round. In 1954 the Hoops progressed to the semi-final of the Cup where they lost 2-1 to old rivals Drumcondra.

In 1955 the first round paired the Hoops and Sligo Rovers. The two sides had also met in the first round the previous year when the Hoops won 2-0 in a replay after a 1-1 draw. This time the first game also ended all square. A crowd of 6,000 witnessed a 2-2 draw at the Showgrounds. The Hoops had been winning by 2-1 until late in the game when Sligo were awarded a penalty which Albert Straka successfully put into the back of the net. At that stage supporters of both sides were crowding around the pitch. Hoops supporter Jimmy Cripps was so incensed with the decision that he ran out onto the pitch and kicked the ball off the penalty spot!

Goals from Coad and Tuohy were enough to see Shamrock Rovers through to the next round after they beat Sligo 2-1 in the replay at Milltown the following Thursday. Rovers then beat old rivals Shelbourne by 3-0 in the quarter-final at Milltown before a crowd of 18,000, the Rovers scorers being Liam Tuohy (2) and 'Maxie' McCann. Longford Town provided the opposition in the semi-final in which Tuohy scored twice and Coad got one also without reply. That game attracted a crowd of 11,120. In the meantime, Drumcondra had won their way through to the final by beating Waterford in the other semi-final after a replay.

A crowd of over 33,000 turned up to witness a disappointing final which the Hoops won 1-0, thanks to Liam Tuohy's goal in the 78th minute. It was the twelfth time for Rovers to win the Cup and a first for all the new players such as Gerry Mackey, Ronnie Nolan, Shay Keogh, Paddy Ambrose etc. In particular, it was a good day for eighteen year old Hughie Gannon, who came to Rovers from junior side Johnville, for he received a late call up following the withdrawal of Paddy Coad due to injury.

The story of the 1956 FAI Cup final will live on forever. 'A Story From A Schoolboy's Magazine Come True' was how the heading in the Irish Independent the following morning described it. The late great W. P. Murphy wrote in the opening paragraph of his match report: 'The present generation will cherish the memory of the day Rovers were two down with thirteen minutes to play.' How right he was, for the story is still told in pubs and clubs around the city of Dublin.

Cork took the lead when, after 34 minutes, John Horgan was fouled by the Rovers left back, Ronnie Nolan. From Paddy Noonan's free kick Jimmy Delaney challenged Christy O'Callaghan and forced him to drop the ball and the 41-year-old Scot knocked it over the line. Two minutes before the interval Cork got their second goal when Jimmy Murphy headed in from Horgan's free kick. In the second half Rovers worked hard to get back into the game but time and time again they were frustrated by the Cork defence. With 13 minutes to go it seemed certain that the Cup would go South. Then Tommy Hamilton made the most of a chance when Coughlan's clearance rebounded off Tuohy and suddenly Rovers were back in contention. Minutes later Rovers were awarded a penalty after a Cork defender had handled the ball and Liam Hennessy did not miss from the spot. All square.

Then in the dying seconds, Ronnie Nolan, who had moved from left full to left half just before the first Rovers' goal, came up to head a brilliant winning goal from Coad's corner kick. The impossible had happened: three goals in less than a quarter of an hour to snatch the Cup.

Cork's Jimmy Delaney had the unusual record of having won national cup medals in Scotland, England and Northern Ireland and had come within thirteen minutes of adding an FAI Cup winner's medal to his collection.

There was another story attached to this Cup final when a director of the Cork club is said to have left the ground with fifteen minutes to go to purchase some champagne in order to celebrate his club's pending victory. However, he was to discover on his way back up the Dalymount Lane that the result was not quite the same as it was when he left the ground! Just how that poor Cork official felt on the long journey home is not recorded.

Ronnie Nolan, the hero of the Cup final, came to Rovers in 1952 from Johnville. He came almost straight into the first team winning honours in his first game which was a President's Cup game against Drumcondra at Dalymount Park in September 1952.

Ronnie won every honour in the domestic game during his sixteen years at the club including full international and inter-League caps. After Rovers, Ronnie joined north city rivals Bohemians where he won another FAI Cup medal in 1970. He won Cup honours with the Hoops in 1955, 1956, 1962, 1964, 1965 and 1966.

'With Rovers the greatest thrill I got was scoring the winning goal in the Cup final against Cork in 1956', said Ronnie during 1991. 'The strange thing about it was that even though we got into lots of Cup finals all we ever did after the games was go home or go to the pictures or whatever; but for some unknown reason for that particular Cup final a dinner had been planned for afterwards.

That was held in the International Hotel in Bray and, as events turned out that day, the function became a huge success. I think we got home at around six o'clock the next morning.'

When he signed for Rovers in 1952 Ronnie was taken on as an amateur. 'I got twenty pounds in an envelope to buy a bicycle for myself', he recalled. 'Three months after I signed professional terms, I got £3 a week plus ten bob a point. My signing on fee was the £20 I received when I signed as an amateur.'

'I had a great career and I was very lucky, I never got injured and I had some marvellous trips abroad with Rovers. I have no regrets. I was lucky to have been with a good club and a good set of lads. We loved the game, we were basically amateurs even though we got paid and the money was helpful but we never got overpaid. Relative to the gates we brought in I think we got poorly paid looking at it, but that was not a key factor to us. None of us were rich but we loved the game and we were happy to be with a successful club.'

Old acquaintances were renewed in the final of 1957 when Drumcondra and Rovers met once again. Drums 'keeper Alan Kelly produced the highlight of the afternoon when he pulled off a near impossible save from a Tuohy header.

For Rovers, 'keeper Eamonn Darcy made a penalty save after 22 minutes from 'Bunny' Fullam but the linesman had signalled that Darcy had moved before the penalty kick was taken and Fullam successfully converted with the second opportunity. The second half was only two minutes old when Drumcondra got their second goal. Darcy had managed to push the ball out following a corner from Stan Pownall but Tommy Rowe succeeded in sending it back in; Mickey Gorman had his shot stopped on the line by Mickey Burke and, amid a crowded goalmouth, Willie Coleman managed to push the ball over the line. It was the fifth (and sadly the last time) that Drumcondra won the Cup.

If Drumcondra were the underdogs that year then Dundalk were even more so a year later in 1958 when they earned their passage to the final without conceding a goal; only the second club ever to do so after Athlone Town in 1924. Ted McNeill was a steadying influence in goal, especially in the second half when he saved an almost certain goal from an Ambrose header. On another occasion it was the outstanding Johnny Robinson, playing in the middle of the field, who cleared off the line when McNeill had been beaten. Robinson was playing in his fourth final and his third against Rovers having lined out in 1948, 1954 and 1955 with Drums.

It was the former Rovers' player, Hughie Gannon, who gave Dundalk victory when he scored the only goal of the game. O'Callaghan had advanced too early and Hennessy had allowed Gannon to push through and he proceeded to head the ball into the net. That was after 17 minutes of the second half. Four minutes later, Rovers had a golden opportunity to draw level when Tommy Kerr handled in the box but Liam Hennessy drove his penalty kick wide.

The biggest shock for many years came when Bohemians beat Rovers 3-2 in the first round of the 1959 competition. The sides met at Dalymount Park on Saturday, 14 February 1959, before a large crowd. Rovers won the toss and Paddy Coad elected to play against the breeze and up the hill. Bohemians made the most of the fierce breeze and stormed into a 3-0 lead by half time. The first goal came after 10 minutes when A. Morahan headed the ball onto P. Webber who headed into the back of Rovers' net. Shortly after that a mistake by Rovers 'keeper Eamonn Darcy let the amateurs in for a second. Darcy dropped the ball after a cross came over from F. Moran and Shay Keogh, in attempting to clear, struck the ball off Morahan and it rebounded into the net. After just 25 minutes Bohs went further ahead when Webber took the ball upfield and finished the move himself by stroking it over the line past Darcy.

It was a typical Cup tie and after the interval Rovers threw everything they could at Bohs. Former Bohs player Mick Lynch, who had joined Rovers only a couple of weeks previously, got one back for Rovers and it looked as though the Hoops might at least get a draw as Hamilton, McCann and Tuohy all went close during a period of intense pressure on the Bohs goal area after Tuohy had made it 2-3. The home defence held well, however, and the final whistle was greeted with wild enthusiasm by the Dalymount faithful.

The teams lined out that day as follows: Bohemians: P. Troy; P. Duffy, J. Connolly; B. Williams, M. Cahill, J. Lowe; M. Hendrick, F. Moran, P. Webber, A. Morahan, M. O'Brien.

Rovers: Darcy; Farrell, Mackey; Nolan, Keogh, Hennessy; McCann, Hamilton, Lynch, Coad, Tuohy.

SPOTLIGHT ON LIAM TUOHY

It was in August 1951 that Liam Tuohy arrived at Milltown. He went into the under-21 team and became the only one from that team to become one of Coad's Colts.

It was not until the closing stages of the 1953/54 season that Liam broke into the first team on a regular basis. 'At that stage I was in between the under-21 and 'B' teams and I did not really command a place until the back end of that season. I started my first game against Sligo Rovers in a replay of the FAI Cup after we had drawn against them at Milltown. We went down to Sligo for the replay and I was introduced to the team. We won that game and I was never off the side after that', explained Liam.

Tuohy remained involved with the first team up to the end of the 1959/60 season after which he was transferred to English First Division side Newcastle United. The outside left returned to Rovers for the 1963/64 season and was influential first as a player and then as a player/coach in yet another successful era at the club.

Liam Tuohy witnessed many great players and many great occasions at the club. Yet he is reluctant to pit teams from one era against those from another, as he explained.

'The way I always look upon it is that certain teams were the best of their era. The 'forties and 'fifties teams in League of Ireland football had big heavy leather boots and the balls were heavy with laces going through them that would cut the head off you. The fellas in the 'sixties and

'seventies did not have to compete with that so you were not always comparing like with like.

In the 'fifties we played with what we called a 'tree ball', that is to say that if it was raining it would soak up the water and by the second half of the game you would nearly need to get onto the terracing to kick a corner ball into the goalmouth. Of course the balls are non-absorbent now and you also have much better grounds. I would say that the Shamrock Rovers' team of the 'fifties was the best team of that era while in the 'sixties there were three particularly good teams in Rovers, Waterford and Shels (the Hannigan/Barber team). Drums were an excellent 'fifties team with players like 'Bunny' Fullam and Tommy Rowe and Dundalk were always there or thereabouts for they always had a strong professional side.'

According to Liam the 'fifties team was special in that they introduced a new style of football. At that stage League of Ireland football consisted of individual players; there was not a lot of passing in it.

'Individuals would get the ball, characters you could say, and they would be encouraged to beat people and so on. Paddy Coad introduced a pattern of play and we were probably the fittest team in the League. We were also a very exciting team and consequently as we went on we were always able to hold our own against other great teams. For example, when Chelsea won the English First Division in 1954/55 they came over here and we beat them 3-2 and so it can be seen that we had a very good side with some exceptional players. We had a pattern of play, we had lovely passing movements, everybody dovetailed for each other. Mickey Burke was a very good attacking full back while Gerry Mackey was a very good defensive full back. Liam Hennessy was a very good attacking wing half while Ronnie Nolan was a very good defensive wing half so we all complemented each other.'

While the 1950s had special memories of their own the 'sixties too were to equal all this with some outstanding memories too. Shamrock Rovers enjoyed their own degree of success and but for a very good Waterford side could have captured the League title on one or two more occasions other than 1963/64. A new crop of players emerged at Milltown in the early 'sixties and, as mentioned above, were to be joined by Liam Tuohy upon his return from Newcastle United.

Liam Tuohy was born in April 1933. When he was finished playing he took over as manager at Dundalk in 1969. For a while he also managed the Republic of Ireland senior team in the early 'seventies and the Irish Youths team in the early 'eighties. He himself was capped by Ireland six times between 1955 and 1956. He made 24 appearances for the inter-League team between 1954 and 1965. He scored 87 League goals during his time at Milltown.

Liam won many honours with Shamrock Rovers including four League medals. He appeared with Rovers in seven FAI Cup finals (including the 1964 replay against Cork Celtic) and he was on three winning sides (he missed out on the 1965 replay against Limerick due to injury).

SPOTLIGHT ON PADDY AMBROSE

Paddy Ambrose was associated with Shamrock Rovers from 1949 to 1973, first as a player and then as coach. That long association began after the late Jimmy Dunne signed him from junior side Clontarf. Dunne wasted no time in putting his new young inside forward into action, including him in the team which played Transport on 28 August 1949 in the City Cup competition.

Later, Ambrose became one of the club's greatest ever centre forwards. During his career at Rovers he chalked up 109 League goals, five more than Paddy Coad, a club record which still stands. He was the leading scorer at the club in 1953/54, 1954/55, 1955/56 and 1960/61.

When Rovers won the title in 1953/54, their first title for fifteen years, Paddy scored 13 goals. His total would probably have been a great deal more had he not broken an ankle half way through the season. Although absent for two months he came back at a crucial time and helped the team effort by scoring six goals. His best tally was the four goals which he scored against Cork Athletic at Milltown on 6 December in a game which the Hoops won 10-2. The other Rovers' scorers that day were Liam Hennessy (4) and Liam 'Mousey' Munroe (2).

Paddy Ambrose won a League medal with Shamrock Rovers four times, in 1953/54, 1956/57, 1958/59 and 1963/64. Even in that latter season, towards the end of his career, he still contributed 11 goals. He played in six FAI Cup finals plus one replay and won four winner's medals in the following years, 1955, 1956, 1962 and 1964. In his fifth final Paddy won his third winner's medal against Shelbourne in 1962 in a game that represented a personal triumph for him. Shels had taken the lead after 33 minutes but Ambrose scored twice before half time to send Rovers on the road to victory. Tommy Hamilton scored twice in the second half to wrap it all up for the Milltown club.

When he played for Ireland against Poland in May 1964 Paddy received an ankle injury which he spent the following summer months nursing. He was fit to return to the Rovers team for the start of the 1964/65 season but disaster was soon to strike. The ankle injury reoccurred after a clash with the goalkeeper in the away European Cup tie against Rapid Vienna. After that Paddy was forced to take a back seat but continued at Milltown as a coach helping to train the reserve and youth teams.

For the man who had a great interest in Gaelic games before he came to Rovers a great career lay ahead of him in association football. Perhaps his greatest love, though, was his pigeons which he used to race and for which he won prizes. Even at the height of his career with the Hoops, Paddy maintained his interest in pigeon racing.

He was the quiet man of the team and kept himself to himself. A former team-mate recalls that Paddy hardly ever spoke to anybody else on the team bus travelling to away venues. 'You could never get Paddy to talk, but mention pigeons and he was away!'

Paddy Ambrose made five international appearances for Ireland and appeared seven times for the League of Ireland at inter-League level.

CHAPTER SIX

SIX IN A ROW

(1 9 6 0 - 6 9)

The departure of Paddy Coad from Milltown to his native Waterford in January 1960 heralded the end of an era at Rovers. The 'fifties team, Coad's Colts, arguably Rovers' finest team, was breaking up and the task of replacing the fine players that had moved on was going to pose a great challenge for both the Cunningham family and Paddy Coad's successors. Gerry Mackey, Christy O'Callaghan, Noel Peyton and Mickey Burke had left the Hoops and Liam Tuohy accepted an offer to join Newcastle United at the end of the 1959/60 season. The previous season Rovers had won their ninth League title and they had been drawn against O.G.C Nice in the first round of the European Cup. The first leg of the tie was played in Nice on Wednesday, 26 August in almost unbearable heat. When Rovers took the field that afternoon the temperature was 98° F; the first time that the Hoops ever encountered such intense heat on a playing pitch. The Rovers' line-up on that stifling afternoon was as follows:

Darcy; Farrell, Hennessy; Nolan, Keogh, Bennett; Turner, Geoghegan, Hamilton, Tuohy and Ambrose. Early injuries to Danny Bennett and Liam Tuohy left Rovers with only nine fully fit players but they battled tremendously against the odds and stunned the French champions after 18 minutes when Tommy Hamilton dribbled through the Nice defence to shoot past Lamia. After 25 minutes the Dutch referee Marten awarded the home team a controversial penalty after the ball had struck Liam Hennessy's arm. The penalty was converted by Nuremberg and two minutes later Foix made it 2-1 for the home side. Liam Hennessy collapsed from the effects of sunstroke at half-time and Rovers had to play the first 16 minutes of the second half with ten players before Hennessy bravely rejoined the fray. Foix dribbled through the Rovers defence to score his side's third goal with 15 minutes remaining. Paddy Coad instructed Rovers to try and slow things down as best they could in the intense heat and the Hoops were rewarded for their gallant efforts when Liam Tuohy lobbed the ball over Lamia from a difficult angle after 85 minutes. Rovers great tradition and fighting spirit kept them going throughout the final minutes and they were utterly exhausted when the final whistle went.

Liam Tuohy had a bone in his ankle chipped during the game and he didn't play again until the return leg at Dalymount Park four weeks later. Tommy Hamilton, who had a splendid game in Nice, was ruled out of the return leg due to a bout of tonsillitis. Sonny Rice and Albie Murphy were signed from Clyde in September and there was an interesting story in the signing of Murphy. Apparently he had opened up a bookmaker's shop near Harold's Cross bridge. However, at that time players in Scotland and England were strictly forbidden to get involved in the betting business. Albie was unaware of this rule when he set up his shop and despite his protests the Scottish League were adamant that he would have to give up the business if he wanted to remain in Scottish football. Albie refused and Rovers were only too glad to avail of the opportunity to sign him.

The return leg against Nice was played at Dalymount Park on Wednesday, 23 September and Jimmy 'Maxie' McCann who replaced Tommy Hamilton was Rovers only change from the first leg. A crowd of just over 32,000 gave Rovers vociferous support throughout the match but unfortunately they didn't get the result they hoped for. After 12 minutes, Liam Hennessy gave the Hoops the lead when he hit a bullet-like shot to the net from fully 40 yards. The French champions equalised after 25 minutes when Faivre shot to the net following a corner. Rovers laid siege to the Nice goal for the rest of the match but they simply couldn't find a way past an inspired Lamia who performed heroics for the French champions. He made an amazing save from Paddy Turner in the second half and on one occasion Liam Tuohy seemed destined to score as he was about to head a cross to the net but Danny Bennett got to the ball before Liam and headed narrowly over the bar. It was a match that Rovers should have won by two or three goals but a combination of great goalkeeping and inadequate finishing deprived them of a famous victory. O.G.C Nice went on to beat the Turkish champions Fenerbahce in the next round before going out to the eventual winners Real Madrid at the quarter-final stage.

Rovers won the President's Cup and the Dublin City Cup that season, beating St Pat's 2-0 after a replay to win the President's Cup and beating Drumcondra 5-2 on corners after a 1-1 draw in the final of the Dublin City Cup. Rovers' form in the Shield in the 1959/60 season was very disappointing as they only recorded two wins from eleven matches finishing in 10th place, ten points behind the winners St Pat's. Rovers were too inconsistent in the League that season. They lost three of their first four matches in the league and although they finished strongly they ended up in fourth place, three points behind the winners Limerick. Shelbourne beat Rovers 3-1 in the Top Four semi-final on 29 April and the Reds also ended Rovers' interest in the FAI Cup, beating the Hoops 3-0 in the quarter-final replay. However Rovers did give their fans something to shout about when they beat Manchester United 3-2 in a friendly at Dalymount Park on 5 April. Liam Tuohy, Tommy Hamilton and Liam Hennessy from a penalty scored for Rovers with Scanlon and Dawson scoring for United. Eamonn 'Sheila' Darcy had an inspired game for Rovers against United as the Reds could have been three or four up at half-time only for Darcy's heroics in goal. Dermot Cross ended the season as Rovers top League scorer, scoring a total of eleven goals in the campaign.

Albie Murphy took over as coach to Rovers in September 1960 and he held this position until Sean Thomas took charge of the team on the American tour in 1961. The 1960/61 season was another disappointing campaign for the Hoops. Shelbourne beat Rovers 3-1 after two replays to win the President's Cup final and Transport ended Rovers interest in the Dublin City Cup on 18 August when they beat Rovers 2-1.

St Pat's beat Rovers 5-1 in the first round of the Leinster

Senior Cup on 19 October and the Hoops only managed four victories from eleven matches in the Shield, finishing in fifth place, six points behind the winners Cork Celtic. Rovers' League form was patchy, containing a mixture of the mediocre and the brilliant. They only managed nine wins from twenty-two matches and they finished in sixth place, eight points behind the winners Drumcondra. Peter Mitchell was signed from Ballymena and scored four times on his debut against Sligo Rovers at Milltown on 26 March 1961 as Rovers trounced Sligo Rovers 8-1. They beat Limerick 1-0 in a replay of their first round FAI Cup match but the Hoops made their exit from the competition in the next round as an own goal from Ronnie Nolan decided the quarter-final match against Waterford.

It was against this background of another dismal season for the Hoops that the Cunninghams asked Sean Thomas to take over as coach to Shamrock Rovers. He readily agreed and took charge of the team for a tour to America and Canada. Three guest players, Liam Tuohy who was with Newcastle United, Johnny Fullam who was with Preston North End and Frank O'Neill who was with Arsenal, joined the touring party. There were a total of sixteen players in the travelling party and they achieved a memorable result against Red Star Belgrade on Sunday 16 July 1961 when they beat the crack Yugoslav side 5-1. Tony Byrne with two goals, Paddy Ambrose, Frank O'Neill and Liam Tuohy were the scorers in what was a famous victory for Rovers.

Rovers also suffered their heaviest defeat when the Czech side Dukla Prague beat them 10-0 but they had a growing injury crisis when they played the Czechs having only nine fully fit players. The tour was a success and two of the three guest players, Johnny Fullam and Frank O'Neill, were signed from their English clubs. Both went on to make an immense contribution to the Hoops over the next decade.

Rovers lost their first competitive game of the 1961/62 season when St Pat's beat them 2-1 after extra time in the Dublin City Cup. Rovers drew three of their first four matches in the Shield competition and those dropped points were to cost Rovers dear as they finished in third place two points behind the winners Drumcondra. Frank O'Neill made his debut for Rovers against Waterford on Sunday, 17 September 1961 and scored twice as the Hoops won 4-0. A heavy defeat by Shelbourne effectively ended Rovers' challenge for the Shield but early injuries to key players disrupted their pattern in that match.

Rovers made an encouraging start to that season's League campaign, taking nine points out of a possible ten before they were beaten by Cork Celtic at Milltown on 10 December. The Hoops suffered another home defeat on 7 January when the eventual champions Shelbourne beat them 2-1 on an occasion that saw Telefis Eireann make their first appearance at a soccer match in Ireland. A further defeat by Transport that month dealt Rovers' title hopes a severe blow but they bounced back with three successive victories over Limerick, St Pat's and Drums to leave themselves well in contention for League honours as the season reached its climax. The victory over Drumcondra on 11 February at Milltown was a tremendous result as Rovers twice came from two down to eventually win 4-3. Ronnie Nolan scored the winner in the last minute in a match where no quarter was asked or given and some of the tackling was of a ferocious nature. Another victory followed over Waterford before Cork Celtic ended Rovers' title hopes with a comprehensive 4-0 win at Turner's Cross on 4 March. Rovers finished in third place that season, four points behind the joint leaders Shelbourne and Cork Celtic. Shelbourne beat Cork Celtic 1-0 in a play-off for the League title at Dalymount Park on Wednesday 2 May.

The cup campaign brought Rovers fourteenth success in the competition. After surviving a pulsating 3-3 draw at the Showgrounds, a solitary goal by Frank O'Neill won the replay. Bohemians were beaten in the quarter-final at Dalymount and the Hoops beat Waterford 5-2 in the cup semi-final replay at Tolka Park. Shelbourne were installed as warm favourites for the final as they had beaten the Hoops twice in the League and once in the Shield that season. However when it really mattered in the final, Rovers produced the goods and ran out convincing 4-1 winners.

Shelbourne gained a little consolation when they beat Rovers 4-1 after extra time in the Top Four semi-final at Tolka Park on 11 May. The referee on that occasion, T. P. Germaine got injured early on and had to be taken to hospital. One of the linesmen, Johnny Igoe, took over and Rovers were the victims of some strange decisions. An Eddie Bailham header was destined for the net until Shelbourne's Paddy Roberts punched the ball out with his goalkeeper beaten and to the amazement of the Rovers' players a corner was awarded. Paddy Ambrose had a goal disallowed and another penalty appeal was turned down when Freddie Strahan fouled Ambrose after 83 minutes. In extra-time Shelbourne were the better side and scored three times without reply.

Tommy Hamilton and Maxie McCann had their benefit match against Sunderland at Dalymount Park on 30 April. Rovers were assisted by guest players Liam Tuohy and Johnny Giles but Sunderland ran out convincing 5-2 winners after McCann and Tuohy had given Rovers an early two-goal lead. That match was Tommy Hamilton's last match for Rovers as he joined Cork Hibernians in a player-exchange deal that brought Jackie Mooney to Milltown.

Rovers first competitive game of the 1962/63 season was a remarkable match in the P. J. Casey Cup against Drumcondra at Tolka Park on 26 August. Pat Dunne and Jackie Mooney made their debuts for Rovers in the match, Pat having been signed during the close season. Jackie Mooney gave Rovers the lead after eight minutes but then Drums scored three in three minutes to lead 3-1. Mooney scored with a header after 22 minutes and just before half-time Eddie Bailham scored with a shot from 30 yards. Right on half-time Rice put Drums 4-3 ahead. Eddie Cowzer equalised after 59 minutes and then after 66 minutes, the same player crossed for Bailham to head the ball to the net. That goal was the only time that Eddie Bailham ever scored with a header for Rovers and Pat Dunne tells a story of Billy Lord throwing some holy water over Eddie's head in the dressing room before the match. Eddie was a Protestant and in the years that followed Billy Lord often used to give him a gentle ribbing over divine inspiration and the only time he ever scored with a header for Rovers. Billy Dixon scored the tenth and final goal of the match after 86 minutes to level the scores at 5-5. The teams for that amazing match were as follows: Drumcondra: Murphy; Fullam, Brennan; Byrne, Smyth, Prole; Keogh, Dixon, Rice, Morrissey, Halpin.

Rovers: Dunne; Farrell, Courtney; Nolan, Cahill, Fullam, O'Neill, Mooney, Bailham, Cowzer, O'Connell, Sub: J. Keogh for Mooney.

Rovers lost their two remaining matches in the P. J Casey Cup to Dundalk and St Pat's and did not qualify for the semi-finals of the competition. Rovers made a good start to the Shield competition winning their first three matches against Shels, Limerick and Cork Hibs before losing 3-1 to Waterford. Bohemians received the backlash the following week as Rovers went on the rampage and won 7-2 at Dalymount Park, Eddie Bailham scoring a hat trick. They had comfortable victories over Dundalk and Drumcondra before they faced Bulgarian opposition in the first round of the European Cup Winners Cup.

Rovers' opponents from Bulgaria were a side called Botev Plovdiv and the Hoops were confident of getting a result when they played them at Dalymount Park on 24 October. However they got a rude awakening from the Bulgarians who ran out comfortable 4-0 winners on the night. The Hoops were no match for the fast fit Bulgarians who put on a very impressive display. The Rovers team that faced the Bulgarians at Dalymount Park was as follows: Dunne; Keogh, Courtney; Nolan, Cahill, Fullam; O'Neill, Mooney, Bailham, Farrell, O'Connell. Rovers performed much better in the second leg in Plovdiv on 14 November losing 1-0, with the solitary goal coming from a penalty awarded after five minutes of play.

The trip to Bulgaria was a bit of a culture shock for the Rovers party. When they landed at Sofia airport they were put on a coach which took six hours to make it to Plovdiv, which was only 150 miles from Sofia but was up in the mountains. The ancient coach really struggled at times to make it up the mountain roads. On occasions, the engine fumes billowed into the coach itself much to the discomfort of the Rovers' players and officials. They eventually made it to Plovdiv but the players insisted on flying back to Sofia.

Their hotel in Plovdiv was a big ugly grey building. John Keogh told the story of how he made the tea the following morning for the breakfast. (The tea they received was only lukewarm.) John boiled the water again over the gas stoves and this time it was acceptable to the players. The Bulgarians had very little but they were very hospitable to the Rovers' party and they gave what they had to their visitors. When Botev had been in Dublin they had run out of money and Joe Cunningham had given them a loan of £400. The Bulgarian players used their money to buy presents while in Dublin and Joe was given his £400 in Bulgarian currency when he arrived in Plovdiv. Unfortunately for Joe, this money could only be spent in Bulgaria and between them all they made a gallant effort to spend as much of the £400 as they could. It wasn't easy.

The players got a major shock when they saw the plane for the flight back to Sofia. They were taken by coach into a field where two twin-engined Dakotas waited. There was no such thing as flight control or air hostesses at all. A big burly Bulgarian official pointed at the two planes and announced that one of the planes was going to Warsaw and the other was going to Sofia. The Rovers party received another shock when they boarded the plane and discovered that there were no seat belts on board. All it would have taken was for one player to stand up and say 'I'm not flying in this' but they all remained silent and the plane took off for the capital. It was a mightily relieved group that reached Sofia safe and sound where they spent a day before returning to Dublin via Amsterdam.

Jackie Mooney and Frank O'Neill went sightseeing in Sofia and as they were ambling through the city's streets they heard the sound of gunfire. The two lads decided to investigate and as they turned a corner they saw two wounded men on the street being treated by a nurse for gunshot wounds to their legs while armed policemen watched over them. The players decided to return to their hotel rather than get any closer to the wounded men. That night Jackie Mooney told their interpreter about what they had witnessed earlier in Sofia only to be told by the interpreter that those type of incidents did not happen in Bulgaria. That was the end of that.

Rovers won their remaining matches in the Shield to finish winners by a comfortable six points margin from Cork Celtic and Dundalk. Waterford were beaten home and away by the Hoops in the Dublin City Cup before Rovers opened their League campaign with a 4-2 win over defending champions Shelbourne at Tolka Park. They then lost their next three League matches before a hat trick from Jackie Mooney gave them an easy win over Bohs at Milltown on 23 December. They lost 2-1 to Shelbourne in the Leinster Senior Cup final on 26 December and the Reds also beat them in the semi-final of the Dublin City Cup on 9 January by three goals to two. Rovers' League form was very inconsistent at this stage but they managed to hammer Shels at Milltown on 27 January by five goals to nil. The Hoops were five up at half-time and they were quite content to play out the second half without inflicting any more damage to a demoralised Shelbourne side. The following Saturday, 2 February 1963, Manchester United played Coventry City in a friendly match at Milltown. The severe winter weather in Britain caused hundreds of postponements that season and the two teams were glad of the opportunity to get in some badly needed match practice. A crowd of just over 20,000 attended the match and it finished in a two-all draw.

Rovers' indifferent League form continued and they took only three points from their next four League matches. They had good wins over Cork Celtic and Bohemians in the Cup and on St Patrick's Day they travelled to Dundalk to take on the League leaders with a side weakened by injuries. To the surprise of many, the Hoops beat Dundalk 3-1 with Eddie Cowzer scoring two of Rovers' goals. The Hoops then had League victories over Drumcondra and St Pat's before Shelbourne ended their involvement with the FAI Cup with a 2-0 win in the semi-final. Rovers' final two League matches that season were against Cork

Celtic and they produced two draws, so that they finished the season two points behind Cork Celtic in fifth place taking a mere 19 points from 18 matches.

During the 1963 close season Liam Tuohy signed for Rovers from Newcastle United and his experience was to prove vital to Rovers over the next six years. Liam had some difficulty persuading Newcastle to release him. He had gone to Newcastle for three years and had made an agreement with Newcastle's manager that he could return to Rovers after that period was over. However the manager with whom he had the agreement was dismissed by Newcastle and his successor was unaware of the arrangement. Eventually it took the persuasive powers of Mrs Cunningham to convince the Newcastle board that Liam was in fact now a Rovers' player again.

Rovers began the 1963/64 season with three victories in the Shield over Bohemians, Limerick and Waterford before Cork Celtic beat them 2-0 at Turner's Cross on 15 September. Three days later, Rovers took on Valencia in the first round of the Fairs Cup at Dalymount Park. Rovers lined out as follows: Dunne; Keogh, Courtney; Nolan, Farrell, Fullam; O'Neill, Mooney, Bailham, Tuohy, O'Connell.

Valencia were the holders of the Fairs Cup for the previous two years yet Rovers had them back pedalling for most of the first half. Tony O'Connell, Ronnie Nolan and Johnny Fullam were outstanding as Rovers proved more than a match for the highly rated Spaniards. Liam Tuohy was narrowly wide with a shot after 14 minutes, Jackie Mooney then missed a great chance after 27 minutes when he headed a cross from Fullam over the bar. Ten minutes after half-time Quincoces almost put Rovers ahead when his attempted clearance narrowly cleared his own crossbar. Valencia scored against the run of play after 72 minutes when Sanchez-Lage set up Suco to shoot to the net from just inside the penalty area. Valencia's keeper Nito made a tremendous save from a free kick by Eddie Bailham in the dying minutes.

Three weeks later Rovers travelled to Valencia for the return leg. In the previous two years no club had even managed to draw with Valencia in the Fairs Cup in Spain. Teams such as Nottingham Forest, Inter Milan, M.T.K Budapest, Barcelona, Celtic, Dunfermline Athletic, Hibernian, A. S Roma and Dynamo Zagreb had all failed in Valencia. There was a setback for Rovers even before the match as both Paddy Ambrose and Johnny Fullam were suffering from the effects of food poisoning and Rovers only had eleven fit players. Johnny Fullam actually played with a temperature of 103. It speaks volumes for his total commitment to the Hoops that he lasted the ninety minutes unscathed.

Rovers attacked from the start and they stunned the partisan 45,000 crowd when Liam Tuohy gave Rovers the lead after 39 minutes. Nine minutes into the second half Jackie Mooney put Rovers two up and a real sensation was on the cards. Guillot then pulled a goal back for Valencia after 62 minutes and had the result stayed like this a third game would have been necessary as the away goals rule was not introduced into European club competitions until the 1965/66 season. After 78 minutes Valencia's left back, Arnal, scored from what every Rovers' player thought was an offside position. However the referee, Henriques from Portugal thought otherwise, and allowed the goal to stand. Jackie Mooney came close twice in the dying minutes but the game finished 2-2 and Rovers, most unluckily, went out on aggregate by three goals to two.

Earlier that month the League of Ireland beat the English League 2-1 at Dalymount Park. Five Rovers players played on the team: John Keogh, Johnny Fullam, Jackie Mooney, Eddie Bailham and Tony O'Connell. Bailham scored the League of Ireland's first goal on the night. Rovers completed the Shield campaign with only one more defeat against Shelbourne to win their fifteenth Shield by a margin of three points from Dundalk. On 16 October the Hoops beat Drums 3-1 in the Dublin City Cup final, two goals from Liam Tuohy and one from Eddie Bailham seeing off Drums' challenge.

Rovers' League campaign began with a 2-1 win over Bohs at Dalymount Park on 8 November. In their next two League matches the Hoops scored fourteen times as they crushed Limerick

6-2 at Milltown and Waterford 8-1 at Kilcohan Park. Rovers had struggled to beat Waterford in the Shield at Milltown in September but on this occasion they took The Blues to the cleaners, being four goals up at half-time and eight goals up with a couple of minutes to go. The match report in the following day's *Irish Times* contained this piece about the game.

'*Shamrock Rovers in their most deadly efficient mood, shattered Waterford with an eight-goal blitz at Kilcohan Park yesterday. In the end, the home team had been reduced to a pitiful, distressed and humiliated group. In fact, in those closing stages when Shamrock Rovers had forced Waterford to their knees they might have aimed at double figures. But Rovers were either being merciful or perhaps the forwards, each of whom played a magnificent part in the annihilation, were so embarrassed as not to permit themselves to inflict further punishment.*'

For the record Rovers' scorers on the day were Bailham (3), Mooney, Tuohy, Nolan, Ambrose and O'Neill.

Rovers played three matches in the Leinster Senior Cup in December, beating Shelbourne 2-1 in the quarter-final replay on the 11th. They then accounted for Drums by a 2-0 margin in the semi-final on the 18th before beating St Pat's 3-0 in the final on St Stephen's day. Jackie Mooney, Paddy Ambrose and Eddie Bailham scored in the final against St Pat's and their line-up that day was by now familiar: Dunne; Keogh, Courtney; Nolan, Farrell, Fullam; O'Neill, Mooney, Bailham, Ambrose, Tuohy. The Hoops went through an indifferent spell of form in the League in December and early January as they only won one of their seven League matches in that period. They drew with Cork Celtic, Cork Hibs, Drums, Drogheda and St Pat's and they lost to Dundalk, their main challengers for the League, at Oriel Park on 5 January 1964.

The match with Drogheda at Milltown on 29 December was a fascinating contest. Drogheda, on their first visit to Milltown, opened the scoring after five minutes, Liam Tuohy equalised after 11 minutes, but by the 23rd minute McGrory and McElroy had put Drogheda 3-1 up. Eddie Bailham scored from a penalty after 28 minutes and just before half-time Paddy Ambrose equalised for Rovers. Two minutes into the second half Jackie Mooney put Rovers ahead only for McCaffrey to level the scores at 4-4 after 57 minutes. Straight from the kick off Drogheda conceded another penalty and Bailham made no mistake from the spot, however four minutes later Dan McCaffrey completed the scoring and the game finished at five goals each.

The following Sunday Rovers went to Oriel Park and a record attendance at the ground paid gate receipts of £640. The match ended controversially as John Keogh was ordered off after 87 minutes. A few enraged Rovers supporters invaded the pitch and chased the referee D. Horgan and linesman J. Meighan to the dressing room. Some of these so-called supporters actually managed to inflict some severe blows on the helpless match officials before they made it to the sanctuary of the dressing rooms. Rovers had started well and missed two great chances in the opening ten minutes. Eamonn Farrell was deputising for the injured Eddie Bailham and his hesitancy in front of goal cost Rovers early on. After 23 minutes, a free kick from Fullam was headed out by Lyons and as the ball dropped Frank O'Neill lobbed the ball over Barron for the lead for Rovers. Just before half-time Tommy Farrell handled a cross from Callan and Callan scored from the spot despite Pat Dunne getting his hands to the ball. Dermot Cross scored the winner for Dundalk after 46 minutes with a brilliant shot past Pat Dunne. Two minutes later Rovers were awarded a penalty when Murphy handled in the area but Frank O'Neill put the penalty too close to Barron who saved comfortably. Dundalk maintained their control of the game in the closing stages and Dunne made great saves from Callan and Fottrill near the finish.

After playing a scoreless draw with St Pat's on 12 January at Inchicore, Rovers played their next two League matches at Milltown and scored seven times against both Sligo Rovers and Bohemians. The match against Sligo Rovers should have been abandoned after 70 minutes as a thick fog was blanketing the ground and the referee ordered the training lights to be turned on to try and improve visibility in the gathering darkness. Rovers coasted to a 7-2 victory although they were only 1-0 ahead at the interval. In the last minute with the Hoops leading 7-1, Tommy Farrell attempted a back pass to Pat Dunne, but he didn't notice that Pat was out of his goal due to the poor visibility and the ball trickled into the net for Sligo's second goal.

The following week Bohs were the victims as Eddie Bailham scored four times in a 7-1 victory. Wins over Limerick and Waterford followed before Rovers flew out to Spain to take on the Spanish 'B' International side a few days before a vital Cup tie against Dundalk at Milltown. The Spaniards won 7-2 and a lot of people questioned the decision of the Milltown mentors to undertake such a trip at an important stage of the season. Some people even thought that the heavy defeat would demoralise Rovers and hand an advantage to Dundalk. As it turned out their fears were groundless: Rovers swamped Dundalk in the Cup match 7-0 with both Jackie Mooney and Eddie Bailham scoring hat tricks and Paddy Ambrose also scoring. Rovers got a crucial victory at Turner's Cross on 23 February as Cork Celtic laid siege to Rovers' goal in the second half. Eddie Bailham scored the only goal after three minutes when he hit a rebound off the crossbar to the net. There was controversy the following week at Milltown when Rovers played Cork Hibs. After 87 minutes Eddie Bailham was involved in an incident with Noel O'Mahony which led to Bailham being sent off by the referee S. Spillane. Rovers' supporters invaded the pitch at full-time and the Rovers' players had to escort the referee to the pavilion. Johnny Fullam scored the only goal of the match as the Hoops began to draw away from Dundalk at the top of the League table. A last minute goal from Eddie Bailham accounted for Limerick in the quarter-final of the Cup at the Market's Field and three victories over Shelbourne, Drumcondra and Drogheda on successive Sundays put Rovers in a commanding position at the top of the League table before they faced Drums in the semi-final of the Cup.

Liam Tuohy scored the only goal of the semi-final after 19 minutes but the Hoops were very fortunate to win as Drumcondra created more chances throughout the game and only a combination of inspired goalkeeping from Pat Dunne and poor finishing from the Drums' forwards kept Rovers' lead intact. The following Thursday, 9 April, Rovers faced Dundalk at Dalymount Park needing a win to clinch their tenth League title. The teams lined out as follows. *Rovers*: Dunne; Keogh, Courtney; Nolan, Farrell, Fullam; O'Neill, Mooney, Bailham, Ambrose, Tuohy.

Dundalk: Barron; Murphy, McKeown; Rowe, Lyons, Harte; Gillespie, Callan, Hasty, Cross, Kennedy.

The first half was scoreless. One minute into the second half Jimmy Hasty scored for Dundalk. Four minutes later Johnny Fullam forced a cross from Paddy Ambrose over the line for the equaliser. Paddy Ambrose then scored twice in two minutes to seal Rovers tenth League triumph.

Rovers completed their League programme by drawing with St Pat's and Sligo Rovers. They finished with 35 points from 22 matches, five points ahead of Dundalk and Limerick. Their only League defeat of the season had been at Oriel Park to Dundalk on 5 January. Eddie Bailham was Rovers' top League scorer with 18 goals with Liam Tuohy next on 13 goals.

Rovers faced Cork Celtic in the Cup final and beat them 2-1 after a replay. A week later Dundalk beat Rovers 3-2 in the semi-final of the Top Four competition. Goals from Hasty and Kennedy put Dundalk two up after 52 minutes, Tony Byrne pulled a goal back for Rovers but almost immediately, Jimmy Hasty scored Dundalk's third goal. Jackie Mooney scored Rovers' second after 64 minutes but although the Hoops laid siege to the Dundalk goal for the remainder of the match they couldn't find a way through and Dundalk foiled Rovers of victory in the final domestic competition of the season.

Sean Thomas, who had guided Rovers to so many triumphs, should have been guaranteed the job of Rovers coach for as long as he wanted it after such a successful season. Amazingly, he joined Bohemians before the start of the 1964/65 season. His departure from Rovers was over who controlled team selection, the coach or the board of directors. Frank O'Neill did not have a good game in the drawn Cup final against Cork Celtic. He had, however, been the inspiration and guiding light of so many Rovers' victories that season with his outstanding wing play that it was correct to assume that he would have a much better game in the replay. Sean Thomas was firmly of that view. However, the directors took the decision to replace Frank with Tony Byrne for the replay. The dropping of Frank O'Neill was the straw that broke the camel's back as far as Sean Thomas was concerned. He did not have complete control over team selection and his fine record at Milltown should have meant that he had.

Jackie Mooney arrived for training one evening at Milltown and was told by Liam Tuohy that all the players were being asked by the directors for their opinions on how things were going for the team. This happened at a time when the Hoops were winning the League and it seemed like an attempt by the directors to undermine the authority of Sean Thomas as coach. Liam Tuohy told the players that they were worth nothing if they sold out Sean Thomas. The players gave their coach their full backing in their conversations with the directors but the directors still weren't happy with the way team matters were being run by Sean Thomas.

The directors were bypassing the coach and picking the team themselves. Players were left out in the final matches of the season and Sean Thomas's protests at this interference in team selection were ignored by the directors. He became very disillusioned but it was the decision to drop Frank O'Neill that really forced his hand to leave the Hoops.

Bohemians, who had finished bottom of the League 28 points behind the Hoops, having won just one match in the competition all season, offered the manager's job at Dalymount Park to Sean Thomas. He knew that he would be going from one end of the League table to the other but as he was born and reared in Connaught Street and would have complete control over team selection and was made a very good offer by Bohemians, he decided to accept their offer and leave Rovers.

His record at Milltown was tremendous. The only thing the Hoops had failed to win in the 1963/64 season was the Top Four trophy and they were most unluckily beaten by Dundalk in the semi-final. Sean Thomas should have been given a long-term contract at Milltown after such a successful season. Instead, he was on his way to Dalymount Park leaving behind him one of the finest teams ever to represent Shamrock Rovers; indeed, in some supporters' eyes that team was the greatest Rovers team of them all.

Liam Tuohy was appointed player-coach in succession to Thomas. Liam took the job on the understanding that he would have complete control over team selection. Some of the directors still wanted to have their say before Liam picked the team but Liam insisted that it was his responsibility alone and the board of directors then gave him complete control over team selection. However, there were still occasions when certain directors tried to influence team selection. For instance, Mick Kearin was signed by Rovers from Bohemians in 1966. At that time Liam Tuohy's local butcher was Mick Kearin's uncle. On some occasions Mick used to work with his uncle in the shop. After Mick Kearin was selected for a match one of the directors, who didn't think highly of him as a footballer, informed Liam after seeing the team selection: 'I see you've picked your butcher again.'

Pat Dunne signed for Manchester United after the Cup final replay. Sunderland were also chasing his signature but Pat opted for United and won a League medal with them in the 1964/65 season before signing for Plymouth Argyle in 1967. The departure of Pat Dunne meant that there was fierce competition from three goalkeepers for the coveted 'keeper's jersey at Rovers. Mick Smyth who was signed from English non-League side Barrow, Paddy Henderson and Jimmy Cummins all played during the 1964/65 season before Smyth established himself as Rovers regular 'keeper. Eddie Bailham left Rovers in September 1964 to take up a job in London, joined non-League team Cambridge City and was a regular goalscorer for them.

Rovers began the new season with a friendly match against Manchester United at Dalymount Park on 14 August. United won 4-2 with Jackie Mooney scoring twice for Rovers; Herd (2),

Charlton and Best scored for United. Five days later Rovers played their first competitive game of the season when they beat Bohs 5-1 in the President's Cup semi-final with Liam Tuohy scoring four times. Rovers began the Shield campaign with another four-goal victory over Bohs but Drumcondra put a stop to Rovers' good start by knocking the Hoops out of the Dublin City Cup on a 2-0 scoreline on 27 August. Three days later, at Milltown, Rovers beat Limerick 3-1 in the Shield and the remarkable fact about this match was that all four goals were scored from penalties with Eddie Bailham, in one of his last games for Rovers, scoring a hat trick from the penalty spot, a most unusual occurrence. Rovers then beat Waterford and drew with Cork Celtic in the Shield before they departed for Vienna for the first leg of their European Cup match with Rapid Vienna.

Just over a year before Rovers played Rapid Vienna, the Irish International side gained a 0-0 draw in Vienna against Austria in the Nations' Cup. Ireland won the return match 3-2 at Dalymount Park to qualify for the quarter-finals. The International match in Austria left a lot of ill-feeling between the two sides and Rovers were to be the victims of some bizarre refereeing decisions during the Rapid Vienna match. The Rovers line-up for that European Cup match at the Praeter Park stadium was as follows: Henderson; Nolan, Courtney; Mulligan, Farrell, Fullam; O'Neill, Ambrose, Mooney, Tuohy, O'Connell. The referee, Ferncl from Czechoslovakia, sent off Tony O'Connell just after half-time for putting his foot over the ball while three Rapid Vienna defenders hacked at his legs. He disallowed a legitimate goal from Jackie Mooney when the match was still scoreless claiming that Jackie was offside. He awarded the Austrians a total of 47 free-kicks in the first half and they led by 1-0 at half-time, their goal coming from a free kick by their centre-half Glechner. Nuske made it 2-0 for Rapid after 56 minutes, and five minutes later Glechner scored from another free kick to put the Austrians three up. Paddy Ambrose and Liam Tuohy limped off with injuries in the second half and Rovers finished with just eight players on the pitch. Rovers played poorly in the return leg at Dalymount Park before a big attendance of 32,000. The Austrians scored twice to run out winners on aggregate by five goals and end Rovers' involvement in European competition for the season.

The Hoops were beaten 4-1 by Cork Hibs on their return from Vienna but they bounced back with an easy 5-2 win over Shelbourne at Milltown on 27 September in the Shield. That match was Eddie Bailham's last for the Hoops and he departed in fine style, scoring a hat trick with Liam Tuohy scoring the other two. Tony O'Connell scored Rovers goal in the drawn President's Cup Final with Dundalk on 7 October. The Hoops' remaining matches in the Shield resulted in wins over Dundalk and Drogheda, a draw with Drumcondra and a loss to St Pat's before they faced Sligo Rovers in their last Shield match at Milltown on 1 November. Limerick and Cork Celtic led the table by one point from Rovers with Drumcondra and Dundalk a further point behind. Rovers could only manage a 2-2 draw with Sligo Rovers, but Dundalk beat Limerick and Drums beat Cork Celtic to ensure a five-way play off for the Shield with all five teams finishing up on 15 points from 11 matches.

In the play offs, the Hoops beat Limerick 6-1 at Dalymount Park on 13 January. They then beat Dundalk 1-0 in the semi-final on 24 February at Tolka Park before winning the final 2-1 against Cork Celtic at Dalymount Park on 17 March. Dundalk beat Rovers 4-2 in the replayed final of the President's Cup on 4 November. Matt Wogan, making one of his rare appearances in the first team, scored Rovers' second goal in the replay but it wasn't enough to prevent the trophy going to Oriel Park. For the record, Ronnie Nolan scored Rovers' first goal.

The Hoops began their defence of the League title with a 2-0 win over Bohs at Milltown. They then lost their next two matches, losing 2-1 to Limerick in the League and crashing out of the Leinster Senior Cup 3-1 to St Pat's at the quarter-final stage. The Hoops took five points from their next three League matches before Shelbourne ensured Rovers' second League defeat of the season with a 3-1 win at Tolka Park. Jimmy Cummins made his debut for the Hoops against Drums the following Sunday at

League of Ireland Champions, 1922/23. Malone (inset). Back row (l. to r.): M. Dunne, Warren, O'Kelly, Marlowe, Byrne, J. Dundon. Front row (l. to r.): Egan, Flood, Fullam, Cowzer, Fagan. Seated: Doyle, Glen.

Action from the 1932 FAI Cup final, Rovers versus Dolphin.

Shamrock Rovers' affiliation to the Leinster Football Association in 1901/02 as
recorded by the secretary of the LFA.

Shamrock Rovers side from the early 1930s. Players only. Middle row
(l. to r.): Daly, Gaskins, McCarthy, Burke, Kinsella. Front row (l. to r.):
Byrne, Glen, unknown, Matthews, Flood, Buchanan, Smith.

No. 36, The Square, where David 'Babby' Byrne lived.

Cup Final Mascots   345&

Mick McCarthy with mascots before the 1932 FAI Cup final. The mascot on the left was Mickey Burke, son of John Burke. Mickey was later to become a member of one of the most successful ever Rovers teams.

Billy Meek (left) gets a header in towards goal watched anxiously by 'Sonny' Molloy (centre) and Dundalk defenders. Joe Ward is the Rovers player on the right.

Rovers team, 1939. Back row (l. to r.): Joe Williams, Jim Blake, Tommy Donnelly, Mick McCarthy, Harry Finnegan, Christy Flood. Front row (l. to r.): 'Sonny' Molloy, Joe Ward, Jimmy Dunne, Billy Meek, Eddie Dunne.

Rovers team 1940/41. Top row (l. to r.): S. Farrelly, 'Marlowe' Dunne, Larry Palmer, J. Smithers, Paddy Doherty, Shay Healy, Mick McCarthy, Podge Gregg, Joe Creevey, Billy Fallon. Second row from top: 'Ando' Byrne, Mattie Clarke, 'Lowry' Maher, Paddy Reynolds, Tommy Pounce, Billy Cameron, Billy Meek, Paddy Murphy, Harry Finnegan, C. Finnegan, Joe Williams, Joe Byrne. Bottom row (l. to r): Capt. Tom Scully, George Price, Jimmy Dunne, Joe Cunningham Snr, Mary Jane Cunningham, Jack McCarthy, Mattie McNevin. Sitting (l. to r.): Kevin Matthews, Joe Ward, Dessie Westby, Paddy 'Sonny' Molloy.

Jimmy Dunne - one of the greatest players to line out for Shamrock Rovers.

Team captain Paddy Coad pictured with the FAI Cup at Dalymount Park after Rovers had beaten Bohemians in the 1945 final. (Irish Press)

Rovers team 1948/49: Back row (l. to r.): Ossie Nash, Tom Dunne, Frank Glennon, Tommy Godwin, Ossie Higgins, Paddy Kavanagh. Front row (l. to r.): Tommy O'Connor, Eugene Kirby, Paddy Coad, Mattie Clarke, Jimmy Gaynor.

Action from the Rovers versus Waterford Dublin City Cup game at Milltown, 21 August 1950. (Evening Herald)

Tommy Eglington (at bottom of steps) followed by Freddie Kiernan and Paddy Coad being welcomed upon their arrival in Austria in 1952.

Ireland's centre half Gerry Mackey heads the ball clear from a corner kick watched by Tommy Taylor of the English League, 19 September 1956. Ronnie Nolan is the player on the extreme left and Noel Peyton stands with his arms akimbo second from left.

Milltown. Goals from Jackie Mooney and Noel Dunne set up a 2-1 win. The following Sunday, 27 December, the Hoops travelled to Drogheda and played a scoreless draw with the home side; this occasion saw Mick Smyth make his debut for Rovers. So on three successive Sundays in December 1964, Rovers played different goal keepers in each match. The Hoops and Jackie Mooney in particular then struck a rich vein of form as Rovers won their next five League matches. Wins over Dundalk, St Pat's, Bohs, Limerick and Waterford put Rovers in with a very good chance of retaining the League title. In those matches they scored fifteen goals and only conceded four, and Jackie Mooney - scoring in each match - helped himself to seven goals over that five-match period.

The Hoops then took on Glasheen in the first round of the FAI Cup. A goal from Noel Dunne after 57 minutes earned Rovers victory. Noel Dunne was the match winner again the following week when the Hoops beat Cork Celtic 1-0 in the League at Milltown. Cork Hibs brought Rovers' run of seven consecutive victories to a halt at Flower Lodge on 28 February when they won 2-0. The Hoops returned to winning ways the following Sunday when they were slightly fortunate to come from behind and beat Dundalk 3-1 in the quarter-final of the Cup. They then beat Shelbourne 3-1 in the League at Milltown before they suffered two disastrous defeats which were ultimately to cost them the League title.

Rovers played Drumcondra at Tolka Park on 21 March and after conceding a goal mid way through the first half they proceeded to dominate the game completely but couldn't force an equaliser. Chance after chance was created but Drums' goal remained intact and then, to add insult to injury, Drums scored again in injury time at the end of the second half to wrap up the points. On Good Friday, 26 March, the Hoops travelled to Sligo and came away empty-handed as Sligo Rovers beat them 1-0. Rovers never got going in this match and they couldn't really complain about the result as they played second fiddle to Sligo for most of the match.

Mick Lynch was signed by Rovers and made his debut against

Drogheda on 28 March. He scored twice as Rovers won 4-1. On Sunday, 4 April, Rovers recorded their first victory at Flower Lodge beating Cork Celtic 3-0 in the semi-final of the FAI Cup. They then beat St Pat's and Sligo Rovers in the League before they travelled to Oriel Park on Monday, 19 April needing to beat Dundalk to force a play-off for the League title with Drums. Rovers' line-up that evening was as follows: Smyth; Mulligan, Courtney; Nolan, Farrell, Fullam; O'Neill, Mooney, Lynch, Dunne, Tuohy.

The Hoops began brightly and forced ten corners in the first half. Frank O'Neill headed a cross from Tony O'Connell against the inside of the post after 28 minutes. Three minutes later, Jackie Mooney headed a free kick from O'Neill to the net to put the Hoops one up. Dundalk piled on the pressure in the second half but Rovers looked to have weathered the storm as the game entered the last ten minutes. However with eight minutes left, Jimmy Hasty equalised for Dundalk when he headed a free kick from Masterson past Smyth.

Drums finished one point ahead of Rovers and the final table for the Top Four was as follows:

	P	W	D	L	F	A	Pts.
Drumcondra	22	14	4	4	35	22	32
Rovers	22	14	3	5	40	22	31
Bohemians	22	10	7	5	38	24	27
Cork Hibs	22	11	5	6	41	29	27

Rovers played Limerick in the FAI Cup final on Sunday, 25 April. Noel Dunne gave the Hoops the lead after 63 minutes but Eddie Mulvey equalised for Limerick eight minutes later. In the replay Johnny Fullam scored the only goal after 55 minutes with a close-range header past Kevin Fitzpatrick.

Rovers beat Bohemians 3-1 in the semi-final of the Top Four competition but Drums beat the Hoops 3-0 in the final at Dalymount Park on 9 May. Jackie Mooney finished the season as Rovers' top scorer in the League with a total of sixteen goals.

The 1965/66 season began with some changes in personnel at Milltown. A serious knee injury had tragically curtailed Jackie Mooney's career and he was to score his last goal for Rovers against Cork Hibs in the Shield at Milltown on 19 September. Bobby Gilbert, Noel Hayes and Brian Tyrrell arrived on the scene and the Hoops made a good start to the season, retaining the Shield by three points. Limerick and Drums beat Rovers in the Shield with Drums' win at Milltown on 3 October being the first home defeat since February 1963. On Wednesday 20 October Bohs beat Rovers 3-2 in the replay of the President's Cup final. It was Bohemians' first trophy since they won the Leinster Senior Cup in 1947. The Hoops had taken a two-goal lead with goals from Tyrrell after 24 minutes and Tuohy after 50 minutes. However Bohs never gave up and were rewarded for all their attacking efforts with three goals in eleven minutes from Jimmy Conway and Ben O'Sullivan.

Rovers signed Bobby Gilbert from Derry City and he made his debut against St Pat's in the Shield at Milltown on Sunday 24 October. Dinny Lowry and the St Pat's defence must have wished that Bobby Gilbert's debut could have been delayed another week because he took St Pat's to the cleaners, scoring in the first minute and three times in total as Rovers crushed Pat's 9-1. Gilbert opened the scoring in the first minute. Tuohy volleyed Mulligan's centre to the net after five minutes and Brian Tyrrell put Rovers three up after 12 minutes. Bobby Gilbert scored his second goal to put Rovers four up after 24 minutes. On 33 minutes O'Connor pulled one back for St Pat's before Fullam and Gilbert scored before half-time to put Rovers 6-1 up. O'Neill after 54 minutes, O'Connell after 55 minutes and Tuohy after 73 minutes completed the scoring. Only heroic goalkeeping by Dinny Lowry and a couple of interventions by the woodwork prevented Rovers from getting into double figures. The Rovers' forwards tried very hard to get a tenth goal and it speaks volumes for their attitude to the game that they never ceased to attack even though they were ahead by such a big margin.

The Hoops clinched their fourth Shield in a row and their eighth in twelve seasons by beating Sligo Rovers 3-1 at the Showgrounds on 31 October. They had scored 36 times in eleven Shield matches and this augured well for the coming League campaign, which Rovers began with a 4-2 win over Bohs at Dalymount Park. They then had wins over St Pat's and Limerick in the Leinster Senior Cup quarter-final and the League respectively before they took on Zaragoza in the second round of the Fairs Cup at Dalymount Park on Wednesday, 17 November. Rovers had been given a bye in the first round and were now drawn against the winners of the 1963/64 Fairs Cup. Their line up on that night was as follows: Smyth; Keogh, Courtney; Mulligan, Nolan, Fullam; O'Neill, Tyrrell, Gilbert, Tuohy, O'Connell.

Snow had fallen the previous day in Dublin and the referee Marcel Deckx from Luxembourg had to inspect the pitch twice before giving the go-ahead for the match to take place because of persistent heavy rain. The wet night cut the attendance to a mere 6,500 but those who stayed away were the real losers as the Hoops gave a great performance. Santamaria, the Zaragoza defender, stopped a piledriver from O'Neill after only five minutes. On 35 minutes O'Neill sliced a Tuohy cross wide after the opening had been created by Fullam. Just before half-time Rovers went ahead when Johnny Fullam crossed for Liam Tuohy to score with a diving header. Liam Tuohy and Bobby Gilbert both came close in the second half with headers before the Spaniards equalised with a long-range shot from full back Reija with only three minutes remaining. A two-goal lead would not have flattered Rovers such was their dominance on the night but they were held to a draw and they had it all to do in the return leg in Spain.

Rovers played Waterford in the League at Kilcohan Park on Sunday 21 November and it was a match full of incident and controversy. The two teams lined out as follows. *Waterford:* Taylor; S. Casey, Morrissey; O'Neill, Griffin, Ryan; Fitzgerald, A. Casey, Lynch, Coad, Wallace. *Rovers:* Smyth; Keogh, Courtney; Mulligan, Nolan, Fullam; O'Neill, Tyrrell, Gilbert, Tuohy, O'Connell.

The referee Patrick Grahame, awarded Rovers a controversial penalty after 65 minutes when Rovers were leading 3-2. The referee alleged that Tommy Taylor had hand-tripped Liam Tuohy. Johnny Fullam scored from the spot and some sections of the Waterford supporters went on the rampage. Stones were thrown at the referee and the players. Billy Lord received a nasty gash on the forehead and was unconscious for several minutes. Thirty garda reinforcements were called in to help the four gardai on duty at the match. It took the referee fifteen minutes to reach the sanctuary of the dressing rooms at full-time as gardai and stewards battled with incensed local supporters. Two early goals from Bobby Gilbert had given the Hoops a good start. Peter Fitzgerald narrowed the gap with a diving header before Gilbert created an opening for Liam Tuohy to put Rovers 3-1 up. Al Casey scored from a John O'Neill cross just on half-time to make it 3-2 for the Hoops at the interval. Peter Fitzgerald scored for The Blues in the dying minutes to leave it 4-3 for Rovers.

The Hoops then travelled to Zaragoza for the second leg of the Fairs Cup match. After ten minutes Mick Smyth came out to gather a corner, was bustled by two of his own players and as he dropped the ball Santos reacted quickly to slam the ball into the roof of the net. Rovers equalised after 21 minutes. Tony O'Connell was fouled and Frank O'Neill's free kick was only half-cleared. Bobby Gilbert crossed the ball and Johnny Fullam headed low to the net. Mick Smyth made two fine saves from Reija and Lapetra before Brian Tyrrell in a breakaway attack was robbed just as he was about to shoot from five yards out. Canario scored the winner for Real Zaragoza after 78 minutes and try as they did Rovers couldn't force an equaliser. Smyth, Courtney, Nolan, Mulligan and O'Neill were outstanding for Rovers; Paddy Mulligan marked the Spanish international Marcelino out of the game completely. Real Zaragoza went on to reach the final that season. Barcelona beat them 4-3 on aggregate after extra time in the second leg of the final.

Rovers beat the two Cork teams, Celtic by 3-1 and Hibs by 2-0 before they were surprisingly beaten 2-0 by Shelbourne in the semi-final of the Leinster Senior Cup at Dalymount Park on Wednesday 8 December. Rovers played Shelbourne in the League at Milltown on the following Sunday but this time there was a totally different result. Johnny Fullam and Liam Tuohy each scored twice and Gilbert, Tyrrell and O'Connell also scored as the Hoops won 7-1. Drumcondra, Drogheda, Dundalk, St Pat's and Sligo Rovers were beaten on consecutive Sundays as Rovers equalled the 29-year-old record of Sligo Rovers in gaining maximum points from the first half of the League. Rovers' twelfth match was against Bohemians at Milltown on 23 January. They took into it a six-point lead over their nearest challengers, Waterford, and seemed poised to take their eleventh League title. They were also trying to set a new record of twelve wins from the opening twelve matches. The line-ups on that January afternoon were as follows. *Shamrock Rovers*: Smyth; Keogh, Courtney; Mulligan, Nolan, Fullam; O'Neill, Dunne, Gilbert, Tuohy, O'Connell. *Bohemians*: Duffy; Young, Wade; Cahill, Browne, Conway; O'Sullivan, Murray, Kearin, O'Connor, Gilmore.

This was a magnificent match as fortunes swayed one way and then the other. Rovers took the lead after 24 minutes when O'Connell passed to Tuohy and as Browne, the Bohs centre half, hesitated Tuohy picked his spot to put Rovers one up. Their lead was short lived. Jimmy Conway, who was having a tremendous tussle with Ronnie Nolan, latched on to a pass from Turlough O'Connor and shot past Smyth for the equaliser. Five minutes later Jimmy Conway was fouled just outside the box and Kevin Murray hit a great shot to the net to give Bohs the lead. Bohs' winger Ben O'Sullivan had injured a hip early in the match and Sean Thomas moved Jimmy Conway up to centre forward where he was causing all sorts of problems for Ronnie Nolan. The Hoops equalised after 50 minutes when Gilbert sent O'Neill away on the right and as Duffy advanced O'Neill chipped him to level the scores. Both sides went all out for the winner and it arrived after 77 minutes. Bohs attacked down the left wing and Kearin placed Gilmore for a shot. The ball hit a defender and broke for Bohs 18-year-old winger Ben O'Sullivan to hit a screamer past Smyth. The large crowd which paid gate receipts of £1,302 gave the two teams a standing ovation at the final whistle for what had been an outstanding game of football.

Rovers then played Limerick at the Market Fields and drew 1-1 but Bobby Gilbert missed a good chance when he was put through by O'Connell but he shot wide. The following Sunday, 6 February, Rovers played their nearest challengers Waterford in a vital League match at Milltown. Waterford wanted the game to be switched to Dalymount Park because of the anticipated huge crowd and there were doubts as to whether or not Glenmalure Park would be able to accommodate all who wanted to see this match. Rovers refused Waterford's request because of (1) the cost of renting Dalymount Park, (2) the cost of stewarding, and (3) the question of whether the players would be prepared to give up home advantage. Waterford had agreed to give 30 per cent of their share of the gate (at that time the visiting side received 30 per cent of the gate) towards expenses. The sides couldn't come to an agreement and the game went ahead as planned at Milltown.

A huge support had travelled from Waterford in four special trains. They arrived so early outside Milltown that the Gardai insisted on the gates being opened at 1 p.m. There were queues a mile long outside the ground ten minutes before kick-off time. A record crowd of 24,000 paid gate receipts of £2,610 to watch a League match that was to have a vital bearing on the destination of the title. The two teams lined out as follows. *Shamrock Rovers*: Smyth; Keogh, Courtney; Core, Mulligan, Fullam; O'Neill, Dunne, Gilbert, Tuohy, O'Connell. *Waterford*: Taylor; S. Casey, Ryan; Maguire, Griffin, McGeough; A. Casey, O'Neill, Lynch, Coad, Wallace.

Waterford, playing with grim determination and no little skill, deserved their success. The only goal of the match came after 39 minutes. Wallace dispossessed Dunne before pushing the ball to McGeough who rounded Keogh before crossing for Al Casey to side foot the ball to the net. Seamus Casey took a curling shot from Frank O'Neill off the line with Taylor beaten. Taylor also made good saves from Johnny Fullam and Bobby Gilbert.

However, Waterford did most of the attacking and John O'Neill hit the post for the Blues. Ronnie Nolan was out injured after he twisted his left knee against Limerick the previous Sunday. Paddy Mulligan, who replaced Nolan, and Sean Core performed as dual centre halves. Mulligan had a great game keeping Lynch, the League's highest scorer, subdued. Vinny Maguire and Johnny McGeough were outstanding for Waterford and Frank O'Neill was the only Rovers' forward who caused serious problems for the Blues' defence. That defeat meant that Rovers now only led Waterford by one point while three weeks earlier there had been a six-point gap between the clubs.

The Hoops beat Cork Hibs 3-1 in the replay of their first round FAI Cup match after a 1-1 draw at Flower Lodge. Rovers dropped another vital League point at Turner's Cross on 20 February before they hammered Cork Hibs 6-1 in the League at Milltown on 27 February. The Hoops then faced Shelbourne three times in eight days. Rovers beat the Reds in the quarter-final of the FAI Cup after a replay but they could only manage a 1-1 draw when the two sides played a League match at Tolka Park on 13 March. Hughie Brophy who had been signed from Bolton Athletic made his debut the following Sunday against Drumcondra at Milltown. Bobby Gilbert scored a hat trick and Liam Tuohy scored twice as Rovers had a comfortable 5-1 win over Drums.

A great one-handed save from Mick Smyth late in the game kept Rovers in the Cup when they drew 2-2 with Waterford at Dalymount Park on 3 April in the semi-final. Ronnie Nolan had an outstanding game in the replay three days later as the Hoops won 4-2. Then calamity struck less than a week later when St Pat's scored a shock win over Rovers at Milltown. Liam Tuohy was injured after three minutes and though Rovers battled very hard they couldn't contain St Pat's who won 2-1 with all the goals coming in the second half. This defeat virtually cost the Hoops the title as it opened up a three-point lead for the Blues.

There was some consolation, however, towards the end of the season. Tony O'Connell and Frank O'Neill scored the goals as the Hoops recorded their 17th FAI Cup triumph with a 2-0 win over

Limerick in a disappointing final.

On 27 April Rovers played Waterford in the semi-final of the Top Four competition and it was a magnificent match. Johnny Fullam, Paddy Mulligan and Hughie Brophy were outstanding for Rovers as Brophy in his third game for the Hoops completely outfoxed Jimmy McGeough. Bobby Gilbert put Rovers ahead after three minutes when he headed Fullam's cross to the net. Waterford then laid siege to Rovers' goal and after Smyth had saved shots from Coad and McGeough he was well beaten by a great rising shot from Mick Lynch after 22 minutes. Rovers then reasserted themselves and Hughie Brophy restored the Hoops' lead after 31 minutes when he beat Tommy Taylor from close range after being put through by Bobby Gilbert. Four minutes after the interval Frank O'Neill, who had moved over to the left wing, crossed for Bobby Gilbert to head the ball down to Tony O'Connell who poked it home from close range. Rovers went 4-1 up after 64 minutes when O'Neill and Brophy set up John Keogh who beat Taylor easily. Al Casey completed the scoring after 79 minutes when he took a pass from Mick Lynch to make it 4-2 for Rovers.

The Hoops then played Bohs in the final. This match went to two replays before the Hoops eventually won by three goals to nil. The first match ended in a 3-3 draw with the Hoops coming back from two goals down. In the first replay the Hoops also had to come from behind to force a 1-1 draw. Rovers had it relatively easy in the second replay winning 3-0 with the goals being scored by Bobby Gilbert (2) and Damien Richardson.

During the 1966 close season Billy Dixon was signed from Drumcondra and Mick Kearin from Bohemians. Rovers kicked off the 1966/67 season with a friendly against F.A Cup winners Everton. The Toffees won two-one with goals from Derek Temple and Mike Trebilcock. Billy Dixon scored on his debut for Rovers and their line-up for that friendly on 5 August was as follows: Smyth; Keogh, Courtney; Mulligan, Nolan, Fullam; O'Neill, Kearin, Gilbert, Dixon, Tuohy.

Rovers played their first competitive match of the 1966/67 season on 21 August losing 2-1 to Bohs in a Shield match. Three days later the Hoops beat Drums 5-2 in the Dublin City Cup and the following Sunday they trashed Limerick 6-0 at Milltown in the Shield with Gilbert scoring four times. Waterford then beat the Hoops 2-0 before Rovers won their next three matches in the Shield, beating Cork Celtic, Cork Hibs and Shels; scoring seventeen times in these three matches and conceding only three. On 14 September the Hoops withdrew from the Leinster Senior Cup competition. Rovers were fined £50 by the Leinster FA over their failure to fulfil a President's Cup tie with Shelbourne. The fine was later reduced to £10.

On Wednesday 28 September the Hoops played Spora Luxembourg in the first leg of their first round European Cup Winners' Cup match at Dalymount Park. Rovers line-up was as follows: Smyth; Mulligan, Courtney; Core, Nolan, Fullam; O'Neill, Dixon, Gilbert, Tuohy, Kearin.

Rovers opened the scoring after nine minutes when Johnny Fullam scored with a shot after Bobby Gilbert had set him up with a neat pass. The Hoops were stunned when Weis equalised for Spora after 27 minutes. Rovers shock was short lived as Billy Dixon regained the lead for them two minutes later with a tremendous shot from the left. After 58 minutes a corner from Frank O'Neill was flicked to the net by Mick Kearin and with 15 minutes remaining the referee Robert Lacoste from France awarded Rovers a penalty after Liam Tuohy was fouled in the area. Frank O'Neill made no mistake from the spot to give the Hoops a 4-1 victory.

The return match was played on 5 October and Rovers, fielding an unchanged side from the first leg had another 4-1 victory. The Hoops took the lead after 16 minutes when Mick Kearin scored with a shot from 35 yards. Joseph Krier equalised for Spora after 35 minutes and Billy Dixon regained the lead for Rovers after 42 minutes. Second half goals from Frank O'Neill and Billy Dixon gave the Hoops an 8-2 aggregate win over the Luxembourg side.

On their return from Luxembourg Rovers had a 4-1 victory over Drogheda in the Shield before they travelled to Oriel Park on

16 October to take on a Dundalk side that needed only a draw to win that competition. A total of twelve special buses left Milltown for Dundalk as interest in the game was huge. A total attendance of 14,000 people paid record gate receipts of £1,430 and the big home crowd were not disappointed as Dundalk won 2-0. Rovers then drew with St Pat's in the Shield before they gained revenge for their defeat at Oriel Park by beating Dundalk 2-1 in the final of the Dublin City Cup on 26 October with goals from Mick Kearin and Frank O'Neill. The Hoops completed their Shield programme with a 3-0 victory over Sligo Rovers at Milltown on 30 October. They finished in third place with 15 points from 11 matches, four points behind Dundalk but still the highest goalscorers with 37 goals, ten more than the trophy winners.

On Wednesday 9 November, Shamrock Rovers faced Bayern Munich in the first leg of the second round of the European Cup Winners' Cup. The two teams lined out as follows. *Shamrock Rovers*: Smyth; Keogh, Courtney; Core, Nolan, Fullam; O'Neill, Mulligan, Tuohy, Dixon, Kearin. *Bayern Munich*: Maier; Novak, Kupterschmidt; Olk, Beckenbauer, Werner; Nafziger, Muller, Olhauser, Koulmann, Brenninger. A crowd of just over 20,000 were enthralled as Rovers attacked from the start. Paddy Mulligan was instructed by Liam Tuohy to stop Franz Beckenbauer from making forays into the Rovers' half and setting up attacks. Mulligan did his job so well that Beckenbauer didn't count as an attacking force at Dalymount Park. O'Neill, Kearin and Fullam all came close in the first half with rasping shots. However, after 17 minutes Bayern took the lead. A corner from Brenninger was punched out by Mick Smyth and as the ball dropped Koulmann volleyed the ball to the net with his left foot. Sepp Maier saved at his near upright from Tuohy and then Billy Dixon hit the crossbar with a tremendous shot. Rovers finally equalised after 63 minutes. Mick Kearin swung the ball over from the left, Liam Tuohy headed it down and Billy Dixon forced it home much to the disgust of Maier who followed the referee to the half-way line claiming that he had been fouled.

A few minutes later with Rovers exerting considerable pressure on the Bayern defence the referee Lee Van Ravens from Holland stopped the game after some missiles had been thrown at Sepp Maier from behind the goal. The referee approached Liam Tuohy and got a message announced over the P.A. system that he would abandon the game if the missile throwing did not stop immediately. The game was resumed after a delay of about four minutes, but those vital four minutes allowed the Germans the opportunity to regain their composure and Rovers were not as dominant when the match restarted. Maier blocked a shot from Tuohy and as Bayern came forward in the last few minutes they were foiled by the excellent defensive play of Ronnie Nolan.

The Hoops began their League campaign with a 2-0 win over Limerick at the Market's Field on 13 November with Frank O'Neill scoring twice. Rovers beat the champions Waterford 2-1 at Milltown the following Sunday with goals from Liam Tuohy and Billy Dixon. It was a match that the Hoops should have won convincingly as they had three goals disallowed and missed a penalty. Rovers then travelled to Munich to take on Bayern in the second leg. The pitch at the Olympic stadium in Munich was frostbound and rock hard. The match was played in sub-zero temperatures and John Keogh recalled that Rovers wore white undershirts underneath their hooped jerseys as a precaution against the freezing weather conditions. The two teams lined out as follows. *Bayern Munich*: Maier; Kupferschmidt, Beckenbauer; Olk, Schwarzenbach, Muller; Koulmann, Nafziger, Roth, Olhauser, Brenninger. *Shamrock Rovers*: Smyth; Keogh, Courtney; Mulligan, Nolan, Fullam; O'Neill, Dixon, Gilbert, Tuohy, Kearin.

Bayern took the lead after five minutes when Brenninger scored from a rebound after Smyth had blocked a shot from Muller. Seven minutes later Olhauser put Bayern two up. After that second goal Rovers rallied and led by Ronnie Nolan and Liam Tuohy they gradually clawed their way back into the game. Liam Tuohy must have given an inspirational half-time pep talk as Rovers came out with all guns blazing in the second half. Bobby Gilbert hit the crossbar with a tremendous shot just after half-time and after 53 minutes he pulled a goal back for the Hoops when his powerful shot ricocheted off Beckenbauer and ended up in the net. Five minutes later Liam Tuohy really put the cat amongst the pigeons when he went by a few defenders before burying a low shot past Maier into the far corner of the net. Rovers were now technically ahead as, with the introduction of away goals counting double in the event of a tie for European club competitions in 1965, Rovers would have gone through had the score remained at 2-2. Bayern Munich didn't know what had hit them and as time ticked away they were becoming rattled and a real upset was on the cards. With seven minutes remaining Liam Tuohy was caught offside just inside the Bayern Munich half and Bayern were awarded a free kick by the Yugoslav referee Konstantin Zecevic. As Franz Beckenbauer came up to take the free he threw the ball in the air in an effort to remove some of the ice and frost from it. Frank O'Neill stood just in front of him but then the Bayern left back took off on a run towards Rovers' goal and Frank O'Neill went back to mark him. Beckenbauer floated the free kick towards the Hoops' penalty area. Ronnie Nolan and Paddy Mulligan both went for the ball with the big Bayern Munich forward Koulmann. Unfortunately for Rovers, Koulmann got to the ball first and flicked it inside to Gerd Muller who beat Mick Smyth from close range. It was a terrible blow for the Rovers defence and especially for Ronnie Nolan, John Keogh and Mick Smyth who had all played magnificently only to be foiled of ultimate victory at the last moment.

John Keogh recalled that the Hoops were not experienced enough in European competition to realise that they should have got more players behind the ball to play out the last few minutes and go through on the away goals rule. Instead they kept going forward and they were caught by that late goal from Muller. Liam Tuohy was lavish in his praise of the Rovers' players after the match. He said 'the lads were magnificent, coming up from behind like that when we were two goals down. If they were full-time players like the Germans and had their training opportunities, I think we could sweep through Europe. I told the lads at half-time that Bayern could be rattled if we scored a goal and they proved it superbly.' Bayern Munich went on to beat Rapid Vienna, Standard Liege and Rangers to win the European Cup Winners' Cup and as they lifted the cup on a May evening in Nuremberg one wonders if their minds went back to the previous November when they were only seven minutes away from being eliminated from the competition by Shamrock Rovers.

On their return from Germany, Rovers drew their next two League matches against Cork Celtic and Cork Hibs before they resumed winning ways with victories over Shelbourne and Drums. The Hoops slipped up on St Stephen's Day when they lost 1-0 at Drogheda. On New Year's Day they beat Dundalk 2-1 at Milltown and included in their line up was Mick Leech who was making his debut. Mick was substituted by Billy Dixon in the second half but it wasn't long before he made a major impact with Rovers.

The Hoops' League form continued to be inconsistent and they could only manage two victories from five matches in January. They beat Shelbourne in the first round of the President's Cup but they were well beaten by Waterford in the League on 5 February, a result which ended any lingering chance they had of making a strong challenge for the title. The following Sunday, a goal from Mick Kearin knocked Shels out of the FAI Cup but the Hoops' indifferent League form continued as they lost to the two Cork sides, Celtic and Hibs. Mick Leech scored his first goal for the club when he got the first of two against Cork Hibs at Flower Lodge on 26 February. Hibs won the match 4-2 and Mick was unlucky not to have scored a hat trick. Two goals from Liam Tuohy saw off the challenge of Home Farm in the quarter-final of the Cup and they also picked up five points from their next three League matches.

The Hoops beat Dundalk 3-0 in replay of the FAI Cup semi-final but they could only manage to win one of their last three League matches. They finished seventh in the League that season, 13 points behind the winners Dundalk. They were beaten 1-0 in the final of the President's Cup by Drums on 12 April and then played St Pat's in their fourth successive FAI Cup final on 23 April. Goals from a Frank O'Neill penalty and from Mick Leech and Billy Dixon saw Rovers record their 18th Cup victory. This was the first televised Cup final which was largely responsible for the reduced attendance. A benefit match for Pat Courtney and John Keogh, who had captained the Hoops to victory over St Pat's in the Cup final, brought West Ham United to Dalymount Park in May 1967. The game finished in an exciting 5-5 draw and it was Rovers' last match before they departed for America for the United Soccer Association League.

The United Soccer Association of America arranged to obtain twelve foreign teams, one to represent each city, for a twelve-game season opening May 26 and finishing on 9 July. Shamrock Rovers were selected to represent Boston and their home matches were played at the Manning Bowl in Lynn, Massachusetts. The other American and Canadian cities in the League were represented by the following clubs. Detroit: Glentoran; New York: Cerro (from Montevideo, Uruguay); Cleveland: Stoke City; Vancouver: Sunderland; Chicago: Cagliari; San Francisco: ADO (Holland); Dallas: Dundee United; Los Angeles: Wolves; Houston: Bangu (Brazil); Toronto: Hibs; and Washington: Aberdeen. The format was that each team met every other team once and played home and away games with its natural city rival. Boston met Detroit on a home and away basis, so the Hoops played Glentoran twice on the tour. Pat Dunne, who was with Plymouth Argyle at the time but was a guest player for Rovers on the tour, described the two matches with Glentoran as mini battles. The Glens adopted a very physical approach from the start and the Hoops responded in kind. The first match between the clubs ended in a 1-1 draw and Glentoran won the return match with a goal nine minutes from time. The Hoops lost four games by one goal and their only bad defeat was against Cagliari who beat them 5-0. Rovers managed to draw 1-1 with Wolves and caused a major upset by beating the Brazilian champions Bangu 3-1 before beating the previously undefeated Aberdeen by two goals to one. The Hoops clocked up 30,000 miles playing from East to West coasts and they acquitted themselves reasonably well, considering that they were after all a team of part-time professionals.

Rovers kicked off the 1967/68 season with a friendly against

Everton at Dalymount Park. Frank Brady, a brother of Liam Brady, made his debut for Rovers and two goals from Joe Royle gave Everton victory. The Hoops' first competitive match was against Dundalk in the Shield and they drew 1-1 at Oriel Park with Billy Dixon getting their goal. Rovers beat Bohs 5-1 in the Dublin City Cup on 24 August and three days later Mick Leech went on the rampage against Shels scoring four times as Rovers won 6-0 while still missing a penalty and getting three goals disallowed for offside! The Hoops then had two wins over Waterford, beating them 3-2 in the Shield at Milltown and 2-1 in the semi-final of the Dublin City Cup. Mick Lawlor scored his first goal for Rovers in the latter match.

On 10 September the Hoops drew 2-2 away to Sligo Rovers. The referee, Pat Brady, was assaulted by Sligo Rovers' fans at the end of the match as he awarded the Hoops a penalty three minutes into injury time which Frank O'Neill converted to secure the draw. The following Sunday, Rovers got the perfect boost for their forthcoming European Cup Winners' Cup match against Cardiff City when they trashed Cork Celtic 6-1 in the Shield at Milltown.

Rovers played Cardiff City at Dalymount Park on 20 September with the following line-up: Smyth; Courtney, Mulligan; Kearin, Nolan, Fullam; O'Neill, Dixon, Gilbert, Leech, Kinsella.

Rovers took the lead mid way through the first half when Bobby Gilbert scored with a bullet-like header from 20 yards. However, they could not add to their lead and they were caught out in the second half when King equalised for Cardiff City. Drums and Drogheda were beaten in the Shield before the Hoops travelled to Cardiff for the second leg. An injury-hit Rovers' side went down 2-0 to Cardiff City who went on to reach the semi-final stage before being knocked out by S. V Hamburg. After the disappointment of their Cardiff defeat the Hoops beat Bohs, Limerick, St Pat's and Cork Hibs to win the Shield by three points from Dundalk. Rovers took 20 points from 11 matches and they were the only unbeaten side in the competition, scoring 34 goals and only conceding 11.

The League campaign began with a 1-1 draw against reigning

champions Dundalk. Mick Leech scored Rovers' goal. Two days later, Ronnie Nolan left the club to join Bohemians as player-coach. Ronnie had been dropped for the cup semi-final replay against Dundalk the previous season and as a result had missed the final against St Pat's. He had given great service to the Hoops and had won six FAI Cup medals with them. Shels and Waterford beat Rovers in their next two League matches and they drew 2-2 with Dundalk in the final of the Dublin City Cup after extra time with Mick Leech scoring twice for Rovers. The Hoops stepped up a gear in their next three League matches, beating Sligo Rovers, Cork Celtic and Drums. Damien Richardson got a hat trick against Sligo Rovers at Milltown on 26 November when the Hoops won 7-0. Rovers then drew with Drogheda and beat Bohs before Limerick beat them 3-2 on New Year's Eve at the Market's Field when a hat trick from Andy McEvoy cancelled out a brace of goals from Mick Leech.

A week later two goals from Frank O'Neill in the last 12 minutes beat St Pat's at Milltown. Later that same week John Keogh and Sean Core were placed on the transfer list. Rovers then beat Cork Hibs 2-0 before defeats by Dundalk and Shelbourne effectively ended Rovers' challenge for the title. The Hoops shocked the League leaders Waterford with a 3-2 win at Milltown on 4 February. Two goals in the last five minutes from Damien Richardson and Liam Tuohy turned defeat into victory.

Rovers began their defence of the FAI Cup at Milltown on 11 February and goals from Mick Lawlor and an own goal from Pat O'Mahony gave the Hoops a 2-0 win over Cork Celtic. Rovers had League wins over Sligo Rovers and Cork Celtic before a goal from Mick Lawlor beat Shelbourne in a very poor game in the quarter-final of the Cup at Milltown. The Hoops' inconsistent League form continued with a 3-3 draw with Drums and a 1-0 defeat by Drogheda.

Rovers played the European Cup winners Celtic at Dalymount Park on Monday 18 March in a friendly match. The two teams lined out as follows. *Rovers*: Smyth; Gregg, Courtney; Kearin, Clarke, Fullam; O'Neill, Richardson, Gilbert, Lawlor, Kinsella.

149

Sub: Hayes for Lawlor. *Celtic*: Simpson; Craig, Gemmell; Murdoch, McNeill, Brogan; Johnstone, Wallace, Chalmers, Gallagher, Hughes. *Subs*: McBride and Lennox for Johnstone and Chalmers.

An attendance of 35,000 saw Rovers appear in blue jerseys which baffled many Hoops fans, as they could never remember Rovers wearing blue before. When the Hoops played Rapid Vienna in the European Cup at Dalymount Park in 1964, Rovers wore yellow shirts and black shorts. So the fans couldn't understand why the Hoops should wear blue of all colours. The explanation was simple. A number of years earlier, Bohemians had played an exhibition match against Arsenal to mark the first match under floodlights at Dalymount Park. The Bohemians selected XI wore blue jerseys with the Dublin City coat of arms. These were the same jerseys that Rovers wore against Celtic.

As for the match itself, Willie Wallace gave Celtic an early lead and only inspired goalkeeping from Mick Smyth kept Rovers in the match. Then McNeill was penalised for a foul on Kearin after 22 minutes and Frank O'Neill's free kick was headed to the net by Bobby Gilbert for the equaliser. Willie Wallace restored Celtic's lead with a neat flicked header after 35 minutes. Mick Smyth kept Celtic at bay in the second half and with 8 minutes remaining a move involving Gregg, Gilbert and O'Neill ended with Tommy Kinsella beating Simpson with a powerful shot. Bobby Gilbert came close to snatching a dramatic winner in the dying seconds but the game finished with honours even at 2-2.

The Hoops had a 2-1 victory over Bohs in the League on 24 March before they beat Dundalk 3-0 in the semi-final of the FAI Cup on 30 March with goals from Mick Leech (2) and Mick Lawlor. Rovers took four points from their three remaining matches in the League, beating Limerick 2-1 at Milltown and drawing with both St Pat's and Cork Hibs. Mick Leech scored a dramatic winner against Limerick with a spectacular scissors kick after 77 minutes. Rovers finished in fourth place seven points behind the winners Waterford, taking 27 points out of a possible 44. It was no great surprise then that Waterford were installed as hot favourites to beat the Hoops in the Cup final. However, in

Cup finals then, Rovers were a law unto themselves. After soaking up Waterford's best efforts in the first half, the Hoops scored three times without reply in the second half to win their 19th FAI Cup by a convincing margin.

Rovers beat Dundalk 13-11 on corners after both sides had ended up sharing four goals after extra time in the Top Four semifinal. On 1 May, the Hoops travelled to Ards and beat the home team 3-0 in the quarter-final of the Blaxnit Cup. Waterford gained a little revenge when they beat Rovers 3-2 in the final of the Top Four competition. Waterford led 3-0 after twenty minutes but goals from Johnny Fullam and Mick Leech before half-time brought the Hoops right back into the match. In the second half Rovers laid siege to the Waterford goal but they couldn't find a way past an inspired Peter Thomas and Waterford held out for a narrow win. The Hoops beat Waterford in the semi-final of the Blaxnit Cup at Milltown on 9 May. A 20-yard shot from Damien Richardson after 16 minutes decided the match. Rovers played Crusaders in the two-legged Blaxnit Cup final. The Hoops won 2-0 with goals from Mick Lawlor and Mick Leech at Crusaders on 20 May and two days later Crusaders beat Rovers 2-1 at Dalymount Park; but the Hoops took the trophy on a three-two aggregate scoreline.

Rovers began the 1968/69 season on 11 August with a 3-2 victory over Dundalk in the President's Cup final. Rovers' goals were scored by Tommy Kinsella, Bobby Gilbert and Billy Dixon. The Hoops won their next three matches beating Dundalk and Shels in the Shield and Bohs in the Dublin City Cup before Waterford beat them 4-2 in the Shield at Kilcohan Park. Mick Leech was in great form that season and in his next two matches he scored two hat tricks as Rovers drew 3-3 with Sligo Rovers in the Shield and beat Cork Hibs 3-2 in the semi-final of the Dublin City Cup. He then grabbed a brace of goals in a draw with Cork Celtic in the Shield before Rovers travelled to Denmark to play Randers Freja in the European Cup Winners' Cup. Their line up was as follows: Smyth; Gregg, Courtney; Fullam, Brady, Dixon; Kinsella, Leech, Gilbert, O'Neill, Richardson.

The Hoops were holding the Danes and looked like getting a scoreless draw until disaster struck in the 89th minute when Gaardsoe scored. Rovers beat Drums and Drogheda in the Shield before they took on the Danes in the return leg at Dalymount Park. Their line up for the return leg was as follows: Smyth; Gregg, Courtney; Richardson, Brady, Fullam; O'Neill, Dixon, Gilbert, Leech, Lawlor. *Subs*: Tuohy and Kinsella for Leech and Dixon. Rovers laid siege to the Randers Freja goal in the first half as they made an all-out effort to get on level terms quickly. The Hoops missed six great chances in the first half and they were stunned when Gaardsoe scored to put the Danes 2-0 up on aggregate. Johnny Fullam equalised from a well-rehearsed free kick routine. Fullam pushed the ball to O'Neill and then moved forward to take the return. O'Neill lobbed the ball over the wall and Fullam left footed the ball to the net. Andersen scored in the dying minutes to give the Danes a 2-1 win at Dalymount and a 3-1 win on aggregate. Rovers were hugely disappointed with the results over the two legs as they were confident that they would progress through to the next round. However, their failure to put away the many chances they created in Dublin in the first half cost them dearly.

Rovers beat Bohemians 4-1 in the Shield and then disposed of Transport in the quarter-final of the Leinster Senior Cup. Limerick and St Pat's were their next victims in the Shield before Cork Hibs beat them 2-0 in their final Shield match. The Hoops finished in third place, three points behind the winners Waterford. Mick Leech, who was having a great season, scored 10 of their 29 goals from 11 matches in the Shield.

David Pugh was signed from Boston and Hughie Brophy was signed for the second time for Rovers from Crystal Palace. They both appeared in Rovers' team for the opening League match against Dundalk at Oriel Park on 3 November. Rovers won 5-1 and Mick Leech grabbed a hat trick with Johnny Fullam and Frank O'Neill getting the other goals. The Hoops beat St Pat's 4-1 in the Leinster Senior Cup semi-final and they had a comfortable 4-0 win over Shels before they played the champions Waterford in the

League at Milltown on 17 November. A huge crowd paid gate receipts of £1,800 but Waterford had the better of the match winning 2-1 with Billy Dixon getting Rovers' goal.

The Hoops then beat Sligo Rovers and Cork Celtic and drew with Drumcondra and Drogheda. They beat Bohs 3-0 twice in the space of four days, first in the League and then in the Leinster Senior Cup final. Mick Leech scored twice in the Leinster Senior Cup final with Frank O'Neill getting Rovers' other goal. A 2-0 victory over Limerick on 29 December was followed by a 6-1 thrashing of St Pat's at Inchicore where Rovers were three up after just three minutes. The Hoops went to the top of the table on 12 January following their 3-1 win over Cork Hibs at Milltown. Rovers now had 18 points from 11 matches and the following Sunday, Mick Leech scored his 38th goal of the season as they beat Dundalk 2-1 at Milltown. Shels were the next opponents at Milltown on 26 January and the Hoops took the Reds to the cleaners romping home with a 7-1 win. They were three up after 29 minutes and five up at half-time; Mick Leech got a hat trick. However, the Hoops came down to earth with a large thud the following Sunday when they were comprehensively outplayed by Waterford at Kilcohan Park. The Blues were five goals to the good before Mick Leech scored his 42nd goal of the season. Waterford were now 2 points behind with a game in hand and it was all to play for as the season neared its climax.

The Hoops began their defence of the Cup with a comfortable 3-0 victory over Dundalk in the first round at Milltown on 9 February. Rovers' next match was against Cork Celtic in the League at Turner's Cross and goals from Leech and Lawlor gave them a 2-0 win. Ringmahon Rangers were beaten 4-0 in the second round of the Cup at Milltown and a 2-0 League win over Drums at Milltown left Rovers in a strong position with five matches remaining. Drogheda put a severe dent in Rovers' title ambitions with a surprise 2-1 win at Lourdes Stadium on 16 March and then the Hoops crashed to a heavy defeat in the Dublin City Cup final when Dundalk swamped them in the second half to win 5-2. The Hoops then drew 2-2 with Bohs before they played arch rivals Shelbourne in the semi-final of the Cup at Dalymount Park on 30 March and Johnny Campbell gave the Reds the lead after 65 minutes. However, the referee Peter Coates awarded Rovers a penalty for hand ball against Newman a few minutes later and Frank O'Neill made no mistake from the spot to earn the Hoops a replay. Mick Lawlor scored the only goal of the replay after 35 minutes to put Rovers into a record-making sixth successive FAI Cup final. The Hoops beat St Pat's 3-0 in the League on 6 April and then they signed Ben Hannigan from Dundalk. Hannigan scored twice on his debut for the Hoops and they beat Sligo Rovers 2-1 at Milltown on 11 April. Rovers finished their League campaign with a 2-0 defeat by Cork Hibs at Flower Lodge. The Hoops finished on 31 points, five behind the champions Waterford. Rovers scored 56 goals in 22 matches and Mick Leech was their top League scorer with 19 goals.

The Hoops played Cork Celtic in the FAI Cup final on 20 April. Things looked bad for Rovers as John Carroll had given Cork Celtic the lead and Frank O'Neill had a penalty saved by Tommy Taylor. With nine minutes remaining Cork Celtic were still holding on to their lead when disaster struck the Leesiders. Rovers forced a corner, and after Taylor had saved from Kinsella the ball broke to Courtney who crossed for Mulligan to head the ball towards the goal. John Keogh was at the post but the ball was marginally too high for him to clear with his foot and he only succeeded in deflecting the ball into his own net for the equaliser. The Hoops made no mistake in the replay winning 4-1 to complete an historic six in a row in the FAI Cup and their 20th Cup victory in all.

Rovers then beat Glentoran 2-0 away in the quarter-final of the Blaxnit Cup with Mick Leech getting both goals. They overcame Dundalk 2-1 in the semi-final of the Top Four competition but lost 2-0 to Waterford in the final on 2 May.

Rovers qualified for the final of the Blaxnit Cup, beating Shels 1-0 in the semi-final. The first leg of the final was played at Coleraine and the Irish League side won 2-1. The second leg was played at Dalymount Park and the Hoops looked set to win the trophy when goals from Lawlor and O'Neill put them two ahead on the night and 3-2 ahead on aggregate. However, Coleraine stunned the Hoops with two late goals, an own goal from Mick Kearin and a very late goal from Dickson, to take the trophy by 4-3 on aggregate.

Mick Leech had a wonderful season for the Hoops in 1968/69. He scored 56 goals in all competitions. All in all, the 'sixties had been a very successful decade for the Hoops: seven Cup wins, five Shield wins and one League title. Moreover, they really should have won the League both in 1965 and 1966 when they were pipped by Drumcondra and Waterford respectively. The 1960s brought good times to Milltown. It was going to be difficult to emulate the achievements of that great Rovers' side in the 1970s.

THE PATH OF THE CUP 1960-69

Rovers' first FAI Cup game of the 1960s was played at Milltown on St Valentine's day. The Hoops faced their old rivals Drums in a first round tie and the referee J. Cook of Yorkshire allowed the game to go ahead despite the fact that most of the pitch was covered in snow which made conditions treacherous for the players. Drums were two up after 23 minutes but Rovers fought back to level by half-time. Dermot Cross scored a great goal after 36 minutes and seven minutes later he was fouled in the penalty area and Liam Hennessy scored from the spot. The second half was scoreless and Courtney, Nolan and Keogh were outstanding for the Hoops. A solitary goal from Paddy Ambrose decided the replay on 25 February at Tolka Park. The Hoops' next opponents were Shelbourne and a crowd of 22,000 attended the quarter-final tie between the arch rivals from Ringsend at Milltown on Sunday 6 March.

Shelbourne took the lead after 15 minutes when Barber passed to Conroy on the left wing, Ollie Conroy sent over a good cross for Jackie Hennessy to head past Eamonn Darcy. Rovers equalised seven minutes later when Tommy Hamilton headed a corner from Liam Tuohy to the net. Hamilton hit the crossbar with a shot after

155

39 minutes and two minutes later disaster struck the Hoops, when Tommy Farrell and Liam Hennessy collided with each other. Farrell had to leave the field and he was brought to hospital where he received eight stitches in a head wound. Liam Hennessy bravely carried on but he was a passenger on the left wing because he was still in a dazed condition. Rovers had to reorganise their depleted team as they now only had nine fully fit players. Albie Murphy went to centre-half, Ronnie Nolan to right full, Paddy Ambrose and Liam Tuohy dropped back to wing halves and Cross, Hamilton and McCann made up the forward line. Young Pat Courtney played brilliantly at left back and as Shels attempted to play the ball down the middle they came up against a stern Hoops defence which gave nothing away. Tommy Hamilton cleverly kept possession up front for long periods in order to take the pressure off his team mates behind him.

Shels put out an unchanged side for the replay the following Wednesday night at Tolka Park while Noel Dunne replaced Tommy Farrell for the Hoops. Rovers had the better of the exchanges in the first half but they failed to make the breakthrough. Shels then took over and three goals in the first 17 minutes of the second half decided the tie. Eric Barber scored twice and Christy Doyle got the other goal. The attendance at the replay was only 10,000 due to very heavy rain on the night. Shels went on to beat Cork Hibernians in the final, winning the Cup for the second time in their history.

The Hoops were drawn away to Limerick in the first round in 1961. The match at the Market's Field attracted a crowd that paid gate receipts of £720 and saw Eamonn Darcy make six brilliant saves to deny Limerick the win that they deserved on the run of play. Limerick hit the crossbar twice and the upright once and Rovers were mightily relieved to hear the final whistle. A headed goal from Paddy Ambrose following a cross from the left by Tony O'Connell after 56 minutes decided the replay. The Hoops made their exit at the quarter-final stage when an own goal by Ronnie Nolan decided the tie against Waterford at Milltown on 12 March.

Rovers began the 1962 cup campaign with a first round tie at

Sligo on 18 February. Sligo were two up after 26 minutes with goals from Turner and Munns. Tommy Hamilton reduced the deficit with a shot after 29 minutes and 12 minutes later they were level when Eddie Bailham blasted to the net after Donaghy had failed to hold a shot from Frank O'Neill. Bailham put the Hoops ahead after 57 minutes when he scored with a low hard shot from 18 yards. Sligo Rovers equalised after 69 minutes when Turner's cross was headed down by Quinn and Munns forced it home. Rovers had a lucky escape in the dying minutes when Blake hit the post with Henderson beaten. A goal by Frank O'Neill after 72 minutes decided what was a poor replay compared to the exciting first match. Ronnie Nolan slammed a free kick to the net in the dying seconds but the referee disallowed the goal having blown the final whistle before the ball entered the net. The Hoops played Bohs in the quarter-final at Dalymount Park on 11 March and Eddie Bailham scored the only goal of the game after 17 minutes. A cross sliced off Billy Young's boot and Bailham beat Cecil Cahill with a low hard shot to the far corner. Tommy Hamilton was outstanding for Rovers and Paddy Henderson did not have a single shot to save although Bohs fought tooth and nail to the finish.

The Hoops' opponents in the semi-final were Waterford. There was controversy before the game when Tommy Hamilton, who was having a great season for Rovers, was dropped in favour of Tony Byrne. Tommy Hamilton had been dropped for the 1957 and 1958 FAI Cup finals for reasons that were a mystery to most fans! Now there was considerable anger when the same sort of thing seemed to be happening again. However, Tony Byrne had a knee injury; he failed a fitness test on the day of the semi-final and Tommy was recalled in his place. Hamilton scored Rovers' goal after five minutes having been set up by Eddie Bailham. The Hoops looked set for the final as they led 1-0 with only two minutes remaining but then Paddy Henderson allowed a weak shot from Sinnott to slip through his legs for the equaliser. The replay was played three days later at Tolka Park and although Waterford scored first through Jim O'Neill after 25 minutes, Rovers equalised before half-time and went on the rampage in the second half, scoring four times and running out comfortable 5-2 winners. Eddie Bailham scored the first when he forced a rebound to the net just on half-time after a shot from Paddy Ambrose had come back off the post. Goals from Ambrose, O'Neill (2) and Bailham gave the Hoops a 5-1 lead after 68 minutes and although Dixon pulled a goal back for the Blues after 71 minutes there was no catching the Hoops who qualified to play Shelbourne in the final.

The Hoops played Shels in a League match at Dalymount Park on 19 April, the night after the semi-final replay against Waterford. Shelbourne scored first and although Rovers equalised and then went ahead with goals from Bailham and Hamilton, Shels equalised before half-time and brushed a leg weary Hoops' team aside in the second half. The Reds scored four times without reply after the interval and it seemed that they had gained a massive boost for the Cup final which was to be played ten days later. Shelbourne were hot favourites going into the Cup final, although not everyone agreed. In his preview of the big match in the *Irish Times*, Seamus Devlin wrote the following: 'I may have cause to regret being out of step in the matter of forecasts, but I do believe that the greater experience of Shamrock Rovers, particularly players like Ronnie Nolan, Tommy Hamilton and Paddy Ambrose, is something in their favour and while I have the greatest respect for this young Shelbourne team I cast my vote in favour of the Milltown club.' Theo Dunne, who had captained Shelbourne to victory over Cork Hibernians in the 1960 final, was injured and he was interviewed by Radio Eireann before the game. Theo said that if Shelbourne didn't keep a close eye on Hamilton and Ambrose they could be in trouble. Subsequent events were to prove both Seamus Devlin and Theo Dunne correct.

A crowd of 32,000 paid gate receipts of £4,600 to watch the third Cup final between the two arch rivals from Ringsend. It was a perfect late spring afternoon with the sun shining brightly and the close cut sod of Dalymount Park in perfect condition. Shelbourne were first to seize the initiative forcing three corners in the first two minutes. Rovers counter attacked and Paddy Roberts kicked a goal bound Hamilton shot off the line. Ollie Conroy then missed a great chance for Shelbourne when he blazed a cross from Hennessy over the bar when he had the time to pick his spot and score. Shels took the lead after 31 minutes when Hennessy and Hannigan combined to give a great through ball to Eric Barber. Tommy Farrell tried to block Barber's goal bound shot but he was unable to do so and Shels took the lead. Paddy Henderson saved another shot from Eric Barber before the Hoops surged forward to equalise after 37 minutes. Frank O'Neill, who was playing splendidly for Rovers, rounded Shelbourne's left back Brendan O'Brien and sent a head high cross into the centre for Paddy Ambrose to nod the ball to the Shelbourne net. A minute before half-time the Hoops took the lead. Tommy Hamilton pulled the Shelbourne defence to one side before sending a delightful lobbed pass into Paddy Ambrose who picked his spot before placing the ball past John Heavey. Ollie Conroy almost equalised for Shelbourne when his lobbed shot beat Henderson but Pat Courtney cleared it off the line.

The Hoops went further ahead after 63 minutes when Ronnie Nolan put Tommy Hamilton through and he gently lobbed the advancing Heavey to score Rovers' third goal. Frank O'Neill had a goal disallowed by referee Sammy Spillane for offside and Tony O'Connell and Eddie Bailham came close for the Hoops before Hamilton sealed victory for the Hoops with his second and Rovers' fourth goal in the 85th minute. So the Hoops triumphed for the 14th time in the FAI Cup and they had now won all three Cup final clashes with Shelbourne. Four Shelbourne players, Freddie Strahan, Eric Barber, John Heavey and Tommy Carroll, had been vaccinated against smallpox for a trip by the League of Ireland side to Italy and all four had suffered ill effects in the week preceding the cup final. It turned out later that the vaccination for entry to Italy was not necessary. While the ill effects of the vaccinations did not help Shelbourne's cause it can't be said that they were the cause of Shelbourne's defeat, as Rovers were by far the better team on the day.

The Cup final was Tommy Hamilton's last competitive game for Rovers. He joined Cork Hibernians in a player exchange deal which took Jackie Mooney to Milltown. The swap was arranged by Ronnie Nolan.

The Hoops started their defence of the Cup in 1963 with a comfortable 3-0 win over Cork Celtic at Milltown on 17 February. Jackie Mooney, Eddie Bailham and Tony O'Connell were the scorers. Rovers played Bohemians in the quarter-final at Milltown on 10 March. This was a very exciting match and Bohs started well, missing three good chances in the first ten minutes. Bohs left back, Grace, twisted his knee in the first half and had to go off after an hour. Johnny Fullam gave Rovers the lead and then Jackie Mooney scored in the 27th and 30th minutes to put Rovers three up. Frank O'Neill scored the fourth goal after 32 minutes with a shot from the edge of the area and although Boyce pulled a goal back for Bohs after 34 minutes, Rovers remained almost completely on top. The Hoops scored twice in two minutes early in the second half when O'Neill sent over pin point crosses for Mooney and Nolan to head to the net. Paddy Ambrose put Roy Paton through to score Rovers' seventh goal and in the dying minutes Maguire scored twice for Bohs to put a more respectable look on the scoreline as the match finished in a comprehensive 7-3 victory for the Hoops.

Shels were Rovers' opponents in the semi-final and the Reds gained revenge for their cup final defeat the previous year with a comfortable 2-0 win at Dalymount Park. Jackie Hennessy scored the goals in the 28th and 83rd minutes and the nearest Rovers came to a goal was when O'Neill hit the crossbar with a shot after 51 minutes. The Hoops' line up for the semi-final was as follows: Henderson; John Keogh, Courtney; Jim Keogh, Nolan, Fullam; O'Neill, Mooney, Ambrose, Paton, O'Connell. The selection of Jim Keogh at centre-half instead of Tommy Farrell was a big surprise as Keogh played very few games for the Hoops.

Rovers' first game in the Cup in 1964 was a first round tie at Milltown against their nearest challengers for the League title that season, Dundalk. The Hoops had played the Spanish International 'B' side on the previous Wednesday in Spain and had been beaten 7-2. There were many people who said that it was sheer folly for

Rovers to play such a match so soon before an important Cup tie. These people reckoned that the Hoops would be demoralised after such a heavy defeat but Rovers rose to the occasion splendidly against Dundalk. The speed and accuracy of Bailham, Mooney and O'Neill riddled the Dundalk defence. Jackie Mooney opened the scoring with a header after nine minutes and Eddie Bailham scored with a low shot to the corner of the net a minute later. Jackie Mooney and Eddie Bailham completed their hat tricks with two goals each in the second half and Paddy Ambrose scored the last goal of the match to give the Hoops an easy 7-0 win. It was a great team performance and Tommy Farrell and Pat Courtney were brilliant in defence for the Hoops.

A goal in the last minute by Eddie Bailham gave Rovers victory over Limerick in the quarter-final at the Market's Field before an attendance of 6,000. Paddy Mulligan made his cup debut for the Hoops in that match.

Drums were the Hoops' opponents in the semi-final at Dalymount Park. It was a very tight battle and the only goal of the game came after 19 minutes. Alf Girvan hit the ball across his own goal area and Paddy Ambrose swooped to send Liam Tuohy in with a clear chance. He made no mistake to send Rovers into the final against Cork Celtic. Pat Dunne had a very good game in the second half and Drums missed a few chances as they fought very hard to try and get an equaliser.

The final at Dalymount Park on 26 April was a very close affair and ended all square. Rovers took the lead after 49 minutes when Courtney's long clearance was picked up by Tuohy on the left, before he passed the ball inside to Ambrose. Paddy Ambrose drew the defence before flicking it to Jackie Mooney who tapped the ball to the net. Cork Celtic equalised after 80 minutes when a corner from Paul O'Donovan was headed to the net by Donal Leahy. Cork Celtic claimed that they should have had a penalty after 32 minutes when Pat Courtney appeared to handle the ball but the referee waved play on. The replay took place under lights at the Phibsboro venue the following Wednesday with a 7.45 kick off. Frank O'Neill was dropped for the replay and was replaced by

Tony Byrne. Johnny Coughlan missed the replay for Cork Celtic and was replaced by George Lynam. Tommy Farrell hobbled off after 20 minutes and was replaced by Sean Smyth. After 68 minutes Ronnie Nolan was fouled by Ray Cowhie in the area and Rovers were awarded a penalty. Kevin Blount stopped Bailham's first shot but Eddie followed up and scored with the rebound. Al Casey equalised after 75 minutes and the game seemed destined for extra time. Then John Keogh picked up the ball outside his own penalty area and ran with it into the Cork Celtic half. He passed to Tony Byrne who made ground along the right wing before passing to Jackie Mooney who found Eddie Bailham and Eddie made no mistake from just inside the penalty area.

Eddie Bailham came to Rovers in 1960 from Cork Hibernians. Before that he had been with Home Farm and had a trial at Manchester United from which nothing materialised. While he was playing with Cork Hibs in a match against Rovers he impressed Joe Cunningham Snr who signed him up shortly after.

His stay at Milltown was not as long as it should have been. In 1963/64, when Rovers won the League Championship, Bailham was the top scorer with 19 goals. 'It was a great team; you could tell that they were all quality players', recalled Bailham from his home in England during August 1991. 'When we played Dundalk in the first round of the FAI Cup in 1964 and beat them 7-0 at Milltown the performance of the Rovers' team that day was really something. It's funny the crowds we used to get, they were nearly all capacity gates or it was a case of the ground being three-quarters full for average games and when we played the top sides it was always packed. Looking back at it you could not walk up the pavement to Milltown, you had to actually walk on the road because there were so many people going up to the game. I will never forget it, even when we won the Cup against Cork Celtic in 1964, Dalymount was packed.'

Eddie Bailham left Rovers in October 1964 and signed for English non-League side Cambridge. Originally it was for business reasons that he went to England but as he was still technically a Shamrock Rovers' player he was unable to sign for any side in the

English League. After three seasons at Cambridge the former Rovers centre forward went to Worchester for a while and then to Wimbledon (then a non-League side) where he remained for about five years. 'I went back to Cambridge for about two years, I had close ties with them.' The highlight of his time at Rovers was, without doubt, the 1963/64 season and two games in particular.

'The day we beat Dundalk in the Cup game by 7-0, I got three goals and Jackie Mooney got three. It was a great performance; Dundalk were a good side and that was some scoreline. I think that every goal was well built up from the back and all were well worked, they were well created and everything seemed to go well for the team that day', he recalled. 'When we won the Cup against Cork Celtic, it was in a replay and it was a real battle, such a battle that we never really got playing the flowing game of football that we normally played but I think that Cork Celtic in those days were probably one of the toughest sides around.' Today, Eddie lives with his wife and family in Wimbledon and is employed by British Telecom.

The Hoops began their defence of the Cup in 1965 with an away tie against Munster League side Glasheen at Turner's Cross on 14 February. However, it was no St Valentine's day massacre as Noel Dunne scored the only goal of the game after 57 minutes when he headed home a cross from Frank O'Neill. Rovers played Dundalk in the quarter-final at Milltown and were fortunate to emerge winners. Jimmy Hasty put Dundalk ahead after 36 minutes. The Hoops pushed Johnny Fullam forward and Paddy Mulligan dropped back into defence. Dundalk's keeper Gerry Maclain made a serious error after 44 minutes and Ronnie Nolan forced the ball home for the equaliser. Jackie Mooney gave Rovers the lead after 57 minutes from a free kick and with seven minutes remaining a chipped cross from Frank O'Neill was helped to the net by two Dundalk defenders. The Hoops travelled to Flower Lodge to take on Cork Celtic in the semi-final on 4 April. Tony O'Connell put Rovers ahead after only three minutes and even though Cork Celtic dominated the remainder of the first half they couldn't find a way past Mick Smyth. Cork Celtic forced 21 corners in the match, 11 of them in the first half but the Hoops with less possession scored three times. Jackie Mooney and Johnny Fullam scored in the second half to give the Hoops a 3-0 win. Peter Mitchell, the former Hoops' player, scored the winner for Limerick against Drumcondra in the other semi-final and the Shannonsiders contested their first FAI Cup final on 25 April 1965 against Rovers, the Cup specialists.

Noel Dunne gave the Hoops the lead after 62 minutes with an angled left foot shot. Limerick equalised nine minutes later when Eddie Mulvey headed Ewan Fenton's free kick past Mick Smyth. Limerick had suffered a terrible blow after 41 minutes when Mick Doyle broke his leg, to be replaced by Denis Linnane. In the replay, Liam Tuohy was forced to cry off the Rovers team through illness and he was replaced by Tony O'Connell. The Hoops had their chances limited by the fine defensive play of Fenton, Finucane and McNamara and the Shannonsiders should really have scored just after half-time when Paddy O'Rourke blazed the ball inches over the crossbar. Ewan Fenton had a goal disallowed for offside and after 55 minutes the Hoops started a five-man move which began with Tony O'Connell and finished with Johnny Fullam heading past Fitzpatrick from close range.

The Hoops were drawn away to Cork Hibernians in the first round of the Cup in 1966. A goal from Tony O'Connell at Flower Lodge gave the Hoops a 1-1 draw and two goals from Frank O'Neill, one from the penalty spot, and a goal from Liam Tuohy gave Rovers a 3-1 win in the replay. The Hoops played Shelbourne in the quarter-final at Milltown on 6 March and looked set for the semi-final when they led Shels 1-0, courtesy of a goal scored by Liam Tuohy after 11 minutes, as the game entered its last minute. However, Shelbourne had other ideas and Eric Barber beat Mick Smyth with a great left foot shot after getting a long ball from Jackie Hennessy. Frank O'Neill scored the winner in the replay from a penalty 13 minutes into extra time after McKeown had handled a tremendous left foot shot from Pat Courtney.

The Hoops met Waterford in the semi-final. Waterford scored twice in the space of a minute mid way through the first half to lead at half-time, their goals coming from Al Casey and Shamie Coad. Liam Tuohy and Bobby Gilbert had replied for the Hoops when a great one-handed save from Mick Smyth with only five minutes left kept Rovers in the competition. Two goals each from Frank O'Neill and Bobby Gilbert gave the Hoops a 4-2 win in the replay after a tremendous match in which Ronnie Nolan had an outstanding game for Rovers. John O'Neill and Jimmy McGeough scored Waterford's goals in the replay and the Blues went on to win their first League championship that season. Limerick were the Hoops' opponents in the final for the second successive year and in a disappointing game goals from Tony O'Connell and Frank O'Neill gave Rovers their 17th FAI Cup victory.

The Hoops' first match in the Cup in 1967 was their clash with Shelbourne at Milltown on 12 February. Mick Kearin scored the only goal of the match and Shelbourne had a penalty appeal turned down by the referee. Two goals from Liam Tuohy saw off the challenge of Home Farm in the quarter-final and Mick Leech made his cup debut for Rovers in the semi-final against Dundalk on 2 April. A crowd of 16,650 at Dalymount Park saw a Mick Leech goal give Rovers a 1-1 draw. Three days later at Tolka Park, the kick off time was put back by ten minutes to allow the capacity crowd get in before the start of the replay. The Hoops took the lead after 15 minutes when Gilbert crossed for Dixon to side foot the ball to the net. Mick Leech sent a great right foot shot past Blount after 37 minutes and Leech completed the scoring after 50 minutes to give the Hoops a comfortable 3-0 win.

Ronnie Nolan was dropped for that semi-final replay and he joined Bohemians as assistant to Sean Thomas the following November. Rovers' opponents in the cup final on 23 April were St Patrick's Athletic in the first Cup final to be televised live, for which RTE paid a match fee of £750. John Keogh captained the Hoops that day and a minute's silence was observed before the kick-off as a mark of respect to the late W. P. Murphy, the chief sports writer of the *Irish Independent*, who had died the day before. It was a special day for Billy Dixon, the Rovers inside right, for the 26-year-old insurance clerk was due to get married the next day.

The Hoops put on the early pressure and had several chances, mainly set up by Frank O'Neill, but Dinny Lowry, in goal for St Pat's, was alert in those early stages. The Inchicore team took the lead after 31 minutes when Mick Kearin attempted a back pass to Mick Smyth but it was intercepted by former Rovers' player Noel Dunne who lobbed the ball over Smyth's head to score. Eight minutes later, the St Pat's centre half, Doug Boucher, handled a cross from Fullam and Frank O'Neill scored from the spot. Just before half-time Vinny O'Reilly, the St Pat's full back, crossed for Noel Bates to head past Mick Smyth and regain the lead for the Inchicore side.

After 50 minutes, Mick Leech equalised for the Hoops when he shot the ball low past Lowry after Kearin and O'Neill had set up the chance. With ten minutes remaining Pat Courtney sent the ball to Billy Dixon and Dixon beat Dinny Lowry with a low 25-yard drive.

The Hoops began their quest for a record equalling five in a row Cup wins with a 2-0 victory over Cork Celtic at Milltown on 11 February. An own goal by Pat O'Mahony after 34 minutes and a volleyed goal from Mick Lawlor after 85 minutes saw the Hoops into the quarter-final at Milltown against Shels where a Mick Lawlor goal after 76 minutes won a poor match for the Hoops. Two goals from Mick Leech and one from Mick Lawlor gave Rovers an easy win over Dundalk in the semi-final at Dalymount Park on 30 March to set the scene for an eagerly awaited Cup final clash with Waterford.

In 1967-68, Waterford won their second League title in three seasons. The Blues were favourites going into the Cup final but everyone knew Rovers' great tradition in the Cup and a near record crowd of 39,128 paid record gate receipts of £8,500 to see the final. John O'Neill created the first real chance after 11 minutes. He passed the ball to Matthews and it went via Hale to Mick Lynch in the inside right position. From the edge of the area Lynch hit a tremendous shot which came back off the upright before being scrambled away for a corner by a Rovers' defender. Johnny Fullam had a good shot saved by Peter Thomas before

Alfie Hale crossed for John O'Neill to head the ball against the post. Just before half-time Peter Thomas did very well to save a headed effort from Bobby Gilbert.

After 64 minutes, Mick Lawlor put a fine pass over the head of Vinny Maguire for Mick Leech to run on to and slip past Peter Thomas for the opening goal. Five minutes later Paul Morrissey's attempted clearance cannoned off Mick Lawlor's foot and ended in the net. Mick Lawlor had now scored in every round of the cup for the Hoops. Rovers then took complete control of the match and Lawlor, Gilbert and O'Neill all went close before Leech dispossessed Jackie Morley in the final minute and put the ball between Peter Thomas's legs for Rovers third goal.

The Hoops began their defence of the Cup in 1969 with an easy 3-0 win over Dundalk at Milltown. Damien Richardson put Rovers ahead after eight minutes, when he took down a cross from O'Neill and scored from just outside the area. Seven minutes later Brennan passed the ball back to Swan and as Swan was about to clear Leech poked out a tentative boot which connected with the ball and sent it to the net. The referee Derry Barrett from Cork allowed the goal to stand and Leech scored another before the finish to seal Rovers' victory. The Hoops played Ringmahon Rangers in the quarter-final and two early goals from Mick Leech did the trick. Richardson and O'Neill completed the scoring to give Rovers a 4-0 win.

The Hoops played Shels in the semi-final at Dalymount Park on 30 March and the Reds looked good for the final when Johnny Campbell gave them the lead after 65 minutes. However, Newman was adjudged to have blocked a speculative shot from Liam Tuohy with his hands while his 'keeper was off his line and referee Peter Coates awarded Rovers a penalty. Frank O'Neill scored from the spot to force a replay at Tolka Park on 2 April. Mick Lawlor scored the only goal of that game after 35 minutes when he latched on to a poor back pass from Walsh and belted the ball to the net.

Rovers' opponents in the Cup final were Cork Celtic and like 1964, the Hoops won the replay after a 1-1 draw. Cork Celtic scored in the first game after 27 minutes when John Carroll blasted the ball to the net from 25 yards. The linesman raised his flag for an offside but the referee allowed the goal to stand as he considered that the player who was deemed offside was not interfering with play. Seven minutes later Tommy Taylor made a great save from a penalty by Frank O'Neill that was awarded after Billy McCullough had handled under pressure from Paddy Mulligan. Rovers equalised after 81 minutes when John Keogh could only turn a goalbound header from Paddy Mulligan into the side of his own net as he made a desperate attempt to clear the ball.

The Hoops made changes for the replay with Damien Richardson replacing Ben Hannigan and Hughie Brophy replacing Tommy Kinsella. Mick Leech, who was taken off after 79 minutes in the drawn match, was back to his best in the replay and scored after 33 and 41 minutes to give Rovers a two-goal interval lead. Mick Kearin scored with a great shot after 53 minutes and although Frank McCarthy pulled a goal back shortly afterwards for Cork Celtic, Damien Richardson scored the Hoops' fourth goal after 59 minutes. Richardson almost added a fifth goal in the dying minutes but Tommy Taylor deflected the ball away from the danger zone. Rovers had now completed an historic six wins in a row in the FAI Cup. It was their 20th success in the Blue Riband of Irish soccer.

The 'sixties were a glorious decade for the Hoops in the FAI Cup with seven wins from seven final appearances. The decade which was to follow that glorious era was going to be the worst in Rovers' history but few could have realised that on that wet Wednesday evening at Dalymount Park in April 1969.

SPOTLIGHT ON FRANK O'NEILL

Frank O'Neill began his career with Home Farm before signing for Arsenal. He was with Arsenal in May 1961 when Sean Thomas, the newly appointed coach of Shamrock Rovers, approached him and invited him to go on Rovers' forthcoming tour of America as a guest player. Frank had been on a one-year contract at Arsenal and he was due to go on tour to Italy with the Arsenal under-21s. Frank went with Rovers to America instead and did so well that the Hoops were anxious to sign him. There was a lot of stalling over the transfer and Frank was almost due to return to London when he was finally signed by Rovers in September 1961 for a fee of £3,000. Frank made his debut in a Shield match against Waterford at Milltown on 17 September 1961.

Frank played as a centre forward in his first match and scored twice as the Hoops beat Waterford 4-0. O'Neill played a major role in Rovers' 14th FAI Cup final win in 1962. The Hoops drew 3-3 with Sligo Rovers in the first round of the Cup and Frank scored the only goal in the replay at Milltown. Rovers were also held to a draw by Waterford in the semi-final of the Cup that year and Frank scored twice in the replay at Tolka Park on 18 April as Rovers won easily by five goals to two. O'Neill made the first goal in the Cup final against Shelbourne when he ran the length of the pitch before crossing for Paddy Ambrose to score. Frank gave the Shels left full, Brendan O'Brien, a very busy afternoon as he created chance after chance for the Rovers' forwards.

Frank O'Neill holds the record for the number of international caps won by a League of Ireland player. O'Neill won all twenty of his caps while with Shamrock Rovers in an international career that began against Czechoslovakia at Dalymount Park in October 1961 and finished against Austria in Vienna in 1971. He was on the Irish team that was narrowly beaten by Spain in Paris on 10 November 1965 in the play-off match for the 1966 World Cup finals in England. Frank played in all Rovers' matches in the European club competitions against sides like Botev Plovdiv, Valencia, Rapid Vienna, Zaragoza, Spora Luxembourg, Bayern Munich, Cardiff City, Randers Freja and Schalke 04 and he scored in both the home and away legs of the European Cup Winners' Cup match against Spora Luxembourg in 1966.

Frank O'Neill had a hugely successful season in 1963/64 when Rovers won five trophies including the League and Cup double for the first time since 1932. Frank was the architect of so many of Rovers' victories that season that it came as a big surprise to many

Hoops supporters to hear that he had been dropped for the replay of the FAI Cup final against Cork Celtic. Rovers won the replay 2-1 but, as we saw earlier, Sean Thomas left the club and took over as manager of Bohemians as he felt that he no longer had control over team selection at Shamrock Rovers.

Frank O'Neill played in the rest of Rovers' Cup finals in the 'sixties and he scored vital goals in those successful Cup campaigns including many from the penalty spot. In 1966, he scored from penalties in the first round replay against Cork Hibs, the quarter-final replay against Shelbourne and the semi-final replay against Waterford. Frank also scored Rovers' third goal in the 4-2 semi-final replay win over Waterford and he went on to score the second goal in the final that year against Limerick. Frank scored from the penalty spot against St Pat's in the 1967 final which Rovers won 3-2 and he was also successful from a penalty in the drawn semi-final against Shelbourne in 1969. His contribution to Rovers' great run of success in the FAI Cup was immense. He won a total of seven Cup medals with Rovers, playing in nine finals including replays.

When Arthur Fitzsimons was dismissed as manager of Shamrock Rovers in October 1969, Frank O'Neill took over as player-manager and remained in the managerial hot seat until the end of the 1970/71 season. Frank readily admits that his play suffered when he was player-manager because he also had to concentrate on how the whole team was playing and often couldn't fully focus on his own game. He didn't have any success in the Cup while player-manager but he guided Rovers to a play-off for the League title with Cork Hibs in 1971 after a disastrous start to the season. The Hoops finished second in the League in 1970, two points behind the champions Waterford.

Frank O'Neill felt that his game improved when he no longer had the additional burden of the manager's job to worry about and he will forever be remembered by Hoops' fans for his ability to beat a full back and cross the ball with pinpoint accuracy just before it went over the end line. The Cunninghams tried to sell him to Limerick towards the end of their last season in charge at Milltown

in 1972 but the deal fell through and Frank remained on at
Milltown until September 1974 when he signed for Waterford.
Frank had a short spell with Athlone Town when Amby Fogarty
was manager there and he finished his League of Ireland career by
playing a few matches for St Pat's in 1980. As an entertainer Frank
had few equals and his outstanding wing play endeared him to
thousands of football supporters throughout Ireland. His record of
twenty international caps for a League of Ireland player will hardly
ever be broken and he will be remembered as one of the greatest
players ever to wear the famous green and white hooped jersey of
Shamrock Rovers.

SPOTLIGHT ON JOHNNY FULLAM

Johnny Fullam began his career with Home Farm before signing
for Preston North End in 1958. In 1961, Mrs Cunningham asked
him to go on Rovers' tour of America and Johnny told her that he
wasn't particularly interested in going as a guest player but he
would go if he was a signed Rovers player. Mrs Cunningham duly
signed him for Rovers and he made his debut for the Hoops on the
tour. Johnny Fullam scored his first goal in a competitive match for
Rovers from the penalty spot against Transport in a Shield match
on 20 August 1961. He suffered a serious knee injury in February
1962 and was out of football for six months, missing Rovers' Cup
final victory over Shelbourne that season.

Johnny Fullam played most of his football as a wing half
although he occasionally turned out as an inside forward for
Rovers. In his second spell at Milltown, he played as a centre half
and his great experience was invaluable to the younger players. He
played in the European matches against Botev Plovdiv in 1962
and he won his first Shield medal in 1962/63. Johnny was a regular
member of Rovers' all-conquering side of 1963/64 when the Hoops
almost made a clean sweep of the domestic trophies. He was one of
five Rovers' players who were on the League of Ireland side that
beat the English Football League side 2-1 at Dalymount Park on 2
October 1963.

Just over a week later Johnny Fullam played against Valencia in the Fairs Cup in Spain having gone down with food poisoning the previous day. He played in that match with a temperature of 103, which speaks for itself. Johnny won the first of his six FAI Cup winners' medals with Rovers in the replayed final in 1964 against Cork Celtic and in the replayed final against Limerick the following year, he scored the winner when he headed home a cross from Noel Dunne. Johnny Fullam scored for Rovers in Zaragoza in the second round of the Fairs Cup in 1965 and only a late goal from Canario knocked Rovers out of the competition on a 3-2 aggregate scoreline.

Johnny also scored in the European Cup Winners' Cup against Spora Luxembourg in 1966 and he had two great games for Rovers against Bayern Munich in the second round when the Hoops were only seven minutes away from winning a sensational victory. He had one of his best ever games for Rovers in the 1968 FAI Cup final against Waterford when playing a sweeper role, he marshalled the Hoops defence superbly as they withstood Waterford's onslaught in the first half before emerging as comfortable winners in the second. Johnny Fullam scored Rovers' goal in the European Cup Winners' Cup match against Randers Freja in October 1968 and two months later he played in a World Cup qualifying round match against Denmark which was also played at Dalymount Park.

A knee injury which Johnny received in March 1969 caused him to miss Rovers' record making six-in-a-row Cup final win over Cork Celtic. He signed for Bohemians shortly afterwards. Johnny always had great admiration for Sean Thomas and when Sean made him a good offer he accepted. In his first season at the Phibsboro' club he won his sixth FAI Cup medal when Bohs beat Sligo Rovers in the final after two replays. Johnny Fullam went on to win a League medal with Bohs in 1975 and he won his seventh FAI cup medal when Bohs beat Drogheda 1-0 in the 1976 final.

Sean Thomas was appointed manager of Shamrock Rovers in 1976 and he enticed Johnny Fullam back to Milltown during the close season of 1976. There was a very young side at Milltown then and Johnny's experience helped young players such as Robbie Gaffney and Larry Wyse considerably. Johnny felt that Sean

Thomas wasn't given enough time at Milltown. He believed that Sean would have produced another fine Rovers side within a couple of years had he been given time and resources. Johnny was part of the full-time experiment when Johnny Giles arrived at Milltown in the summer of 1977 but this was abandoned after the end of the 1978/79 season which was also Johnny's last at Milltown.

Johnny captained Rovers to victory in the 1978 FAI Cup final against Sligo Rovers and thus emulated the great achievement of Sacky Glen in winning eight FAI Cup medals. He was given a free transfer by Johnny Giles at the end of the 1978/79 season; many Rovers' fans thought that this was a mistake at the time as there were not enough experienced players left to help the young hopefuls make the breakthrough. Johnny was critical of the style of play Johnny Giles employed, feeling that it was too predictable and very easy to defend against.

Johnny Fullam finished his career in the League of Ireland with Athlone Town. He had played for Rovers for a total of eleven seasons in his two spells with the club and he is remembered with great affection by many Hoops' fans. He was a worthy recipient of the Shamrock Rovers Supporters Club 'Hall of Fame award' in 1991. Indeed, many Rovers' fans would regard Johnny, along with Frank O'Neill and Pat Byrne, as one of the three best players who have played for the Hoops in the last thirty years.

CHAPTER SEVEN

THE BLEAK YEARS

(1 9 7 0 - 7 6)

The 1969 close season brought about many changes at Milltown. Liam Tuohy resigned as coach because of work commitments and went to Dundalk as manager. He was working as a group manager for HB ice cream and the area he was responsible for were counties Louth, Roscommon, Cavan and Monaghan amongst others. It meant that Liam had to do a lot of travelling in these counties and he simply would not have been able to attend the training sessions at Milltown. He realised that if he couldn't attend all Rovers' training sessions he couldn't continue as Rovers' coach. Dundalk made Liam an offer which he accepted because he was based in Dundalk. Johnny Fullam signed for Bohemians and David Pugh returned to his native Sligo.

Arthur Fitzsimons, who had been capped 28 times for the Republic, was appointed manager of Shamrock Rovers in July 1969 in succession to Liam Tuohy. Arthur Fitzsimons had been player-manager of Drogheda for two years prior to getting the Rovers' job. Eric Barber signed for the Hoops and their first competitive game of the season was against Drogheda in the first round of the President's Cup. It finished scoreless but Rovers won 14-7 on corners and then beat Dundalk 4-3 in the semi-final. The Hoops won the Cup by beating St Pat's 4-3 in the final on 10 August. Mick Leech with two goals, Mick Lawlor and Eric Barber scored in the final.

The Shield was divided into two sections of six teams with the top two from each section qualifying for the semi-finals. Rovers began well with wins over Athlone Town and Cork Celtic but St Pat's beat them by two goals to one at Inchicore on 7 September and although they beat Limerick 4-0 in their next match, their chances of qualifying were dealt a severe blow when they lost 1-0 to Cork Hibs at Milltown on 28 September. Rovers travelled to Waterford on 9 October needing a win to qualify for the semi-finals but they could only manage a 2-2 draw and they were eliminated from the competition.

The Hoops played Schalke 04 in the first round of the European Cup Winners' Cup at Dalymount Park on Wednesday 17 September. Rovers line-up on that very foggy night was as follows: Smyth, Gregg, Canavan, Kearin, Mulligan, Richardson, O'Neill, Leech, Hannigan, Barber, Dixon. *Sub:* Haverty for Dixon. The referee Frede Hansen from Denmark allowed the game to proceed even though visibility was down to sixty yards and the situation got worse in the second half. The Schalke 04 manager Rudi Gutendorf was most annoyed that the game went ahead. He felt that the referee cheated the fans because they could hardly see the play in the fog. Gutendorf felt that the game should have been postponed until the following night as they had no game at the weekend. Schalke 04 went ahead after 35 minutes when their left winger Pickner scored from close range against the run of play. Six minutes later Eric Barber had the ball in the net but the goal was disallowed for offside. In the second half Rovers continued to force the pace and in the 71st and 72nd minutes two mighty roars from out of the blackness shrouding Schalke's goal signalled first an equaliser and then the lead for Shamrock Rovers. The first Rovers' goal started with Mick Kearin finding Frank O'Neill on the right wing and Hannigan running deep into the open space. He took the ball through to tangle with goalkeeper Nigbur before laying it square for Barber who tapped it to the net. The move for the second goal was started by substitute Joe Haverty who had replaced Billy Dixon after 57 minutes. Haverty passed to Leech who sent a long ball through the middle to Hannigan. Ben Hannigan dummied to unhinge the Schalke defence and Barber pounced to beat Nigbur from close range.

Joe Sherwood in the following night's *Evening Press* described the match as the best match he never saw. There were four goals in the match, one of which was offside, and Joe saw none of them or even the shot or header leading up to them. Pat Courtney missed the match through injury, the first time that Pat had missed a European match for the Hoops. Rovers were beaten 3-0 in the second leg at Gelsenkirchen on 1 October. The Germans scored after six minutes and they could afford to miss a penalty after 77 minutes and still win 3-0 on the night to go through to the next round on an aggregate score of 4-2.

The Hoops began their League campaign with a 2-1 win over Bohemians at Milltown on 5 October with Frank O'Neill and Ben Hannigan getting the goals. One week later the Hoops drew 2-2 with Athlone Town at St Mel's Park and the following Thursday, Arthur Fitzsimons was dismissed as manager of Shamrock Rovers. When Fitzsimons reported for training on Thursday 16 October he was handed a letter by club chairman Joe Cunningham which informed him of his dismissal. When questioned on the reason for his dismissal Arthur Fitzsimons said: 'It appears I was sacked because I acted as a manager should - discuss tactics with his team. I was instructed by the board not to lay down any tactics for our match with Athlone last Sunday. But naturally I gave certain orders to my players prior to the match, and this I feel was one of the causes for my sudden dismissal. In addition I requested that one of our players, an international forward, be dropped from the first team as he was going through a bad patch. This, I feel, did my image little good. Yet I honestly believed that this player was not giving of his best, and I acted as any manager worth his salt would have done. If I had been given full control at Milltown I would have swept the boards. Of that I am convinced. As it was, I had virtually no power. In theory I selected the team, but invariably the team was altered by some members of the board prior to the match.'

The old story of directors interfering with team selection had surfaced again and had put paid to another manager of Rovers. Frank O'Neill was appointed player-manager from 19 October and in his first match in charge the Hoops beat Sligo Rovers 4-1 at Milltown with Mick Leech grabbing a hat trick and Mick Lawlor getting the other goal. Paddy Mulligan signed for Chelsea on 22 October for a fee of £17,500. He had almost signed for Everton the week before but he was not satisfied with the terms Everton offered. Rovers drew 2-2 after extra time with Athlone Town in the quarter-final of the Leinster Senior Cup but Athlone won the replay 3-2. The Hoops took four points from their next four League matches, beating Cork Celtic 2-0 at Turner's Cross before losing 1-0 to Limerick at the Market's Field. They then drew with Shels and Dundalk to have nine points from their first seven matches.

League champions Waterford were Rovers' next opponents at Milltown on 23 November and a big crowd who paid gate receipts of just over £2,000 saw the Hoops win by four goals to one. Rovers inconsistency was to continue despite the fine win over Waterford and they drew four of their next five League matches to leave themselves four points behind the leaders Cork Hibs after 13 matches. The Hoops began the new year well with wins over Bohs at Dalymount Park and over Athlone Town at Milltown. They travelled to Sligo on 18 January and were comprehensively beaten 3-1 by the home side before slumping to another 3-1 defeat the following Sunday at Milltown when Cork Celtic beat them.

The Hoops great run of 32 matches undefeated in the FAI Cup was brought to an end by Shelbourne at Milltown on Sunday 1 February. Two goals in three minutes from Brendan Place and Brian Delargy in the second half gave Shels a 2-1 win over Rovers. The Hoops returned to winning ways with a 2-0 win over Limerick the following Sunday at Milltown, but Shels set back Rovers' title challenge considerably when they beat them 1-0 at Tolka Park on 15 February. Rovers beat Athlone Town 9-7 on corners after a 1-1 draw after extra time in the quarter-final of the Dublin City Cup but they made their exit from this competition at the semi-final stage when Limerick beat them 3-2 at Dalymount Park.

Rovers then made a late determined bid for the League title. They took 13 out of a possible 14 points from their last seven League matches, the highlight of that good run being their 4-2 win over League leaders Waterford at Kilcohan Park on 1 March. However, Rovers made that run just a little too late and Waterford won the League by two points. The top four League positions were as follows:

	P	W	D	L	F	A	Pts.
Waterford	26	16	6	4	55	33	38
Shamrock Rovers	26	14	8	4	55	29	36
Cork Hibernians	26	13	9	4	35	20	35
Limerick	26	12	6	8	35	24	30

Waterford beat Rovers 3-1 in the semi-final of the Top Four competition at Tolka Park on Sunday 26 April. They went on to win the final two weeks later when they beat Cork Hibs 6-2. Eric Barber finished as Rovers' leading League scorer with 15 goals.

Denis Stephens was signed during the close season from Drums and the Hoops' first match of the 1970/71 season was a friendly against English League champions Everton at Glenmalure Park on 2 August. Everton won 4-2 and both Rovers' goals came from penalties converted by Damien Richardson. Ball, Whittle, Newton and Royle from a penalty scored for Everton. Rovers line-up in that match was as follows: Smyth, Gregg, Courtney, Fagan, Canavan, Dixon, Brophy, Richardson, Leech, Stephens, Lawlor. *Subs*: Haverty for Canavan; Byrne for Lawlor.

Rovers' first competitive match of the season was the President's Cup quarter-final against Dundalk on 6 August and goals from Ben Hannigan and Mick Leech (2) gave the Hoops a 3-0 win. Rovers beat Athlone Town 1-0 in the semi-final and a penalty converted by Damien Richardson three minutes into injury time gave them a rather fortunate 3-3 draw with Drogheda in the final on 12 August. They beat Drogheda 3-1 in the replay with goals from Damien Richardson (from a penalty), Mick Leech and Hughie Brophy.

For the second successive year the Hoops played Finn Harps in the first round of the Dublin City Cup. On 17 August 1969, Finn Harps playing their first competitive game in the League of Ireland were trounced 10-2 by Rovers at Ballybofey. The goalscorers on that bleak day for Finn Harps were Mick Leech (5), Ben Hannigan (4) and Eric Barber, Rovers led 7-1 at half-time. On 16 August 1970, the Hoops beat Finn Harps 6-3 in the Dublin City Cup having lead 5-0 at one stage of the game.

The Shield was divided into two groups of seven teams and Rovers made an encouraging start taking five points from their first three matches against Athlone Town, Cork Celtic and St Pat's. However, the Hoops hit a run of poor form then and lost their remaining matches in the group to Limerick, Waterford and Cork Hibs. The Limerick defeat was a particularly poor performance as Limerick romped to victory with a decisive 4-0 win. Rovers beat Ards 6-4 on aggregate in the first round of the Texaco Cup. They won the first leg at Castlereagh Park 4-1 with goals from Lawlor (2), Hannigan and Brophy, but Ards won the second leg at Dalymount Park 3-2.

The Hoops' start to the League campaign was a total disaster. They lost their first three matches to Bohemians, Athlone Town and Sligo Rovers respectively. They then drew 1-1 with Cork City at Milltown before recording their first League success on 1 November with a 3-1 win over Limerick. Rovers line-up that day was as follows: Smyth, Gregg, Courtney, Fagan, Canavan, Kearin, O'Neill, Brophy, Richardson, Lawlor, Stephens. *Sub*: Dixon for Fagan. The win over Limerick was the Hoops' first win over League of Ireland opposition since 30 August. Rovers beat St Brendan's 7-0 in their first match in the Leinster Senior Cup but lost to Derry City 5-3 on aggregate in the second round of the Texaco Cup. They went down 4-0 in the first leg at the Brandywell but then made a great start to the second leg at Dalymount by scoring twice through Richardson and Stephens in the first 10 minutes. Rovers missed a great chance to go three up after 14 minutes, but Derry scored again and although Richardson got a third near the finish, the Hoops went out of the competition.

Rovers' next League match after their first victory against Limerick was at Tolka Park on 8 November against Shelbourne. Mick Smyth had a diabolical game in goal for Rovers although he didn't get too much help from his defenders. A rampant Shels' forward line took the Hoops apart and won 5-0 to leave Rovers with a mere three points from their opening six matches in the League. Rovers' player-manager Frank O'Neill approached the Cunninghams about the need to get a new goalkeeper and plans were set in motion to buy former Hoops' keeper Pat Dunne from Plymouth Argyle. Rovers drew their next two League matches, against Dundalk at Milltown and away to Waterford, and TEK United were beaten 4-1 in the quarter-final of the Leinster Senior Cup. Frank O'Neill introduced young players Paul Martin and Eddie Byrne to the team but their biggest problem was at centre half and numerous players were tried throughout the season. It was very hard to replace players of the calibre of Johnny Fullam, Paddy Mulligan and David Pugh who had left the club in the previous eighteen months.

Pat Dunne was signed from Plymouth Argyle for £3,000 and made his debut for Rovers against Finn Harps on Sunday, 29 November at Milltown. Two goals from Damien Richardson and one from Paul Martin gave the Hoops a 3-1 win. The following Saturday, Rovers went to Flower Lodge and beat the leaders Cork Hibs 1-0 with a late goal from Paul Martin. Despite their dreadful start, they were now only five points behind the leaders Cork Hibs after ten matches.

Mick Leech returned to the side after a long lay-off through injury and scored as Rovers beat St Pat's 4-2 at Milltown on 13 December. The Hoops dropped a point to Drumcondra the following Sunday. Mick Leech had given Rovers the lead in the first half but Drums fought back to take the lead and the Hoops could only manage a draw through a late penalty from Damien Richardson. Rovers played Dundalk in the final of the Leinster Senior Cup on St Stephen's Day and Dundalk won comfortably 5-2 with Turlough O'Connor grabbing a hat trick. Damien Richardson, from a penalty, and Mick Leech scored Rovers' goals.

The following day, the Hoops played Drogheda in the League at Milltown and they tried out Sandy Smith at centre half. Mick Brazil and Christy Canavan had been tried there but had failed to solve this problem position for Rovers. Billy Dixon was also tried as a sweeper that season and they did have some success with this move. Mick Kearin was also tried in this role.

Second-half goals from Richardson and Brophy gave the Hoops a 2-0 win over Drogheda and they began the second half of the League campaign with a match against Bohs at Milltown on 3 January. Mick Smyth had joined Bohs after Pat Dunne had signed for the Hoops and he was given a warm welcome by the Rovers' fans at the match. Paul Martin gave the Hoops an early lead but Bohs equalised before half-time. Mick Leech put Rovers 2-1 up in the second half and then the referee E. Farrell disallowed a goal from Damien Richardson for offside. That would have given Rovers a 3-1 lead and in the last minute Pat Dunne allowed a shot to slip from his grasp and Bohs equalised, thus taking a vital point from Rovers.

On 10 January, the Hoops travelled to Athlone and won 4-2 while Cork Celtic travelled to Sligo and beat the home side 6-1. Rovers' next match was against Sligo Rovers at Milltown on 17 January and they were fairly confident that they would get the two points. The Hoops took the lead in the first half when Mick Lawlor's header from a corner was deflected into his own net by Burns. Rovers should now have won easily but they became careless and didn't press home their superiority on the pitch. Mick Leech was brought down in the penalty area but got up and hit a shot against the upright. Perhaps if he had stayed down Rovers might have got a penalty and sealed the match. Their attitude was unprofessional. They should have scored three goals and then played out time. They were caught badly in the last three minutes when Sligo Rovers scored twice to shock the Hoops. This defeat ultimately cost Rovers the title, as they lost a match that they should have had sewn up by half-time.

The Hoops took three points from their next two matches against Cork Celtic and Limerick to leave themselves five points behind the leaders Cork Hibs with eight matches to go. Rovers beat Cork Celtic in the first round of the Cup at Milltown on 7 February, Mick Leech scoring the only goal after 25 minutes.

Rovers then hit a good run of form and they took maximum

points from their next four matches to keep the pressure on Cork Hibs. On 14 February, a goal from Mick Leech after 53 minutes beat Shelbourne at Milltown. Rovers then beat Dundalk 2-1 at Oriel Park and Waterford 2-0 at Milltown in front of a large crowd that paid gate receipts of £1,650. First half goals from Paul Martin and Mick Leech saw off the challenge of Waterford who made a great effort in the second half to try and stay in the hunt for a fourth successive League title. On 7 March, Rovers travelled to Ballybofey and after taking an early 2-0 lead, they were pulled back to parity by Harps mid way through the second half. Finn Harps went all out in search of their first win over the Hoops, but with two minutes remaining, Mick Leech scored the winner to secure two valuable points for Rovers.

The following Sunday, Drogheda came to Milltown for a quarter-final Cup tie and recorded their first win at Glenmalure Park by sensationally beating Rovers 5-2. Their young centre forward Pat Cullen had a field day scoring a hat trick but Rovers badly missed Sandy Smith who was ruled out through injury. Rovers were now out of the Cup and they were three points behind the leaders Cork Hibs with four matches left. Rovers had their biggest gate of the season against Cork Hibs on 14 March. The crowd paid gate receipts of £2,526 and the Hoops line up was as follows: Dunne, Fagan, Courtney, Dixon, Smith, Kearin, O'Neill, Byrne, Leech, Martin, Richardson. *Sub*: Stephens for Smith. Sandy Smith got injured early on and Rovers had to re-shuffle their forces. The game was a very tame affair with few chances created. Eddie Byrne cleared a header from Tony Marsden off the line in the first half and Billy Dixon almost sent Mick Leech through but his pass was cut out by the Hibs' defence. A controversial incident happened in the first half when the referee disallowed a goal from Mick Leech. Joe Grady, the Cork Hibs' goalkeeper, threw the ball in the air as he was about to kick it down the field. Mick Leech who was standing beside the goalkeeper got his foot to the ball and flicked it round Grady before putting it into the net. As Mick Leech had made no contact with the 'keeper the goal should have stood. Dave Bacuzzi, the

Cork Hibs player-manager, was sent off in the dying minutes but the game finished scoreless.

Rovers took maximum points from their remaining three matches against St Pat's, Drums and Drogheda while Cork Hibs dropped three points to Waterford and Shelbourne in their last two matches to end up like Rovers on 35 points from 26 matches. The top four in the League finished up as follows:

	P	W	D	L	F	A	Pts.
Cork Hibernians	26	12	11	3	38	17	35
Shamrock Rovers	26	14	7	5	49	38	35
Waterford	26	13	8	5	49	34	34
Bohemians	26	12	9	5	38	25	33

The play-off for the title between Cork Hibs and Shamrock Rovers was played at Dalymount Park on Sunday, 25 April 1971. However, with twenty minutes to go before kick off not one Rovers player was togged out as there was a dispute over a win bonus. The players were looking for a win bonus of £25 a man and the directors flatly refused it. There had been discussions with the directors on the previous Thursday at training but they still hadn't conceded. There were more than 28,000 people at the play-off match and Rovers were on a third of the gate receipts, so the players' demands for a win bonus were not unreasonable. It was definitely not the right type of atmosphere to have in a dressing room before a match of such importance. The Hoops had come from a hopeless League position to be now within 90 minutes of the title and the last thing Frank O'Neill should have had was disgruntled players in the dressing-room before the play-off. The two teams lined out as follows. *Rovers:* Dunne, Fagan, Courtney, Dixon, Canavan, Kearin, O'Neill, Leech, Richardson, Byrne, Lawlor. *Sub:* Smith for Lawlor. *Cork Hibs:* Grady, Bacuzzi, O'Mahony, Connolly, Herrick, Sweeney, Lawson, Dennehy,

Marsden, Wiggington, Wallace. It's difficult to imagine how Frank O'Neill would have been able to prepare Rovers for such an important match in such trying circumstances. It's impossible to say whether the result would have turned out differently had there been no friction in the Hoops' camp before the match. On the day Cork Hibs were clearly the better team and won comprehensively 3-1. In the first half Hibs forced nine corners to Rovers one and they missed a few chances before Miah Dennehy gave them the lead after 35 minutes. Mick Leech equalised after 65 minutes and for a while it was anybody's game. Sandy Smith had come on for Mick Lawlor and Frank O'Neill thought about moving Billy Dixon back to sweeper to bolster the defence. However, O'Neill decided not to change things and after 71 minutes, Miah Dennehy scored again to regain the lead for Cork Hibs. Seven minutes later Tony Marsden scored Hibs' third goal from close range and Rovers' last chance was gone.

The controversy in the Hoops camp before the League play off with Cork Hibs was to play a major role in the decision of the Cunningham family to sell the club just over a year later in 1972. Three days later, on 28 April at Tolka Park, Cork Hibs beat Rovers 2-1 in the semi-final of the Top Four competition. Damien Richardson finished the season as the Hoops' leading League scorer with 15 goals.

Billy Young was appointed manager of Shamrock Rovers during the 1971 close season and the Hoops first match of the 1971/72 season was a friendly against Everton at Dalymount Park on 30 July. The line-up was as follows: Dunne, Gregg, Smith, Fagan, Keogh, Kearin, O'Neill, Leech, Richardson, Byrne, Stephens. *Sub*: Lawlor for Fagan. Rovers were most unlucky not to beat Everton both of whose goals came from defensive mistakes. Frank O'Neill and Mick Lawlor scored for the Hoops and the Rovers' fans were most encouraged by this fine performance. The Hoops' first competitive match of the season was on Friday, 6 August; Bohs beat them 1-0 in the first round of the President's Cup.

The Shield was again divided into two sections and Rovers

played six matches in their section. They won only two. There were ugly scenes on the terraces at Milltown on 26 September at the Dundalk match. Paddy Turner scored from an offside position but the referee allowed the goal to stand. Almost immediately a vicious brawl erupted on the terraces and a few people had to be treated for facial injuries. Rovers beat Coleraine 8-1 on aggregate in the first round of the Texaco Cup, winning the first leg at Dalymount Park on 15 September 5-1 and the second leg 3-0.

Goals from Richardson, Leech and Martin gave the Hoops a 3-1 win over Waterford at Kilcohan Park in the first round of the Dublin City Cup. Rovers began their League campaign with a visit to Dalymount Park on 3 October when two goals from Damien Richardson gave them a 2-2 draw, but for the second successive week there was trouble on the terraces and the gardai had to intervene to restore order. The Hoops lost their next two League matches to Sligo Rovers and Cork Celtic respectively and the first leg of their second round Texaco Cup match to Portadown 4-1 at Shamrock Park. The second leg was played at Tolka Park on 3 November and they could only manage a 1-1 draw. The Hoops at last struck some good form in the League and won their next four matches. A very tall gangly centre forward named Con O'Donoghue scored in three of those matches. He later emigrated to the USA and played in American Football as a goal kicker.

Mick Leech had been the subject of much press speculation about a possible transfer to an English club during 1971. Mick had played for the League of Ireland against the Football League at Lansdowne Road in May 1971 and had done very well. Harold Shepherdson, who was Alf Ramsey's No. 2 and assistant to Stan Anderson at Middlesborough, came to Tolka Park on 3 November with Stan Anderson to watch the Hoops play Portadown. Billy Young, Rovers' manager, was playing Mick in midfield and Harold Shepherdson told a Rovers' director that he had come over to watch a striker not a midfield player. The directors tried to get Billy Young to move Mick Leech up front but Billy Young kept Mick in midfield. Rovers travelled to Waterford on 21 November and lost 3-1 to the home side who were the League leaders at that time. Two days later Billy Young was sacked as Rovers' manager. Like Arthur Fitzsimons in 1969, Billy had been given insufficient time to prove himself as manager, and he suffered the same fate as Fitzsimons with the directors trying to interfere with his team selections. Paddy Ambrose took over as caretaker manager until the end of the season. The following Sunday, the Hoops played Finn Harps at Milltown and the Donegal side recorded their first victory over Rovers with a 3-1 win. Unfortunately football hooliganism reared its ugly head again and some so-called Rovers' fans tried to attack the referee and the Finn Harps supporters after the game. John Redmond wrote in the *Irish Press* on 22 November: 'Meagher was the centre of controversy because of a penalty award from which Finn Harps scored their first goal. At the final whistle, the referee and linesmen stayed on the field surrounded by six gardai until the angry crowd left the ground. The referee was smuggled out of the ground afterwards.'

On 5 December, Rovers lost their third successive League match when they were beaten 3-1 by Cork Hibs. The Hoops took seven points from their next four matches and they were still in with an outside chance of the title as they trailed leaders Waterford by seven points with twelve matches remaining. Rovers had beaten Bohs 1-0 at Milltown on 2 January but their League form then became very inconsistent as they won three and lost three of their next six League matches. The Hoops beat Athlone Town 5-0 in the replay of their first round Cup tie at St Mel's Park on 17 February after a 0-0 draw at Milltown. Waterford came to Milltown on 27 February for a vital League game and Johnny Matthews scored the winner early in the second half after Mick Lawlor had equalised an early goal from Alfie Hale. However, the abiding memory of that game were two world class saves from Peter Thomas to deny Mick Lawlor and Denis Stephens late in the game. A header from Stephens seemed destined for the net but Thomas, turning his body in mid air, somehow managed to flick it over the bar to the amazement of the large crowd. Finn Harps completed the League double over the Hoops with a 5-3 win at Ballybofey on 5 March.

The Hoops' season was now dependent on the Cup for success but St Pat's repeated their Leinster Senior Cup success over Rovers in the FAI Cup when a goal from a free kick by Kevin Murray won the quarter-final at Richmond Park on 12 March. Cork Hibs then beat Rovers 4-1 in the semi-final of the Dublin City Cup at Flower Lodge on 29 March. The Hoops took six points from their last four matches in the League and their last home match of the season was against Drumcondra on Sunday 2 April. This was to be Drumcondra's second last match in the League of Ireland as Sam Prole sold the club to Home Farm later that month. It was therefore Drums' last visit to Glenmalure Park and the two teams lined out as follows. *Rovers*: Doyle, E. Gregg, J. Gregg, Hamilton, Keogh, Fagan, O'Neill, Leech, Richardson, Lawlor, Davis. *Drums*: Scothorn, Tuck, Colwell, Vance, Place, Masterson, Martin, Garvan, McArdle, Devlin, Hamill.

Rovers won the match 4-1 and Damien Richardson scored all four goals, one of which was from a penalty. Appearing at left back for Drums was Joe Colwell who was to become a director of Shamrock Rovers in 1988. (Drums' last game in the League was a 1-1 draw with Shelbourne at Tolka Park on 5 April.) The Hoops' final League match of the season was at Lourdes Stadium on 9 April and Rovers finished the season with a 3-3 draw. Frank O'Neill was their leading League goalscorer that season with 11 goals. The Hoops finished fifth; the top five positions were as follows:

	P	W	D	L	F	A	Pts.
Waterford	26	21	2	3	66	35	44
Cork Hibernians	26	19	2	5	70	17	40
Bohemians	26	16	5	5	45	24	37
Finn Harps	26	18	0	8	62	34	36
Shamrock Rovers	26	12	4	10	52	41	28

The huge gap between Rovers and Waterford represented just how much the Hoops had fallen back since the great days of the late 1960s. During the 1972 close season the Cunningham family ended a long association with Shamrock Rovers by selling the club to the Kilcoyne brothers, Barton, Louis and Paddy. Louis Kilcoyne was already involved in football through a sports agency; he felt that in order to make a more serious contribution to football in Ireland they would have to take over a club. The Kilcoynes had a series of meetings with Sam Prole in the spring of 1972 and they had agreed to purchase Drumcondra. However, at the eleventh hour Sam Prole, according to the Kilcoynes, changed his mind and sold to Home Farm instead.

Weeks later, Louis Kilcoyne met Des Cunningham and the club was sold to the Kilcoyne brothers within a week. Des Cunningham appointed Liam Touhy as manager of Rovers in June 1972 so that there would be an experienced manager at Milltown to help the Kilcoyne brothers as they started off in football. It is believed that the club changed hands for a fee in the region of £35,000. Shamrock Rovers F. C Ltd, which had been set up in August 1935, was now liquidated but the final winding-up of the company did not take place until 10 January 1978. The records of Shamrock Rovers F. C Ltd in the Companies' Office reveal that the company had a total of £27,583.13 in the bank on 30 November 1972, proof that there had been good money in football in Ireland in the 1960s although not enough, it would appear, to make the running repairs needed at the time. Glenmalure Park had hardly changed for decades. Ground improvements were not made; facilities which were inadequate were not improved. The state of the ground in 1972 left an awful lot to be desired and Glenmalure Park was in a sorry state when the club was taken over by the Kilcoyne brothers.

Louis Kilcoyne had the following to say about his first couple of years at Milltown.

'Rovers were in disarray financially; the crowds had stopped coming to football; by the late 'sixties and early 'seventies Rovers were down to

about 2,000 per game. Players were getting wiser and more shrewd and demands were becoming unreasonable. In our first years we found it difficult to come to terms with the running of a football club, i.e we found it difficult to apply a business strategy to the peculiar business that football is and had similiar difficulties with player demands. The pitch and the ground were in a poor state when we took over. Under the stand was overgrown with prize fungi. After the first season we pulled down the old terracing which was dangerous and replaced it with a car park. At the same time we gutted the grandstand and built two new bars, a social club (namely a night club and members' bar) at a cost of £100,000.'

The pitch, which had once been the finest in Ireland, was in poor shape also but it wasn't until the arrival of Johnny Giles, five years later, that anything major was done to restore it.

Rovers' first competitive game of the season was a first round President's Cup match against Bohemians at Dalymount Park and goals from Denis Stephens and a penalty from Damien Richardson gave them a 2-0 win. The Hoops beat Home Farm-Drumcondra 2-1 in the semi-final and in the final at Dalymount Park on 13 August, they beat Dundalk 3-1. Their line-up in the final was as follows: Dunne, E. Gregg, J. Gregg, Byrne, Keogh, Tuck, Stephens, Lawlor, O'Neill, Richardson, Leech. *Sub*: Kearin for Stephens. Leech and Lawlor, who scored twice, were the goalscorers.

The Shield was again divided into two sections of seven but from this season the winners of the Shield no longer qualified for the UEFA Cup. This position now went to the runners-up in the League. Rovers began the Shield well with wins over Finn Harps, Shelbourne and Drogheda. Eugene Davis, who had been signed by Liam Tuohy during the close season, scored his first goal for the club in the Finn Harps match. The Hoops then drew with Sligo Rovers and Home Farm and had only to avoid a three-goal defeat by Dundalk in their last match to qualify for the semi-finals. Dundalk won 1-0 and qualified with Rovers on eight points from six matches.

The Hoops beat Waterford 1-0 in the first round of the Dublin

City Cup and they faced Bohemians in the first League match of the season at Glenmalure Park on 8 October. Their line-up for the match was as follows: Dunne, E. Gregg, Keogh, Kearin, J. Gregg, Fagan, Lawlor, Byrne, O'Neill, Leech, Richardson. *Sub*: Daly for Richardson. The game ended in a disappointing 0-0 draw with few chances being created by either side. Damien Richardson scored in Rovers' next two League matches, away to Athlone at St Mel's Park where the Hoops won 2-1 and twice at Milltown when they beat Sligo Rovers 3-0 with Lawlor getting the other two. This was Richardson's last match for Rovers; he signed for Gillingham in the following week. The Hoops continued their good form in the League with wins over Cork Celtic, Limerick and Dundalk. Cork Celtic managed to gain revenge for their League defeat when they beat Rovers in the Dublin City Cup on 7 November but the Hoops qualified for the final of the Leinster Senior Cup when they beat Dundalk 2-1 in the semi-final.

Rovers then hit a run of poor form which saw them lose to Dundalk, Waterford and Finn Harps. Finn Harps hammered them 5-0 at Ballybofey on 3 December. It would be another seventeen years before Rovers suffered a five-goal defeat again. They drew their next two games against Cork Hibs and St Pat's at Milltown. Pat Dunne, Rovers' goalkeeper, scored from a penalty against Cork Hibs on 10 December and John Herrick was signed from Cork Hibs and played against St Pat's on 17 December. The Hoops beat Home Farm 4-0 on Christmas Eve and Leo Kearns scored the fourth goal. Bohs beat Rovers 3-1 in the final of the Leinster Senior Cup on St Stephen's Day and the Hoops' inconsistent form continued when they beat Drogheda 3-1 but then lost 3-2 to Bohs at Dalymount after being 2 up with less than 20 minutes remaining.

Charlie Hendricks and Frank McEwan were signed to try to strengthen the team. Later that month, David Parkes joined from Bohs while Mick Kearin and Eamon Gregg signed for the Phibsboro club. Pat Whelan from Sallynoggin signed for Rovers as the Hoops attempted to build a formidable side for the FAI Cup. The club's League form remained patchy as they managed only five points from five matches before they began their Cup campaign.

On 18 February, a goal from Mick Leech gave Rovers a 1-1 draw in the first round of the Cup against Dundalk. It took three matches to decide this Cup tie with the Hoops eventually winning 3-0 in the second replay at Dalymount Park on 26 February. Rovers then had a marathon with Athlone Town in the second round before emerging to play Limerick in the quarter-final, two days after their fourth Cup match with Athlone Town. Limerick beat them 1-0 but the Hoops were rightly aggrieved at the fact that they had to play the match at all, as it was their ninth match in twenty-two days.

Rovers had a very good win in Waterford on 4 March, but they only managed two wins from their last six League matches. They had a great 6-0 win over Dundalk on 4 April when the goalscorers were Mick Leech (2), Frank O'Neill (2), Terry Daly and Eugene Davis. O'Neill scored a hat trick in Rovers last League match of the season at Glenmalure Park when the Hoops beat Drogheda 3-0. Rovers finished fifth in the league, 12 points behind the winners Waterford. Mick Leech was Rovers leading League goalscorer with 10 goals. The top five in the League finished as follows:

	P	W	D	L	F	A	Pts.
Waterford	26	20	2	4	67	21	42
Finn Harps	26	19	3	4	59	32	41
Bohemians	26	16	5	5	46	25	37
Cork Hibernians	26	13	8	5	53	27	34
Shamrock Rovers	26	12	6	8	45	32	30

Rovers played Athlone Town in the semi-final of the Shield and it turned out a bit like their FAI Cup tie. The Hoops this time took three matches to beat Athlone Town with a 4-0 win in the second replay on 2 May. Two nights later Cork Hibs beat Rovers 1-0 in the final of the Shield.

The Hoops began the 1973/74 season with a friendly against Celtic at Glenmalure Park on 25 July. Rovers wore white jerseys with green collars and cuffs, a set of jerseys that were borrowed from the Offaly Gaelic football team. They lined up for the match as follows: Dunne, Herrick, Fagan, Whelan, Parkes, McEwan, Lawlor, Davis, O'Neill, Leech, Daly.

Bobby Lennox scored the only goal of the game after 27 minutes, although Rovers were most unlucky after 54 minutes when Eugene Davis scored with a shot from 20 yards which the referee disallowed for offside although the Rovers' player who was adjudged to have been offside was out near the touchline and could hardly have been interfering with play.

The Hoops lost to Hull City and Bohs and drew with Preston North End in friendlies played in August. Rovers signed Harry Voakes from Athlone Town and John Herrick returned to Cork Hibs. Tony Ward, later to win fame as a rugby international, played in the friendly against Bohs. The Hoops' first competitive game of the season was on 26 August at Oriel Park when they lost 3-1 to Dundalk in the Leinster Senior Cup. The Shield was replaced with the League Cup competition, and there were six teams in Rovers' group. The Hoops won one, drew two and lost two and did not qualify for the semi-finals. Rovers beat Dundalk 4-3 in their first ever League Cup match to record their only win in the group. They lost 6-3 to Portadown on aggregate in the first round of the Texaco Cup, drawing 2-2 in the first leg at Shamrock Park but losing the return leg 4-1.

Rovers began their League campaign on 7 October with a 1-0 defeat by Sligo Rovers at the Showgrounds. The Hoops played a scoreless draw with Athlone Town on 14 October and the following evening they played Manchester United in a friendly at Dalymount Park. Rovers line-up against United was as follows: Dunne, Kearns, Fagan, Voakes, Parkes, McEwan, Collins, O'Neill, Smith, Lawlor, Daly. *Subs*: Leech for Smith, Davis for McEwan, Doyle for Dunne. United won 2-1. Frank O'Neill scored Rovers' goal from a penalty and Brian Greenhoff and George Graham scored for United. Bobby Collins guested for Rovers in this match and he was to sign for the Hoops the following month. Donal Murphy was signed from Coventry City and Douglas Wood was signed from Athlone Town.

Donal Murphy scored on his debut against Cork Celtic in a 1-1 draw but after eight matches the Hoops had only five points. Tony Ward made his League debut in a scoreless draw against Home Farm and the following week Rovers lost 5-3 to Waterford at Milltown. After that match, Tommy McConville joined Rovers from Waterford and Mick Leech signed for the Blues. Tommy McConville made his debut for the Hoops against Dundalk at Oriel Park on 16 December when Rovers won 3-1 with the goals coming from Donal Murphy (2) and Eamon Fagan.

The following Thursday, 20 December, Liam Tuohy resigned as manager of Shamrock Rovers. Paddy Ambrose was coach to the first team and Hughie Fleming was coach to the 'B' team. A representative of the board went to Liam Tuohy and told him that the playing staff was costing too much and that they wanted to make cut-backs. The board wanted to get rid of Paddy Ambrose and Hughie Fleming. Liam Tuohy approached the two coaches and, like the great club men that they were, they said that they would do their jobs without pay - as many League of Ireland players have done when times were bad. But the board insisted that they had to go. 'They don't figure in our plans' was a phrase repeated four times by Louis Kilcoyne to Liam Tuohy. Paddy Ambrose was a lifelong friend of Liam Tuohy and Tuohy decided there and then to resign. Paddy Ambrose and Hughie Fleming left with him. Shay Keogh, who had been in the position of technical advisor to the club, was appointed manager with Douglas Wood but Shay Keogh resigned two days later. Shay Noonan, Dick Giles and Douglas Wood looked after team affairs from then until the end of the season.

Drogheda beat the Hoops 2-1 on 23 December and Rovers then hit a run of good form taking nine points from their next five matches. Tony Ward scored his first goal for Rovers in a 2-1 win at St Mel's Park against Athlone Town on 13 January. Mick Lawlor signed for Shelbourne in January 1974 and so another member of the great 'sixties team parted company with the Hoops. Rovers lost 4-0 at Turner's Cross on 10 February to the League leaders Cork Celtic and the following week they travelled to Waterford to take on the Blues in the Cup. A goal from Eamon Fagan gave Rovers a replay but Mick Leech, playing against his old club, scored the only goal of that replay to knock the Hoops out of the Cup.

Rovers won five of their remaining eight matches to finish in seventh position, a considerable distance behind winners Cork Celtic who had four points to spare over Bohemians and Cork Hibernians. The Hoops' League record for the season was as follows:

	P	W	D	L	F	A	Pts.
Rovers	26	11	5	10	31	33	27

Mick Meagan and Theo Dunne were appointed during the 1974 close season to the positions of manager and assistant manager. Liam Tuohy had not been given enough resources to build a good team. Mick Meagan was to be similarly handicapped. Players like Brendan Bradley, Tony Macken and John Minnock were available but Rovers didn't make high enough bids to secure their services. At the start of the 1974/75 season there was a pay dispute over bonuses for the League Cup competition. Six players - Charlie Hendricks, Pat Whelan, Eugene Davis, Tommy McConville, Eamon Fagan and Terry Daly - refused to re-sign for the club. Eventually a compromise was reached but Terry Daly and Eugene Davis left for Athlone Town. These two young players were a great loss. A greater effort should have been made to keep them at the club.

The Hoops began the 1974/75 season with a League Cup match against Shelbourne at Milltown which they won. Their line-up was as follows: Dunne, Miller, Parkes, Meagan, Kearns, McEwan, Ward, Cooke, Murphy, Smyth, Lawlor. *Sub*: Molloy.

They played seven matches in the League Cup and finished with ten points to secure second place in the group. However, the League of Ireland management committee ruled that Eddie Miller was ineligible to play as his registration had not been cleared following a period on trial at Leeds United at the end of the previous season. The club was fined £50 and deducted one League Cup point which was enough to enable Sligo Rovers to meet Finn Harps in the semi-final.

Frank O'Neill left Rovers after thirteen outstanding seasons and signed for Waterford. On his debut for the Blues, he scored twice - as did Mick Leech - as Waterford beat Shelbourne 6-1 at Kilcohan Park.

The Hoops began the League campaign with a 4-1 win over Sligo Rovers at Milltown on 6 October. They lost their next three League matches before goals from Tommy McConville and Frank McEwan gave them a 2-1 win over St Pat's at Milltown on 3 November. They qualified for the semi-finals of the Leinster Senior Cup by beating St Pat's and Bluebell United. Rovers then drew with Cork Celtic and beat Finn Harps before they lost to the League leaders Bohs 2-0 at Dalymount Park on 24 November. They then had two wins over Home Farm, the second of which enabled them to qualify for the final of the Leinster Senior Cup.

Rovers' League form was very much mid table stuff and in the seven League matches they played in December and January, their record was 2 wins, 2 draws and 3 defeats. Players like Dermot O'Shea, Tony Ward and Alan Lyons were getting regular runs in the team but Rovers were still a long way from being a good side. They drew 0-0 with Parkvilla in the first round of the FAI Cup at Oriel Park on 16 February. Rovers won the replay 5-1 at Milltown the following Thursday when Donal Murphy grabbed a hat trick. The Hoops beat Finn Harps and lost to Bohemians in the League before Shelbourne beat them in the quarter-final of the Cup with a goal in the last minute from a free kick.

Bohs beat the Hoops in the replay of the Leinster Senior Cup final at Tolka Park on 20 March. Gerry Ryan scored the only goal after five minutes, but Rovers were a little unlucky as they hit the crossbar and missed a penalty in the second half. The Hoops took eight points from their last six matches to finish in 8th place, 17 points behind the winners Bohemians. Rovers' final League record for 1974/75 was as follows:

	P	W	D	L	F	A	Pts.
Shamrock Rovers	26	10	5	11	40	38	25

Robbie Cooke finished as the club's top League goal scorer with seven goals, Tommy McConville, Tony Ward and Donal Murphy all finishing with six goals each.

Joe Cunningham died in April 1975 at the age of 82.

A Shamrock Rovers' selection of golden oldies played the reigning All-Ireland football champions, Dublin, at Milltown in June 1975 in a charity match in aid of the Simon Community. Michael O'Hehir was also present that evening and he gave a commentary on the match from the press box.

Rovers began the 1975/76 season with a friendly against West Bromwich Albion at Milltown. The line-up for the friendly was as follows: Dunne, Whelan, Parkes, Miller, Synnott, Fagan, McEwan, McGrath, Murphy, O'Connor, Cronin. The pitch was in an absolutely disgraceful condition for this match: there were bald patches in many areas. An own goal from Eamon Fagan decided the issue in West Brom's favour.

Donal Murphy went back to Coventry City and Tommy McConville signed for Dundalk. Frank McEwan, Eamon Fagan, Tony Ward and David Parkes were put on the transfer list. The club introduced a youth policy and practically the whole Cherry Orchard youth team was signed up. Home Farm had won the FAI Cup in 1975 with a very young side and obviously the board at Shamrock Rovers was going to try to emulate Home Farm.

The Hoops went on a tour of Japan and played the Japanese national side twice, winning one of the matches 3-2 and losing the other 1-0. They beat Japan 3-2 on 11 September and Robbie Cooke (2) and Jackie Jameson were Rovers' goalscorers on that occasion. Frank McEwan had gone to Boyne Rovers and Eamon Fagan went to Beggsboro and the club had a young, inexperienced side as they began the 1975/76 season with a League Cup match against Home Farm on 21 September. The line-up for the Hoops in that match was as follows: Dunne, Lindsay, Whelan, Synnott, Miller, Burke, Jameson, Kenny, Cooke, Lyons, McNevin. *Sub*: Magee for McNevin. Home Farm beat the Hoops 2-1, with Jackie Jameson getting Rovers' goal. The League Cup was organised on a knockout basis in season 1975/76. The first round matches consisted of home and away ties, while the remaining matches were organised on a single match knockout format. Home Farm crushed Rovers 5-1 in the second leg on 24 September to win 7-2 on aggregate and qualify for the quarter-finals. The Dublin City Cup was organised that season for teams who failed to make it to the quarter-finals of the League Cup and the Hoops played St Pat's in the first round on 27 September. St Pat's won 4-1; Rovers' goal came from a penalty scored by Pat Dunne. The Hoops made their exit from the Leinster Senior Cup at the first hurdle on 2 October, losing 4-0 to Shelbourne.

Needless to say optimism was not high amongst Rovers' dwindling band of supporters as they prepared for a League season with the youngest and most inexperienced League side ever fielded by the club. Their support had fallen to a small hardcore of die-hards who supported the club through thick and thin. But who could blame the vast majority of Rovers' supporters from turning their backs on the club at this stage? The Hoops lost many supporters in the mid 1970s who were lost forever to the domestic game.

Mick Meagan and Theo Dunne worked very hard at Milltown but their hands were tied behind their backs as they had no money to buy players. How could they succeed if all they had was virtually a schoolboy team, who would sign for other clubs after spending a few seasons at Milltown? The once-proud Shamrock Rovers had gone from riches to rags in next to no time; indeed, the club was almost on its knees in that wilderness period of the mid 1970s. The decline on the pitch was mirrored in a sad loss of tradition off it. Many old pictures of famous Rovers' teams from previous decades and many historic pennants that Rovers had received from clubs throughout the football world were destroyed or discarded during this depressing few years.

After seven matches in the 1975/76 League, the Hoops' record was one win, three draws and three defeats with their one win coming against Limerick at Milltown on 26 October when a solitary goal from Pat McGrath gave them victory. The Hoops played the League champions Bohs at Milltown on Sunday, 23 November with a kick-off time of 11.30. Robbie Cooke scored the only goal of the game to give Rovers a morale boosting win. They then hit a poor run of form and they could only manage four points from their next eight League games. They drew with Waterford and Home Farm and beat Cork Hibernians on the Cork club's last visit to Milltown with the help of an own goal scored by Hibs' goalkeeper Gerry Spillane. Alan O'Neill made his League debut for Rovers in this match. The Hoops completed a League double over Limerick when they beat them 2-1 at the Market's Field on 25 January with Robbie Cooke and Alan Lyons scoring. Rovers lost their next two League matches to St Pat's and Cork Celtic before they made the short journey to Inchicore to take on St Pat's in the first round of the Cup. It was a draw but St Pat's, inspired by Barry Bridges, won the replay 3-1 at Glenmalure Park on 19 February.

The club now faced the prospect of having to re-apply for membership of the League of Ireland for the only time in the club's history. Rovers had to take a minimum of five points from their remaining seven matches but they could only manage two draws against Finn Harps and Cork Hibs, while Bohemians, Shelbourne, Waterford, Dundalk and Drogheda United beat them to ensure bottom place for the Hoops for the only time in the clubs proud history. Mick Meagan and Theo Dunne had resigned in April 1976, before the end of the season, and Sean Thomas was appointed manager. His first game in charge was the Drogheda

United match on 8 April, which was played at Tolka Park. Rovers had to win their last two matches to avoid seeking re-election and things looked good when goals from Magee and Dardis gave them a two-goal lead. However Drogheda fought back and won 3-2 and it was a deeply depressed group of Rovers' supporters who made their way out of Tolka Park that April evening, knowing that the Hoops would now have to seek re-election to the League. Their final game of the season was also Cork Hibs' final game in League of Ireland football and a goal from Paul Magee gave Rovers a 1-1 draw. The Hoops' League record for season 1975/76 was as follows:

	P	W	D	L	F	A	Pts.
Shamrock Rovers	26	4	7	15	27	49	15

Robbie Cooke finished as Rovers' leading League goalscorer with seven goals. Their full record for the season, including friendlies, was as follows:

	P	W	D	L	F	A
Shamrock Rovers	36	5	8	23	35	66

It was truly a very poor record, winning a mere five matches out of thirty-six.

Billy Lord's testimonial match was held on 7 May when a Shamrock Rovers' selection of players from the 'fifties and 'sixties took on a Drumcondra selection from the same period. A crowd of around 2,000 people turned up to pay tribute to one of the greatest servants of Shamrock Rovers.

During the close season of 1976 Sean Thomas signed both Johnny Fullam and John Doran from Bohemians. John Conway had been signed the previous February by Mick Meagan, so badly needed experience was being added to the young side at Milltown. The League Cup was divided into four groups of four and Rovers' opponents in their group were Home Farm, Shelbourne and Dundalk. The Hoops' first competitive game of the season was a League Cup match against Home Farm at Milltown on 5 September. Their line-up was as follows: Dunne, Doran, Lindsay, Synnott, Fullam, Conway, Cooke, Cash, Gaffney, Dardis, Magee. *Subs*: Donoghue, Lyons.

A goal from Gerry Lindsay gave the Hoops a 1-0 win. Goals from Robbie Gaffney and John Conway saw off the challenge of Dundalk and Shelbourne were beaten 2-0 in the final group match with Paul Magee and Noel Synnott scoring the goals. Mick Leech and Brendan White were signed and Mick Leech scored on his reappearance for the Hoops as they beat Cobh Ramblers 3-0 in the semi-final of the League Cup.

A good crowd paying gate receipts of £1,124 saw Rovers play Sligo Rovers in the League Cup final at Dalymount Park on 6 October with the following line-up: O'Neill, Doran, McNevin, Wyse, Synnott, Fullam, Leech, Conway, Meagan, Lyons, Gaffney. *Sub*: Paul Magee for Mark Meagan. A goal from a tremendous thirty-yard shot from Mick Leech in the last minute gave Rovers a famous victory. It was their first and only success in the League Cup; they have been unsuccessful in four finals since then. That was also Mick Leech's 250th goal in senior football.

The Hoops began their League campaign with a 2-1 win against Albert Rovers, the successors of Cork Hibs, on 3 October. Mick Leech and Larry Wyse scored in this match. Rovers then hit a poor run of form, losing their next five matches in the League. Sean Thomas made more signings: Con Martin and Tom O'Dea came to Milltown. Harry McCue and Hughie Brophy played in the Rovers' side that lost to Bohs at Dalymount Park on 7 November. The Hoops recorded their first victory since the opening League game of the season when they beat Finn Harps 3-1 at Milltown the following week. They then took four points from their next three matches before hitting another poor run of form when they lost four matches in a row.

The Hoops got back on the winning trail when they beat Dundalk 3-2 at Oriel Park. Rovers' form was better away from home that season and they beat Shelbourne at Harold's Cross in between losing home matches to Waterford and Bohemians. Rovers made the short journey to Dalymount Park on 13 February to take on the holders Bohs in the Cup and emerged with a praiseworthy 2-2 draw. Ten days later, however, Rovers suffered their heaviest defeat ever in the Cup at Milltown when Bohs romped to a 4-0 win.

Rovers' League position was again looking a bit precarious and it now became more dodgy as they lost their next four matches. There was a particularly bad defeat at Milltown on 20 March when Limerick beat them 4-0. Rovers took on Home Farm the following week at Tolka Park desperately needing a win to try and pull clear from the re-application zone. They won 2-1, but it was a close-run thing, with their goals coming from Tony Ward and an own goal from Home Farm defender McDonnell. Still, any win was welcome.

Rovers' last home League match was played on Saturday 2 April. They were having a miserable run at Milltown, not having won at home since 28 November when they had beaten St Pat's 1-0. Since then, they had played eight times at Milltown with the best result being a scoreless draw with Home Farm on 12 December. They had lost seven matches in a row and needed both points to have any chance of avoiding having to reapply for admission to the League. Both Albert Rovers and Limerick were ahead of them in the table. The match kicked off at 2 p.m. and a goal from Paul Magee gave Rovers victory - in front of a crowd of 63 paying customers! The Hoops' final match was away to Sligo Rovers at the Showgrounds and the home side won 3-1 to win the League title. Rovers finished in 11th place, one point ahead of both Limerick and Albert Rovers and five points ahead of Home Farm who finished bottom. The Hoops' League record for the season was as follows:

	P	W	D	L	F	A	Pts.
Shamrock Rovers	26	7	3	16	26	46	17

Mick Leech finished as top League goalscorer with eight goals. Rovers did not participate in the Leinster Senior Cup that season as the competition was confined only to all the Leinster Senior clubs and two League of Ireland clubs, the previous season's League champions and Cup winners, Dundalk and Bohemians. For the record Dundalk beat Bohemians 1-0 in the final at Tolka Park on Friday, 22 April.

THE PATH OF THE CUP 1970-77

Rovers had completed a history-making six FAI Cup final triumphs in a row in April 1969 in the replayed final against Cork Celtic. They had now gone 32 games without defeat in the Cup and they were drawn at home to Shelbourne in the first round in 1970. The match was played on Sunday 1 February and the two teams lined out as follows: *Rovers*: Smyth, Dixon, Courtney, Richardson, Canavan, Kearin, O'Neill, Leech, Barber, Lawlor, Gregg. *Sub*: Brophy for Leech. *Shelbourne*: Roche, Gannon, O'Brien, Murray, Place, Dunning, Wallace, Delargy, O'Connor, Core, Campbell. *Sub*: Ennis for O'Connor.

Rovers took the lead after 12 minutes when Eric Barber headed home a cross from Mick Lawlor. Three minutes later the Hoops almost sealed victory but Paddy Roche somehow managed to touch a fierce shot from Barber on to the crossbar and Mick Gannon completed the clearance by heading the ball off the line. This save turned the match as Shelbourne grew in confidence and they had Rovers on the defensive for the remainder of the first half. Shelbourne forced thirteen corners in the first half yet Rovers went in at the interval still a goal ahead. Shelbourne kept up the pressure in the second half and it finally told after 70 minutes. From Shelbourne's seventeenth corner, the Reds' centre half Brendan Place forced the ball home in a crowded goalmouth. Three minutes later, after Rovers had cleared a corner, Johnny Campbell floated over a cross which was met with a diving header by Brian Delargy to give Shelbourne the lead. The Hoops almost snatched a late equaliser when Paddy Roche cut out a cross from O'Neill with Barber and Dixon waiting to apply the finishing touch.

So ended Rovers great Cup run and Shelbourne fancied themselves then to go all the way - the last two times they had beaten Rovers in the Cup they had gone on to win it. However, Shelbourne's next opponents in the Cup, Bohemians, had other ideas and beat the Reds 1-0 in the quarter-final before going on to beat Sligo Rovers 2-1 in the second replay of the final.

The Hoops began their Cup campaign in 1971 with a first round home match against Cork Celtic on 7 February. Mick Leech scored the only goal of the game after 25 minutes, but Cork Celtic were unlucky to have a goal disallowed by referee John Carpenter after seven minutes when he adjudged McCarthy to have handled the ball before it finished up in the net. Rovers' opponents in the quarter-final were Drogheda whose player-manager Mick Meagan later bacome manager at Rovers. Drogheda had never won at Milltown so the Hoops got a rude awakening when Drogheda went three goals up after 37 minutes. Paul Martin pulled a goal back just before half-time and when Eddie Byrne scored Rovers' second goal after 52 minutes it looked as if they might yet save the day. The Hoops laid siege to the Drogheda goal for the next twenty minutes but they could not force a way through. After 73 minutes, disaster hit Rovers when McEwan intercepted a pass from Pat Dunne to Damien Richardson and crossed for Pat Cullen to score his third and Drogheda's fourth goal. Two minutes later, it was all over for the Hoops when Ronnie Whelan headed Drogheda's fifth goal. Drogheda had become the first side ever to score five goals in a Cup tie against Shamrock Rovers at Milltown. (Only one other side had ever before scored five goals against the Hoops in a Cup tie - Shelbourne, who won 5-2 in a first round tie on 13 March 1947.) Rovers line-up for that Cup tie was as follows: Dunne, Gregg, Courtney, Fagan, Richardson, Kearin, O'Neill, Byrne, Leech, Lawlor, Martin. *Sub*: Dixon for Gregg (80 mins). That was Pat Courtney's last Cup appearance for Rovers: he was given a free transfer at the end of the season, his 13th for the Hoops, and decided to hang up his boots. Mick Meagan told an amusing story about the match. Apparently, three Drogheda directors, Tom Munster, Charlie Hurley and Vincent Kerins, left the ground after Rovers scored their second goal as they couldn't bear the tension. They went into the church at Milltown just down the road from the ground and while they were there they heard two loud roars. They left the church just after full time convinced that the Hoops had won the match 4-3. However, when they saw the smiles on the faces of the Drogheda supporters leaving the ground they knew that their team had prevailed. Sandy Smith, Rovers' centre half, was out injured and his steadying influence was badly missed at the heart of the Rovers' defence.

Drogheda went on to reach the Cup final that year but they were beaten 3-0 by Limerick in the replayed final. Rovers were drawn at home to Athlone Town in the first round in 1972. They drew 0-0 at Milltown and four days later, on 17 February, Rovers hammered Athlone Town 5-0 in the replay. The goalscorers were Paul Martin (2), Mick Lawlor, Damien Richardson and an own goal from Jackie Quinn. The Hoops lost 1-0 away to St Patrick's Athletic in the quarter-final. A first-half goal from a free kick by Kevin Murray decided the tie in St Pat's favour. Rovers' fans knew it wasn't going to be their day when Damien Richardson missed a penalty in the second half. It was the first time that Damien Richardson had ever missed a penalty for Rovers, having been successful from the spot on twelve previous occasions. He always put the ball to the keeper's left and Tom Lally went the correct way to bring off a good save. St Pat's were beaten 1-0 in the semi-final by the eventual winners that year, Cork Hibs. Rovers' line-up for that quarter-final tie at Richmond Park was as follows: Dunne, E. Gregg, Fagan, Keogh, J. Gregg, Hamilton, O'Neill, Leech,

Richardson, Lawlor, Stephens. *Sub*: O'Donoghue for Stephens (76 mins).

In 1973, Rovers played eight Cup ties in the space of twenty-two days and did not even make the semi-finals of the competition. Their odyssey began with a first-round tie at home to Dundalk on 18 February. A goal from Mick Leech gave Rovers a 1-1 draw and four days later the teams played a scoreless draw in the replay at Oriel Park. Rovers won the second replay 3-0 at Dalymount Park on 26 February, with the goals coming from Mick Leech, Terry Daly and Mick Lawlor.

On 1 March they travelled to St Mel's Park to take on Athlone Town in the second round. Terry Daly gave the Hoops the lead after 21 minutes but Ivan Parke equalised for Athlone Town just before half time. The first replay was played on 7 March at Dalymount Park and finished in a scoreless draw. The second replay was played the following evening at the same venue and produced another scoreless draw even after two periods of extra time. The sides had to return to Dalymount Park yet again the following evening, Friday 9 March, where the gate receipts were £900, up £100 on the previous evening. Despite an appeal by both clubs that the game be postponed, the secretary of the FAI Mr Peader O'Driscoll, stated that the association could not rescind a decision by the emergency committee who had deemed that the tie take place as proposed. The quarter-finals were due to be played two days later and the winners of the Rovers/Athlone tie were drawn away to play Limerick at the Market's Field. The problems endured by the clubs involved were further illustrated by the failure of Athlone Town to secure the release of two of their players from work for the third replay.

Eugene Davis gave Rovers the lead after 20 minutes and nine minutes later Mick Lawlor made it 2-0 for the Hoops. Athlone Town's player manager Dougie Wood pulled a goal back in the second half but Eugene Davis sealed victory for Rovers with a goal two minutes from time. There was a nice touch after the game when Athlone Town director, the late Seamus O'Brien, walked into the Hoops' dressingroom carrying two bottles of champagne and a bottle of whiskey.

A meeting of the FAI emergency committee took place after the match at Dalymount Park under the chairmanship of Charlie Walsh after Rovers had requested a postponement of the quarter-final tie on the following Sunday. Gerry McKeever (Dundalk) was absent from the meeting and the committee voted by five votes to four that the cup tie on Sunday had to go ahead as planned. Those who voted in favour of the match going ahead were: Liam Rapple (hon. sec., Bohs); Dick Doran (hon. treasurer); Eddie Halpin (Bohs); Jack Traynor (Shels); and Donie O'Halloran (FAI chairman). Those who voted against were Vere Deane, Charlie Liddy, Louis Kilcoyne and Martin Dunne (St Pat's). The FAI obviously did not give sufficient consideration to the fact that soccer in Ireland is a part-time game. It was totally unreasonable to expect part-time footballers to play four matches in five days. Mick Leech had considerable difficulty in even getting out of bed on Sunday morning, having played three Cup matches in three days. He could not possibly give of his best at the Market's Field due to extreme tiredness. Rovers were missing three of their regular back four players, John Herrick, Charlie Hendricks and Pat Whelan and a gallant Hoops' team went out of the Cup 1-0. Rovers line-up in the quarter-final against Limerick was as follows: Dunne, Tuck, Parkes, Gregg, Fagan, McEwan, Lawlor, Davis, O'Neill, Daly, Leech. *Sub*: Cummins for Leech.

Limerick were beaten by the Cup holders Cork Hibs in the semi-final and Hibs went on to beat Shelbourne 1-0 in the replayed final, thus becoming the only side other than Shamrock Rovers to retain the FAI Cup.

In 1974, Rovers were drawn away to Waterford in the first round of the Cup. After securing a 1-1 draw at Kilcohan Park through a goal from Eamon Fagan on 17 February, the Hoops lost the replay three days later at Milltown. A goal from ex-Hoops favourite Mick Leech, when he headed a corner to the net in the first half, decided the tie. Waterford were beaten by Drogheda in the quarter-final and Finn Harps went on to win the Cup, beating Drogheda's conquerors St Pat's 3-1 in the final. Rovers line-up against Waterford was as follows: Dunne, Hendricks, Meagan,

McConville, Parkes, McEwan, O'Neill, Kearns, Murphy, Fagan, Collins. *Sub*: Daly for O'Neill (49 mins).

The Hoops began their Cup campaign in 1975 with a scoreless draw against Parkvilla in the first round at Oriel Park on 16 February before winning the replay four days later at Milltown by five goals to one, with Donal Murphy scoring a hat trick and Alan Lyons and Frank McEwan getting the other goals. Donal Murphy thus became the first Rovers' player to score a Cup-tie hat trick since Jackie Mooney and Eddie Bailham got three apiece in the Hoops' 7-0 demolition of Dundalk eleven years earlier. (It was to be another sixteen years before a Rovers' player scored a hat trick in a Cup tie. Like the previous three, it was scored in a first-round tie and the honour fell to Derek Swan when Rovers beat Finn Harps at the RDS on 10 March 1991.) The Hoops' opponents in the quarter-final were Shelbourne and the Reds shocked Rovers with a goal in the last minute after Rovers had created most of the chances in the match but had failed to take them. Shelbourne reached the final that year where they were surprised by a very young Home Farm side who beat them 1-0. The Hoops line-up against Shelbourne was as follows: Dunne, Kearns, Whelan, McConville, Parkes, Fagan, McEwan, R. Cooke, Murphy, Lyons, M. Cooke. *Sub*: Ward for Lyons (73 mins).

Rovers were drawn away to St Pat's in the first round of the Cup in 1976. The Hoops were rank outsiders that year and surprised quite a few people by getting a 1-1 draw at Richmond Park thanks to a Magee goal. Four days later St Pat's won the replay 3-1 with Robbie Cooke getting Rovers' goal from a penalty. History was made for Rovers, however, with the presence of a father and son combination in their line-up. Mick Meagan, player manager of the Hoops, and his son Mark played in both Cup ties against St Pat's. Drogheda beat St Pat's in the next round and went on to reach their second FAI Cup final where they were beaten by Bohemians 1-0.

In 1977 Rovers were drawn away to the holders Bohemians in the first round of the Cup. The tie was played at Dalymount Park on 13 February and a goal from Mick Leech and a penalty from

Johnny Fullam gave Rovers a 2-2 draw in a very exciting match. The Hoops were never at the races in the replay and Bohs won comprehensively 4-0. This was Rovers' heaviest defeat ever in a Cup tie and their line-up on that bleak day was: Dunne, Doran, O'Dea, Fullam, Lyons, Gaffney, Ward, Leech, Synnott, Conway, McCue. *Subs*: Martin for Synnott (half-time), Magee for Martin (81 mins).

So ended Rovers' most unsuccessful period in the FAI Cup. In eight seasons between 1970 and 1977, they played in a total of 23 cup ties and their record was as follows:

	P	W	D	L	F	A
Shamrock Rovers	23	5	10	8	27	26

The most formidable team in the FAI Cup had become a pale shadow of the once feared force throughout the country. After the demoralising 4-0 first round replay defeat by Bohemians, it seemed that success in the Blue Riband trophy of Irish soccer was light years away for the Hoops. However within fourteen months of that depressing February afternoon at Milltown, Shamrock Rovers would lift the FAI Cup for the 21st time.

SPOTLIGHT ON MICK LEECH

Mick Leech was signed by Paddy Ambrose and Liam Tuohy for Shamrock Rovers in November 1966 from junior side Ormeau. The deal was completed in the North Star Hotel in Amiens Street and Mick received a signing-on fee of £300, half of which he gave to Ormeau. He spent six weeks in the reserves before he made his first team debut against Dundalk at Glenmalure Park on New Year's Day, 1967. Rovers drew 1-1 in this match and Mick was substituted by Billy Dixon in the second half. Leech scored his first goal for the Hoops on 26 February 1967 when he scored twice but

Rovers lost 4-2 to Cork Hibs at Flower Lodge. He played his first Cup tie for the Hoops in the semi-final against Dundalk and scored Rovers' goal as they drew 1-1. The Hoops made no mistake in the replay and Leech scored twice as Rovers won 3-0. Mick scored Rovers' second equaliser in the final against St Pat's and a late goal from Billy Dixon gave Rovers the cup and Mick Leech his first FAI Cup medal while still a teenager.

The following year, 1968, Leech again stamped his mark on the Cup, scoring twice both in the semi-final against Dundalk and the final against Waterford. It was during the following season, 1968/69, that Mick really stormed on the scene as he notched up an incredible total of 56 goals during the season. He scored two in the FAI Cup final replay against Cork Celtic and his tremendous form that season should have had the English managers queueing up to sign him.

However the move to full-time football in England never materialised and Mick became very disillusioned with the game. Liam Tuohy is of the view that Mick Leech was good enough to play at any level of football. He had tremendous ball control, a brilliant first touch and great positional sense. He could run onto a ball and hit it without changing his stride and he had all the attributes of a top-class striker. Liam felt that at that time in English football, too much emphasis was being placed on work rate and because Mick Leech was a very skillful player and not a workhorse he didn't get away to England. Liam Tuohy managed the Irish team that took part in the mini World Cup in Brazil in 1972 and two of the best players he had were Mick Leech and Mick Martin. Mick Martin was signed by Manchester United shortly afterwards but Mick Leech remained in Ireland. There was speculation about West Ham in 1967 and Middlesborough in 1971 but it came to nothing.

Mick became disheartened and he left Rovers for Waterford in December 1973. He returned to Milltown in September 1976 when Sean Thomas signed him and the following month, he scored his 250th goal in senior football when his 30-yard shot in the last minute beat Sligo Rovers in the League Cup final. Johnny

Giles took over as manager of Rovers the following season. Mick Leech didn't figure in his plans and he was on his way to Bohemians shortly after Giles took over at Milltown.

Mick won international caps and numerous inter-League caps while at Rovers and he was a great crowd pleaser at Milltown. He was a great opportunist in the penalty area and his goalscoring feats made him one of the greatest strikers ever to wear a Rovers' jersey.

SPOTLIGHT ON PAT DUNNE

Pat Dunne began his football career at Everton during the 1958/59 season when he was 16. When he signed as a professional at 18 there were five other goalkeepers at Goodison Park, among them Irish international Jimmy O'Neill, Albert Dunlop and a young Welsh goalkeeper named Williams who later went on to be capped by Wales at full international level. It was hardly surprising that Pat found it difficult to break through to the first team. Pat Dunne played for the first team at Everton twice, although those two games were representative matches against the RAF and the Army.

In the summer of 1961, Pat injured an arm badly in an accident and he spent a total of eight weeks in hospital. When he returned to Everton, Harry Catterick had taken over as manager from Johnny Carey. Shortly afterwards Pat Dunne was released by Everton. He was ready to give up football then as he was still worried about whether his injured arm would ever be right again. Sean Thomas persuaded him eventually to come to Milltown and he signed for the Hoops in the summer of 1962.

Pat Dunne made his competitive debut for Rovers in a memorable P. J Casey Cup match against Drumcondra at Tolka Park on 26 August 1962 which ended in a 5-5 draw. He played in the European Cup Winners' Cup matches that season against Botev Plovdiv from Bulgaria and had a good run in the team before Sean Thomas decided it was time to give him a break from first team football and replaced him with Paddy Henderson. As a young goalkeeper Pat was now very determined to regain his place after being dropped and he became Rovers first choice goalkeeper for season 1963/64. He played in the Fairs Cup matches against Valencia and in all 22 of the Hoops' League matches that season. They almost carried off the grand slam that season, the Top Four trophy being the only domestic trophy that they failed to win.

Rovers suffered only one League defeat in 1963/64 and Pat Dunne is of the opinion that it was the greatest Rovers' team of them all. Manchester United, who had Pat watched by Billy Behan, who incidentally was indirectly responsible for getting Pat Dunne away to Everton back in 1958, approached him through Matt Busby after the drawn 1964 FAI Cup final with Cork Celtic and made him an offer to transfer to Old Trafford. Between that match and the replay the following Wednesday, Sunderland also came in with an offer but he signed for the Manchester club in May 1964.

Pat won a League championship medal with Manchester United in his first season at Old Trafford and he spent another full season at Old Trafford before signing for second division side Plymouth Argyle during the 1966/67 season. Pat was a guest player on Rovers' American tour in 1967 and he was voted goalkeeper of the tournament. He rejoined the Hoops in November 1970 when player-manager Frank O'Neill signed him from Plymouth Argyle for a transfer fee of £3,000.

The Hoops qualified for a play-off for the League title later that season with Cork Hibernians but the Cork side won the play-off 3-1 at Dalymount Park on 25 April. Pat had played a large role in getting Rovers to the play-off as he helped considerably to steady a shaky defence which had conceded twenty goals in their first eight League matches. That was the nearest Pat came to winning a major honour with Rovers in his second spell at the club as the club then went through its bleakest period in the mid 1970s.

Pat Dunne became the first player to be shown a red card in League of Ireland football when John Carpenter sent him off on 1 September 1974 in a League Cup match against Shelbourne at Milltown. Despite this lapse, he gave the Hoops great service in those depressing years and he even started taking penalties for the club. He scored his first against Cork Hibs at Milltown on 10 December 1972 and he was also successful with penalties against St Pat's on 27 September 1975 and against Sligo Rovers on 5 October 1975. The question as to what would happen if Pat Dunne missed a penalty was answered at Milltown on 12 October 1975. Rovers were awarded a penalty against Athlone Town and Mick O'Brien saved Pat Dunne's shot. Pat then rushed in and grabbed O'Brien in a bear hug, preventing him from kicking the ball down the field. The referee awarded a free kick to Athlone Town and had severe words with Pat but did not book him, preferring instead to give him a stern lecture.

Pat Dunne travelled to Japan in September 1975 with the Rovers team that played three matches on that tour and they beat the Japanese international side 3-2 in one of them. He vied with Alan O'Neill for the goalkeeping spot over the next two seasons but when Johnny Giles arrived in the summer of 1977 it wasn't long before Pat was on his way from Rovers. Pat Dunne and Johnny Giles never quite saw eye to eye and Pat disapproved of Johnny's style of football. Pat played in the first League match of the season against Dundalk in August 1977 but he left during the season and became player-manager of Thurles Town. He enjoyed a memorable win over Rovers at Milltown in February 1979 when Thurles Town won 2-1 but he will always be fondly remembered by Rovers' supporters and during the lean years and sparse crowds of the mid 'seventies at Milltown his roars of 'out, Rovers, out' to his defenders could be heard all around Glenmalure Park. Pat Dunne is still playing football today and turns out regularly in the United Churches League.

CHAPTER EIGHT
THE GILES ERA
(1 9 7 7 - 8 3)

Themost kept secret in Irish football was broken in July
1977 when it was revealed that Johnny Giles was to
return from England to become manager of Shamrock
Rovers. Sean Thomas, who had slowly but surely brought
improvements to the Rovers' team, quit as manager shortly before
Giles returned. At that time a piece written by Jimmy Meagan
appeared in the *Irish Press* and it contained the following:

'*Shamrock Rovers are to seek planning permission to transform
Milltown into a super-sports stadium which may become the official
headquarters of Irish soccer when finished. Club officials couldn't be
contacted today, but I understand that a formal application to carry out
major reconstruction at Glenmalure Park is about to be made. If
permission is granted, and there is nothing to suggest it will not,
Milltown will cater for something in the region of 50,000 spectators,
most of whom will be seated. Floodlights, too, will be erected and the
Shamrock Rovers club will include other sporting amenities, probably
squash courts, plus bar and restaurant facilities. The project should be
completed some time in 1979, with the new-look Milltown in which the
FAI will play a part becoming one of the most impressive stadiums in the
country, superior to either the IRFU headquarters, Lansdowne Road, or
the GAA Mecca, Croke Park. It will mean the end of Dalymount Park
as an international venue and Lansdowne Road as an alternative or vice
versa.*'

Subsequent events at Milltown meant that the modern
stadium that Jimmy Meagan wrote about never appeared.

Having spent very little money on Rovers in the previous two
seasons the Kilcoyne brothers now invested heavily in a full-time

structure at Milltown. Johnny Giles had the option of acquiring 50 per cent of the club but he never exercised his option. He believed that he could apply professional logic with which he was familiar in England to the League of Ireland. However he was handicapped by the fact that no other club attempted to complement his ideal and as a result he was always going to be fighting an uphill battle. Giles aimed to have a side capable of winning the European Cup in 1985. His long-term plans were admirable if ultimately unattainable.

Johnny Giles brought the nucleus of a very experienced squad to Milltown. Ray Treacy and Eamon Dunphy joined him and other experienced players were signed during the season. Giles signed 17-year-old Pierce O'Leary and he also signed up Steve Lynex, who had been with him at West Bromwich Albion. The Hoops first successful match under Johnny Giles took place on 14 August 1977 when they beat Finn Harps 2-0 at the opening of the Cramford sports complex in Co. Donegal. Mark Meagan and Paul Magee were the goalscorers in this match.

Rovers' first competitive match under Giles took place at Oriel Park on the evening of Sunday, 28 August when they took on the Cup holders Dundalk in the first League match of the season. Their line-up was as follows: Dunne, Doran, Kearns, Dunphy, Synnott, Fullam, Gaffney, Leech, Treacy, Giles, Meagan. Mick Leech scored the only goal of the game after 54 minutes.

Johnny Giles had introduced a full-time set-up at Milltown but this didn't suit either Mick Leech or Pat Dunne, both of whom were in full-time employment at the time. Pat Dunne also did not approve of the style of football that Giles played with Rovers, feeling that it was far too concerned with avoiding defeat rather than going all out for a win. Pat Dunne and Johnny Giles did not hit it off and it wasn't surprising that Pat left Rovers shortly after Giles took over. Johnny Giles told Mick Leech that he did not feature in his plans for the club and the great goalscorer and huge favourite of Hoops' fans soon departed to play out the end of the 1977/78 season with Bohemians. Mick Leech and Pat Dunne gave Rovers great service, especially during the wilderness years of the early and mid 'seventies. It was unfortunate that both had to leave just as things were looking brighter for the Hoops.

Rovers' first home League match of the season attracted a crowd that paid gate receipts of £1,968 and saw them draw 1-1 with Waterford, with Ray Treacy scoring for Rovers. The Hoops then took five points from their next three League matches, beating Limerick and Shelbourne at Milltown and drawing with Athlone Town at St Mel's Park. The match with Athlone drew a gate of £1,500 to St Mel's Park, Athlone's biggest gate in two seasons. Ray Treacy scored a hat trick in the 4-1 win over Shels on Saturday, 24 September and the Hoops had eight points from their five League matches. On 2 October, a crowd paying gate receipts of £2,200, the biggest gate for years at Richmond Park, saw St Pat's beat Rovers 1-0, with Gordon Banks on loan from his American club Lauderdale making his only appearance for the Inchicore side. Banks pulled off a tremendous save from Dunphy in the dying minutes to ensure victory for the home side.

Denis Burnett, the former West Ham and Millwall star, appeared for Rovers in the St Pat's match and made a few more appearances for the Hoops during the season, as did Eoin Hand who made his debut for Rovers against Sligo Rovers at Milltown on 9 October. This match attracted a crowd of 8,500 who paid gate receipts of £3,035, a new record which beat the previous best of £2,610 for the Rovers and Waterford match in February 1966. A spectacular header from Ray Treacy late in the game gave the Hoops a 2-1 win over the reigning League champions. The following Sunday, Rovers travelled to Flower Lodge and played out an uneventful scoreless draw with Cork Albert. Cork Albert only finished mid table that season but Rovers went to Cork with the intention of avoiding a defeat and in the process bored both sets of supporters. The Hoops' attitude should have been far more positive as they had a much better team on duty that day than Cork Albert had. This attitude of avoiding defeat at all costs and playing for draws away from home was to cost Rovers the chance of winning the League title. The Hoops qualified for the semi-final of the Leinster Senior Cup by beating Arbour United 4-1 and

Shelbourne 2-1, but Dundalk beat them 1-0 in the semi-final at Dalymount Park on 1 December. After the Cork Albert game, Rovers' League form was not good enough to sustain a serious title bid and they dropped four points from their next six matches. They lost 3-0 to the leaders Bohemians at Dalymount Park on 30 October which left them trailing Bohs by four points after ten series of matches. Mick Gannon was signed from Shelbourne in November and a centre forward, David Irving, joined Rovers from Fort Lauderdale, an American club side. Irving was to play for the club for three months only, but he made a very big impression on the fans in that short time with his courageous, all-out attacking style.

Rovers beat Cork Celtic 4-0 at Milltown on 4 December and then they played in Zone D of the League Cup against Home Farm, Shels and Dundalk with the top side from the group qualifying for the semi-finals. Rovers had a dismal time of it in the League Cup scoring just one goal in three matches, losing to both Dundalk and Shelbourne and drawing with Home Farm. Ronnie Whelan, later to win fame with Liverpool, scored Home Farm's goal in the 1-1 draw with Rovers on 11 December and former Celtic star, Jimmy Johnstone, scored the winner for Shelbourne against the Hoops at Tolka Park on 27 December. Rovers beat Dundalk 2-0 on New Year's Day 1978 in a controversial match which saw two Dundalk players, Paddy Dunning and Noel King, as well as Hoops' player Dave Irving ordered off by the referee. Eamon Dunphy and Ray Treacy were the goalscorers in this match. The Hoops could only manage three points from their next four matches: after losing to Waterford by a single goal at Kilcohan Park, Rovers then drew with Limerick, Athlone Town and Shelbourne on successive Sundays. It was this inability to beat teams that were clearly inferior that cost the Hoops the title in Johnny Giles's first season. Rovers beat St Pat's 2-1 at Milltown on 5 February before they travelled to Ballybofey the following Sunday to take on Finn Harps in the first round of the FAI Cup. The Hoops got a scoreless draw and beat Finn Harps 3-2 after extra time in the replay at Milltown on 1 March.

Rovers beat Cork Albert and drew with Drogheda United in

the League before they took on the leaders Bohemians at Milltown on 19 March. A big crowd paying gate receipts of £3,350 saw the two sides play out a scoreless draw to leave Bohs five points ahead with six matches left to play. Rovers qualified for the semi-final of the FAI Cup by beating Dundalk 1-0 in the quarter-final replay after a scoreless draw in Oriel Park in the first match. The Hoops won 2-0 away to Thurles Town on 26 March and played Galway Rovers at Milltown on 2 April at Milltown, a week before they were due to play Waterford in the semi-final of the Cup. The Galway Rovers match at Milltown on 2 April made history of a kind. It was the only match ever at Glenmalure Park where a section of the crowd literally turned their backs in disgust at the football that the Hoops were playing. In the first half Johnny Giles and Eamon Dunphy, in particular, had bored many people to distraction with their continuous passing of the ball sideways and backwards. Rovers' efforts in that first half were so pathetic that as they attacked the Gonzaga end of the ground, the crowd at that end eventually just turned around to watch a rugby match which was being played in an adjacent field.

Rovers eventually won that match 2-0 with second-half goals from Steve Lynex and Ray Treacy but the fans were far from happy leaving the ground. The Hoops qualified for the FAI Cup final when goals from Mark Meagan and Steve Lynex cancelled out an early strike from Waterford's Syd Wallace. Rovers lost their unbeaten home League record in their last home match when they lost 1-0 to Finn Harps on Sunday 16 April. Even though they dominated most of the match and although Finn Harps missed a penalty in the first half, Rovers should have had the game wrapped up before Harps stunned them with a late winner. Uwe Seeler, the former West German international, turned out for Cork Celtic against Rovers at Turner's Cross on 23 April and scored twice. However the Hoops went on the rampage and scored six times through Lynex (2), Treacy (2), Meagan and Myers. Their last League match of the season was at Tolka Park on 25 April where they drew 0-0 with Home Farm. Rovers finished fourth in the League, four points behind Bohemians. The top four finished as follows:

	P	W	D	L	F	A	Pts.
Bohemians	30	17	10	3	74	25	44
Finn Harps	30	19	4	7	60	38	42
Drogheda United	30	15	10	5	53	27	40
Shamrock Rovers	30	14	12	4	45	22	40

The Hoops drew twelve matches in 1977/78 and it was the loss of those 12 points that ultimately cost them the title. Too often, they played for draws when a more adventurous approach might have yielded them more points.

Rovers won the Cup for the twenty-first time when they beat Sligo Rovers 1-0 in the final at Dalymount Park on 30 April. Rovers' goal came from a penalty three minutes into additional time at the end of the first half and it was converted successfully by Ray Treacy.

The Hoops then competed in the Tyler Cup which was contested by the top four teams in the League of Ireland and the Irish League. Rovers beat Glenavon in the quarter-final at Milltown on 2 May and Drogheda United 4-2 on penalties after a 1-1 draw in the semi-final. They played Finn Harps in the final at Milltown on 17 May and a headed goal from Steve Lynex in the second half gave Rovers a 1-0 victory.

The Hoops began the 1978/79 season with a Spanish tour in August 1978. They played four matches, winning two and losing two. They beat Academia of Portugal 1-0 with Ray Treacy scoring the goal, they then lost 3-0 to Burgos and 2-0 to Jerez before completing the tour with a 1-0 win over Salamanca with John Cervi scoring their goal. A number of signings had been made during the close season. John Cervi came from Home Farm and Noel King from Dundalk. Bobby Tambling had a short stay at Rovers during the 1978/79 season and John Osborne was signed with the European matches in mind, as Alan O'Neill had picked up a knee injury in Spain and would not play again for five months.

The Hoops' first competitive game of the season was the President's Cup Final against Bohemians which Bohs won 3-1. The League Cup for season '78/79 was organised on a knockout basis and the Hoops beat St Pat's 1-0 in the first round at Milltown on 3 September with Bobby Tambling scoring the winner. Goals from Jackie Jameson and Larry Murray gave Rovers a 2-1 win over Shelbourne in the second round on 6 September and the Hoops started their League campaign with a home match against Dundalk on 10 September. Dundalk won 2-1 and three days later Rovers played their first European match at Milltown when they played Apoel Nicosia in the first leg of the European Cup Winners' Cup first round. Rovers' line-up on that historic occasion was as follows: Osborne, Gannon, O'Leary, Fullam, Synnott, Dunphy, Giles, King, Cervi, Treacy, Lynex. The Hoops won 2-0, with the goals coming from Johnny Giles just before half-time and from Steve Lynex in the second half. A goal from Steve Lynex gave Rovers a 1-0 win in the second leg.

The Hoops lost 2-0 to Waterford in the League at Kilcohan Park but two goals from Steve Lynex gave Rovers a 2-1 win over Athlone Town at Milltown on 1 October. This was to be Rovers' last win over Athlone Town until Jim McLaughlin's Hoops side beat them 4-0 on 18 March 1984. Rovers' League form became very patchy after that win and in their next six matches they took only five points, losing three matches in a row to Cork Alberts, Drogheda United and Bohemians. Part of Rovers' problem in the League that season was that they never had a settled side: a total of 29 players played for the club in that season's League championship.

Rovers played St Francis in the third round of the Leinster Senior Cup on 11 October. Alan Campbell made his debut for Rovers in this match and scored twice as the Hoops won 5-1. Campbell was also on the mark in the quarter-final against Dunleary Celtic when he scored from a penalty as Rovers won 2-1 to qualify for the semi-final.

The Hoops were drawn against Banik Ostrava in the second round of the European Cup Winners' Cup and the formidable Czech side won both legs of the tie, winning 3-0 in Czechoslovakia and 3-1 at Milltown where Richie Bayly, at sixteen years old, became the youngest player ever to play for the Hoops in a European tie. Eddie Byrne had been signed for the club and he fitted comfortably into a striker's role in the side, especially after Steve Lynex returned to England in December.

Rovers qualified for the League Cup final by beating Sligo Rovers 2-0 on aggregate and their League form improved as they managed to take ten points from six matches before they travelled to take on the leaders Dundalk at Oriel Park on 24 December. Rovers were now five points behind the joint leaders Dundalk and Bohs and they simply had to get a result at Oriel Park to bring themselves back into contention. But they lost 3-2 to Dundalk after playing most of the match with ten men after Ray Treacy had been sent off following an altercation with Dermot Keely. Rovers were ahead until the last eight minutes when Dundalk scored twice to snatch both points and open up a seven point lead on Rovers.

The Hoops dropped out of contention for the League when they lost 2-0 to Athlone Town on 7 January. Eamon Dunphy retired from the game to pursue a career in journalism. Gerry Clarke, Eddie O'Sullivan and Terry Byrne were all tried at full back as Giles strove to find a winning side at Milltown.

Rovers qualified for the final of the Leinster Senior Cup by beating Home Farm 4-1 after extra time in the semi-final on 18 January and also began to show an improvement in the League winning five of their next six matches. Alan O'Neill had returned from injury and he played a splendid game in the first round of the FAI Cup against Shelbourne at Milltown on 11 February where two goals from Eddie Byrne gave Rovers a 2-1 win. They beat Drogheda United 2-1 at Milltown and then they put a severe dent in Bohemians' title challenge by going to Dalymount and winning 1-0 on 25 February, Rovers' first victory over Bohs in ten matches.

The Hoops then proved just how inconsistent they were that

season by losing 2-1 to Thurles Town at Milltown the following Sunday before qualifying for the semi-final of the FAI Cup by beating Limerick 2-0 at Milltown with goals from Eddie Byrne and Robbie Gaffney. The Hoops won three of their remaining four matches in the League to finish in fifth position, eight points behind the winners Dundalk. The top five finished as follows:

	P	W	D	L	F	A	Pts.
Dundalk	30	19	7	4	57	25	45
Bohemians	30	18	7	5	53	21	43
Drogheda United	30	17	6	7	60	40	42*
Waterford	30	17	8	5	48	32	42
Shamrock Rovers	30	17	3	10	45	25	37

* *Two points were awarded to Drogheda United from Finn Harps.*

Bohemians beat Rovers 2-0 in the League Cup final at Dalymount Park on 22 March. The Hoops played Waterford in the semi-final of the FAI Cup at Dalymount Park on 8 April and a late penalty from Syd Wallace gave the Blues a 2-1 win after Johnny Giles had scored Rovers' goal, also from a penalty. Rovers' final competitive match of the season was the Leinster Senior Cup final which was played at Dalymount Park on 11 April and the Hoops lost 2-1 to Bohs with Paul Murphy scoring for Rovers.

During the 1979 close season, Liam Buckley was signed by Rovers from Shelbourne and Paddy Mulligan also joined the club. Johnny Fullam, who had played for the Hoops for eleven seasons over two periods at Milltown, was given a free transfer by Johnny Giles and joined Athlone Town. Johnny Fullam had given the club tremendous service and Giles was perhaps a little hasty in letting Fullam go as his influence over the younger players in the side was enormous and young players were able to develop their game in leaps and bounds when they played alongside Fullam in the Rovers' defence. Ray Treacy had suggested to Johnny Giles at the end of the 1977/78 season that he should buy Dermot Keely, as he was exactly the type of player that the club needed if they were to win the League. Keely was a very good League of Ireland player, who knew how to look after himself on the pitch, and Treacy realised that you needed about two of these players on your side to give you the necessary hard qualities on heavy pitches in the depths of winter. However, Johnny Giles didn't act on Ray Treacy's suggestion. Jim McLaughlin signed Keely instead and Dundalk proceeded to win the double in the 1978/79 season. There was a feeling that Giles probably underestimated the challenge that faced him when he sought to build a side capable of competing regularly in the European Cup and dominating the League of Ireland scene.

All League of Ireland clubs like to put one over on Rovers because for years they were the glamour side in football and clubs invariably got their biggest gate when they played Rovers. The fact that Johnny Giles was now player-manager of the Hoops gave a lot of teams a double incentive to beat Rovers and most Hoops' matches were like Cup finals. Johnny Giles rarely varied his style of play; the Hoops played the same away from home as at Milltown, and as a result Rovers became very predictable. Teams found it easy to play against them. Johnny Fullam stated that in his first match for Athlone Town against Rovers at St Mel's Park he was strolling around the pitch for most of the match as he knew exactly what the Hoops would do when they got the ball and it was very easy to intercept a pass when you knew exactly where it was going.

Rovers began the 1979/80 season with a first round Tyler Cup match against Portadown at Shamrock Park on 4 August. They won 3-1 with Larry Murray, Richie Bayly and Eddie Byrne scoring the goals. Cliftonville came to Milltown on 8 August to play Rovers in the second round of the Tyler Cup and they brought a fair sized support with them. Unfortunately a considerable number of the Cliftonville supporters spent most of the match chanting obscene slogans at Johnny Giles. Giles gave them the perfect answer when he scored the only goal of the game with a shot from outside the penalty area after 88 minutes of play. Rovers played Athlone Town in the semi-final of 12 August but despite another goal from Giles, Athlone Town won 2-1 and went on to beat Drogheda United 4-3 on aggregate in the two-legged final.

The League Cup was organised on a knockout basis and Rovers beat Shelbourne 3-0 in the first round on 26 August at Milltown. The following Sunday, they qualified for the semi-finals of the League Cup when they beat Drogheda United 5-4 on penalties after a 0-0 draw. The Hoops beat Bray Wanderers 2-1 in the Leinster Senior Cup on 5 September but they were sensationally beaten 3-2 by Dunleary Celtic in the quarter-final on 31 October.

The Hoops began their League campaign with a home game against Sligo Rovers on 9 September. University College Dublin (UCD) had been elected to the League to replace Cork Celtic, Cork Alberts changed their name to Cork United and Limerick changed their name to Limerick United. Rovers line-up for their opening League match against Sligo Rovers was as follows: O'Neill, Mulligan, Burke, Synnott, O'Leary, Gannon, Treacy, Gaffney, Meagan, Gavin, Campbell. *Subs*: Byrne, Kavanagh. Johnny Giles had picked up a serious ankle injury and this injury was to keep him out of football for almost a year. Rovers won the match 4-0 with both Robbie Gaffney and Alan Campbell scoring twice for the Hoops. Rovers drew their next three League matches 1-1 against Cork United, Drogheda United and Thurles Town respectively and the Hoops' old failing of not being able to beat teams whom they dominated for most of the match was resurfacing again. Rovers took seven points from their next four matches before they travelled to Oriel Park to take on the reigning champions Dundalk on 11 November.

Dundalk won the match 1-0 with a goal from Pop Flanagan eight minutes from time. That defeat left Rovers three points behind the joint leaders Limerick United and Dundalk after nine series of matches. St Pat's beat them 2-1 in the semi-final of the League Cup on 14 November. Alan Campbell was then brought back into the side and he managed to score in nine of the next ten

League matches. He started his scoring run with the equaliser in the match against Waterford at Milltown on 18 November. Pierce O'Leary scored the winner against Waterford from a penalty after Ray Treacy had been floored with a punch from Tommy Jackson in an off-the-ball incident in the penalty area. Tommy Jackson was shown the red card by the referee as was another Waterford player for persistent arguing after the penalty had been converted by Pierce O'Leary. The League leaders Limerick United came to Milltown the following Sunday and went away with both points following a 2-1 win after an excellent match. Athlone Town trounced the Hoops 4-1 at St Mel's Park on 2 December but then Rovers won their next five League matches. They got six goals on successive Sundays in late December against Sligo Rovers and Cork United.

Rovers' run of five consecutive victories was brought to a halt on 6 January when they drew 1-1 with Drogheda United at United Park. The following Sunday, the Hoops drew 1-1 with Bohemians despite dominating the match for long periods. Alan Campbell gave Rovers the lead in the first half and Pierce O'Leary gave Bohemians an unexpected reprieve when he headed the ball past Alan O'Neill under no pressure whatsoever, late in the second half. The Hoops won their next two League matches against Thurles Town and Galway Rovers before they faced Bohemians in the first round of the FAI Cup at Milltown on 10 February. Kieron Maher had made his debut for Rovers against Galway Rovers on 27 January while Larry Murray and Mark Meagan left Milltown for Waterford. Bohs beat Rovers 2-0 in the Cup at Milltown; they were deserving winners on an afternoon where little went right for the Hoops.

Harry Kenny had played against Bohs in the Cup at right back due to an injury to Paddy Mulligan and had a fine game against Finn Harps the following Sunday as Rovers beat the Donegal side 2-0 with goals from Buckley and Campbell. Paddy Mulligan played his last match for the club against St Pat's at Inchicore on 24 February. He injured his hamstring early in the first half and was substituted, and then took up an offer in Greek football. So another experienced player was lost. Rovers' title challenge fell away in March when they only managed to pick up three points from four matches. The title race was now between Limerick United and Dundalk.

On 7 April 1980, Athlone Town came to play Shamrock Rovers at Milltown. In the Athlone Town line-up that day was Johnny Fullam who had played for Rovers for eleven seasons. This was Johnny's last season in football and the Rovers' match was his last appearance in Dublin. Both the Shamrock Rovers and Athlone Town teams lined up to applaud Johnny Fullam on to the pitch for his last competitive game in Dublin. Louis Kilcoyne presented him with a bouquet of flowers on the half-way line. A bouquet of flowers was a most unusual presentation to give to a footballer at the best of times, but this was no ordinary bouquet. They were in fact plastic flowers which had been hurriedly taken from a vase in the office at Milltown! Clearly, it had not occurred to anyone to organise a proper presentation, so the plastic flowers were resorted to in order to hide Rovers' embarrassment. Johnny gave the 'bouquet' to his wife who had come to see her husband's last game in Dublin. Incredibly, the 'flowers' were then taken back from Johnny's wife and returned to the vase from which they had been removed shortly before. It was a strange way to bid farewell to one of the greatest players ever to wear the Shamrock Rovers' jersey. In May 1991, Ciaran Byrne the chairman of the Shamrock Rovers Supporters' Club, presented Johnny Fullam with the Supporters' Club's 'Hall of Fame Award'. Johnny Fullam was the fifth winner of this award and it was a fitting tribute to a player who had given magnificent service both to Shamrock Rovers and Irish football. His contribution to the game certainly warranted more than the temporary loan of a bouquet of plastic flowers.

Athlone Town beat Rovers 1-0 in that match and six days later the Hoops took on UCD in their last home League match of the season. Alan Campbell went into the UCD match as joint top scorer on 18 goals with Tony Morris of Limerick. The *Soccer Reporter* magazine had offered a prize of £1,000 to the first player to score 20 goals that season and as Limerick, who were League leaders at the time, were playing Home Farm at the Market's Field it was felt that Tony Morris might score a few. Rovers beat UCD 7-1 at Milltown and Limerick beat Home Farm 4-0 at the Market's Field. Alan Campbell managed to score four against UCD while Tony Morris failed to score at all for Limerick. Alan Campbell checked the time of his second goal against UCD with referee John Carpenter - he was taking no chances whatsoever - but as it turned out he won the award comfortably.

The Hoops lost their final game of the season when Home Farm beat them for the first time in a League match, 2-0 at Tolka Park on 16 April. Rovers final League position was fourth, nine points behind the winners Limerick United. The Hoops had drawn ten of their thirty matches in the League and once more this high figure had cost them many vital points. The top four finished as follows:

	P	W	D	L	F	A	Pts.
Limerick United	30	20	7	3	67	24	47
Dundalk	30	20	6	4	59	13	46
Athlone Town	30	16	7	7	60	24	39
Shamrock Rovers	30	14	10	6	61	29	38

Johnny Giles had resigned as manager of the Irish international side in March 1980 and Rovers' supporters naturally hoped that he would now be able to concentrate all his energies on restoring Shamrock Rovers to their former greatness. However, in his latter years at Milltown, Johnny Giles was to spend more and more time with Vancouver Whitecaps in the North American League.

Ray Treacy went to Drogheda United during the close season of 1980 as player-manager. Rovers had some good young prospects in the reserves, and players like Des Kavanagh, Joe Mooney, Mick Savage, Gary Barrett and Jim Beglin were ready to stake a claim for regular first team football. Rovers began the 1980/81 season with a friendly against Southampton at Lansdowne Road on 23 July. Their line-up for that match was as follows: O'Neill, Kenny, Kavanagh, Gannon, Synnott, O'Leary, Maher, Campbell, Buckley, Giles, Bayly. Southampton won 3-1 with Alan Campbell scoring Rovers' goal.

The Hoops' first competitive game of the season was the first round of the Tyler Cup on 26 July when they beat Ballymena 2-0 with goals from Campbell and Maher. The Hoops beat Portadown at Shamrock Park in the second round 1-0 with a goal from Liam Buckley and they played Athlone Town in the semi-final at Milltown on 6 August. This was Rovers first home match of the season and the pitch was in an immaculate condition. Johnny Giles had insisted when he took over at Rovers that the condition of the pitch would have to be improved dramatically so that good football could be played on it. The Kilcoyne brothers saw to it that the pitch was the finest in Ireland and the groundsman Matt O'Toole did an excellent job in producing an almost carpet like surface at Glenmalure Park. It was a pity that only a few clubs followed Rovers' example of getting the playing pitch right, as far too often players were expected to play on pitches that were more like ploughed fields than football pitches.

Athlone Town beat the Hoops 2-0 in the semi-final of the Tyler Cup and the midlanders were beaten by Linfield 2-1 on aggregate in the final. Shelbourne shocked Rovers with a goal in extra time to beat the Hoops 1-0 in the first round of the League Cup at Milltown on 24 August. A goal from Liam Buckley gave the Hoops a 1-0 victory over Cherrywood in the Leinster Senior Cup on 28 August before Rovers travelled to Sligo on 7 September to begin their League campaign. The Hoops won this match 3-0 with the goals coming from Liam Buckley (2) and Alan Campbell. Rovers won their first home League match 2-0 against Cork United.

Rovers beat AIB 2-1 in the quarter-final of the Leinster Senior Cup but they were beaten 3-2 in the semi-final by UCD. The students went on to win the trophy by beating St Pat's 2-1 in the final. Rovers lost their first League game of the season when they were beaten 2-0 by Drogheda at United Park on 21 September. They then drew 2-2 with Bohs at Milltown on 28 September after being two goals ahead at half-time. Cathal Muckian was signed for the club and he made his debut in the Drogheda match on 21 September. The Hoops beat Thurles Town 3-2 on 5 October but their inconsistency was there for all to see when they were beaten 2-1 by Galway Rovers at Milltown on 12 October. Alan O'Neill injured his knee in this match and missed the next five months of the season.

Dave Henderson took over in goal and Rovers won their next two League matches against Shelbourne and Finn Harps.

Rovers' championship hopes were in tatters by the end of November when they were nine points behind the leaders Limerick Utd after thirteen matches. November was a very bad month, producing only one victory out of five games.

Johnny Giles played his last match for Shamrock Rovers in a dreadfully boring 0-0 draw with UCD at Milltown on 14 December. Rovers' form continued to fluctuate as they took four points from their next four League matches. They were drawn away to Waterford in the first round of the Cup on 8 February and their form in the three weeks prior to that Cup tie was encouraging as they recorded victories over Thurles Town, Galway Rovers and Shelbourne. Their season was effectively ended when the Blues beat them 2-1 after an excellent Cup tie.

The Hoops were now just playing out the season from a mid table position and they gave runs in the first team to a number of promising young players. Dave 'Dotsy' Kelly, Mick Savage and Jim Beglin were three such players, and they benefited from the experience of getting a prolonged run in the first team. Dotsy Kelly scored the winner for Rovers on successive Sundays in March against Waterford and Limerick and the Hoops completed the season with a highly creditable draw against Athlone Town at St Mel's Park and a win over Home Farm at Milltown on 7 April. Athlone Town needed to beat Rovers on 29 March to clinch the title but the young Hoops' side put up a spirited display to snatch a

1-1 draw and delay Athlone's celebrations for a week. Mick Savage scored Rovers' equaliser. Goals from Dotsy Kelly and Paul O'Neill gave the Hoops a 2-0 win over Home Farm in their final game of the season and Rovers finished in fifth place, fifteen points behind Athlone Town. The top five League positions for season 1980/81 were as follows:

	P	W	D	L	F	A	Pts.
Athlone Town	30	23	5	2	67	22	51
Dundalk	30	20	5	5	63	28	45
Limerick United	30	17	7	6	47	25	41
Bohemians	30	10	16	4	38	25	36
Shamrock Rovers	30	14	8	8	37	29	36

During the 1981 close season Rovers signed Derek O'Brien from Bohemians but the side was still young and inexperienced. Francis Burns, the former Manchester United player and Scottish international, was signed later in the season to give the side a badly needed old head who could slow things down in vital matches. Rovers began the 1981/82 season with a friendly against Ards which they won 2-1. Their first competitive game of the season was a League Cup match against St Pat's at Richmond Park. This went into extra time before the Hoops won 3-2 with the goals coming from Liam Buckley (2) and Alan Campbell. Paul McGrath made his debut for St Pat's in this match and he made a big impression with his pace and ability on the ball.

The Hoops beat Railway Union and AIB to qualify for the semi-final of the Leinster Senior Cup. They also qualified for the semi-final of the League Cup when they beat Shels 8-7 on penalties after a 0-0 draw on 5 September. The Hoops began their League campaign on 13 September with a 7-0 win over Thurles Town at Milltown. The goalscorers were Liam Buckley (3) Alan Campbell (2, 1-Penalty) and Gary Barrett (2). For that season the

League of Ireland introduced a new points system for the League. It worked as follows: four points for an away win; three points for a home win; two points for an away draw; and one point for a home draw. The biggest flaw with this system was that an away team could come and put up a blanket defence, get away with a scoreless draw and still get one more point than the home team for their efforts. It also widened the gap considerably between the top and bottom sides in the league.

On 20 September, the Hoops travelled to Dalymount Park to take on Bohs and things looked good for Rovers when Liam Buckley scored within the first half minute of the game. However, Bohs gradually got back into the match and a goal from Jacko McDonagh from a free kick had Bohs level before half-time and they scored twice without reply in the second half to win 3-1. Rovers won their next four matches by the only goal of the game in each case against Drogheda United, Waterford, Sligo Rovers and UCD respectively. In the Sligo Rovers match at Milltown on 11 October, Harry Kenny was most unfortunate to break his leg after a clash with Liam Patton after 88 minutes. Harry was 19 at that time and it was quite possible that he would have gone to have a career in England only for that unlucky break.

The Hoops continued their good form with a 2-0 win away to Home Farm on 23 October and they then beat Limerick 4-0 in the League Cup semi-final at Milltown on 26 October with the goals coming from Buckley, Bayly, Maher and an o.g from Tommy Gaynor. Rovers were then brought back down to earth when Athlone Town, Rovers' bogey side, hammered them 3-0 at Milltown and the Hoops lost for the second successive week in the League when Limerick United beat them 2-1 at the Market's Field on 8 November.

Peter Eccles had taken over the right back position from Harry Kenny and Ronnie Murphy and Derek O'Brien had also established themselves as regulars in the team. Francis Burns was the old head amongst the players and his experience and motivational qualities were a big help to the young Hoops side. Rovers got back on the winning trail in the League when two goals from Alan Campbell gave them a much needed win at Milltown on 15 November, Rovers then qualified for the final of the Leinster Senior Cup when they beat CYM 4-0 in the semi-final at Tolka Park on 17 November with goals from Paul O'Neill (2), Buckley and Campbell from a penalty. Michael Giles, the son of manager Johnny Giles, made his debut for Rovers in this match. Rovers then travelled to Oriel Park and a goal from a great header by Liam Buckley after 66 minutes gave them four precious points. Alan O'Neill was outstanding for the Hoops in this match, making four brilliant saves to foil McConville, Carlyle, Flanagan and Kehoe. He got a standing ovation from the Rovers' fans as he left the pitch after a marvellous display. The Hoops kept up their challenge for the title with three wins on successive Sundays against Cork United, Galway United, who had changed their name from Galway Rovers at the start of the season, and Thurles Town.

Rovers played Athlone Town in the League Cup final at Tolka Park on 1 January and despite dominating the match for the entire first half the Hoops failed to score, missing three good chances. Athlone Town scored from a corner in the second half and they could even afford to miss a penalty just before the end as they held out for a 1-0 win. This was a very disappointing defeat for the Hoops but they failed to beat Athlone Town that season in their four encounters with the midlanders.

Two days later, Rovers played Bohs in a crucial League match at Milltown. Going into that match Bohs had 45 points from 16 matches, Dundalk had 40 points from 15 matches and Rovers had 38 points from 14 matches. A win for Bohs would have put the Phibsboro' side in a commanding position, even though the Hoops still had two games in hand. A very big crowd turned up for the match and things looked bleak for the Hoops when Terry Eviston gave Bohs the lead just before half-time. The referee played three minutes of additional time at the end of the first half and in the third minute of additional time Liam Buckley headed a free kick from Francis Burns past Dermot O'Neill for the equaliser. There had been very little stoppage time in the first half so it seemed strange that the referee played an extra three minutes but Liam Buckley and the Rovers' fans weren't complaining. Alan Campbell scored the winner from a penalty in the second half and the Hoops got a tremendous ovation from the shed as Francis Burns led the team over to acknowledge the great support that the team had got throughout the match.

Bad weather caused the postponement of Rovers' next two League matches and Ray Hankin had been signed from Vancouver Whitecaps for a short spell when Rovers took on Sligo Rovers at the Showgrounds on 24 January. He scored the only goal of this match to give the Hoops yet another 1-0 win.

Rovers lifted their first trophy since winning the FAI Cup in 1978 when they beat Dundalk in the Leinster Senior Cup final at Tolka Park on 27 January. Goals from a penalty by Alan Campbell and from Liam Buckley gave the Hoops a comfortable two-goal interval lead and although Dundalk pulled one back in the second half, Rovers held out. Their line-up for the Leinster Senior Cup final was as follows: O'Neill, Eccles, Murphy, Synnott, Barrett, O'Brien, Stiles, Greenhough, Campbell, Buckley, P. O'Neill. *Subs*: Giles, Gaffney.

Rovers dropped a vital two points at Belfield on 31 January when UCD equalised a goal from Gary Barrett in the last minute. They then faced Drogheda United in the first round of the FAI Cup and it took the Hoops three games before they eventually beat Drogheda United 4-1 in the second replay. The months of February and March 1982 were hugely disappointing ones for Rovers' Cup and League challenges. In those months, they played seven League matches and their record was two wins, two draws and three defeats. They were comprehensively beaten by both Athlone Town on 21 February and St Pat's on 14 March when Paul McGrath had an outstanding game for the Inchicore side and John Cleary grabbed a hat trick. The Hoops were unfortunate to lose in Cork on 28 March when they had seemingly valid claims for a penalty turned down by the referee.

Athlone Town put paid to their Cup hopes when they beat the Hoops 1-0 in the quarter-final at St Mel's Park on 7 March, but

Rovers were unlucky not to have got at least a replay as they dominated the match for long periods and hit the woodwork twice. Dundalk played Rovers in the League at Milltown on 21 March in a match the Hoops simply had to win: they were nine points behind Dundalk even though they still had two games in hand. The match finished in a 1-1 draw with Sean Byrne scoring for Dundalk and Liam Buckley equalising for Rovers with a great header. Alan Campbell sent a penalty wide before Buckley equalised, a penalty miss that proved most costly for the Hoops. At this point, Johnny Giles left for Vancouver to take over the managership of Vancouver Whitecaps in the NASL. This was a pity, for he was leaving Milltown as the season neared its climax and when his shrewd guidance would be most missed.

After the Dundalk match, the Hoops lost to Cork and were now thirteen points behind Dundalk with two games in hand on them but with only six matches left in the League. Rovers then managed to put a good run together and won their last six League matches. They beat Finn Harps on 4 April at Ballybofey 2-0 with the goals coming from Alan Campbell and Paul O'Neill. Shelbourne were then beaten home and away over the Easter weekend and Rovers followed this up with victories at home over Waterford, Galway United and Finn Harps.

Floodlights, which had been sought by the Floodlight Committee and the Development Association for years, finally made their appearance at an exhibition match against the AUL at Milltown on 20 April. Jimmy Keane, currently a director at Shamrock Rovers, had approached the Kilcoynes in 1980 with a view to getting floodlights installed at Milltown. Inflation, which was running at almost 20 per cent in the early 'eighties, meant that they would have to be erected quickly, lest the costs spiral. The Floodlight Committee approached a contractor, Brendan Hall of South East Electric, and were quoted a price of £80,000 to erect floodlights at Milltown. The committee, which was to be superseded by the Development Association, had raised £15,000 in the six to nine months immediately after first seeking permission to install floodlights. The Development Association felt that if the decision wasn't taken there and then to proceed, the costs would increase dramatically and the £15,000 already raised would be wasted.

A deposit of £15,000 was paid to South East Electric with the balance of £65,000 to be paid on completion of the floodlights. The Development Association sought to raise another £15,000 through fund raising efforts and to borrow £50,000 from the bank. The banks were prepared to grant the Shamrock Rovers Development Association, which was a separate body from the club, a loan of £50,000 on the strength of six guarantors: Brian Murphy, Michael Corby and Jimmy Keane who were patrons of the club at that time; Louis and Paddy Kilcoyne, directors; and Jimmy Shiels, general manager.

Having borrowed the £50,000 the Development Association paid this over to the contractor. However, the ESB insisted on a new fuse box going into Milltown as the old one wasn't suitable for the installation of floodlights. Between the new fuse box and VAT and having paid the contractor £80,000 already, the Development Association now had to raise another £13,000. This was paid a year after the floodlights were installed so it meant that the banks were owed more than the £50,000 originally borrowed after the first year of payments on the overdraft. The Development Association had been promised 10 per cent of the gate of floodlight matches but very few such matches were arranged. The only contribution the club made to the cost of erecting the floodlights was £4,000 which they gave to the Development Association from the proceeds of the gate for the Liverpool match on 23 November 1982.

The Development Association worked very hard over the next few years raising funds for the floodlights and they managed to get the figure owed down to just over £24,000 before Rovers left Milltown. When Rovers left Milltown no payments were being made by the Development Association on the overdraft for the lights. The bank relieved Michael Corby, Brian Murphy and Jimmy Keane as personal guarantors for the money borrowed from the bank and the Kilcoyne brothers sold the lights in 1988.

The AUL beat Rovers 2-1 on 20 April and four nights later Rovers took on Finn Harps in their last League match of the season. It was great to see the whole Milltown skyline lit up by the new floodlights and both teams raised their game to give the fans very good entertainment. Rovers went into the match with a two-point lead over Bohemians in third place but Bohs had a match in hand. Rovers beat Finn Harps 3-1 with Liam Buckley scoring twice. Robbie Gaffney scored the other goal with a diving header just after half-time.

That win put Rovers level on top of the table with Dundalk and five points ahead of Bohemians. Bohs had to get at least a draw in Cork in their second last match of the season to deprive Rovers of the UEFA Cup spot but they lost 2-1 and so the Hoops had the runners-up position. Rovers would have qualified for a play-off for the League title with Dundalk had Dundalk lost in Athlone in their last match of the season. Dundalk won 2-1 after being a goal down at half-time and Jim McLaughlin had now steered Dundalk to three League triumphs. The top four League positions were filled as follows:

	P	W	D	L	F	A	Pts.
Dundalk	30	20	6	4	61	24	80
Shamrock Rovers	30	21	3	6	50	23	76
Bohemians	30	17	9	4	50	18	72
Athlone Town	30	18	3	9	70	42	67

Liam Buckley finished as Rovers' top League goalscorer with 21 goals. Rovers had lost the League title by a margin of four points and it was their inexperience that finally told against them. They were a young, fairly lightweight side and they needed a couple of more experienced players to bolster their challenge for honours. To this end, in the close season of 1982, the Hoops signed Jacko McDonagh from Bohemians, Denis Clarke from

Athlone Town and Tommy Gaynor from Limerick. Gerry McGowan also signed; Kieran Maher and Dave Henderson went to St Pat's, and Richie Bayly went to Drogheda.

Rovers' first match of the 1982/83 season was a friendly against Ards on 7 August at Milltown. Rovers won 3-0 with the goals coming from Gaynor, Buckley and O'Brien. Their line-up was as follows: O'Neill, Synnott, Beglin, O'Brien, McDonagh, Murphy, Campbell, Gaffney, Buckley, Clarke, Gaynor. Rovers then signed former goalkeeper Mick Smyth in August 1982 and defeated Newry Town 1-0 in another pre-season friendly. Their first competitive match of the season was a Leinster Senior Cup tie against Bluebell United on 28 August which they won 4-0 with goals from Campbell (2 - 1 penalty), Buckley and Gaynor; they qualified for the semi-final when they beat Shelbourne with a goal from Liam Buckley at Milltown on 4 September. The League Cup was organised into four groups of four with the winners from each group qualifying for the semi-finals. Rovers were drawn in Section A with Bohs, St Pat's and UCD. They drew 0-0 with St Pat's, lost to Bohs 2-1 at Milltown on 17 September (Bohs' last win at Milltown) and beat UCD 7-3 at Milltown on 25 September. St Pat's qualified from the section and were beaten in the semi-final by Dundalk who in turn were beaten 2-1 by Athlone Town in the final.

The Hoops had been drawn against Fram Reykjavik of Iceland in the UEFA Cup and the first leg took place in Reykjavik on 22 September. Rovers line-up for the match was: O'Neill, Eccles, Synnott, Murphy, Beglin, Gaffney, McDonagh, Clarke, Campbell, Buckley, Gaynor. *Sub*: O'Carroll for Synnott. Ronnie Murphy scored with a shot from just inside the area mid way through the first half and Alan Campbell put Rovers two up with a close range header just before half-time. Tommy Gaynor sealed victory when he added a third in the last minute. The return leg was played at Milltown eight days later and goals from Gay O'Carroll, Liam Buckley, Jim Beglin and Tommy Gaynor gave Rovers a 7-0 win on aggregate, the highest aggregate win ever by an Irish club in European competition.

The League of Ireland scrapped its multi-point system after just one year and for season 1982/83 they introduced three points for a win and one point for a draw. Rovers began the League season with three successive draws against Sligo Rovers, St Pat's and Shelbourne. Athlone Town, meanwhile, had got off to a flying start and had won their first three matches to leave themselves six points clear of Rovers after only three matches.

The Hoops played Universitatea Craiova of Romania in the second round of the UEFA Cup and the first leg of the tie was played at Milltown on 21 October. The Romanians shocked the Hoops by taking an early lead and although Rovers created two very good chances in the first half, Silviu Lung in the Craiova goal kept his net intact. (Eight years later, Silviu Lung played for the Romanian team against Ireland in Genoa and was the goalkeeper who stood between Ireland and a place in the quarter-finals of the World Cup. He wasn't as successful on that evening as he had been at Milltown.) Craiova scored a second goal in the second half and even though John Stiles, son of former England international Nobby and nephew of Johnny Giles, came on in the second half there was no way through the Romanian defence and they held out for a 2-0 victory.

Three days later, Rovers got their first League win of the season when goals from Buckley (2), Clarke and Campbell gave them a 4-0 victory over Limerick. The Hoops played in the Leinster Senior Cup semi-final against Drogheda United and there was considerable anger amongst Rovers' fans over the team that the club put out that night. The Hoops' line-up was as follows: Smyth, Gaffney, McGowan, O'Callaghan, McDonagh, Moore, Campbell, Gaynor, Breslin, Stiles, Coady. *Subs*: K. Ward for Breslin, Andrews for Gaynor.

Rovers fielded an experimental side minus seven first team regulars and Drogheda United had little difficulty in winning 3-0. Drogheda United were beaten 3-2 by St Pat's in the final. On 31 October, Rovers made the short journey to Belfield where they drew 2-2 with UCD. John Coady, who was making his League debut for Rovers, played up front and scored both goals. The

Hoops then travelled to Craiova for the second leg and were beaten 3-0 to go out on a 5-0 aggregate to the side who got as far as the semi-final stage of the competition that season. Rovers lost to Galway United 2-0 at Milltown on 7 November following their return from Romania and this defeat left the Hoops trailing Athlone Town by eleven points after six matches.

Rovers won their next four League matches, beating Finn Harps, Bohemians, Home Farm and Waterford to begin to make their way up the table. Harry Kenny played his first match for the Hoops in thirteen months when he lined out against Bohs on 19 November. Rovers won this match 3-0 and Jacko McDonagh scored a great goal for the Hoops in the second half. A cause of irritation for Rovers' fans at this time was their side's appearance in an all-white strip at some of their home matches. The Bohs' match was the fourth time that season that Rovers had worn the all-white strip when there was no clash of colours. The fans let their feelings be known but the team still appeared three more times in the all-white strip, much to the annoyance of the supporters.

After the four successive League victories, Rovers then drew their next two matches against Drogheda and Dundalk. They played the runaway League leaders Athlone Town at Milltown on 26 December. Rovers badly needed a win to have any chance of getting back into the League race. Athlone Town had 32 points from 12 matches going into that match with the Hoops 11 points behind them. Noel Larkin gave Athlone Town the lead from a penalty in the first half and Liam Buckley equalised for Rovers early in the second, also from a penalty. Athlone Town were reduced to ten men mid way through the second half but the nearest Rovers came to a winner was when Jim Beglin fired in a great shot which rebounded off the crossbar. The game finished 1-1 and Rovers' chances of the title were now very slim.

Alan Campbell had been transfer listed at his own request in November but a deal with Dundalk fell through at the last minute in December. It was an indication of how things had gone wrong at Milltown that the top scorer of the 1979/80 season now wanted to leave the Hoops. On Sunday, 2 January Rovers played Sligo

Rovers at Milltown and the referee P. J. Walsh from Limerick sent off Graham Fox of Sligo Rovers after 49 seconds for a foul on Liam Buckley. Two more Sligo players were sent off during the match so that the visitors finished with only eight players. Mick Smyth played in goal for Rovers that day and the Hoops won 3-1, with goals from Tommy Gaynor, Liam Buckley from a penalty, and Harry Kenny.

The Hoops showed just how inconsistent they had become when they won two and lost two of their matches in January. After the Sligo Rovers match, Rovers lost 1-0 to St Pat's at Inchicore and then hammered Shelbourne 6-1 at Milltown. However, after that excellent display, Rovers were beaten 2-0 by Limerick at the Market's Field in their next match.

Sean Carroll, who had been secretary of Shamrock Rovers F. C., died in January 1983 after devoting many years of his life to his beloved Hoops. Sean had been instrumental in getting Sean Thomas to take the position of coach at Rovers in 1961 and had given great service to Rovers. It was a terrible pity that he didn't live to see Rovers regain the premier spot in Irish football.

Johnny Giles resigned as manager on Thursday, 3 February 1983. The great experiment of a full-time set-up in the League of Ireland had been abandoned after a couple of years and Giles had ultimately failed in his aim of having a side capable of winning the European Cup by 1985. Many reasons were advanced as to why Giles failed in his aims. Some felt that he underestimated the challenge of the opposition in the League of Ireland. Teams like Dundalk, Bohs, Athlone Town and Limerick proved that in winning the League you needed a side that had a good mixture of youth and experience. In his first season, Giles did have some very experienced players, but his obsession with not losing away from home cost Rovers dearly when a more attacking, cavalier approach might have yielded the Hoops the extra points they needed to win the title.

When the experienced players left, Giles didn't replace them, embarking instead on a full-scale youth policy. He introduced many fine young players to the game and had them playing a neat possession game but they were too light and small for the very physical challenge that the League of Ireland presents. It is one thing to have a young, lightweight team playing attractive football at Milltown in September, but will those same players be still able to produce that type of play at St Mel's Park in December and at the Showgrounds in January? Johnny Giles and the Kilcoynes did great work on the pitch at Milltown but regrettably few clubs did likewise with their pitches. The same can be said for the original full-time set-up at Milltown: if the other clubs had followed Rovers' example maybe it could have worked, but they didn't and the experiment failed.

Noel Campbell had taken over team affairs in March 1982 when Giles left for Vancouver and the Hoops won their last six League matches that year. Rovers played with more adventure and flair under Noel Campbell than was normally the case under Giles. Rovers were too often predictable in the Giles years. Pat Dunne tells a story to illustrate this point. In February 1979, the Hoops played Thurles Town at Milltown and Rovers' attacks in the second half consisted of the ball being played out to the left full, Eddie O'Sullivan, who would then send over a cross for the strikers. The Hoops were attacking into the Gonzaga end and Eddie O'Sullivan was not having a good day with his crosses. Pat Dunne recalled that there was an old man behind him on the terraces who caught more balls in the second half than Pat himself did as Eddie's crosses ended up on the terraces more often than they landed in the penalty area. The point that Pat Dunne was making was that even though Rovers' attacking plan wasn't working, Giles was loathe to change it. In his time as manager of Rovers he rarely made a substitution or changed tactics during a match and it was this failure to change when things weren't going right that made Rovers terribly predictable and very easy to play against.

The Giles experiment while it ultimately ended in failure was a brave new departure on the League of Ireland scene and one in which the Kilcoyne brothers had invested heavily, as they sought to make Rovers the top side in the country. After running the club on a shoestring in the mid 'seventies, turning out virtual schoolboy teams, the Kilcoynes had invested a good deal of money, time and effort since Giles took over and they must have been sorely disappointed when he resigned. The pitch, having been in a disgraceful condition in 1976, was now the best in the country and the facilities at the ground had improved although the toilets and the dressing rooms still left a bit to be desired. The car park which replaced the terracing on the reserved side in 1973 was used as a five-a-side pitch in training and thus the pitch was preserved for match days.

Noel Campbell once again took charge of team affairs when Giles resigned but it remained to be seen whether or not he would be appointed as manager of Shamrock Rovers. The Hoops began the month of February with a 2-0 win over Ringmahon Rangers in the first round of the FAI Cup. Rovers' League form continued to slump and they could only manage one win from their four League matches in February as Galway United, Finn Harps and Bohemians managed to beat them. The season now depended on the Cup but they had no joy in this competition either as a late goal from a Tony Fagan free kick gave Sligo Rovers a 2-1 win in the quarter-final at the Showgrounds on 6 March. Rovers' season was now over but they managed to take seven points from their next three matches as they beat Home Farm and Dundalk and drew with Waterford. The win over Dundalk at Milltown on 27 March was marred by a dreadful leg injury to Noel Synnott who was the victim of a terribly crude tackle from Mick Fairclough.

The Hoops completed their League season in April with two defeats against Athlone Town and Drogheda United. Athlone Town were presented with the League trophy for the second time in three seasons after the Rovers' match and Drogheda United clinched the UEFA Cup spot when a goal from Gerry Martin in the second half gave them a 1-0 win at Milltown on 16 April.

Rovers finished in sixth position in the League, a staggering 27 points behind Athlone Town. The midlanders had a 100 per cent home record. The next best home record was that of fifth placed Shelbourne who took 28 out of the available 39 points. All this meant that Athlone Town had a huge lead over the pursuing clubs. The top six finished as follows:

	P	W	D	L	F	A	Pts.
Athlone Town	26	20	5	1	61	24	65
Drogheda United	26	14	7	5	43	18	49
Dundalk	26	14	6	6	32	17	48
Bohemians	26	13	7	6	42	26	46
Shelbourne	26	13	5	8	50	45	44
Shamrock Rovers	26	10	8	8	39	25	38

Liam Buckley finished as Rovers' top League goalscorer with a total of 11 goals. The Giles era at Rovers was now over. In his six seasons at Milltown, the Hoops won the FAI Cup once in 1978 and the Leinster Senior Cup once in 1982.

THE PATH OF THE CUP 1977-83

The Johnny Giles era at Milltown in 1977/78 began well as he guided the Hoops to victory in the FAI Cup final of 1978. A controversial penalty awarded to Rovers was enough to secure victory against Sligo Rovers. The road to success began on Sunday, 19 February, when Rovers travelled to Ballybofey to take on Finn Harps. The Donegal side were having a very good season and were pushing Bohemians very hard at the top of the League table. The game attracted the biggest crowd of the day. Gate receipts amounted to £1,040, but the tie finished scoreless.

The replay took place on Wednesday, 1 March at Milltown. Charlie Ferry gave Finn Harps the lead with a great rising shot to the roof of the net from just outside the penalty area after 27 minutes. Eamon Dunphy retired injured at half-time. Rovers' performance improved considerably in the second half. They kept up the pressure and got the equaliser after 66 minutes when Mark

Meagan shot home from eight yards. Finn Harps were awarded a penalty after 75 minutes when Johnny Fullam was adjudged to have fouled Jim Smith and Joe Healy scored from the penalty. Rovers laid siege to the Finn Harps goal for the remaining 15 minutes but the Harps goal remained intact and things looked bleak for the Hoops as the game entered its second minute of injury time.

Then Noel Synnott got the ball on the half way line and sent an outswinging cross into the Harps' penalty area. Eddie Mahon, the Harps' goalkeeper, failed to gather it and Ray Treacy dashed in to hit the ball to the net for the equaliser. Treacy then scored the winner in extra time, netting the rebound from close range after Mahon failed to hold a shot from Giles. Rovers' line-up for that dramatic Cup tie was as follows: O'Neill, Gannon, O'Leary, Synnott, Fullam, Dunphy, Giles, Meagan, Murray, Treacy, Lynex. *Sub*: Gaffney for Dunphy.

All roads now led to Oriel Park for the quarter-final tie on Wednesday, 15 March. As in the first game with Finn Harps the game finished scoreless and a second meeting was necessary to settle the tie. Only one goal was required to decide who would go through to the semi-final and that came after 26 minutes from Steve Lynex. He received a pass from Giles in the semi-circle, took off at speed towards goal sending both Tommy McConville and Paddy Dunning the wrong way before sending a great shot to the corner of the net from 25 yards which left Richie Blackmore helpless. It was a goal of real quality and deserved every bit of the rich applause it received.

The semi-final against Waterford attracted a crowd of 18,000 to Dalymount Park on 9 April. Waterford shook Rovers by taking the lead after two minutes through Syd Wallace. An injury to Johnny Matthews early in the first half unhinged Waterford and Rovers began to get on top at midfield. They equalised on the half-hour through Mark Meagan and early in the second half a long range shot from Steve Lynex rebounded off the post and hit Peter Thomas before ending up in the net for a bizarre goal. There was no further scoring: Rovers had qualified for their first FAI Cup final in nine years.

Sligo Rovers qualified for the final by beating St Pat's, Cork Alberts and Drogheda United. This was the second time that the two clubs had met in the final. In 1940 Sligo Rovers lost their second cup final in successive years when the Hoops beat them 3-0. On the day of the big game itself there were few goalscoring chances and controversy raged afterwards regarding the four minutes of extra time which had been added on at the end of the first half by Dublin referee John Carpenter. It was during this period of time added on that the Hoops scored from the penalty spot through Ray Treacy after Sligo Rovers full back Paul Fielding was adjudged to have fouled Steve Lynex. Ironically, Mr Carpenter explained afterwards that he had added on extra time at the end of the first 45 minutes as a result of delays by Shamrock Rovers when taking throw-ins. Ray Treacy had practised taking penalties the day before. Ray normally placed the ball to the 'keeper's right but he spent half an hour at Milltown trying to hit the back stanchion to the 'keeper's left. When he took the penalty on Cup final day he hit the back stanchion to the 'keeper's left while Alan Patterson, the Sligo Rovers goalkeeper, dived to his right. Five of the Hoops' players who played that day were aged thirty or over while another five were under twenty, illustrating the mix of players that Giles had assembled at the club. Johnny Fullam had returned to Rovers from Bohs and by winning another Cup medal he brought his total to eight and thus equalled the personal record of William "Sacky" Glen. It was Rovers 21st FAI Cup triumph.

The Hoops began their defence of the cup in 1979 with a 2-1 win over Shelbourne in the first round at Milltown. Alan O'Neill made a tremendous save from a Liam Buckley shot before Eddie Byrne scored the first of his two goals to give Rovers a half-time lead of a single goal. A superb through ball from Johnny Fullam enabled Eddie Byrne to put Rovers two up early in the second half. Con Martin was sent off and ten-man Shelbourne reduced the arrears when Eric Barber scored late in the game. Limerick were Rovers' opponents in the quarter-final and first half goals from Eddie Byrne and Robbie Gaffney gave Rovers a 2-0 win.

For the second successive year Rovers met Waterford in the

semi-final and Syd Wallace again gave Waterford the lead with an early goal. Rovers equalised from a Johnny Giles penalty after Noel Synnott had been fouled. Then Eddie O'Sullivan was penalised for handling in the dying minutes and Syd Wallace scored from the spot to give Waterford a 2-1 win. Dundalk completed the double by beating Waterford 2-0 in the final. Rovers line-up in the semi-final on 8 April was as follows: O'Neill, Gannon, Fullam, Burke, O'Sullivan, Bayly, Meagan, Byrne, Synnott, Giles, Gaffney.

Rovers were drawn against their arch-rivals Bohemians in the first round of the Cup in 1980. The game was played at Milltown on 10 February and a large crowd of over 6,000 attended the match. Goals from Gino Lawless and Anto Whelan gave Bohs a deserved 2-0 victory. Bohs reached the semi-final where they were beaten by St Pat's who were then beaten by Waterford in the final.

The Hoops also made an early exit from the 1981 competition as Waterford beat them 2-1 in the first round at Kilcohan Park on 8 February. A big crowd paying gate receipts of £3,200 saw Liam Buckley give Rovers a first half lead but two goals in the first ten minutes of the second half from Brian Gardiner and Donie Madden overturned that lead. Waterford went on to reach the semi-final where they were beaten after a replay by Sligo Rovers. Dundalk beat Sligo Rovers 2-0 in the final.

In 1982 it took three games to settle the first round tie between Rovers and Drogheda United. Rovers included in their side the former Leeds striker, Ray Hankin, and Francis Burns who had played with Manchester United in the 'sixties. Hankin scored Rovers' equaliser in the first match with Drogheda United at United Park which finished in a 1-1 draw. The first replay took place at Milltown and the game finished scoreless after extra time. The Hoops had been reduced to ten men in the second half when referee Eamonn Farrell had sent off Michael Giles for an over the ball tackle. Rovers won the second replay 4-1 at United Park on 17 February with the goals coming from Campbell, Buckley (2) and Gaffney.

The Hoops were drawn away to their bogey side that season, Athlone Town, in the quarter-final. A crowd paying gate receipts of £4,500 attended the match at St Mel's Park on 7 March and saw a goal from Frank Devlin after 7 minutes give victory to the midlanders. Rovers were very unlucky not to have forced at least a replay as they hit the woodwork twice and dominated the match for long periods. Athlone Town were beaten after a replay in the semi-final by Limerick who went on to beat Bohemians in the final. Rovers line-up for the quarter-final against Athlone Town was as follows: O'Neill, Eccles, Synnott, Murphy, Beglin, O'Brien, Bayly, Campbell, Buckley, Gaffney, Barrett.

Rovers beat Ringmahon Rangers, the Munster senior League side, 2-0 in the first round of the 1983 cup in a poor game. The goals were scored by Noel Synnott and Alan Campbell, and Liam Buckley missed a penalty. In the quarter-final Rovers were drawn away to Sligo Rovers. The match was played on 6 March and Harry McLoughlin gave Sligo Rovers an early lead. Andy Elliot missed a penalty for Sligo Rovers just before the interval, a miss that appeared costly when Liam Buckley equalised for Rovers in the second half. However, with six minutes remaining, Tony Fagan scored for Sligo Rovers with a long-range free kick and the westerners went on to win the FAI cup by beating Cobh Ramblers in the semi-final after four matches and then Bohemians in the final after a terrific contest. Rovers' line up in the quarter-final was as follows: O'Neill, Eccles, Synnott, McDonagh, Murphy, Giles, Gaffney, Campbell, Buckley, Clarke, O'Carroll. *Sub:* McGowan for Giles.

Rovers' success rate in the FAI Cup during the Giles era had not been high; their record in the Cup during those six seasons was as follows:

	P	W	D	L	F	A
Shamrock Rovers	17	8	4	5	21	16

SPOTLIGHT ON ALAN CAMPBELL

Alan Campbell made his debut for Shamrock Rovers in a Leinster Senior Cup match against St Francis on 11 October 1978, scoring twice as the Hoops won 5-1. He made his League debut against Galway Rovers on 18 March 1979 at Terryland Park and scored one of the goals in the Hoops' 2-0 win. Alan really came to the fore the following season, 1979/80, when he scored ten goals in seven consecutive matches. He finished that season as the League's top scorer with 22 goals, scoring four against UCD at Milltown in April 1980 when the Hoops won 7-1. The Hoops struggled the following season but in 1981/82 they claimed the UEFA Cup spot and Alan Campbell's prolific partnership with Liam Buckley saw many defences breached by Rovers. The 1982/83 season was an unhappy one for Alan as he was placed on the transfer list at his own request and almost departed for Dundalk.

Jim McLaughlin took over as manager of the Hoops in 1983 and he was to transform Alan's career. He restored Alan's confidence and helped him once again to become the most feared striker in the League of Ireland. His tremendous speed tormented many a defence and he finished the 1983/84 season with a League medal and as top scorer with a staggering total of 24 goals from 26 matches.

Alan Campbell left Rovers in the summer of 1984 and signed for Racing Club Santander in Spain. He also played for Logrones before moving on to Belgium and signing for Berchen. He was capped at full international level in 1985 by Eoin Hand and after leaving continental football he joined Scottish side Dundee. Alan spent two seasons there before moving to Forfar Athletic where he is still finding the net.

Alan Campbell was a big favourite with the fans at Milltown and his goals in the 1983/84 season played a major role in the Hoops' League title triumph.

SPOTLIGHT ON ALAN O'NEILL

Alan O'Neill was signed by Rovers' B team manager Shay Noonan from St Malachy's in 1973. Pat Dunne was the regular 'keeper at that time and Alan made his League debut for the Hoops on Sunday, 28 December 1975 when Rovers beat Cork Hibernians 1-0 at Milltown. Sean Thomas was appointed manager of Shamrock Rovers in April 1976 in succession to Mick Meagan and Sean gave Alan an extended run in the first team in the early part of the following season. During this period Rovers won the League Cup for the only time in the club's history when a thirty-yard shot from Mick Leech in the last minute beat Sligo Rovers in the final at Dalymount Park on 6 October 1976.

Pat Dunne recaptured the goalkeeper's jersey shortly after the League Cup final and there was keen competition for the goalkeeping spot between Pat and Alan over the next year. Sean Thomas departed at the end of the 1976/77 season and Johnny Giles returned from England to take over as manager of Rovers. Alan recalled that Giles was always very thorough in his preparation for matches and he learnt an awful lot about the game from Giles. Alan felt that Johnny Giles never got the credit for what he attempted at Rovers, feeling that Giles made a huge contribution to the game of football in Ireland.

Rovers ended a nine-year barren spell in the FAI Cup with their 21st triumph in 1978. Alan recalled that the feeling in the Hoops' dressing room after the match was more one of relief than elation that Rovers had won a trophy in their first season with Giles as manager. Even before they went up to collect the trophy, Giles pointed out to players what had gone wrong on the pitch and Alan felt that this was an example of Giles' professionalism - that even after winning a Cup final he could still point out what needed improving in Rovers' play.

Alan suffered two serious injuries at Rovers which ruled him out of football for just over four months each time. He was injured on a pre-season tour of Spain in August 1978; Dave Henderson took over in goal for Rovers until Alan returned the following January. In October 1980, Alan was in the international panel for a World Cup match against Belgium but a knee injury sustained on the previous Sunday against Galway United ruled him out of football until the following February. O'Neill had a very good season in 1981/82 and his performance against Dundalk at Oriel Park in November 1981 when Rovers won 1-0 was arguably his finest display for the Hoops. Rovers finished second to Dundalk in the League and qualified for the UEFA Cup.

Alan O'Neill played in the UEFA Cup matches against Fram Reykjavik and Universitatea Craiova in the autumn of 1982 and this made up to some degree for the disappointment in missing the European matches in which Rovers had played when he was injured in 1978. Rovers had an unsuccessful season in 1982/83 and Jim McLaughlin was appointed Rovers manager in June 1983. Alan failed to see eye to eye with McLaughlin and this ultimately led to his signing for UCD. Alan's first meeting with Jim McLaughlin was a bit of a disaster: a misunderstanding developed between them, and when Dermot Keely - the newly appointed player manager of UCD - made an approach for Alan, he signed for the Belfield side. A mutual respect later developed between Alan O'Neill and Jim McLaughlin, a fact proved when Jim picked Alan for several inter-League sides when he was manager. Jody Byrne, who replaced Alan at Milltown, became a very good goalkeeper and Alan O'Neill proved both at UCD and later at Dundalk that he was still one of the best goalkeepers in the country.

A lot of Rovers' fans were deeply disappointed to see Alan leaving Milltown and the Hoops' supporters gave him a tremendous reception, one that he will never forget, before the start of the 1984 FAI Cup final when UCD shocked the Hoops by winning 2-1 after a replay. Alan O'Neill played a major role in UCD's win and won the 'Man of the Match' awards in both games despite being hampered by an ankle injury. He went on to sign for Dundalk at the start of the 1985/86 season and won all the domestic honours with the Oriel Park side.

Alan made a major contribution to Shamrock Rovers during the Giles' era. It was unfortunate that he was not still at Rovers when they dominated the League of Ireland in the mid 'eighties.

CHAPTER NINE

THE MCLAUGHLIN ERA

(1 9 8 3 - 8 6)

In May 1983, Noel Campbell was sacked and Jim McLaughlin, the Dundalk manager, was appointed in his place. The 1983 close season was a very busy period for Jim McLaughlin and Shamrock Rovers in the transfer market as McLaughlin sought to strengthen the squad at Milltown.

Jim McLaughlin adopted a different approach to Johnny Giles. McLaughlin had a much greater understanding of the part-time game and of part-time footballers than Giles had. McLaughlin knew that in order for Rovers to challenge for the title he would have to have the nucleus of a very experienced side at Milltown. McLaughlin's critics have always claimed that he is a cheque book manager but the secret of his success has been his ability to buy wisely and his great man management ability which enables him to get the best out of players.

McLaughlin has always operated on the principle that he alone is the boss and his track record in the League of Ireland as a manager is second to none. Jim McLaughlin brought Jody Byrne, the Dundalk reserve goalkeeper, to Milltown. Jim's first meeting with Rovers' 'keeper Alan O'Neill did not go well and O'Neill sought and was granted a transfer which led to him signing for Dermot Keely who had just been appointed manager of UCD. Jim McLaughlin also brought Noel King from Dundalk. Jim and Noel worked very well together at Milltown with King doing the coaching and most of the training as assistant coach and McLaughlin concentrating on the man management side. Mick Neville was signed from Drogheda United and Terry Eviston was signed from Bohemians.

Anto Whelan, who had started his League of Ireland career with Bohemians and had been transferred to Manchester United, returned home and he also signed for Rovers. Liam O'Brien, who also had started his League career with Bohs, signed for Rovers as did Neville Steedman. McLaughlin's best signing was the capture of Pat Byrne from Scottish Premier side Hearts. Pat Byrne became the engine of McLaughlin's team and it is doubtful whether any of the successes under McLaughlin would have been achieved if Pat Byrne had not been guiding the Hoops' midfield. Kevin Brady was also signed from Bohemians. Thus seven of the nine players that McLaughlin brought to Milltown had been on the books of Bohemians at some stage of their careers.

With McLaughlin bringing in nine players it was inevitable that there would be almost as many departures from Milltown. Alan O'Neill and Robbie Gaffney were transferred to UCD, Denis Clarke returned to Athlone Town and both Derek O'Brien and Tommy Gaynor signed for Dundalk. Gerry McGowan left and Michael Giles went to UCD. It was almost like Spaghetti Junction at Milltown with all the comings and goings.

Rovers' first match of the season was a friendly against Newry Town which the Hoops drew 3-3 with Pat Byrne scoring twice and Alan Campbell getting the third. Tommy Gaynor scored twice in a 2-2 draw with Oxford United at Milltown shortly prior to his departure. The Hoops' first competitive game of the season was a Leinster Senior Cup match against Hammond Lane on 24 August which the Hoops won 4-0. The Kilcoyne brothers had now invested a considerable sum of money in new players for the 1983/84 season, although this outlay was offset to some degree by the sale of full back Jim Beglin to Liverpool. Rovers were to receive additional payments when he made a certain number of first team appearances for Liverpool and when he gained an international cap. The signing-on fees that the Kilcoynes were paying for players were sometimes on the high side and it led some Rovers' critics to say that the Hoops were buying up the best available talent in the League. Their point was that large signing-on fees could only be afforded by the bigger clubs and would lead to a situation where only a few clubs could compete realistically in the transfer market. Thus the gap between the top three or four clubs and the rest would widen considerably.

The Dublin City Cup was played under a new format in season 1983/84. The six Dublin clubs, Dundalk and Drogheda United competed in the competition which was played with experimental rules and a shortened playing time. Rovers' first match in this competition was on Friday, 2 September when they beat Shelbourne 1-0 in a torrential downpour. Neville Steedman made his debut for the Hoops in this match when he replaced Anto Whelan after 55 minutes. Steedman had been playing reserve team football for Bohs and Athlone Town and was actually thinking of playing rugby for Old Wesley when he received a letter from Jim McLaughlin. The manager had originally wanted him as cover but such was the impression Steedman made that he became a regular first team player that season. His outstanding play on the right wing contributed enormously to the club's success.

The Hoops beat UCD in a play-off before they went on to beat Dundalk 4-2 on penalties in the final after a 0-0 draw. The League Cup was again organised into four groups of four and, as in the previous season, Rovers were grouped with St Pat's, UCD and Bohs. The Hoops didn't do well in the League Cup, losing to both St Pat's and Bohs and only beating UCD. Jody Byrne struggled in his first few games. His was a difficult task. Replacing a crowd favourite like Alan O'Neill wasn't going to be easy and some fans were not slow to criticise Jody when he made some early blunders. Slowly but surely, however, Jody won the confidence of his defenders and of the fans and the fact the Shamrock Rovers Supporters' Club voted him as their player of the year in 1987 and 1989 says a lot about the respect in which Jody Byrne was held by the Hoops' followers.

A testimonial game was held for Noel Synnott on 21 September when the Hoops beat a League of Ireland selection 5-0. Unfortunately the crowd was very small; Noel Synnott deserved better than that, as he had given great service to the Hoops over a number of seasons. Rovers qualified for the semi-final of the Leinster Senior Cup when they beat Dunleary Celtic 3-0 on 27 September.

Five days later the Hoops began their League campaign with a home match against Drogheda United. Their line-up on that occasion was as follows: J. Byrne, Hyde, Whelan, McDonagh, Eccles, P. Byrne, King, Steedman, Campbell, Buckley, Eviston. Rovers won 2-0 and Liam Buckley scored both goals. What was significant about that line-up was that only four of the team had been regulars the previous season; McLaughlin had brought in the remaining seven. The Hoops scored four times in their next two League matches, away to St Pat's and home to Galway United. Alan Campbell scored in both of those matches; it was a remarkable tribute to McLaughlin's managerial skills that he was able to restore Campbell's confidence considering that Alan had been transfer listed the previous season. The 23-year-old striker rediscovered his scoring touch and was a revelation during the 1983/84 season.

Rovers next travelled to Ballybofey and although they played very well they were caught twice on the break by Harps' veteran striker Brendan Bradley. Jacko McDonagh scored for the Hoops and Declan McIntyre had a great game in the Finn Harps' goal. McLaughlin left Ballybofey that October afternoon knowing that although he had most things right on the pitch, the centre of his defence still needed attention. It wasn't long before he had a remedy for that problem.

The Hoops travelled next to Dundalk and a goal from Alan Campbell gave them a 1-0 win; then a last minute equaliser from John Reynor gave Bohs a 1-1 draw at Milltown and three nights later the Phibsboro' club beat Rovers 3-2 at Tolka Park in the semi-final of the Leinster Senior Cup after a very good match. The Hoops had wins over Waterford and Home Farm in the League before Jim McLaughlin made one of his most important signings as Rovers' manager when he persuaded the UCD player-manager, Dermot Keely, to sign for the Hoops. McLaughlin's team was now complete. Keely made his debut for Rovers against Athlone Town in a 1-1 draw with Liam Buckley scoring for the Hoops. They had a big 5-0 win the following week against Sligo Rovers at Milltown, with Liam Buckley scoring a hat trick and Alan Campbell scoring twice. The team was now playing very well and it was a nicely balanced side. The centre half partnership of Keely and McDonagh operated well - a combination of a stopper and a ball player. McDonagh's forays up front often gave Rovers an extra attacking option and Keely held the line when McDonagh went forward. The midfield partnership of Pat Byrne and Noel King worked well and Pat Byrne's great ability to deliver the telling pass deep inside the opposition's half made a huge contribution. It has often been said about those years at Milltown that Pat Byrne was the difference between the Hoops winning the League and finishing second or third. He was the engine of that Rovers' team and his willingness to go into the positions where it hurt the opposition led to many goals. Neville Steedman was a revelation on the right wing and his ability to take on and beat defenders before sending over accurate crosses made lots of chances for Buckley and Campbell. Liam O'Brien, Mick Neville and Terry Eviston competed for the other midfield position and all three were given opportunities to play alongside Noel King and Pat Byrne. The competition for places meant that no one could rest on his laurels and as a result the players gave their all on the pitch. Moreover, it was obvious that all the players wanted to play for the club and the manager.

Rovers made the short journey to Harold's Cross on 11 December and Shelbourne won by the odd goal in five after one of the best games in the League of Ireland for years. John Delamere gave Shelbourne a two-goal interval lead after Pat Byrne had missed a penalty when Shelbourne were one up. Noel King pulled one back for Rovers before Mick Byrne scored a terrific goal for Shelbourne. Dermot Keely scored his first goal for Rovers to make it 3-2, but there was no further scoring and Shels held out to win. Neville Steedman had a great game for the Hoops on the wing and the big crowd who paid gate receipts of £3,600 got terrific value for money.

Rovers' final League game of the year was against UCD at Milltown on 18 December and they won it 2-1 with the winner coming from Alan Campbell in the last minute. UCD had a very good defence and they were very hard at times to play against, but the Hoops got the points after falling behind to a goal from Robbie Gaffney in the first half. Rovers now led the League with 18 points from 12 matches, two ahead of Bohs and four ahead of Limerick City who had two games in hand.

Rovers travelled to Limerick on New Year's Day and a goal from Liam Buckley and a penalty save from Jody Byrne gave the Hoops a valuable 1-0 win. Rovers were on top in the month of January. After beating Limerick, they accounted for Drogheda United, Galway United and Finn Harps to consolidate their position on top of the table. Drogheda United had paraded the League Cup, which they had just won before they played the Hoops on 8 January, but goals from Campbell (2), Buckley, King, Steedman, O'Brien and Byrne gave Rovers a 7-0 win. Bohemians then lost at Limerick to slip four points behind the Hoops. Alan Campbell grabbed a hat trick as Rovers beat Finn Harps 5-1 and the partnership of Buckley and Campbell had now scored 13 goals each from Rovers' total of 42 goals in 16 League matches.

The Hoops next travelled to St Mel's Park and beat non-League St Mary's 3-0 in the first round of the Cup. Rovers were then involved in an extraordinary match with Dundalk at Milltown on 12 February. Dundalk took the lead in the first minute. Martin Lawlor was sent off for a second bookable foul on Neville Steedman. Kieron Maher was sent off in the second half and Dundalk were reduced to eight men when the referee sent off Paul McLaughlin for reasons best known to himself. The Dundalk directors left the ground in disgust at this decision but their team fought a great rearguard battle and Noel King only equalised against the eight men with four minutes remaining. Arch rivals Bohemians completed their third victory of the season over Rovers when a last minute header from Paul Doolin gave them a 2-1 win over the Hoops, which reduced Rovers' lead at the top over Bohs to two points with eight matches remaining.

Liam Buckley injured his collar bone in a clash with Tony Dunphy after two minutes of the Rovers and Waterford match on 26 February. Liam O'Brien replaced Buckley and Terry Eviston went into the centre with Alan Campbell. Waterford had two players sent off in the match before Alan Campbell scored two late goals to give the Hoops victory. Three nights later another goal from Alan Campbell gave Rovers a rather fortunate 1-0 win over St Pat's at Milltown and Campbell showed great form when he notched a hat trick against Home Farm on 4 March; the highlight of this match was a spectacular goal from Neville Steedman. The Hoops beat Limerick City by a single goal in a very tight cup tie at the Market's Field before the Hoops gave their best performance of the season at Milltown on 18 March.

Rovers' line-up for that match against Athlone Town was as follows: J. Byrne, Neville, Keely, McDonagh, Coady, O'Brien, P. Byrne, King, Steedman, Campbell, Eviston. *Sub*: Eccles for Eviston. Rovers had not beaten Athlone Town since two goals from Steve Lynex gave them a 2-1 victory over the midlanders at Milltown on 1 October 1978. Athlone Town had then gone fourteen games without defeat against the Hoops, so this match was going to be a real test for Rovers. The Hoops got on top early on and in the first half hour they played some of the best football ever seen at Milltown. Noel King scored the first goal and then Alan Campbell chipped Jim Grace after a neat one-two with Noel King for Rovers' second. In the 25th minute the Hoops scored a spectacular third goal after Coady sent Eviston away on the left; his cross was met by a diving header by Liam O'Brien and the ball flashed into the net past a helpless Jim Grace. Liam O'Brien scored his second and Rovers' fourth goal in the second half when the Hoops could have scored many more as they created and missed numerous chances.

Rovers were eliminated from the Shield by Bohs two nights later when a weakened side was beaten 1-0. The Hoops beat Sligo Rovers 2-0 at the Showgrounds on 25 March with goals from Campbell and Steedman but Liam O'Brien injured his ankle after 18 minutes and was replaced by Pat O'Toole. That ankle injury ruled Liam O'Brien out for the rest of the season and it came at a bad time for him as he was just establishing a regular first team place for himself in the team.

On 1 April 1984, Rovers clinched their first League title in 20 years when they beat Shelbourne 3-1 at Milltown and Limerick City lost 3-0 to Galway United at Terryland Park. Rovers line-up for the Shelbourne match was as follows: J. Byrne, Whelan, Keely, McDonagh, Coady, King, Byrne, Neville, Campbell, Eccles, Eviston. *Sub*: O'Toole for Eccles. Alan Campbell gave the Hoops the lead after two minutes and scored his second after 30 minutes. John Coady sealed victory with a third goal in the second half and though Mullen scored from a penalty for Shelbourne late in the game, the Hoops finished comfortable 3-1 winners. The celebrations that followed lasted long into the night and it seemed even at that early stage that this Rovers team would dominate for a few years to come. The crowds that supported Rovers that season at Milltown were not as big as they should have been, however. With the modern emphasis on participation in sport, many hundreds of would-be Hoops' supporters were playing football on Sundays.

A goal 15 minutes from time by Peter Eccles gave Rovers a 1-1 draw in the semi-final of the FAI Cup against Shelbourne although Paul Newe missed a great chance for Shels in the dying minutes. Liam Buckley, having broken his collar bone six weeks earlier, was now fit to return to action and he was on the bench for the replay. He came on for the injured Peter Eccles and scored the winner after 50 minutes when he flicked a cross from Steedman from the right to the net. Rovers completed their League programme with a draw against Limerick City at Milltown on 15 April and a 2-0 win over UCD at Belfield on 17 April. They were presented with the League trophy after the Limerick City match and in a nice gesture before the match, Billy Lord - then approaching his 94th birthday - led the Hoops on to the pitch. Alan Campbell finished the season as Rovers top League goalscorer with 24 goals and the top four in the League finished as follows:

	P	W	D	L	F	A	Pts.
Shamrock Rovers	26	19	4	3	64	15	42
Bohemians	26	13	10	3	39	20	36
Athlone Town	26	15	4	7	44	28	34
Limerick City	26	13	7	6	38	26	33

Rovers drew 1-1 with Derry City in a friendly at the Brandywell on 21 April and then faced UCD in the final of the FAI Cup on 29 April. The cup final ended in a 0-0 draw and five days later a goal six minutes into injury time from Ken O'Doherty gave UCD a 2-1 win in the replay. In July 1984, the draw for the first round of the European Cup paired Rovers with the Irish League champions Linfield with the first leg taking place at Windsor Park. Jim McLaughlin's worst nightmare had been confirmed as he was manager of Dundalk when they played Linfield in the European Cup in 1979 and the game at Oriel park was played in a terrible atmosphere. The last thing Jim McLaughlin wanted was a repeat of that awful night but it was now staring him in the face. The close season of 1984 had seen the transfer of Rovers' striking duo of Buckley and Campbell to continental clubs. Liam Buckley went to Waregem in Belgium and Alan Campbell to Santander in Spain. The transfer fees involved for the two players were believed to be in the region of £130,000.

The sale of these two fine players left Jim McLaughlin with the problem of finding adequate replacements for them and it took him quite a while to do so. The Hoops' first competitive game of the season was a Leinster Senior Cup tie on 17 August against Hammond Lane and the Hoops won 3-1 with new signing Mick Byrne from Shelbourne getting one of the goals. Rovers beat UCD 3-2 in the President's Cup final at Tolka Park on 22 August; Neville Steedman played a major role in this victory when he took over in goal from the injured Jody Byrne and brought off some fine saves. Liam O'Brien, Terry Eviston and Pat Byrne, from a penalty, scored Rovers' goals in this match. Paul McGee, the much travelled forward, signed for the Hoops in August and made his debut against Home Farm in the League Cup on 29 August. Paul McGee scored twice on his debut as Rovers won 4-2 with the other goals coming from Liam O'Brien and Pat Byrne. Rovers were in a group of four in the League Cup with Shelbourne, UCD and Home Farm. They beat Shelbourne 3-0 and drew 1-1 with UCD to qualify for the semi-finals.

The Hoops began their defence of the League with a match against Bohemians at Dalymount Park on 16 September. Bohs won 2-0, Bohs' seventh match in a row without losing to the Hoops. Little did their supporters realise then that it would take them another six years before they were to celebrate another victory over Rovers. The Hoops travelled to Belfast to take on Linfield in the first leg of the European Cup first round match and got a 0-0 draw but Paul McGee missed a great chance near the finish. Linfield had George Gibson sent off early in the second half and Rovers should have really pushed forward in greater numbers and gone all out for a win. But they were quite content to gain a draw in the hope that they would win the second leg in Dublin. They won their next two matches against Longford Town and Limerick City and then faced Linfield at Milltown on 3 October.

The game took place at 2.30 in the afternoon and strict security measures were taken by the Gardai to prevent a recurrence of the trouble that had flared before, during and after the Bohemians and Rangers match two weeks previously at Dalymount Park. No tickets for the return match had been sent to Linfield and only about 150 Linfield supporters managed to get tickets for the match. David Jeffrey gave Linfield the lead after 28 minutes when Rovers failed to clear a corner: his shot took a deflection in the crowded goalmouth and ended up in the net. Noel King had a headed effort taken off the line by a Linfield defender and John Coady was inches over with a tremendous shot from 35 yards. Bobby Browne replaced Neville Steedman and Peter Eccles replaced Mick Neville as the Hoops fought to get back into the match.

Mid way through the second half, Peter Eccles scored for the Hoops when he headed home a rebound from a fierce shot from Jacko McDonagh which had come back off the underside of the crossbar. Rovers pushed forward in search of the winner and they should have scored with ten minutes remaining when Peter Eccles was waiting at the far post to head a dropping ball to the net, with George Dunlop stranded at the other post, but Liam O'Brien jumped in on top of Peter's shoulders and the chance was lost. Linfield held out and went through on the away goals rule. Rovers had been handicapped by the loss of Mick Byrne but they missed their chance in Belfast and went out of the competition.

There were a few unsavoury incidents after the match but the Gardai intervened quickly and nothing serious happened. The loss to Linfield was a huge disappointment to the Hoops' supporters and was a far greater loss than the defeat by UCD in the FAI Cup final the previous May. Indeed, one black mark Jim McLaughlin's side had was their poor European record. League titles and FAI Cups are one thing but the true measure of a team's quality in Ireland is progress in European club competitions. Teams from Denmark, Sweden and Greece have reached the last four of a European club competition and that is what League of Ireland teams should be aspiring to.

After their European Cup exit, Rovers beat Finn Harps 3-2 at Milltown before they lost their second League game of the season when UCD beat them 1-0 at Belfield. The Hoops then had two wins over Shelbourne in three days at Milltown, in the League and in the quarter-final of the Leinster Senior Cup. They then drew 2-2 with Waterford United on 28 October to leave themselves two points behind the leaders Bohemians after seven series of matches. The Hoops then put a good run of League form together, winning their next seven League matches against Dundalk, Sligo Rovers, Home Farm, Drogheda United, St Pat's, Cork City and Galway United. Jim McLaughlin made one of his most valuable signings when he persuaded Noel Larkin to come out of retirement in November. Big Noel made his debut against Home Farm on 18 November when they regained the lead in the League race by beating Home Farm 2-0 while Bohs were losing 2-1 in Limerick. He then scored on his home debut on 2 December against St Pat's and he was to prove to be a great signing by McLaughlin and a ready replacement for Paul McGee who had departed for Preston North End.

The Hoops qualified for the Leinster Senior Cup final when they beat St Pat's 4-2 on penalties after a 1-1 draw and they consolidated their position at the top of the League on 23 December by drawing away to Athlone Town while Bohs were losing to Finn Harps. A weak Rovers side lost 2-0 to Waterford in the semi-final of the League Cup at Kilcohan Park on 26 December but three days later they ended Bohemians unbeaten run against them with a convincing 2-0 win in the League at Milltown. Goals from Pat Byrne and Noel Larkin gave Rovers victory before a very big crowd and opened up a six point lead over Bohemians at the top of the table. Rovers had now gone nine League matches without conceding a goal but Longford Town gave them a surprise when they opened the scoring in their League match, which was moved to the Longford Rugby club ground because Abbeycarton was unplayable. However, goals from Noel Larkin and Pat Byrne gave the Hoops victory in the second half. Rovers then took part in an indoor football tournament in Berlin and in their next League match Rovers drew 1-1 with Limerick City at Milltown on a pitch that was covered with frost and ice and was positively dangerous in places. The two teams emerged with great credit for being able to play football at all on such a surface and a late equaliser from Liam O'Brien gave the Hoops a 1-1 draw.

Rovers next had two victories over UCD in the League and in the Leinster Senior Cup final at Tolka Park. The League match at Milltown was decided by a back header from Mick Byrne after 54 minutes and two goals from Pat Byrne, one of which was from a penalty, gave Rovers a 2-1 win over the students in the Leinster Senior Cup final. The next match against Shels at Harold's Cross was one of the worst ever played in the League, ending in a 0-0 draw and cheating the spectators of their hard-earned cash.

Rovers then played Bohs in the Cup and the tie went to three matches before the Hoops finally won through on a 1-0 scoreline. Rovers beat Waterford United and Sligo Rovers and drew with Dundalk in the League before Home Farm became the first team to beat them at Milltown in the League since Jim McLaughlin became manager when they beat the Hoops 2-0 on 10 March. The club had gone 24 League matches at home without defeat before the Home Farm match. Rovers returned to winning ways, beating Drogheda United 3-2 in the quarter-final of the FAI Cup on 17 March with two goals from Noel Larkin and the other from Mick Byrne. Then the second League title in a row was clinched with four wins in 17 days over Drogheda United, St Pat's, Finn Harps and Cork City.

Neville Steedman played a vital part in Rovers' victory over Finn Harps. Con McLaughlin gave Harps the lead after 18 minutes and they held out until Steedman equalised after 75 minutes, before setting up the winner for Noel Larkin after 87 minutes. Two days later Rovers made certain of the title with a 3-1 win over Cork City at Milltown. Noel King gave them the lead after 34 minutes and second half goals from Noel Larkin and Mick Byrne sealed victory for the Hoops. The following Friday, 12 April, Rovers played Athlone Town in the FAI Cup semi-final and Neville Steedman was surprisingly dropped from the team. Rovers qualified for the final with a 2-1 win; the goals came from Liam O'Brien and Mick Byrne. Jacko McDonagh missed a penalty in the second half. Rovers completed their League campaign with victories over Athlone Town and Galway United and finished six points ahead of runners-up Bohemians. The top four positions in the League were as follows:

	P	W	D	L	F	A	Pts.
Shamrock Rovers	30	22	5	3	63	21	49
Bohemians	30	19	5	6	57	29	43
Athlone Town	30	17	6	7	54	28	40
UCD	30	12	14	4	41	26	38

Mick Byrne finished the season as Rovers' leading League goalscorer with 12 goals. The Hoops won the FAI Cup for the 22nd time when they beat Galway United 1-0 in the final at Dalymount Park on 28 April. Noel Larkin scored the only goal of the match after 57 minutes.

During the 1985 close season both Noel King and Jacko McDonagh left Rovers and signed for French clubs. Noel King was to return to Ireland in November when he accepted the position as manager of Derry City. There was intense speculation that Pat Byrne was about to sign for Cork City but the deal fell through and Jim McLaughlin's most valuable player remained at Milltown. Paul Doolin came from Bohemians and made a major impact in his first season at Milltown. Fran Hitchcock was signed, but only lasted a few months at Milltown, and Michael O'Connor arrived from Athlone Town. Terry Eviston had signed for Athlone Town during the 1984/85 season. Of the side that won the League in 1985, only two players, Jacko McDonagh and John Coady, were first team players at Milltown before Jim McLaughlin arrived. That gives an indication of how many changes in personnel McLaughlin made in his first two years at Milltown. He never hesitated to make changes if he thought that new players could improve his team.

Billy Lord died in July 1985 and his passing truly marked the end of an era at Milltown. How many times did Hoops' fans see Billy Lord run on to the pitch in his Aran sweater and treat injured Rovers' players? There are numerous stories about his prowess as a masseur and the times when ash from his Woodbine

Action from Rovers versus Bohs at Dalymount, 1956. (Independent Newspapers)

Rovers team, 1958. Back row (l. to r.): Liam Hennessy, Gerry Mackey, Ronnie Nolan, Eamonn Darcy, Paddy Coad, Shay Keogh. Front row (l. to r.): 'Maxie' McCann, Noel Peyton, Hughie Geoghegan, Tommy Hamilton, Liam Tuohy. (Evening Mail)

League and Cup 'double' winners 1963/64. Back row (l. to r.): Billy Lord,
Sean Smyth, Ronnie Nolan, Pat Courtney, Pat Dunne, Eddie Bailham,
Paddy Ambrose, Tommy Farrell, Joe Byrne. Front row (l. to r.):
Jackie Mooney, Johnny Fullam, John Keogh, Liam Tuohy,
Frank O'Neill, Tony Byrne.

Rovers goalkeeper Pat Dunne makes a save during a game at Milltown watched
by Johnny Fullam (on left) and John Keogh. (Irish Press)

1967 FAI Cup final: Frank O'Neill takes on
the St Patrick's defence. (Independent Newspapers)

Action from a Rovers versus Sligo game at Milltown during the mid seventies. (Irish Times)

Peter Eccles scores against Linfield during the European Cup first round, second leg tie at Milltown, October 1984. (Independent Newspapers)

Pat Dunne punches clear from Gerry Ryan and Pat Byrne at Dalymount Park in an FAI Cup game, February 1977.

Team captain John Keogh receives the Cup from Donogh O'Malley TD after the 1967 FAI Cup final against St Pat's. The other Rovers players in the picture are (l. to r.): Johnny Fullam, Pat Courtney, Mick Leech, Paddy Mulligan, Billy Dixon, Mick Kearin, Bobby Gilbert, Frank O'Neill, Tommy Kinsella, Liam Tuohy, Mick Smyth.

Tommy McConville (far left) gets his toe to the ball and shoots for goal against Finn Harps, February 1973. (Irish Times)

Rovers team 1971/72. Back row (l. to r.): Sandy Smith, Jimmy Gregg, Liam Keogh, Pat Dunne, Terry Daly, Eddie Byrne. Front row (l. to r.): Mick Lawlor, Frank O'Neill, Denis Stephens, Mick Leech, Damien Richardson, Eamonn Gregg.

Noel Larkin holds the FAI Cup aloft after victory against Waterford in the 1986 final. Pat Byrne is on the right. (Sportsfile)

Rovers team 1986/87. Back row (l. to r.): Mary O'Connor (physio), Keith Dignam, Mick Neville, Anto Whelan, Kevin Brady, Jody Byrne, Robbie Horgan, Paul Doolin, Brendan Murphy, Derek Rodgers, Paddy Dunning, Dr Ronan O'Callaghan. Front row (l. to r.): Liam Brien, Peter Eccles, John Coady, Dermot Keely, Pat Byrne, Noel Larkin, Harry Kenny, Mick Byrne, Eoin Monaghan, Dinny Lowry. (Sportsfile)

Glenmalure Park - its fate had been decided and soon houses would be
built there.

Mick Byrne (Rovers) and Damien Byrne (St Pat's) challenge for the ball
during the opening game at the RDS on 30 September 1990. (Sportsfile)

Much respected broadcaster and lifelong Rovers supporter Philip Greene
performs the opening of the Programme Shop at the RDS, 10 January 1993.
(John Quirke)

Rovers team, 1988/89. Back row (l. to r.): Howard King, Ricky McEvoy, Paddy Joyce, Jody Byrne, Andy Moore, Barry Murphy, Wayne Cooney. Front row (l. to r.): John McDaid, Stephen Craig, Roddy Collins, Noel King, Harry Kenny, John Mannion. (Peter Hughes)

Opening Day at the RDS, from left: Michael Hyland (President of the FAI), Michael Donnelly (Lord Mayor of Dublin), Brian Lenihan TD (Minister for Defence) and Rovers Chairman John McNamara. (Peter Hughes)

would fall on a player's leg and Billy would rub it into the leg telling him that it would do him no harm at all. Nor, it seems, did it. He was a living legend at Milltown and Glenmalure Park was all the poorer for his departure.

The Hoops first competitive game of the 1985/86 season was the President's Cup final against Bohs at Milltown on 3 September which Rovers won 1-0 after extra time with Mick Byrne getting the winner. Liam O'Brien had missed a penalty after 79 minutes and Rovers had to play with only ten men from mid-way through the second half after Harry Kenny was sent off for a reason that only the referee knew. Prior to the President's Cup final Rovers had been in Portugal and Spain where they gave a good account of themselves. In the tournament in Portugal, Rovers beat Sporting Lisbon 1-0 with a goal from Harry Kenny and the Hoops lost to Benfica on penalties in the final after a 0-0 draw. Rovers then travelled to Santander and participated in their tournament losing their two matches to Santander and Atletico Madrid by 2-0 margins.

The Hoops were in the same group in the League Cup as Dundalk, Drogheda United and Bray Wanderers. They had a poor League Cup campaign, winning only once in six matches as the teams played each other on a home and away basis. They drew once and lost their other four matches in the group and lost all three matches at Milltown. Dundalk qualified from this group and made it to the final where they were beaten 2-0 by Galway United.

The Hoops beat Home Farm and Longford Town in the Leinster Senior Cup before losing to Drogheda United in the semi-final. Rovers were drawn against the Hungarian champions B. P Honved in the European Cup and the first leg took place in Budapest on 18 September: The line-up for that match was as follows: J. Byrne, Kenny, Brady, Keely, Eccles, Coady, Steedman, Larkin, Hitchcock, Doolin, O'Brien. Jody Byrne had an inspired game in goal for Rovers and with 15 minutes to go the Hoops were only a goal down. Fran Hitchcock then missed a great chance to equalise when his goal-bound shot was taken off the line by a Honved defender. Honved scored their second goal in the dying minutes of the match when a shot took a wicked deflection to beat Jody Byrne. Two weeks later, in the second leg at Milltown, Noel Larkin had the ball in the net after 21 minutes but the referee disallowed the goal for offside. Paul Doolin and Kevin Brady went close with long-range shots in the first half before Lajos Detari struck twice in the space of three minutes as the game entered its last quarter to seal the tie for the Hungarians. John Coady pulled a goal back for Rovers when he volleyed a cross from Paul Doolin to the net. However the Hungarians scored their third goal a minute later to finish up 5-1 winners on aggregate.

The Hoops began their defence of the League title on 20 October in Rathbane but they suffered another defeat when Limerick City beat them 3-1 and a lot of people questioned Rovers' ability to complete a record-equalling three League titles in a row. Rovers had now lost five times in domestic competitive matches that season. Rovers' critics were given their answer, however, when the Hoops hammered Bohs 3-0 at Milltown on 27 October. Liam O'Brien scored an amazing goal in the first half when his shot from 35 yards dipped at the last minute and ended up in the top right corner of the net. Rovers took over completely after that and only some good goalkeeping from Dermot O'Neill and poor finishing from the Hoops' forwards prevented a complete rout. Second-half goals from Paul Doolin and Pat Byrne sealed Rovers' victory against the Phibsboro' side.

The Hoops beat UCD 4-1 on 4 November and before their next League match at home to Waterford on 10 November, there was intense speculation that Jim McLaughlin was about to quit the club and take over as manager of Derry City. But Jim decided to stay at Milltown and Noel King returned from France to take over at the Brandywell. Michael O'Connor scored his first goal for the club against Home Farm at Tolka Park on 17 November when the Hoops were a bit fortunate to emerge 3-2 winners, with Noel Larkin scoring the other two goals.

League leaders Galway United came to Milltown on 24 November and departed with a point after a very good match ended in a 2-2 draw. Rovers then won their next five League matches to go two points ahead of Galway United with the Westerners having a game in hand on the Hoops. Rovers had good wins over St Pat's and Athlone Town before an own goal from Dave Connell gave them a 1-0 win over Dundalk who missed a penalty in the second half. Mick Byrne grabbed a hat trick as the Hoops beat Cork City 3-0 and a goal from Neville beat Shelbourne at Milltown on 29 December on a frostbound pitch that should not have been passed fit to play on; the players found it extremely difficult to keep their feet in the treacherous conditions.

A goal in the dying minutes from Noel Larkin at Harold's Cross gave Rovers an equaliser against Shelbourne in their second meeting within a week and the Hoops were very fortunate a week later when an own goal from Alec Ludzic was all that separated them from Limerick City. The Hoops took on Bohs at Dalymount Park the following Sunday and looked up against it after just four minutes when Harry Kenny was shown the red card by referee Paddy Daly. But Rovers battled very well and Liam O'Brien gave them the lead after 49 minutes. The Hoops really had their backs against the wall when Dermot Keely broke his leg after 75 minutes. A reshuffled defence conceded a goal two minutes later to Eugene Davis but the game finished 1-1. Dermot Keely was ruled out for the rest of the season meaning that Mick Neville would now play at the heart of the defence. In fact, he performed superbly in that role for the rest of the campaign.

Rovers had another single goal victory at Milltown on 26 January when Michael O'Connor's score decided the match against UCD. The Hoops began their defence of the FAI Cup with a comprehensive 4-0 win over Home Farm at Milltown on 2 February. Rovers then lost their second League match of the season when Waterford beat them 1-0 at Kilcohan Park but returned to winning ways with another 4-0 win over Home Farm, this time in the League. They qualified for the quarter-final of the Cup when they beat Newcastle United 2-1 at Milltown on 23 February.

Rovers played Arsenal in a friendly at Glenmalure Park on 25

February and the line-up that night was as follows: J. Byrne, Kenny, Coady, Neville, Eccles, P. Byrne, O'Connor, Larkin, Mooney, Doolin, O'Brien. A headed goal by Noel Larkin after 28 minutes gave the Hoops a 1-0 win on a bitterly cold night. Charlie Nicholas hit the post for Arsenal but that was the nearest the Gunners came to scoring. The Hoops were worthy winners on the night. Five days later Rovers travelled to Galway and won 3-1 in a vital League match. First-half goals from Liam O'Brien, Paul Doolin and Harry Kenny put them in a commanding position and although Paul McGee pulled one back late in the game, the Hoops won 3-1 and Galway United had lost their first League match of the season. Galway United then lost to Bohs and Dundalk and Rovers, surprisingly, lost 1-0 at home to St Pat's on 9 March, only their second home League defeat since Jim McLaughlin had taken over.

The Hoops qualified for the two-legged semi-final of the FAI Cup when they beat Bohs 2-1 at Dalymount Park in the quarter-final on 16 March. They then beat Athlone Town 3-2 at St Mel's Park, leaving them to win just one point from their last two League matches to secure their third League title in a row. Dundalk forced Rovers to put the champagne on ice when they won 1-0 at Oriel Park the following week with a late goal from Tom McNulty. Rovers qualified for the FAI Cup final when they beat Cork City 8-3 on aggregate in the two-legged semi-final.

The Hoops now needed that elusive point from their last League match against Cork City at Milltown on 20 April. Their line-up on that Sunday was as follows: J. Byrne, Kenny, Neville, Eccles, Brady, Doolin, P. Byrne, O'Brien, Coady, Larkin, M. Byrne. John Coady gave Rovers the lead mid way through the first half and second-half goals from Paul Doolin and Mick Byrne (2) brought a comfortable 4-0 win and their 13th League championship success. Rovers won the League with two points to spare from Galway United, their narrowest winning margin during their four years as champions. Mick Neville had played a major role in this victory; he had held the defence together after Dermot Keely had broken his leg. He deservedly won the Shamrock Rovers

Supporters' Club player of the year award for 1986. Rovers' final record in the League that season was as follows:

	P	W	D	L	F	A	Pts.
Shamrock Rovers	22	15	3	4	44	17	33

Paul Doolin finished as top League goalscorer with eleven goals.

However, the crowds at Rovers' matches at Milltown for the historic three-in-a-row were disappointing. Home attendances in 1985/86 were down on the previous season, while the crowds in 1984/85 had been slightly down on those for 1983/84. There were quite a few factors in the decline in attendances but one was that many people felt that the League had lost its competitive edge. The Hoops had opened up a gap on the other teams which too many people felt wouldn't be closed - in other words that they had become too good for the rest of the opposition in the League. Hoops teams in the '50s and '60s had competition from the likes of Waterford, Drums, Shelbourne, Cork Celtic, Cork Hibs and Dundalk but the team of the mid '80s was not pushed as hard by their rivals. They won successive League titles with a bit to spare.

Some of Rovers' critics argued at the time that when a Rovers' player was transferred to an English club, Jim McLaughlin then went out and signed the best available player in the League to replace him. Rovers had been offering big signing-on fees to players with the result that they had a near monopoly on the finest talent in the League. From the League winning side of 1986, only three players - Peter Eccles, Harry Kenny and John Coady - were regulars at Milltown before Jim McLaughlin took over. This meant that the Hoops had bought in eight of the eleven players who won the League that season, the criticism was that Rovers bought the League. The critics also argued that Billy Young introduced most of Rovers' team to League of Ireland football only for Jim

McLaughlin to buy them at a later stage and win the major honours with them.

The problem of falling crowds was not addressed by the club during this period of great playing success. There was little in the way of positive marketing or PR. A trophy was never taken to a single southside classroom and the Cup and League trophies never did the rounds of the local pubs. A team can achieve all the success possible on the playing field and still fail as a club, unless it takes itself to the fans and encourages their involvement. On the night that Rovers won the third League title in a row the bar was shut at Milltown shortly after 6 p.m.

The big crowds of the '50s and '60s were a thing of the past. Social values and pastimes had changed. In the old days there weren't many alternatives to a place on the terraces for a match on a Sunday afternoon. Many people now had cars and they had many more choices for their leisure time. Facilities at some grounds had not changed an iota in decades and people were no longer prepared to put up with primitive conditions. Televised matches also put a big hole in League crowds.

The Hoops won the FAI Cup for the 23rd time on 27 April when they beat Waterford United 2-0 in the final at Dalymount Park. On 13 May 1986 Jim McLaughlin left Rovers to accept the post of general manager at Derry City and three days later Dermot Keely was appointed as manager in his place.

The McLaughlin era at Rovers was now over. His time at Milltown was hugely successful. He won the League three times and the FAI Cup twice in the space of three seasons. His only black mark was a poor European record; the loss to Linfield in October 1984 was a major setback. McLaughlin's proven ability to get the best out of players and his astute dealings in the transfer market made him one of the best managers in the League. Alan Campbell and Neville Steedman were transformed players in 1983/84 when they both made huge contributions to Rovers' first League title win in 20 years. Jim McLaughlin must take the lion's share of the credit for the success of those two players that season but it has to be said that he always had the resources available if and when he wanted to strengthen the team.

Rovers' managers like Liam Tuohy and Mick Meagan in the 1970s didn't have such resources and one wonders how they might have got on had there been more money available. However, Jim McLaughlin's record in the League of Ireland speaks for itself and there were many disappointed fans when his departure for Derry was announced.

THE PATH OF THE CUP 1983-86

At the end of the 1982/83 season Johnny Giles had departed for the United States and when Jim McLaughlin took over in 1983/84 he put a side together that was to emulate the great sides of previous eras. With the League title won for the first time in 20 years the question was whether the FAI Cup could be added to secure the double for the 1983/84 season. Many felt that when UCD made it into the final along with Rovers that there would be no stopping the Hoops. How wrong they were proved to be.

The Cup run began with a 3-0 win away to St Mary's of Athlone, with that game being staged at St Mel's Park on 5 February. Rovers' goals were scored by Liam O'Brien, Alan Campbell and Jacko McDonagh from a penalty. This was followed up with a 1-0 win against Limerick City in the quarter-final at a packed Market's Field stadium on 11 March. Terry Eviston got the winner for the Hoops although the goal had some controversy about it, as the throw in which led to the goal should have been awarded to Limerick City.

There had been some trouble between rival fans before the game and this developed more seriously afterwards with serious clashes between the factions. The local Gardaí exonerated Shamrock Rovers for the ugly scenes which took place that day. The Shamrock Rovers' team bus, a Mercedes which had been hired out from PMPA Coaches in Dublin, was attacked when leaving the city and the Hoops' players were forced to lie on the floor to avoid injury. They had to proceed to Portlaoise where they were transferred to a replacement coach. It may have been a long journey home for the team, considering the circumstances, but the road to the Cup final remained hazardous in itself.

There was plenty of drama in the semi-final at Dalymount Park but thankfully it was all confined to the pitch. A crowd of almost 15,000 turned up on Friday, 6 April, to witness a cracking game under lights between Rovers and Shelbourne. Shels had been out of the limelight for some years but under manager Johnny Byrne they were experiencing a revival. Paddy Joyce gave Shels the lead in the first half but Peter Eccles equalised for the Hoops after 75 minutes. The replay was staged the following Wednesday evening at the same venue before a crowd of 10,300 but the fare was not as good as the first game. Liam Buckley scored the only goal of the game after he came on as a substitute for the injured Peter Eccles. Buckley was making his return from an injury which had kept him out of the game for six weeks and his return was greeted loudly by the Hoops' fans as he had always been a big favourite at Milltown.

By winning the League title Rovers had already qualified for Europe so UCD automatically qualified for the Cup Winners' Cup when they overcame Waterford in the other semi-final. The Cup final itself was a boring affair and it ended scoreless. UCD goalkeeper Alan O'Neill had won a winners medal with Rovers in 1978 against Sligo Rovers and his departure from the club upon the arrival of Jim McLaughlin caused consternation amongst the Hoops' supporters. O'Neill played no small part in preventing Rovers from scoring in the drawn game. He was responsible for a particularly good save from Buckley and then another from Alan Campbell late in the game.

In the replay at Tolka Park there was a marked improvement in the standard of play from both sides. After 41 minutes UCD went ahead with the Hoops having enjoyed most of the play up to then. A brilliant run by Joe Hanrahan ended with the Limerickman scoring for the students. Right on the stroke of half time UCD were awarded a penalty after Noel King had fouled John Cullen but Ken O'Doherty had his penalty kick saved by Jody Byrne. Jacko McDonagh equalised for Rovers after the interval, also from the penalty spot after Paddy Dunning had upended Liam Buckley in the box. Neville Steedman missed a great chance for the Hoops in the dying minutes when he shot wide with Alan Campbell unmarked and on his own in the penalty area.

Five minutes of injury time was added on at the end of normal time arising out of an injury to O'Neill after he had saved from Pat Byrne. It was during this period that UCD were awarded a free kick which was taken by Keith Dignam and his floated effort was met by O'Doherty who made amends for his earlier misdemeanour by heading the ball past Jody Byrne for the winner.

The early rounds of 1985 were marked by a dispute between the Professional Footballers Association of Ireland and the FAI over the alleged failure by the parent body to contribute a reasonable sum to a benefit fund for injured players. As a result the RTE cameras were unable to bring highlights of the first round game between Bohemians and Rovers at Dalymount Park on 10 February. Viewers missed nothing worthwhile as the game turned out to be a boring scoreless draw and the tie required two replays before Mick Byrne scored the only goal of the game in the second replay. Later in that game Rovers' goalkeeper, Jody Byrne, brought down Rocky O'Brien in the box but Jackie Jameson had his penalty kick saved by Jody Byrne.

A thrilling quarter-final game between Drogheda United and the Hoops at United Park on St Patrick's Day ended in a 3-2 victory for Rovers. Drogheda United led twice through Paddy Dillon but the Hoops came back twice, first through Mick Byrne and then through Noel Larkin. Larkin then got a second to secure victory for Rovers. The Hoops' second equaliser was one of the quickest goals ever scored as Rovers put together four passes which culminated in Noel Larkin blasting the ball to the net for the equaliser less than eight seconds after the tip-off. The Drogheda United players were stunned with the speed of Rovers reply to their second lead goal and shortly afterwards Noel Larkin struck again to put the Hoops into the semi-final.

Already League champions, Rovers could afford to concentrate solely on their Cup fortunes when they met Athlone Town in the semi-final at Dalymount Park on 12 April. Rovers won 2-1, their goals coming from Liam O'Brien and Mick Byrne. Denis Clarke had equalised for Athlone Town just after Jacko McDonagh had missed a penalty for the Hoops but a few minutes after Clarke's equaliser Mick Byrne scored the winner. History was made when Galway United (formerly Galway Rovers) overcame the challenge of Limerick City in the other semi-final to qualify for their first ever FAI Cup final. The final was televised live and this, combined with dreadful weather conditions, reduced the crowd to an all-time record low of just 7,000. Galway included in their side 18-year-old Johnny Glynn who was to play for Shamrock Rovers two seasons later. Absent from the Galway United side through injury was top scorer Mickey McLoughlin.

The Rovers centre halves Jacko McDonagh and Dermot Keely put up a stern rearguard action which frustrated the Galway forwards. Dennis Bonner and Brian Gardiner did likewise for Galway. John Coady set Noel Larkin up for the only goal of the game in the 57th minute but the outcome could have been different for Galway had their captain, Kevin Cassidy, made the most of a good chance in the second half. He would almost certainly have scored but he hesitated and Mick Neville got back to take it off the line.

The League was won for the third season in a row in 1985/86 and there was now the chance to achieve the 'double double'. Rovers overcame the challenge of Home Farm in the first round of the Cup on 2 February. The Hoops won 4-0 and the goals came from Mick Byrne (2), Peter Eccles and John Coady. Rovers beat Newcastle United 2-1 in the second round on a bitterly cold afternoon at Milltown on 23 February. The first division side from Newcastle West in Co. Limerick held out until the second half when Noel Larkin put Rovers ahead. Liam O'Brien then put the Hoops two up when he hit a great shot to the net from thirty yards, Newcastle United pulled a goal back before the finish but Rovers advanced to play Bohemians in the quarter-final at Dalymount Park on 16 March.

There was some controversy in the quarter-final as Bohs claimed that they should have had a penalty in the first half and they also claimed that the free kick that led to the winning goal should not have been taken as there were two Bohs players lying injured at the time. Noel Larkin put Rovers ahead after 19 minutes when he blasted a cross from Pat Byrne to the roof of the net. Eight minutes later Bohs equalised when, after John Coady had blocked a shot from Eugene Davis, Gino Lawless hit the rebound to the net. Bohs then appealed loudly for a penalty when the ball struck Peter Eccles just before half time but the referee awarded a corner. Ronnie Murphy was sent off after 48 minutes following a trip on Liam O'Brien but Bohs kept battling and came close to scoring twice before Liam O'Brien hit the winner for Rovers. There were two Bohs players on the ground injured when Noel Larkin spotted O'Brien free on the left of the penalty area and he made no mistake with a well-placed shot.

The FAI decided that the semi-finals would be staged on a two legged home-and-away basis and Rovers were drawn against Cork City with the first game at Milltown on 6 April. A crowd paying gate receipts of £6,700 saw the Hoops win convincingly 4-1 with the goals coming from Liam O'Brien, Paul Doolin and Noel Larkin (2). The wisdom of the two-legged arrangement was called into question as a crowd of only 700 turned up to see the second leg at Flower Lodge a week later which Rovers won 4-2 with their goals being scored by Liam O'Brien (2), Mick Byrne and Paul Doolin.

In the final against Waterford United, Rovers took a two-goal lead after just 13 minutes. After seven minutes Pat Byrne took a short corner to Kevin Brady and his shot spun out of Dave Flavin's hands and over the line for the lead for the Hoops. Six minutes later disaster struck the Blues when Noel Synnott, the Waterford United centre half and former Hoops' player, headed a cross into his own net to put Rovers two up. While the Blues came back into the game before the interval Rovers gradually took control and after that the outcome was never in doubt. One Hoops' player who had every reason to be pleased with himself that day was midfielder Paul Doolin who had appeared in the 1982 and 1983 finals with Bohemians but had only two losers' medals to show for his efforts. Now he had Cup and League medals after his first season with the Hoops.

That was Jim McLaughlin's last competitive match as manager of Shamrock Rovers and his record in the FAI Cup in the three seasons he was in charge at Milltown was as follows:

	P	W	D	L	F	A
Shamrock Rovers	18	13	4	1	32	11

SPOTLIGHT ON PAT BYRNE

Pat Byrne began his football career with schoolboy side Rangers before signing for Bohemians. He won League and Cup medals with Bohemians before joining American side Philadelphia Furies in 1978. Pat had spells with Leicester City and Hearts before he signed for Shamrock Rovers in August 1983. Pat Byrne has been described on many occasions as the engine of the Rovers' four-in-a-row side. There is little doubt that he has been far and away the best midfield player in the League of Ireland for the last twenty years. His influence on Jim McLaughlin's team was profound and his ability to make the telling pass deep inside the opposition's half won many a match during his four-year stay at Milltown. Pat Byrne's contribution to the success of Jim McLaughlin's team was enormous. He was the difference between Rovers winning the League and Rovers finishing a few points behind the winners. Pat almost joined Cork City during the 1985 close season and the Rovers' supporters were mightily relieved when the proposed deal fell through as there was no way that the Hoops would have retained the League title without him. Pat was capped against Denmark at Lansdowne Road in November 1985 and he won numerous inter-League honours as well. His ability from dead ball situations was legendary and one free kick that will always live in the memory was that against Bohemians at Milltown on 4 January

1987. Bohs were leading 2-1 with ten minutes remaining when Pat curled a free kick from the left hand edge of the penalty area just inside the top right-hand corner for a marvellous goal. Pat Byrne left the Hoops at the end of the 1987/88 season and became player-manager of Shelbourne. He joined the select band of people who have captained and managed League winning sides when Shelbourne won the League in 1992. Pat Byrne gave outstanding service to Shamrock Rovers during the Hoops' four years at the top and his brilliant midfield play will always be cherished by Rovers' supporters.

SPOTLIGHT ON LIAM BUCKLEY

Liam Buckley began his League of Ireland career with Shelbourne and signed for the Hoops in the 1979 close season. He scored his first goal for the Hoops against Shelbourne at Milltown on 21 October 1979 and he went on to score another seven League goals that season. In 1981/82 Liam Buckley finished the season as Rovers' top scorer with 21 goals and his ability in the air coupled with Alan Campbell's pace caused problems for many defences in the League of Ireland. The 1982/83 season was disappointing for Rovers but Liam's partnership with Alan Campbell really blossomed the following season as the Hoops won their first League title in 20 years. Liam had scored 13 League goals before he broke his collar-bone against Waterford at Milltown on 26 February. He returned to action less than six weeks later and scored the winner in the replay of the FAI Cup semi-final against Shelbourne. The Hoops failed to sparkle in the cup final against UCD and Liam missed out on a Cup winner's medal. Liam was capped at full international level against Poland and Mexico in 1984 and in July 1984 he was transferred to Belgian club Waregem. He was transferred to Racing Club Santander for the 1986/87 season and later moved on to Swiss side Montreaux where he spent two seasons. Liam Buckley signed for the Hoops again in 1989 but a series of unfortunate injuries prevented him from establishing a regular first team place at Rovers. He was released at the end of 1991/92 by Ray Treacy but his ability in the air and his great headed goals will always be remembered by Rovers' fans.

CHAPTER TEN

THE LEAVING
OF MILLTOWN

Dermot Keely was appointed as manager of Shamrock Rovers in succession to Jim McLaughlin in May 1986 and two months later Rovers were drawn against Celtic in the first round of the European Cup. There was much speculation in the media as to whether or not the match would take place at Milltown but Louis Kilcoyne stated that it would, thus ending press speculation about it being moved to Dalymount Park. Rovers had to make some alterations to the stands and to create another exit on the unreserved terrace to comply with the Chief Fire Officer's new safety regulations.

Rovers played a total of eight friendlies in July and August in preparation for the Celtic game on 17 September. They played their first competitive game of the 1986/87 season against Limerick City at Rathbane in the League Cup on 7 September, winning 5-3 after being two goals down at one stage. Four days later they won the President's Cup for the third year in a row when they beat Dundalk by the odd goal in five in the final at Oriel Park.

Rovers' last match before they played Celtic was a League Cup match against Monaghan United at Milltown on 14 September. Harry Kenny got injured early on in this match, adding to the already long list that the Hoops had as they prepared to take on the Scottish champions. They drew 2-2 with Monaghan United, their goals coming from Eoin Monaghan and Mick Byrne who scored from a penalty.

A crowd of just over 20,000 people packed into Glenmalure Park on the night of 17 September for the first leg of the first round European Cup match between Shamrock Rovers and Celtic.

The two teams lined out as follows:

Rovers: J. Byrne, Neville, Brady, Keely, Eccles, P. Byrne, Coady, Larkin, M. Byrne, Doolin, O'Brien.

Celtic: Bonner, W. McStay, McGrain, Aitken, McGugan, Grant, P. McStay, McClair, Johnston, MacLeod, Burns. *Sub:* O'Leary for McGugan (28 mins).

Rovers came close to scoring twice in the first 20 minutes when Bonner made good saves to deny Noel Larkin and Liam O'Brien. McClair hit the upright for Celtic just before half-time when he should really have scored. Mick Byrne, normally very reliable in front of goal, missed two great chances in the second half and Celtic replied with a shot from Johnston which struck the post. Rovers continued to press forward and Bonner did well to save from O'Brien after the Rovers midfielder had been set up by Mick Byrne. Rovers had been the dominant team for most of the match and would not have been flattered with a two goal lead but with seven minutes to go Celtic struck for the winner. A poor corner taken by Rovers was cleared to Peter Grant. Grant moved forward before passing to Murdo McLeod who outpaced the Hoops defence before shooting past Jody Byrne for the only goal of the game. Celtic thus became the last team to beat Shamrock Rovers at Glenmalure Park.

Temporary stands had been erected on the reserve terrace side of Glenmalure Park specially for the Celtic match and the workmen who assembled them were still working on them just a few hours before the game kicked off. The view from the temporary stand was poor and many supporters of both clubs complained bitterly about the poor value they got from buying a temporary stand ticket as most of those people had to stand behind the goals to get a decent view of the match. The atmosphere inside the ground was electric and Rovers were unfortunate not to get at least a draw. The pitch was like a billiard table and it was tragic that this was the last European club match ever to be played at Glenmalure Park. Both sets of supporters enjoyed the occasion and Milltown was a sight to behold on that balmy September evening.

The Hoops were ravaged by injuries for the second leg at

Parkhead but they still fielded the same side that started the first leg, but on this occasion Eoin Monaghan and Anto Whelan, who had been signed from Cork City, replaced Pat Byrne and Liam O'Brien during the match. Celtic performed much better at home but Mick Byrne missed a great chance to level the tie after only 20 minutes. Packie Bonner fumbled a cross from Liam O'Brien but Mick Byrne struck the shot from four yards off the goalkeeper and over the crossbar. Mick Byrne missed another great chance after 54 minutes when Coady and Doolin combined well after a bad error from Aitken to set up Mick Byrne, but with only Bonner to beat from close range Byrne saw his shot turned round the post by the Celtic 'keeper.

Mo Johnston opened the scoring after 28 minutes when he was on hand to finish off a good run and cross from McInally. After 60 minutes, Johnston completed the scoring when he met a cross from Willie McStay with a looping header which gave Jody Byrne no chance. Byrne performed very well in goal for Rovers and the injury-hit Hoops' side were by no means disgraced by the final score. About 400 Rovers' fans made the trip to Parkhead and enjoyed themselves thoroughly. After the game they swapped hats, scarves and badges with the Celtic supporters.

Dermot Keely, Rovers' player-manager, when interviewed for this book about the Celtic matches a few years after they had taken place, said:

'The first game was a disappointing outcome but it was a great occasion at a packed Glenmalure Park. There was something special about Milltown on European Cup nights. An immaculate pitch as green as green can be, beautifully lit up and a special stand for the Celtic game. With the crowd that was packed in for that game it really felt as if there was a 100,000 people there. It was fantastic. We played out of our skins and we should have beaten Celtic. We got caught with a sucker punch with only a few minutes to go. I had a cartilage injury myself and I still think that had I been fully fit I would have been able to prevent the goal but even at that stage with just minutes to go we had ten men up in their box, that's how much we were on top and they were a relieved side after they had scored.

'We should have won it. I don't think we would have been flattered to have won 2-0 that night. That would have set up a big confrontation at Parkhead. I suppose that on the night we just felt we were going to win. When you think of a League of Ireland team being that confident and having a side like Celtic under the sort of pressure that they were, and yet we really had no thoughts about it. In hindsight it was a bit rash, unlike me really. Normally I would stay back and I would have killed the game at that stage. If we had tried to settle for a 0-0 draw then you could say that there would have been no emotion in the game but that is the difference when you are out there. We felt it was there and had we scored we would have been heroes.

'On the evening of the first leg at Milltown the team met at the Deerpark Inn in Clonskeagh and we had a cup of tea there. We organised it that way just so that the players would have no problem in getting up to the ground. The place was packed and everything was cordoned off.

'It was super arriving at the ground in a coach with the Gardaí outriders escorting us with their blue lights flashing, it all added to the occasion. Pat Byrne was injured, Liam O'Brien was injured, I played with a cartilage, got it out after the first leg and then played in the second leg at Parkhead. I still have the damage which was done then. It was a crazy thing to do but the adrenaline was going then. We struggled badly with injuries for the second leg. You could not afford to lose players like Pat Byrne or Liam O'Brien and survive. We would have struggled in the League of Ireland in a situation like that and with a side like Celtic we were really up against it.

'At Parkhead we missed a great chance early on when Packie Bonner made a superb save from Mick Byrne; that would have made it 1-1 on aggregate at that stage and it would have frightened them but they came down and Mo Johnston got a good goal and a second one and for us it was all over. The crowd were great. We did not feel as though we had lost; they cheered us throughout the whole game and they would not let us leave the pitch at the end. If we had had a full team in the second leg we would have had a real go at it. We went out very weakly in the end for after we lost two good players we just had not got the necessary talent left to do the job.'

Liam O'Brien was transferred to Manchester United after the Celtic match in Glasgow and he watched Rovers' League Cup tie at Milltown on 5 October against Limerick City from the stand. Rovers had signed the former UCD players Keith Dignam and Brendan Murphy, and Dignam scored twice on his debut for Rovers as the Hoops came from behind twice to win 3-2. They qualified for the League Cup semi-final by collecting nine points from six matches and began their bid for a record-breaking forth League title in a row with a 2-1 win over Limerick City at Milltown on 19 October, with Mick Byrne and Noel Larkin scoring their goals.

The Hoops played five League matches in November and took eight points from those matches beating Athlone Town, Bray Wanderers and Galway United and drawing with both Waterford and St Pat's. The victory over Bray Wanderers was very satisfying for Hoops fans as it made amends for the drubbing the Hoops had taken at the Carlisle grounds a month earlier in the Leinster Senior Cup quarter-final.

Six Rovers players played on the Irish Olympic side that lost 2-1 to Hungary at Milltown that month. Mick Byrne gave Ireland the lead just after half-time but the Magyars hit back to score twice and snatch a win before the finish. John Coady had a very good match at left back and it was on the basis of this display that John Hollins, the Chelsea manager, signed him for the London club a month later. Rovers were now joint leaders of the League with Waterford United and the two clubs played a thrilling League Cup semi-final at Kilcohan Park on 27 November when the match finished in a 3-3 draw with the Hoops coming back from two goals and one man down to level things in the second half. Waterford were 3-1 up at half-time having been completely on top in the first half and when Paul Doolin was ordered off on the stroke of half-time things looked bleak for the Hoops.

In the second half Rovers attacked Waterford from the start and goals from Noel Larkin and Peter Eccles made it 3-3 and just before the end of the match Jody Byrne made a tremendous tip over save to deny Waterford United the winner. The Hoops won the replay 2-0 at Milltown on 3 December with goals from Mick Byrne and John Coady. The following Sunday, Rovers took Dundalk to the cleaners as they hammered the lilywhites 5-0 with goals from Mick Byrne (2), Pat Byrne (2) and Peter Eccles. The scoreline was very harsh on Dundalk as the Hoops led 2-0 at half-time despite Dundalk having had most of the play in the opening half. Dundalk gave as good as they got in the second half but Rovers finishing was deadly that day. John Coady was transferred to Chelsea that month and Keely had problems filling his position on the left side of midfield: both Brendan Murphy and John Glynn were tried without success in that position. Brendan Murphy eventually made it his own as he gradually came to grips with the task.

The Hoops beat Sligo Rovers and Home Farm in the League before they then drew with arch rivals Bohemians at Dalymount Park on 28 December in the first of their back-to-back League meetings with the Phibsboro' club. Rovers lost the League Cup final to Dundalk on 1 January at Dalymount Park with Dundalk's goal coming from a controversial penalty awarded by referee Pat Kelly. Three days later Rovers took on Bohemians at Milltown in the League with the following line-up: J. Byrne, Kenny, Keely, Eccles, Brady, Doolin, P. Byrne, Neville, Glynn, Larkin, M. Byrne. *Sub*: Murphy for Glynn (73 mins). Bohs took the lead after eight minutes when Jackie Jameson scored and even though Noel Larkin equalised from a corner after 26 minutes, Bohs regained the lead when a cross from Noel Reid cannoned off Peter Eccles and ended up in the net after 64 minutes. Dermot O'Neill made a great save to deny Mick Byrne after 77 minutes and Bohemians appeared to have weathered the storm as the game entered its final ten minutes. Barry Murphy was penalised for a foul on Noel Larkin and Pat Byrne curled a superb free kick in to the top right hand corner of the net. Two minutes later, disaster struck Bohs when Brendan Murphy was fouled 25 yards out and Pat Byrne rolled the free kick to Mick Neville who hit a great shot to the bottom left-hand corner of the net. There wasn't enough time for Bohs to grab an equaliser and they were fairly shattered at the final whistle.

Rovers had now opened up a three point lead on Waterford United who were beaten by Dundalk at Kilcohan Park that day. The Hoops were now odds-on favourites to win the League for the fourth year in a row.

Rovers won their next three League matches against Limerick City, Cork City and Athlone Town and began their defence of the FAI Cup with a convincing 6-0 win over Tullamore at Milltown on 30 January. They then beat Bray Wanderers and Waterford United in the League at Milltown; the win over the Blues virtually sealed the League. Their good form continued with wins over St Patrick's Athletic in the League at Inchicore and over Limerick City in the second round of the Cup at Rathbane. The Hoops clinched their 14th League title when they beat Galway United 3-1 at Milltown on 8 March with goals from Mick Byrne, Brendan Murphy and Paul Doolin. The Hoops then made the short journey to Inchicore and drew 0-0 with St Pat's in the quarter-final of the Cup. On 18 March, goals from Noel Larkin and Mick Byrne gave them a 2-1 win over Manchester United at Milltown. It was the Hoops' second victory over United that season and even a change in the managership at Old Trafford couldn't alter the fact that United still couldn't beat the Hoops at Milltown.

Although the title was safely won, there were still three matches left in the League. The Hoops suffered their first League defeat at Oriel Park on 22 March when two goals from Terry Eviston gave victory to the home side. In an interview with the authors of this book in 1992 Dermot Keely said: 'My one regret of that season is that we didn't finish unbeaten in the League. I would have liked that because people had said that after the departure of Jim McLaughlin the team was gone. We were very determined as a team as I was as manager to show people that we could go on winning Leagues and Cups at Milltown. The team got better and better throughout the season and they were practically unbeatable.'

The Hoops qualified for the semi-final of the FAI Cup when a great goal from Mick Byrne in the second half gave them victory over St Pat's in the quarter-final replay at Milltown on 25 March.

Two days later, the following headline appeared in the *Evening Herald*: 'Rovers deny move to share Tolka'. An article written by Karl MacGinty speculated that Rovers were having talks with Home Farm with a view to sharing Tolka Park for season 1987/88. When the question was put to both Louis Kilcoyne and Brendan Menton Jnr about the talks, Louis Kilcoyne denied that there had been any talks and Brendan Menton Jnr stated that there had been no official contact between the two clubs. Most Rovers' fans did not believe the article as it seemed incredible to them that the Hoops would leave Milltown. The Hoops beat Sligo Rovers 4-1 in the last League match at Milltown; Paul Doolin (2), Noel Larkin and Keith Dignam were Rovers' goalscorers. The following Sunday, they drew 0-0 with Sligo Rovers at the Showgrounds in the first leg of the FAI Cup semi-final and then on the following Friday morning, 10 April 1987, Charlie Stuart broke the story in the *Irish Press* that stunned Hoops' fans everywhere, 'Goodbye to Milltown'.

Charlie Stuart went on to state in his article that Rovers' ground was to be sold and that the Hoops would be sharing Tolka Park with Home Farm next season. Rovers' fans first reacted with incredulity to the news but once the shock abated their reaction changed to one of deep anger at the prospect of Glenmalure Park being lost to football. Louis Kilcoyne confirmed Charlie Stuart's story and the biggest controversy in Rovers' history had begun. Sean Ryan of the *Sunday Independent* asked if it was 'possible to save this historic ground' and he added 'spare a thought for the loyal supporters of Shamrock Rovers through whose efforts many new facilities, such as floodlights, were provided at the ground. How must they feel at the sudden move to Tolka Park?' Con Houlihan, Sean Kilfeather, Gerry Thornley and Alan Dalton took up the fight for the retention of Glenmalure Park as a soccer ground. However, apart from the above mentioned people, the majority of the soccer writers in Ireland had little to say about it.

Shamrock Rovers and Sligo Rovers played a 1-1 draw in the second leg of the Cup semi-final at Milltown on 14 April. It was to be the last time that the Hoops' first team played at Glenmalure

Park and Mick Byrne scored their last goal at Milltown. The second half was delayed due to an occupation of the pitch by protesting Hoops' fans. The Sligo Rovers fans showed their solidarity by joining in the protest and they led the singing of 'We love you Milltown, we do'. This tremendous gesture by the Sligo Rovers' supporters was deeply appreciated at the time by the followers of Shamrock Rovers.

The demonstration on the pitch, which was called off after Dermot Keely pleaded with the fans, received saturation coverage on TV and in the newspapers and showed that the campaign to save Glenmalure Park had begun. Jimmy Keane, a lifelong Rovers' supporter and patron of the club and member of the Shamrock Rovers Development Association, arranged a meeting with Louis Kilcoyne and Jimmy Sheils, the general manager of the club, for 10.30 the following morning, Monday, 13 April at the Burlington Hotel. Accompanying Jimmy was Ed Kenny, another member of the Shamrock Rovers Development Association, and together they opened up talks with the Kilcoynes.

Jimmy Keane and Ed Kenny tried to persuade Louis Kilcoyne and Jimmy Sheils to postpone the proposed move for a year. Jimmy Keane told them that they would have talks with the Shamrock Rovers' supporters club about raising the extra money that the club needed to run Milltown, but Louis Kilcoyne told them that the move was final. Kilcoyne then agreed to a meeting with the full board of Shamrock Rovers later that day at 5 p.m. in 46, Upper Mount St, which was where Healy Homes Ltd had their offices. At this meeting, Jimmy Keane and Ed Kenny met Paddy Kilcoyne who stated that the reason for leaving Milltown was to safeguard Rovers' future in football. He claimed that the Hoops would get more support at Tolka Park and that the running costs there would be lower. He also said that the final decision had been taken and he refused point blank to postpone the decision for a year.

There was a meeting with the patrons of the club at Milltown that same day at 8 p.m. The meeting had been hastily arranged when the story broke the previous Friday. Paddy Kilcoyne chaired this meeting and he again stated the reasons for moving to Tolka

Park and he outlined the advantages of such a move. Jim Colhoun, a patron of many years standing, said that the proposed move was a disgrace and he attacked it vehemently and at the end of the meeting Jimmy Keane put it to Paddy Kilcoyne that he should accept one of the compromise proposals or else sell the club. These proposals included the possibility of postponing the move for a year while the patrons and supporters' clubs would attempt to raise the finance needed to keep the Hoops at Milltown. Paddy Kilcoyne did not say whether the club was for sale or not but he agreed to meet Jimmy Keane and Ed Kenny again within a week.

In an interview with the authors of this book in 1992 Louis Kilcoyne said the following about the Milltown controversy. 'By the time the fourth League title was won crowds averaged about 1,200.' Exasperated by now, the Kilcoynes decided that after seventeen years with a near perfect success formula and no serious public interest, enough was enough.

'We announced that we would sell Milltown and would transfer the activities of the club to Tolka Park which ironically we had tried to buy in 1972. The two things that attracted us to Tolka were that there was greater support potential for soccer on the northside and secondly it made good economic sense to share the cost of maintaining a stadium with another club. The public which had not supported the Hoops in arguably its most successful period reacted with shock and horror at the thoughts of the one-time mecca of Irish football being closed down. The decision to sell off Glenmalure Park was taken only weeks before the end of the season. I believe that the corporate and business people who have responded to the recent success of the international team under Jack Charlton had no cause to be attracted to soccer in the years preceding that. In point of fact this is evidenced by the fact that only two or three clubs had any serious level of sponsorship.'

The agreement with Home Farm at Tolka Park was long term. The club immediately invested £10,000 in improving the ground.

The Kilcoyne brothers Louis and Paddy, attended a meeting with Joe Veselsky, another Rovers' director, at the Mansion House on Tuesday, 14 April to launch a press conference about 'Tolka Park, a stadium for the future'. Also present were the Mentons representing Home Farm. The Kilcoynes failed to detail any plan for the future of Milltown and they stated that both Shamrock Rovers and Home Farm had set themselves the objective of developing Tolka Park into a modern all-seater stadium worthy of soccer in Dublin in the 1990s. The Kilcoynes stated that they had a two year lease with an option on a further three-year lease agreement. Many Rovers fans were furious with Home Farm FC for offering the Kilcoynes the use of their facilities at Tolka Park.

If the club didn't have the option of moving to Tolka Park it would have been very difficult to find another ground. Later that day, 14 April, the Hoops played their final League game of the season when they beat Home Farm 3-1 at Tolka Park. Rovers finished on 39 points from 22 matches, nine points ahead of Dundalk. The Hoops' complete League record for the season was as follows:

	P	W	D	L	F	A	Pts.
Shamrock Rovers	22	18	3	1	51	16	39

Mick Byrne finished the season as the club's top League scorer with 12 goals. Rovers then beat Sligo Rovers in the Cup semi-final replay at the Showgrounds on 15 April. Noel Larkin scored the winner with a header in the last minute.

Brian Murphy, the chairman of the patrons' committee at Milltown, had been away on business in London and had not been present for the meetings with Paddy and Louis Kilcoyne. Brian Murphy had been informed by Jimmy Keane that the Kilcoynes were not budging an inch from their decision to leave Milltown and so they decided to form a group to oppose the move from Milltown. Jimmy Keane came up with the name KRAM (Keep Rovers at Milltown) and this organisation, along with the

Shamrock Rovers' supporters club, led the campaign to preserve Glenmalure Park as a football ground.

On 26 April, the Hoops completed their third double in a row and their 24th success in the FAI Cup when they beat Dundalk 3-0 in the final at Dalymount Park. The Hoops fans held a protest march to Dalymount Park and they staged another peaceful demonstration on the pitch at half-time. Some of the Dundalk supporters let their club down very badly by throwing stones and bottles at the demonstrators and there were ugly scenes on the terraces before order was restored by the Gardai. Dermot Keely and his team had achieved a historic treble double and it was a terrible pity that the team's great success in April 1987 was overshadowed by the controversial move from Milltown.

Prominent Rovers' patrons and supporters joined KRAM and people such as Jim Colhoun, Des Richardson, Ed Kenny, Gerry Mackey, Gerry Brennan and Liam Christie helped to form the organisation's first committee. Brian Murphy brought in Paul Dillon from Hill & Knowlton, the PR company, and KRAM was launched at the Mansion House on 5 May. Gerry Mackey, the spokesman for KRAM, outlined why the organisation was set up and what their objectives were. KRAM was a club comprising supporters of Shamrock Rovers, football fans and sporting enthusiasts. It had a constitution similar to that of other sports clubs and was formed with the primary objective of keeping Shamrock Rovers at Milltown by acquiring ownership of the club and its grounds at Glenmalure Park.

On 11 May 1987, KRAM launched an appeal for funds to buy the Shamrock Rovers' club and grounds at a meeting at the Clarence Hotel. KRAM had three tiers of membership, ordinary, five-year and life membership which cost £250, £1,000 and £5,000 respectively. Membership entitled members to a stand seat in the patrons' section of the grandstand at Milltown with bar and other facilities if their bid was successful. If their bid was unsuccessful all donations over £20 would be refunded less a pro rata reduction for administration expenses. A total of £68,000 was pledged at that meeting and KRAM continued to raise funds for their bid for

Glenmalure Park. There was widespread media interest in KRAM's proposed bid for Glenmalure Park and there was intense speculation in football circles in Dublin as to whether or not it would be successful. There was a lot of hope and good comradeship amongst the supporters; many believed that KRAM would be able to save Milltown.

However this hope was not universal. On Sunday, 10 May 1987, Eamon Dunphy wrote an article in the *Sunday Independent* called 'Why KRAM's mourning is so irritating'. Eamon Dunphy was well known for his low opinion of the League of Ireland so it was hardly surprising that he was unimpressed by the attempt to save Glenmalure Park. This article, coupled with the fact that Louis Kilcoyne was quoted elsewhere in the same newspaper as saying that the club was not for sale, dismayed a lot of Shamrock Rovers' fans.

KRAM now met with an accountant from Simpson Xavier and, based on the money that had been collected and pledged to KRAM, he was able to put a financial offer together when KRAM met the Kilcoynes on 18 May. The Kilcoynes, for whom Paddy did the talking, were not prepared to postpone the move from Milltown for a year so KRAM made an offer for the club and ground. They made two bids on that night. Their initial figure of £250,000 was refused. The KRAM executive and the accountant then withdrew from the room for a short while before returning with a revised offer of £300,000 for the club and ground. Paddy Kilcoyne first asked how this money would be paid before rejecting it. Jimmy Keane then asked directly what figure Paddy Kilcoyne had in mind and he replied that the ballpark figure was £600,000 to £700,000. Jimmy Keane felt that this was a maximum figure and he believed that Paddy Kilcoyne would probably have done a deal for the club and grounds for a sum in the region of £450,000.

The Kilcoynes had been trying to buy Glenmalure Park since 1980 and the Jesuits finally agreed to sell the ground in the spring of 1984. Protracted negotiations then took place between the Jesuits and the Kilcoynes and a deal was finally agreed in February 1986. At this point, everyone, the Kilcoynes as much as anyone else, believed that Glenmalure Park would always be a football ground. Fourteen months later, however, circumstances had changed.

The Kilcoynes agreed to buy the ground from the Jesuits for £160,000. The first £15,000 was paid in July 1986, the next £15,000 was due in July 1987 and the balance of £130,000 was paid on 23 September 1988. Instead of getting £5,000 rent a year the Jesuits were going to get 32 years' rent in the space of just over two years.

On 12 October 1988, the Kilcoyne brothers put the ground up for sale by public tender. Two brothers from Tyrone bought the property for £925,000 on 29 November 1988. The Jesuits had already received the first payment for Milltown when the story about the club's departure from Milltown broke in April 1987 and once the Jesuits had entered the agreement they were legally obliged to complete it and sell Glenmalure Park to the Kilcoyne brothers even though, as Fr Fergus O'Donoghue S.J. said, they were 'shocked, surprised and saddened' by Rovers' move from Glenmalure Park. He added that if they had known what Milltown's ultimate fate would be 'we would not be in the present agreement'.

The Jesuit community had been very generous to Shamrock Rovers over the years and the rent they received for Milltown was very low. The Kilcoynes paid an annual rent of £5,000 for Glenmalure Park and the lease was up in 1999. The Jesuits didn't raise the rent as they felt that in leasing the ground to Shamrock Rovers, they were providing a social service for the people of Dublin.

On Sunday 24 May 1987 the Shamrock Rovers supporters' club called a meeting at Liberty Hall at which Louis Kilcoyne would be given a chance to state his case about the move from Milltown to Tolka Park. Louis Kilcoyne attended the meeting with Jimmy Sheils, the general manager of Shamrock Rovers and Kilcoyne outlined the reasons for moving to Tolka Park. A question-and-answer session followed after the meeting and the supporters let it be known in no uncertain terms that they would not be going to Rovers' matches in Tolka Park. Louis Kilcoyne pleaded with the fans to support the Hoops at Tolka Park but his appeal didn't go down too well with the people at the meeting. Mr Jimmy Mallon, a Rovers' fan of many years' standing, asked a question about the future of Glenmalure Park. Louis Kilcoyne stated that it would be sold for property development. This was the first time in the whole affair that there was any reference to the development of Glenmalure Park.

The Kilcoynes' position was that they had lost several hundred thousand pounds because of their involvement with Shamrock Rovers. Certainly, investment levels had fluctuated over the years. In the mid 1970s, hardly any money was invested in the team or the pitch, especially in season 1975/76 when Rovers practically had a schoolboy team on the park. But the Kilcoynes invested heavily when Johnny Giles came in 1977 and while the gates were good in Giles's first season, the decrease in support in the following seasons meant that during the Giles' era at Milltown, the Kilcoynes would have been considerably out of pocket for their investment in the club. The full-time experiment at Milltown in the early years of Giles' reign was a brave attempt to improve standards in the League of Ireland. However this experiment failed as very few clubs followed Rovers' lead and it was impossible to play neat possession football on some of the League's most notorious pitches. The full-time experiment was abandoned after two seasons. Johnny Giles resigned as manager of Rovers on 6 February 1983.

The appointment of Jim McLaughlin in 1983 was a master stroke by the Kilcoynes, as his deep understanding of the part-time game brought great success to Shamrock Rovers. The Kilcoynes again invested heavily during the McLaughlin era at Milltown and though the team was very successful it didn't attract the support it deserved. The gates in season 1986/87 were 50 per cent down on those in season 1983/84 when the Hoops won the League for the first time in 20 years. The club did, however, receive some return on their large investment when seven players were sold to English and continental clubs during the 1980s for considerable sums of

money. The club also benefited from the lucrative European Cup
fixture against Celtic as well as friendlies against Arsenal and
Manchester United.

A number of people at the meeting queried the practicality of
moving from Milltown to Tolka Park. Most of them felt that the
running costs at Tolka Park would be as high as they were at
Milltown so why move there at all. The notion of sharing the
ground with Home Farm didn't appeal to many fans as Rovers
would only be tenants of the amateur club who could refuse to
renew the agreement because they no longer wanted the Hoops as
tenants and Rovers would then have to find another ground.
Paddy Kilcoyne stated that there was more support for soccer on
the northside but, as Con Houlihan wrote at the time, you didn't
need mounted police to control the crowds going to watch
Bohemians and Home Farm on the north side of the city. About
30 per cent of Rovers' fans were from the north side but these
people were as vehemently opposed to the move as the Hoops' fans
from the south side were. The greatest opposition of all came from
those Rovers' supporters who had done so much voluntary work
for the club at Milltown. The Floodlight Committee and the
Shamrock Rovers' Development Association had raised the
finance for the floodlights leaving the club needing to find a
residue of only £4,000 to complete their installation at Milltown.

KRAM called a public meeting at Liberty Hall on Tuesday 2
June 1987 to try and get public support for the campaign to save
Glenmalure Park. A number of public representatives from various
political parties attended and pledged their support for the
campaign and members of the KRAM committee stated that they
would fight any planning proposal for Glenmalure Park. The pitch
itself was zoned for recreational amenity including open spaces but
the 1963 Planning Act allowed for an application to change the
permitted use of the property to residential development.

The Shamrock Rovers' supporters' club voted overwhelmingly
to boycott Rovers' matches at Tolka Park and almost all the club's
patrons publicly stated that they would not attend games at Tolka
Park and withdrew their support completely. KRAM had had no

further contact with the Kilcoynes since the rejection of their offer of £300,000 for the club and ground in May and KRAM now felt that the only way to force the Kilcoynes back to the negotiating table was to starve them of finance at Tolka Park. Besides, many Rovers' fans felt that the club had left its supporters when they left Milltown. These fans could not bring themselves to support the Hoops at Tolka Park as they regarded Milltown as Rovers' natural base. To bring the Kilcoynes back to the negotiating table or to force them to sell the club and ground was ultimately KRAM's aim and to be successful in this aim they would have to ensure that the Hoops did not succeed at Tolka Park.

The last competitive match involving a Shamrock Rovers' side at Milltown was the League of Ireland Combination Subsidiary Cup match which was played on 19 May. The Hoops beat Shelbourne 1-0 with a Neville Steedman penalty after 42 minutes. The Hoops' line-up on that day was as follows: Horgan, Toal, Nolan, Matthews, Dunning, Coleman, A. Murphy, Glynn, Kearney, Steedman, Monaghan. *Subs*: B. Murphy, Doolin.

The Hoops went on a pre-season tour in South Korea and performed poorly. KRAM and the Shamrock Rovers' supporters' club held meetings during the close season and the support for the boycott of Tolka Park was very firm amongst the membership of both clubs. Both the supporters' club and KRAM genuinely felt that the move of the Hoops to Tolka Park would damage the club.

Dermot Keely strengthened the Hoops' squad during the close season by signing Damien Byrne, Paul Carlyle and Vinny McCarthy. Robbie Lawlor was also signed and with the clubs now playing each other three times a season instead of twice it was felt by many people that the additional League matches would enhance the Hoops' chances of winning the League title.

Rovers began the 1987/88 season with a friendly against Linfield at Windsor Park which the Belfast club won 2-1. The first competitive match of the season was a Leinster Senior Cup tie on 20 August. Rovers beat Ballyfermot United 3-0 at Richmond Park. The Hoops had been drawn at home for the tie but had conceded home advantage. Consequently, the vast majority of supporters boycotted the match. There were pickets at the match and there was a verbal confrontation between Rovers' manager Dermot Keely and some of the people on picket duty outside the ground.

Dermot Keely recalled:

'The idea of moving from Milltown and going to an all-purpose stadium at Tolka Park is the sort of thing that happens in a lot of European cities where two clubs share a top-class ground and unemotionally that sounded okay to me. But I didn't realise the depth of feeling about Glenmalure Park and all I wanted to do was to win the League for Shamrock Rovers. I now go past Milltown every day and it is a terribly sad sight but at that time I wanted to keep the club going and I felt that if the fans could keep supporting the team at Tolka Park then maybe we could change things at the end of the season. I still object strongly to the tactics used and to the abuse I personally took and my family took, but I can understand the deep feelings that put it there and I was the focal point for a lot of resentment from the fans but all I wanted to do was to keep the club going and win the League for Rovers at Tolka Park.'

The Hoops were drawn with Longford Town, Athlone Town and Shelbourne in the League Cup with the top team from each of the six groups plus the two best losers qualifying for the quarter-finals. The Hoops beat Longford Town 2-0 in their first match and five days later they took on Athlone Town in their first match at Tolka Park. Their line-up for that match was as follows: J. Byrne, Kenny, Lawlor, D. Byrne, Brady, Doolin, P. Byrne, Neville, McCarthy, Larkin, M. Byrne. *Subs*: P. Carlyle for Lawlor, O'Connor for Brady.

The Hoops won the match by 4-1 and the scorers were Noel Larkin (2), Paul Doolin and Paul Carlyle. However the result was not important that night. The real result was at the turnstiles: only a little over 200 people paid gate receipts of £511. The Hoops qualified for the quarter-finals by beating Shelbourne 2-0 in their last group match and they went on to beat Bohs 3-0 in the quarter-final at Tolka Park on 6 September. The crowd for the Bohs' match was very poor: it was the first time for years that there were more Bohs' fans than Rovers' fans at a match between the two clubs. The Hoops began their defence of the League title at Rathbane on 13 September with a comfortable 4-1 win over Limerick City.

Three nights later the Hoops took on Omonia Nicosia in the first leg of the European Cup first round match at Tolka Park. This was going to be a real test of the effectiveness of the boycott and the night turned out to be a disaster for the Kilcoynes. A total of 2,489 people paying gate receipts of £4,805 went into Tolka Park that night, the lowest crowd ever to watch Shamrock Rovers in a European match. The Hoops lost 1-0. Rovers qualified for the final of the League Cup when they beat Fannad United 4-1 in the semi-final in Donegal. Dermot Keely encountered some verbal abuse at this match from some Rovers' supporters. Moreover, he had to get his phone number changed as his family were receiving abusive phone calls. The KRAM committee issued a condemnation of the people making the abusive phone calls to Dermot Keely and appealed to them to cease their activities.

The Hoops suffered their first home League defeat of the season in their opening match at Tolka Park on 22 September when a goal from Bobby Browne, the former Rovers' player, gave Shelbourne a 1-0 win. Before travelling to Cyprus for the return leg of the European Cup match the Hoops beat Bohs 4-1 at Dalymount Park on 27 September with Noel Larkin scoring a hat trick of headers and Vinny McCarthy getting the other goal. The Hoops played a scoreless draw in Cyprus against Omonia Nicosia and therefore went out of the competition by the goal that the Cypriots had scored at Tolka Park.

The Hoops played six League matches in October, of which four were at Tolka Park, taking eight points from those matches. They lost 4-2 to St Pat's after extra time in the Leinster Senior Cup semi-final at Tolka Park on 7 October and 1-0 to Cork City in the final of the League Cup at Turner's Cross on 21 October. The attendances at the five matches at Tolka Park in October were paltry proving beyond doubt that the pickets were hurting the

Kilcoynes financially. When the Hoops played Derry City at Tolka Park on 26 October only 2,000 attended the match. About 70 per cent of them were Derry City supporters and when you include the neutrals it meant that there were very few Rovers fans present. The defeat by Dundalk at Tolka Park on 30 October meant that the Hoops had lost as many League matches at Tolka Park in six weeks as they had in the previous four seasons at Milltown.

For KRAM to succeed they needed to make Rovers' stay at Tolka Park an unsuccessful one and the boycott which was led by the supporters' club was slowly but surely achieving this objective. In November, the Hoops won their only trophy of the season when they beat Dundalk 4-2 on penalties after a scoreless draw in the President's Cup final at Oriel Park. The Hoops had wins over Bray Wanderers and Limerick City and they drew twice with Cork City in back-to-back League matches. In the match with Cork City at Tolka Park on 15 November, the Hoops drew 2-2 and in the *Irish Times* the following day there was a picture of Mick Byrne running towards the stand after scoring the first goal for Rovers. The stand was deserted and this picture showed just how effective the boycott of Tolka Park was.

Enda McGuill, the president of the League of Ireland, appealed to the Hoops' fans to cease their activities for the month of December as the fans protested outside a special League of Ireland meeting. The fans ignored this request. They were dissatisfied with the League's response to the whole Milltown issue.

The Hoops had a bad run in December when they only managed to pick up four points from five matches and they were now six points adrift of the leaders Dundalk. They picked up seven points from their five matches in January, winning away to Limerick City and Derry City and drawing with Dundalk away while beating Bray Wanderers and losing to St Pat's at Tolka Park. Louis Kilcoyne denied that there was a cash or confidence crisis at the club. This statement was surprising considering the fact that Pat Byrne had been left out of the side for the Derry City match at the Brandywell and that Damien Byrne, Michael O'Connor, Vinny McCarthy and Paul Carlyle were being let go by the club.

The defeat by St Pat's at Tolka Park on 15 January was Rovers' third League defeat of the season at the Drumcondra venue, which was proving to be a graveyard for their title hopes. The Hoops beat Shelbourne 2-0 in the League at Tolka Park on 5 February and then six nights later Rovers were sensationally eliminated from the Cup after an unbeaten run of 20 matches when UCD beat them 2-0 in front of the smallest ever crowd to watch the Hoops play in an FAI Cup tie. The students were a mid-table first division side and the seriousness of Rovers' defeat was underlined when UCD lost at home to Longford Town in the next round. Dermot Keely admitted what most fans had suspected for some time, that some players had not been able to adjust to the move from Milltown. The Hoops picked up six points from their next four matches and Eamonn Gregg joined the Hoops from St Pat's and made his debut against Bohs at Dalymount Park on 19 February.

Mick Byrne had been transferred to Den Haag in Holland and the Hoops all-conquering four-in-a-row team was beginning to break up. Joe Hanrahan, who had signed for the Hoops in October 1987, scored a marvellous solo goal against Bohs at Dalymount Park but Bohs equalised and the match finished in a 1-1 draw damaging both sides' League title chances. The Hoops lost their next two League matches, away to St Pat's and home to Dundalk, and the loss to Dundalk meant that the Hoops relinquished their hold on the League title. Rovers beat Bray Wanderers at the Carlisle Grounds on 4 April but two days later Derry City inflicted a fifth League defeat at Tolka Park that season when they won 3-1.

The Hoops' final League game of the season was played at Tolka Park on Friday 8 April. They beat Cork City 2-0 with the goals being scored by Mooney and Neville. Rovers line-up for what turned out to be their last home League match at Tolka Park was as follows: J. Byrne, Gregg, Neville, Larkin, Brady, Nugent, Doolin, P. Byrne, Balmer, Hanrahan, Mooney. *Subs*: Nolan for Balmer, Lawlor for Gregg. The crowd that night numbered less than a hundred. There were more people on the picket line outside Tolka Park than went in to see the match. The Rovers' fans on picket duty took great delight in loudly counting out the number of spectators who had gone to the match as the spectators left the ground. The boycott of matches in Tolka Park was succeeding.

Relations between the Hoops' fans who were on the picket line and the small group of fans who went in to Tolka Park were often strained during that season. A lot of friendships came to grief. There was a certain amount of verbal abuse of some people who went in to the ground by some people on the picket line and it took a long time before relations between the two groups became cordial again. The Kilcoyne brothers, in particular, were the subject of much verbal abuse before and after matches at Tolka Park. The gardai made only one arrest outside Tolka Park all season and that was of a fan wearing the Derry City colours who dropped his trousers outside the ground on 26 October when Derry City played the Hoops.

Later on the evening of Friday 8 April 1988, as the Hoops' fans who had been on picket duty outside Tolka Park headed back to the White Horse on George's Quay, a phone call to the bar in the White Horse informed the assembled fans that Dermot Keely had resigned as manager of Rovers. The fans now felt that the Kilcoynes would soon be putting up the club for sale. Dermot Keely had done very well in his first season at Rovers, guiding the club to the double and winning the tactical battle with Turlough O'Connor in the FAI Cup final of 1987. Despite all the controversy about the move to Tolka Park, Dermot Keely worked very hard to keep the team together and to keep them winning. Despite an almost impossible situation, Keely nearly retained the League title and he deserves great credit for being able to manage the club in such trying circumstances. Time heals a lot of disputes and Dermot Keely has won the admiration and respect of a lot of Rovers' supporters since that troublesome season at Tolka Park.

The Hoops finished in fourth position in the League five points behind the winners Dundalk. The top four in the League finished as follows:

	P	W	D	L	F	A	Pts.
Dundalk	33	19	8	6	54	32	46
St Pat's	33	18	9	6	52	25	45
Bohemians	33	17	11	5	57	32	45
Shamrock Rovers	33	16	9	8	53	30	41

The Hoops had dropped a total of 14 points in 17 League matches at Tolka Park, whereas they had only dropped 10 points in 50 matches at Milltown when they won the four in a row. Louis Kilcoyne was stunned with the shock resignation of Dermot Keely and he told the newspapers, 'I don't know what we are going to do.' He added, 'Shamrock Rovers will definitely be playing in the League at Tolka Park next autumn; there is nothing more certain than that.'

But within weeks offers were being made to the Kilcoynes for the club and it was now a matter of time before they ended their association with Rovers. Meanwhile Glenmalure Park was left to grow derelict. Very little care was taken of the ground and it was quite easy to gain access to the ground. In March 1988, some Rovers' fans found memorabilia at Milltown. A trophy which Real Zaragosa had presented to Shamrock Rovers in November 1965 after the Fairs Cup tie between the two sides was found discarded behind the goal at the Gonzaga end of the ground, left there presumably by intruders who had been in the bar area, access to which was quite open. The pennant for Rovers match with OGC Nice in the European Cup in 1959 was found behind the main stand at Milltown. The owners of the club should have ensured that trophies and pennants were kept in a safe place and the Rovers' supporters were shocked to find such valuable memorabilia lying discarded at Glenmalure Park.

On Sunday, 8 May 1988, Liam Christie, Robbie Murphy and Paddy Malone of the Shamrock Rovers supporters' club met with two members of the King family who were at that time interested in buying the club. The Kings stated that the Kilcoynes had gone public on the negotiations but that they were still interested. Noel King was invited to a committee meeting of the supporters' club and he put his case very well. He reminded the committee that there was a danger of Rovers going out of existence and he appealed to them to keep Rovers alive. It now seemed that Shamrock Rovers and Glenmalure Park were two separate issues. The Kilcoynes had stated publicly that while they were trying to sell the club, they would not sell the ground.

The King family wanted Rovers to remain in Tolka Park. This condition was unacceptable to the supporters. If the Rovers' supporters had agreed to lift the boycott of Tolka Park just because someone other than the Kilcoynes was running Rovers, certain sections of the media wouldn't have been slow to tell all and sundry that the Hoops fans were just running a personalised campaign against the Kilcoynes. The King family then dropped their interest, so that the Kilcoynes were still without a buyer.

A rally was held outside Milltown on Sunday 29 May and the League of Ireland's AGM was picketed on the same day. At the AGM, it was decided to freeze the transfer of players from Shamrock Rovers until Rovers clarified their future position.

In June 1988, John McNamara, a Dublin accountant, attempted to buy Shamrock Rovers. In an interview for this book in 1991, John McNamara disclosed the following details about his bid to buy the club:

'I was a patron of Shamrock Rovers during the 1980s and when Rovers were playing in Tolka Park all patrons were offered free patronship for the first season at Tolka Park. I had met Joe Veselsky several times. I used to go to London by Ryanair every week and used to meet Joe Veselsky and I often talked to him about what would happen to the Hoops. When things were bad at Rovers, when the team was out of the championship race and had been knocked out of the Cup by UCD there were widespread rumours that the Hoops were going to go out of existence and I said to Joe that we could not let that happen and that maybe we could put a consortium together and would he approach the Kilcoynes to set up a meeting.

So, we met some time in early June and at this meeting Louis and Paddy Kilcoyne indicated that there was another party called Joe Colwell who was interested in forming a partnership so we said we would meet again in the Westbury Hotel. There was Joe Veselsky, Joe Colwell, myself, Louis and Paddy Kilcoyne. I agreed to buy Shamrock Rovers, Joe Colwell and Joe Veselsky said that they would back me up. I said "let us negotiate" but I had only agreed on the condition that I could get the boycott lifted, if it was there I would not buy Rovers, it was never my intention to go to Tolka Park. I met the League of Ireland executive at a hastily arranged meeting at Dublin Airport as they were on their way to Geneva for the European club competitions draw and I put my plans to them. These were to have the boycott lifted in order for me to rebuild Rovers and while it was at the death knell of Rovers I would decide in the long term what to do but in the short term I wanted to keep the club in existence. The League of Ireland had blocked the transfer of any Rovers players and in the mind of the Kilcoynes, the League had no authority to do that as the players would have been sold anyway, so the Kilcoynes were under pressure on a number of fronts.

We started several meetings with the supporters' club and KRAM at that time under the control of the League of Ireland and I think we went through three meetings and all the time I decided that I would make the final decision. Joe Colwell had at that stage decided to pull out of it because of the hassle. Joe Veselsky and I had met Noel King in the Stillorgan Orchard Inn and I had offered Noel King the manager's job at Shamrock Rovers. Noel had been offered the job of manager of Galway United which at that stage was much more secure than Rovers were but Noel was determined to take the Rovers' job and people should not underestimate the major role Noel King played in saving the Hoops from extinction.'

The first meeting between the new owner of Shamrock Rovers and KRAM and the supporters' club took place at Merrion Square on Monday, 18 July and went on for just over two and a half hours without reaching agreement. The supporters' club and KRAM wanted a commitment from the new owner to bring football back to Milltown. If the deal fell through, Bray Wanderers would retain their place in the Premier Division and Limerick United would be brought in to the first division. Dr Tony O'Neill was quoted in an article by Jimmy Meagan in the *Irish Press* on Tuesday 19 July as saying the following: 'Our role has been to smooth the way to a solution. It's a very delicate issue, and our role was one of liaising between the groups.'

The League of Ireland represented by Enda McGuill, Dr Tony O'Neill and Des Casey, had met both KRAM and the supporters' club at the FAI headquarters in Merrion Square on Friday 15 July. The League of Ireland representatives wanted to meet the two groups separately. The supporters' club and KRAM refused to be split into two different groups so the League of Ireland had to meet both groups together. At the first meeting on 15 July, both Tony O'Neill and Des Casey tried to get the boycott of Tolka Park lifted. They read the riot act to KRAM and the supporters' club about the boycott of Tolka Park. They said that the draw for the League of Ireland championship for the 1988/89 season had been made and that the League Cup competition would be starting within a few weeks. The Kilcoynes had stated that they were not prepared to carry on as owners of Shamrock Rovers and there was a new man ready to take over the club provided the boycott was lifted. Des Casey said that if the boycott was not lifted then Limerick United would be brought in to the League and Rovers would be out of football.

The meeting broke up quickly after that. The supporters' club and KRAM made it perfectly clear that there was no way that they were going to lift the boycott of Tolka Park. The League of Ireland did not have the three people present who were supposed to be buying Shamrock Rovers. Jimmy Keane stated to the League of Ireland representatives that both KRAM and the supporters' club would have to meet Mr McNamara, Mr Veselsky and Mr Colwell to see what their plans for the club were. KRAM and the supporters' club met John McNamara and Joe Veselsky for the first time on Monday, 18 July at Merrion Square. John McNamara and

Joe Veselsky were told that they as the prospective new owners of Shamrock Rovers must pursue a return to Glenmalure Park as a primary objective. They must object to any planning permission for Glenmalure Park and they must insist that there would be no involvement from the Kilcoynes in Shamrock Rovers.

KRAM also wanted the FAI to object to any planning permission for Milltown. At the end of the meeting, KRAM gave John McNamara a list of six points which he was to consider before resuming the talks the following Wednesday. On the Wednesday, John McNamara informed KRAM that he couldn't sign that kind of an agreement as it contained too many guarantees and he was still negotiating with the Kilcoynes. Liam Christie informed McNamara that the supporters would not go into Tolka Park and that Rovers would have to move into another ground for next season.

The following is John McNamara's account of how the deal to secure Rovers' future in League of Ireland football was finally agreed:

'At the meeting in Merrion Square on Wednesday 20 July was Brian Murphy, Jimmy Keane, Ronan O'Donoghue, Ed Kenny, Liam Christie and Dick Dolan. Gerry Mackey came into the meeting at a later stage. The meeting was going well until we got down to the hard core. We had already approached Bohemians in the meantime and had agreed to pay £12,500 rent to them if Rovers could move to Dalymount Park. If the meeting at Merrion Square had fallen through Rovers would have gone out of existence. We could not get agreement.

We went into a back room. I wanted complete control of Rovers and I wanted no input into it by anybody else because it was my money: I was the one taking all the risks. There were people who were very conciliatory to me at that meeting from KRAM and the supporters' club and there were people who were very, very hostile and at one stage I thought that the meeting had fallen through.

I was up with Noel King and the rest of them in the back room at Merrion Square. We had agreed to adjourn and talk away from the League of Ireland representatives. There was a serious disagreement at *that stage of the negotiations but Ronan O'Donoghue intervened to defuse a potentially disastrous situation. I thought that Rovers were finished and Noel King said "let's go" but Ronan O'Donoghue stepped in and acted as a broker. After that I knew it was going my way. There was a lot of distrust there but it was a situation where you had your back to the wall and wanted to survive and wanted to do well.'*

The terms of the agreement which were eventually agreed to after almost four hours of negotiations on 20 July were as follows:

1. Shamrock Rovers, under the new owners will build a successful team to compete in the Premier Division of the Opel League of Ireland.
2. The new owners will offer public support for the return of Shamrock Rovers to Milltown.
3. Shamrock Rovers have entered into negotiations with Bohemians to play their home games at Dalymount Park in season 1988/89.
4. No members of the previous owners will participate in the future operations of the club.
5. The existing boycott of Shamrock Rovers home games will be lifted immediately and the new owners will enjoy the full support of the Shamrock Rovers supporters' club and KRAM.

'In the end we all just had to sit down and work together. I remember that there were only two weeks before the new season kicked off and the deal was ratified at a meeting in the Clarence Hotel of KRAM and the supporters' club on Tuesday, 26 July and we had a friendly match arranged for Fairview Park the following Saturday and we did not know what the team would be. Dinny Lowry decided immediately to come back and help us and that was a great help to us. I had to go to Premier Dairies and get the sponsorship arranged, in the meantime I sold Joe Hanrahan to Limerick City for £9,000 which gave us a little cash flow.

Eamon Dunphy wrote an article in the Sunday Independent *at that time called "An open letter to John McNamara", in which Dunphy stated that John McNamara would last about six weeks at Rovers and*

he concluded by saying "I and a lot of other people think that with your
£20,000 you've got no chance. You will be gobbled up, and spat out." I
had to get public and employer liability insurance, that was one of the
first things and that cost us about £7,000 we had no money for that as
we had other things to do. I got an agreement with a reputable bank with
easy payments over eight months and the morning after this article
appeared, the bank withdrew the easy payments. They restored the
terms later that day after much effort on my part but it was a problem I
could have done without just then. Bohemians were very helpful and co-
operative; they now had a tenant for the ground who was paying
£12,500 a season plus expenses. Bohs leased the ground for the money,
not for the love of Shamrock Rovers and they received £27,500 for the
Hoops' two-year stay at Dalymount Park.'

Glenmalure Park was now a separate issue from Shamrock
Rovers. While the Kilcoynes had sold the football club to John
McNamara they still owned Glenmalure Park. On 12 October
1988, the Kilcoynes put Glenmalure Park up for sale by public
tender. Charlie Stuart wrote an article which appeared in the *Irish
Press* on 13 October under the headline 'Rovers set to return'. In
the article John McNamara was quoted as saying: 'I believe that
we have put together a fantastic financial package to purchase the
ground. We will be making a substantial bid when the tenders are
made.' Charlie Stuart wrote that Louis Kilcoyne had confirmed
the previous night that the ground was up for sale; he refused to
elaborate on the details but it was now on the cards that the
family's Dublin soccer pitch would not be used for property
development. KRAM who had collected £100,000 to keep soccer
at Milltown, would go ahead with a series of planning appeals if
property developers were to outbid the new Rovers management
set up. 'Politicians of all parties, influential sporting personalities
and even local residents are all in favour of a return to Milltown.
With the ground in a state of total disrepair at the moment, it may
cost in the region of £1m. to put the house back in order again. At
the end of the day, football and Shamrock Rovers will be the real
winner.' The closing date for receipt of tenders was Friday, 18

November 1988 and the selling agents for Glenmalure Park were the auctioneers, Sherry Fitzgerald.

However, on 27 October 1988, Bohemians put Dalymount Park up for sale by public tender. The FAI had been negotiating with Bohemians to purchase Dalymount Park, but the negotiations had broken down. Bohemians' action did not help Rovers. People could now say that soccer was finished in Dublin with grounds for sale all over the city. It made it easier for a developer to put in a bid for Glenmalure Park. The earlier controversy about Milltown had made developers reluctant to get involved.

On Saturday 20 May 1989, Charlie Stuart wrote an article in the *Irish Press* which stated that the GAA was set to buy Tolka Park. He went on to say that a deal was being worked out between the GAA, Home Farm and the Jesuit Order who control Belvedere College grounds beside Croke Park. The GAA wanted access for the building of the New Cusack Stand through the Belvedere grounds and the Jesuits had intimated that they would be willing to provide this once an alternative playing field was made available to them. Instead, later that day, Dr Tony O'Neill and Fran Fields from the FAI approached Home Farm and informed them that Shelbourne were interested in buying Tolka Park. Shelbourne paid £150,000 up front and the FAI guaranteed the remaining £100,000 which Shelbourne paid at a later date. Around the same time the FAI intervened to save United Park in Drogheda. The FAI bought United Park for £43,000 and Drogheda United were given the option of buying the ground back from them at a later date. The FAI then came to an agreement with Bohemians over the future of Dalymount Park in which the FAI decided not to proceed with the purchase of Dalymount Park but agreed to give Bohemians an interest-free loan of £225,000 so that Bohemians could clear their debts. Thus three grounds, Tolka Park, United Park and Dalymount Park were saved for soccer by the intervention of the FAI. It was regrettable that they didn't try to intervene and save Glenmalure Park which was acknowledged as the finest pitch in the League of Ireland.

John McNamara and Bill Tormey put together a financial

package to buy Glenmalure Park and bid £475,000 for the Milltown site. The bid by the club for their former grounds was unsuccessful, for when the decision was announced as to the outcome of the tender on Tuesday, 29 November 1988, it was revealed that a developer who had bid £925,000 was successful.

The identity of the developer remained a secret until Brent Homes lodged an application with Dublin Corporation on Thursday, 30 March 1989 to build 78 dwellings at Glenmalure Park. Brent Homes was owned by the Nugent brothers from Cookstown, Co. Tyrone and there was widespread media speculation as to whether or not their bid for planning permission would be successful. Although the Corporation's planning and development committee had indicated that it wanted the grounds to be kept for amenity purposes, it was open to Brent Homes to seek planning permission for a residential development.

There were a total of eighteen members on the planning committee of Dublin Corporation. Seven were from Fianna Fail, four from Fine Gael, two from the Workers' Party, two Independents, and one each from Labour, Sinn Fein and the Progressive Democrats. The members were drawn from all parts of the city and represented all shades of political opinion. On Friday 9 June 1989, they voted unanimously against the application from Brent Homes to build 78 dwellings on Glenmalure Park. It was rejected because it would be contrary to proper planning and development in the area and would materially contravene the zoning objectives of the 1980 city development plan.

Brent Homes Ltd appealed against the decision on 30 June 1989. An Bord Pleanala decided to hold an oral hearing of the appeal on Wednesday, 25 October 1989 at 10.30 a.m. in their offices at the Irish Life Mall. On the morning of the appeal an article by Sean Kilfeather appeared in the *Irish Times*. Dr Bill Tormey, a director of Shamrock Rovers, had told the *Irish Times* that an accountancy firm and a property development firm were willing to put together a package which could have saved the ground for soccer. The plan was to make an offer to the Jesuits for the lands which they owned bordering the Glenmalure Park site.

A spokesman for the Jesuit order, Fr Fergus O'Donoghue, confirmed that the offer made on behalf of Shamrock Rovers had been turned down. Fr O'Donoghue said, 'The land for which the offer was made is at present being used for recreation purposes and it is not intended to sell it. We have agreed to sell a parcel of land in the vicinity to the Corporation for the purpose of building four houses for travelling families, but it is not intended to offer any further land for sale.' John McNamara's plan was to swap the land bought from the Jesuits for Glenmalure Park, if he could persuade Brent Homes accordingly, but as the Jesuits refused to sell the land to Rovers the plan fell through.

The oral hearing was chaired by the planning inspector Mr Padraig Thornton. Defending the Corporation's decision of 9 June were representatives of Dublin Corporation, Shamrock Rovers and KRAM as well as some elected representatives. Cllr Joe Doyle TD of Fine Gael stated that the proposed development was a material contravention of the 1980 Dublin city development plan. He said that the city council did not favour any amendment to its development plan and he urged Bord Pleanala to refuse any planning permission for Milltown.

Mr Thornton then asked the Brent Homes' representatives to begin their appeal. Brent Homes were represented by a senior counsel, a planning consultant, an architect, a traffic consultant and a consultant engineer. Mr T. C. Smyth SC, for the company, questioned the reasoning behind the zoning of the site for amenity use. He said that this zoning, under the 1987 draft development plan, was 'merely a recognition of historical fact'. He stated that the stadium was not a public amenity in the real sense as the public were only admitted on certain conditions with admission charges.

Mr McDonnell, the architect, said that the proposed development of three-storey houses around a square was in tradition with many squares in Dublin 6 such as Kenilworth, Belgrave etc. He added that the area would be well served by open spaces. Mr Delaney the planning consultant stated that Glenmalure Park should be compared with noxious industry rather than a general amenity. Mr McNicholas the traffic consultant talked about road plans for the Milltown area and he claimed that the people in the new development would use the improved public transport system when the new road system came into operation.

The planning officer then asked the planning officials of Dublin Corporation to make their case for refusing planning permission for Glenmalure Park. The main speaker representing the Corporation was Ms Gabrielle McKeown who highlighted the shortage of open space in the Milltown/Ranelagh area. She said that the provision of zoning and open space are major issues concerning Dublin Corporation. Ms McKeown also said that the development of Glenmalure Park would materially contravene the zoning objectives of the city's 1980 Development Plan. She added that the proposed housing units would be contrary to any proper planning and development of the area.

Cllr Frank Buckley of the Labour Party, who had made a joint submission to Bord Pleanala with his fellow party councillor Eithne Fitzgerald, spoke of the loss of amenity if Glenmalure Park were lost and he stated that the proposed development would seriously worsen traffic conditions in the Milltown area. Fr Fergus O'Donoghue of the Jesuit community spoke of his objection to the reduction of the height of the wall bordering the Gonzaga end of Milltown. He said that the low walls would increase both the security problems and the possibility of damage to the playing fields. There were two nuns from the local convent at the hearing and when asked by a Rovers supporter at the hearing about their views on it they replied that they wanted to see a housing development at Milltown.

The three main speakers for KRAM - Mr Philip O'Sullivan SC, Mr Brian Murphy and Mr Gerry Mackey - spoke in the afternoon. Mr O'Sullivan spoke for about 20 minutes. He stressed the importance of the 1980 development and 1987 draft development plans. He also said that with the introduction of the new planning bill the company would not be eligible for compensation if their appeal failed. This bill would become effective from before the date of Brent Homes' purchase of the site.

This, along with the existing zoning regulations should ensure the non-payment of compensation. Brian Murphy, the chairman of KRAM, then stressed the importance of Glenmalure Park to the social fabric of south Dublin. He said that at Milltown, unlike some other sports venues, people from all walks of life were united in a common cause. In his speech he cleverly blended the emotional and legal reasons why the ground should be retained as a sporting amenity.

Gerry Mackey, a former Rovers' international and executive member of KRAM then spoke briefly but effectively on a similar theme. John McNamara, secretary/director of Shamrock Rovers, then made an important point. He put the record straight by stating that he had made a bid to purchase Milltown when it was put on the market. In the Brent Homes submission they claimed to be the only interested party when they bought the ground in November 1988. Other prominent speakers for the KRAM cause were their planning consultant Kieran O'Malley, Cllr Tom Hand of the Fine Gael party and John Gallagher of An Taisce.

The planning inspector then asked Mr Smyth to end the proceedings on behalf of Brent Homes. Mr Smyth concluded by saying that the land was going to be either developed by his clients or left derelict with the doors closed. He added that they were only interested in developing the site and not in compensation.

The months that followed were full of rumour and counter-rumour about how the decision would go. There were many theories put forward about how the residents of Ramleh Park, which was opposite Glenmalure Park in Milltown, viewed the proposed development. It is probable that some of the residents were against it while some others would have been in favour of the development on the ground that their houses would increase in value. Speculation about the decision reached fever pitch in February when it was believed that the decision was imminent. The now defunct Century Radio announced on one of its news bulletins in February 1990 that planning permission had been turned down for Glenmalure Park but their news was a bit premature.

The decision, when it came on Friday 16 March 1990, was a devastating blow to all Rovers supporters. They had heard the rumours; they believed that planning permission was going to be turned down. Now their hopes were cruelly dashed.

The decision was a very sad day for the game of football in Dublin. When Dublin Corporation refused the Brent Homes application for planning permission they did so unanimously. That 18-0 decision was given by people who represented all shades of political opinion in the city of Dublin. An Bord Pleanala said however that the development of the Milltown site would not contravene the policies of the 1980 development plan and the 1987 draft development plan. Brian Murphy described the decision as 'tragic' and added, 'It's just inexplicable to me that an area zoned as an amenity is to get 78 houses.'

The ground could and should have been saved but at the end of the day, the people who really mattered weren't interested in saving Glenmalure Park. The government could have passed a by-law in 1987 making Glenmalure Park a designated amenity area only or they could have put a compulsory purchase order on it. But the government didn't care about Milltown. There weren't many votes in Glenmalure Park and if Wood Quay couldn't be saved in 1978, it was highly unlikely that the government would save Milltown. The nauseating sight of politicians from the major parties in College Green in July 1990 trying to get on the platform as the Irish team arrived from Italy was in stark contrast to their efforts to preserve Glenmalure Park as an amenity for the people of Dublin.

The building of 78 houses on what was one of the finest playing surfaces in Europe was a tragedy for both Shamrock Rovers and Irish football. It can be argued that the owner of Shamrock Rovers before the Kilcoynes acquired it in 1972, Joe Cunningham, could have done a lot more with Glenmalure Park than he actually did when he was in charge. It is quite conceivable that in different circumstances a fine all-purpose stadium would now be situated on the Milltown Road instead of a housing development.

The April 1990 issue of *Soccer* magazine contained an article

called 'Milltown Disgrace'. The article accurately summed up the
anger and frustration of Rovers' fans at the planning decision.

*'Politicians, both local and national, we are told, reflect the wishes
of the people. They are elected by the people to oversee the quality of life
of the nation. These public figures in their wisdom correctly zoned
Glenmalure Park as an amenity area not to be developed for housing.
The Kilcoyne family sold Milltown to developers who knew that the site
had been zoned so. The developers knew that even if they failed to get
planning permission they would be compensated. Wonderful planning
laws, aren't they? Sadly Shamrock Rovers, KRAM and the supporters'
club have wasted a lot of energy fighting their noble battle. Perhaps,
when this energy is harnessed to develop a new home all will not be in
vain. Glenmalure Park was, no is, part of dear old Dublin. Its passing
just adds to the disillusionment people have with the way they are
governed. As a friend of mine once said, never confuse justice with the
law. Seems he had a point.'*

Just over five months later, Shamrock Rovers moved into the
RDS in Ballsbridge which has been their home since. Rovers' fans,
can now live up to the memory of people like Billy Lord, Sean
Carroll and Paddy Coad and make the Hoops a force in Irish
football again. John McNamara and his fellow-directors deserve
the support of every Hoops' fan. Given time, Rovers will recapture
the glorious deeds of great Hoops' teams of the past.

On that opening day in September 1990 at the RDS, Ciaran
Byrne, the chairman of the Shamrock Rovers' supporters' club,
writing in the match programme, summed up the mood of Rovers'
fans correctly in saying: 'Today is the day we can finally close the
cover on the darkest chapter in our club history. On behalf of all
Shamrock Rovers' supporters I wish to extend our sincere gratitude to
the board of Shamrock Rovers FC for delivering our club from exile
and returning us to the south side. It is now the duty of all Rovers'
supporters to give the club every possible support and assistance.'

THE PATH OF THE CUP 1986/7 & 1987/8

The Hoops began their bid for their 24th FAI Cup with a first round tie against non-League Tullamore Town at Milltown on Friday, 30 January. Rovers had a comfortable 6-0 victory over the non-League side with goals from Noel Larkin (2), Brendan Murphy, Paul Doolin, Mick Neville and Mick Byrne. The second round draw saw the Hoops travel to Rathbane to take on Limerick City and the Shannonsiders gave Rovers an early shock when Johnny Walsh put them ahead after 49 seconds. Pat Byrne equalised for the Hoops a few minutes later and then Noel Larkin put Rovers ahead with a tremendous headed goal from the edge of the penalty area.

Pat Byrne put the Hoops two ahead with a great goal from a free kick after 62 minutes and although Limerick City pulled a goal back late in the game and the Hoops were reduced to ten men when Dermot Keely was ordered off in the dying minutes, Rovers progressed to the quarter-final on a 3-2 scoreline. The Hoops were drawn away to St Pat's in the quarter-final and Jody Byrne made a couple of crucial saves in the first half to deny St Pat's. Mick Byrne missed a good chance in the second-half but he made amends for that miss with the winning goal in the replay at Milltown on 25 March. There appeared to be no danger when Paul Doolin passed the ball to Mick Byrne after 75 minutes of the replay. There were two St Pat's defenders behind Mick Byrne when he received the ball but he turned swiftly and hit a brilliant shot into the top right hand corner of the net at the Milltown Road end of the ground giving Jim Grace no chance at all of stopping it.

The semi-final draw saw the Hoops going to the Showgrounds for the first leg of the tie against Sligo Rovers on Sunday, 5 April. Former Hoop John Burke almost gave the Sligo team a shock win when his headed effort came back off the crossbar with five minutes remaining. The second leg was played at Glenmalure Park, the following Sunday, two days after the story broke that the Kilcoyne brothers were going to sell Glenmalure Park and move the Hoops to Tolka Park. It was to be the last time Rovers ever played a competitive match at Glenmalure Park and a crowd of just over 6,000 paid gate receipts of £11,500 to witness the historic last game at Milltown. Tony O'Kelly gave the Westerners a shock lead after seven minutes but Mick Byrne equalised 20 minutes later. There was a protest and sit-in staged by the fans at half-time and the second-half was delayed until the fans left the pitch after Dermot Keely had pleaded with them to call off their protest. Amid an unreal atmosphere the two teams seemed content to play out a draw. A third game was required and this was played at the Showgrounds on 15 April.

Sligo Rovers had the Hoops under considerable pressure during the third game but they were unable to make this pressure tell. With less than a minute remaining and extra-time beckoning the Hoops strung a great move together which culminated in Noel Larkin heading a cross from the left to the net to put the Hoops through to their fourth FAI Cup final in a row.

The scene was set for the clash of the big two, Rovers versus Dundalk in the final at Dalymount Park on 26 April. The two sides had met in the League Cup final at the same venue on 1 January when Dundalk won 1-0. Player/manager Dermot Keely was suspended for the final and Mick Neville dropped back to partner Peter Eccles in the centre of the Hoops' defence where both players gave outstanding performances. Dundalk failed to rise to the occasion and the Hoops always seemed in control. The first goal came ten minutes before the interval when Joey Malone upended Brendan Murphy in the box at the school end and Harry Kenny converted from the spot when he beat former team mate Alan O'Neill in the Dundalk goal. Rovers controlled every sector and stamped their class on the match with two late goals from Mick Byrne and Noel Larkin. It was a dream come true for Hoops midfielder Keith Dignam who had won a Cup medal when he was on the UCD side which beat Rovers in 1984. His home had been broken into and his medal stolen. He had now at least one medal to cherish from two Cup winning performances. His career in the League of Ireland was brief for he hung up his boots at the age of 27 in order to concentrate on his business career.

The comprehensive Cup final win by Rovers over Dundalk was a personal triumph for player/manager Dermot Keely who won the tactical battle over his Dundalk counterpart Turlough O'Connor. The Hoops played a lot of long balls from right to left that day instead of their normal short passing game. Noel Larkin and Mick Byrne left the space on the left for Brendan Murphy to run into and he gave Gino Lawless the run around as Rovers destroyed Dundalk on the day. Dermot Keely never got the credit he deserved for that success as he won the double in his first season as manager. He was under enormous pressure to succeed after Jim McLaughlin had left and he certainly proved that he was the right man for the job when he led the Hoops to their third double in a row in 1987.

A marvellous unbeaten run of twenty matches was brought to an end when UCD caused the shock of the 1988 competition by beating a more fancied Rovers at a soulless Tolka Park. The last time that the Hoops had lost a Cup tie was in the replay of the final in 1984 when beaten at the same venue by UCD. Then the students had a side which contained five or six professional players but now the team consisted of young college players who had been struggling in the first division. Mick Kavanagh and Mark McKenna scored for UCD in the first half. After just four minutes of the game had elapsed the Hoops must have thought that they were on their way to victory when Shane Leonard upended Kevin Brady but Mick Byrne had his penalty kick saved by Paul Kavanagh. The game was witnessed by the smallest crowd ever to watch Rovers in an FAI Cup tie. The receipts totalled £810 which represented a crowd of less than 500, a result of the picket placed on the ground by supporters protesting at the closure of Glenmalure Park. Rovers line-up for that FAI Cup tie at Tolka Park on 11 February 1988, was as follows: J. Byrne, Kenny, Larkin, Eccles, Brady, Doolin, P. Byrne, Neville, Nugent, M. Byrne, Hanrahan. *Sub*: Swift for Nugent.

CHAPTER ELEVEN

STARTING OUT
ALL OVER AGAIN

(1 9 8 8 - 9 3)

The 1988/89 season began in the unlikely surroundings of 'Red Cow', the home of non-League side Bluebell United. Shamrock Rovers had been drawn against the home side in the first round of the Leinster Senior Cup.

That game took place on Wednesday, 10 August and finished scoreless after extra time with Rovers winning the penalty shoot out by 2-0. It may not have been a very glamorous victory, especially when compared to the recent exploits of the 'four-in-a-row' team, but it was a vitally important win for Noel King and the 'New Shamrock Rovers'.

The historic team that evening was: Jody Byrne, Harry Kenny, Mick Gorman, John Toal, Noel Synnott, Noel King, John Clarke, Ricky McEvoy, Mick Byrne, Paddy Joyce, Alain Ruiz. *Subs*: Stephen Craig for Toal, David 'Dax' Kealy for Ruiz.

In the quarter-final the Hoops were beaten by Bray Wanderers at the Carlisle Grounds. Richie Parsons scored for Bray after 14 minutes with Mick Byrne equalising 20 minutes later. Bray won on penalties by 5-4.

On Sunday, 14 August the Hoops played their first home game at Dalymount Park. Longford Town provided the opposition in the first round of the League Cup.

The *Irish Press* correspondent, Charlie Stuart, noted in his match report of 15 August that 'a disappointing crowd of no more than one thousand still managed to create more atmosphere than all the Hoops' games put together at Tolka Park last season'.

Barry Murphy and Jimmy Donnelly were playing in their first game for Rovers. The first goal at Dalymount was scored five minutes into the second half from a free kick which was taken by Noel King. Rovers won the game 2-0 after Mick Byrne had given them their second goal after sixty minutes.

The Hoops qualified for the quarter-finals after they had drawn with Shelbourne and Athlone and topped the Group Four table. They were beaten 2-0 by Dundalk in the quarter-final game at Oriel Park. After that game Mick Byrne was transferred to Huddersfield Town for a fee of £20,000.

The first League game of the season saw Athlone beat Rovers by 1-0. Wayne Cooney and Andy Moore made their debut in this game. Dundalk beat Rovers by 2-1 in the next game at Oriel Park. The first points came to the club after Rovers beat Waterford by 1-0 at Dalymount Park following a goal by McEvoy in the 29th minute.

The first impressive display of the season came on Friday, 30 September when Rovers beat Bohemians 3-1 at Dalymount. For the record, Rovers were the 'home' side on this occasion. After eight games Rovers were in joint fourth place just three points off the next placed teams, St Pat's, Derry City and Dundalk.

St Pat's beat Rovers 4-0 on 30 October, the first time since the match against Athlone in December 1979 that the Hoops conceded four goals in a League game. Because it was a bank holiday weekend the Hoops were required to play another League game the following day. Following that drubbing by St Pat's they could hardly have been looking forward to their trip to the Brandywell, especially as the Derry side contained so many of the players who had previously brought success to Milltown.

Noel King and the Derry City manager, Jim McLaughlin, once great friends, were now bitter rivals and the game was billed, rightly or wrongly, as a grudge match. Four minutes from half time Jonathan Speak headed in a corner by John Coady to open the scoring for Derry. Roddy Collins was sent off in the 70th minute for a late tackle on Stuart Gauld. Noel King introduced Larry Murray into the ten-man Hoops side in place of himself and with just minutes remaining Murray set up McEvoy for a dramatic equaliser. Although the game ended 1-1 it was considered to be a moral victory for Rovers.

After that the Hoops went through a disastrous period sustaining defeats at the hands of Athlone, Waterford, Galway, Limerick, Cobh Ramblers and Derry City.

On 22 January 1989, they finally broke their bad run of fifteen games without a win when they beat Athlone 2-1 at Dalymount. When they met Bohs again, on 10 March, the Hoops won by 3-0 thanks to a second-half hat trick by striker Peter Mumby. By now Rovers were well safe from relegation.

The most dramatic game that season was at the Brandywell on 2 April. Derry City needed just one point to be sure of winning their first Premier Division title but a crowd of ten thousand, mainly partisan supporters, were stunned into silence when 'Dax' Kealy scored the only goal of the game after 53 minutes. Jimmy Donnelly and John Mannion received injuries and had to depart from the field. Donnelly was absent from the game for fourteen months as a result. Derry went on to win the title afterwards and Rovers finished the season in seventh place.

Noel King had been offered the position of player/manager at Galway United at the start of the season but chose Shamrock Rovers instead.

'I hung on for Rovers and I lost the Galway opportunity because of it but there was no choice really. Rovers are Rovers. Conceivably, I could have ended up with nothing but that did not matter', said Noel.

When the green light was given for Rovers to go ahead under the new structure, King was faced with the task of having to find a panel of players just as the season was ready to begin. Gone from 1987/88 were Dermot Keely, Kevin Brady, Peter Eccles, Mick Neville, Pat Byrne, Paul Doolin, Vinny McCarthy, Paul Carlyle (both of whom had gone back to Waterford and Derry City respectively during the course of 1987/88), John Nolan, Noel Larkin, Tommy Mooney and Martin Nugent. There were no reserve players from whom to choose. Jody Byrne, Harry Kenny and John Toal did remain from the previous season, though Mick Byrne returned to the club from Dutch side, Den Haag, but shortly afterwards left for Huddersfield.

Another player, Joe Hanrahan, was still in contract from the previous season. The Limerickman, however, refused to play for Shamrock Rovers again. 'Joe Hanrahan obviously had offers from somewhere else', recalled King. 'He did not want to play for Rovers again so we sold him back to Limerick City. He did not have a particularly good year with Rovers and he had been with Limerick before when they were struggling and now it looked as though he might have been in for a relegation battle with Rovers which he did not want. He wanted to further his career so we let him go.

'Most of the other managers had their work done from the end of the previous season. All the good players had left Rovers and all the rest of the good players in the League had signed for other clubs so really we were faced with the task of putting together whatever we could. There were some players who did well for us but in normal circumstances maybe they would not have been given the opportunity to play at all.'

Noel King himself was, of course, eligible to play and the trio of Byrne, Kenny and Toal were joined by others. Mick Byrne came in and John Clarke, who had previously been on loan from Huddersfield Town, signed a contract. Soon they were joined by Stephen Craig, Barry Murphy (Bohs), Wayne Cooney (Norwich City), Andy Moore, Jimmy Donnelly (Waterford), Ricky McEvoy (Luton Town), Paddy Joyce, Howard King (Home Farm), Larry Murray, Derek O'Neill and Tommy McDermott (Bray Wanderers).

Craig, Murray, Joyce, Moore and O'Neill were all unattached when they signed for Rovers. Later in the season the panel was strengthened with the inclusion of John Mannion (Galway), Roddy Collins (Mansfield Town) and Peter Mumby (on loan from Leeds United).

Tommy McDermott cost £1,000 from Bray Wanderers while £8,000 was paid to Galway for John Mannion. Dundalk were also after Jimmy Donnelly but Rovers just pipped them for his signature.

'In the history of Shamrock Rovers it could well have been the most successful season in a sense even though there were no major trophies won. It was excellent in relation to what had happened.

The club was formed at the last hour yet we ended up seventh in the League and we got to the semi-final of the FAI Cup', said Noel King.

King had already played for Rovers in different periods. He was at the club during the Giles era and was on the successful teams which won the League in 1983/84 and the League and Cup in 1984/85. During his career Noel also played for Home Farm, Bohemians, Dundalk and Waterford. In May of 1985 Noel went to the continent to further his coaching career and while in France played for second division side Valenciennes. Upon his return he took up the position of player/manager at Derry City on the recommendation of Jim McLaughlin. Later on Noel was appointed as national coach by the Football Association of Ireland.

The start of the 1989/90 season saw several players depart from the club. Andy Moore was released and returned to England, John Clarke and Paddy Joyce went to Waterford and Howard King to Bray Wanderers. The season saw the long awaited debut of former Arsenal and Irish international star John Devine. As the weeks rolled on several new signings were made, some young, some new and some familiar old faces. The Hoops welcomed back Peter Eccles who had returned from Leicester to Dundalk and Liam Buckley returned to the club from Montreux in Switzerland. Former Bohs full back Dave Connell returned from the States and signed for the Hoops while youngsters Barry O'Connor (Cherry Orchard), Derek Tracey (Belvedere) and Sean Byrne (St Malachy's) were to emerge as the season went on. Full back 'Gino' Brazil came to Rovers from first division side Finn Harps at the start of the season and Vinny Arkins signed for Rovers from Dundee United in October. He had been with the Scottish club for two seasons but due to personal differences with United manager Jim McLean he returned home to Dublin.

'Arkins had come home during the summer. He was homesick', recalled Noel King. 'We brought him training and put him on the FAS scheme and then we signed him. It went on for months and months; negotiations were tedious to say the least and Jim McLean was very difficult to deal with.'

At the start of the season Rovers introduced a new scheme in conjunction with FAS, the state training authority, where some of the younger players signed had the opportunity to train further, develop their game and study several courses at the same time.

The Hoops did not qualify for the quarter-finals of the League Cup in 1989/90 and went out of the Leinster Senior Cup when they were beaten by St Patrick's Athletic 3-2 on penalties in the semi-final.

They got off to a dreadful start in the League, picking up just one point in their opening four games. During that time Noel King had brought in two players on loan from Torquay United, striker Carl Airey and midfielder Ian Weston, but it was an experiment which did not work out and both players were soon dispatched back to the UK. During those opening games the Hoops suffered a 5-0 drubbing at the hands of Derry City at the Brandywell. Not since 3 December 1972, when Rovers were beaten 5-0 by Finn Harps at Ballybofey, had they suffered such a defeat. Although the Hoops had a depleted side on duty at the Brandywell, the defeat sent shock waves through the supporters. However, matters improved somewhat in the following weeks.

Rovers beat UCD 2-1 on 1 October and the following week had a very impressive 3-0 win against St Pat's at Harold's Cross. Barry O'Connor scored twice and Wayne Cooney got onto the scoresheet in between with a tap-in from a McEvoy free. It was undoubtedly Rover's best performance for quite a long time. McEvoy, in particular, had a brilliant game but unfortunately he seldom reproduced such a performance again during his time at the club.

After six games Bohs and Derry shared the lead on 11 points each. Bohs had scored ten goals and conceded just two in the process. The scene was set for a big confrontation between the 'Gypsies' and the Hoops on 15 October. In the previous 19 meetings between the sides Bohemians had failed to register a single victory. McEvoy gave Rovers an early lead which was later cancelled out by Derek Murray but goals from Eccles and O'Connor gave Rovers victory.

When Rovers lost 4-1 to Shelbourne at Dalymount Park it looked as though they were slipping back to their poor early season form but the following week they beat Shels 3-1 at Tolka Park in a back-to-back fixture. The Hoops went on for a further 15 games without defeat and before losing to St Pat's at Harold's Cross on 4 March.

In the big game at Harold's Cross Rovers took the lead after just nine minutes, John Devine scoring with a blistering shot from a corner which stunned the St Pat's supporters in the crowd of 5,000. The 'Saints' equalised after 32 minutes when Mick Moody, despite claims that he was offside, received the ball from a long Henderson kick out and was allowed by the referee to run on unhindered to beat Jody Byrne in the Rovers' goal. St Pat's never looked back after that and scored twice more through Mark Ennis and Mick Moody again. The Rovers' team that day was: Byrne, Brazil, Murphy, Eccles, Cooney, Connell, Craig, Devine, Mannion, Arkins, Tracey. *Subs*: Robb for Devine, O'Connor for Tracey. At the end of the season Rovers finished in fourth place.

Several players were welcomed to the club as the 1990/91 season got under way. 'Keeper Paul Kavanagh was signed from UCD as Jody Byrne left to join rivals Shelbourne. Full back/centre half Neil Poutch came from Luton Town and Mick Byrne came back from Huddersfield. As the season went on there were further arrivals in the shape of ex-Bohs' forward Derek Swan from Port Vale, Pat Dolan who was previously with Arsenal, Walsall, St Pat's and Galway, and midfielder David Campbell who had been on loan to Derry City from Bradford City and was now on loan to Rovers. Wesley Robb departed to St Pat's while Larry Murray retired from the senior game.

There was to be no luck for Rovers in the Leinster Senior Cup. They were beaten by St Pat's in the semi-final in controversial circumstances. Joe Lawless had given the 'Saints' the lead eight minutes into the game. Derek Swan made his debut for the Hoops in this game and he almost grabbed a second-half equaliser but his effort was saved by 'Chippy' Devlin. Not long after that Swan was involved in the build-up to the equaliser after he set Vinny Arkins up to score with a header. Despite a Rovers' player lying injured on the pitch the referee allowed play to continue during which he awarded a penalty to St Pat's after midfielder Tony O'Connor had been taken down in the box by Neil Poutch. Mark Ennis stepped up to score from the spot to win the game for St Pat's.

The incident incensed Hoops player/manager Noel King to the degree that he made remarks to the referee after the game, a verbal protest as it were. As a result the referee reported King in his match report and the Hoops player/manager was heavily penalised by the Leinster Football Association. As a direct result of the action taken by the LFA it was decided by the directors of SRFC not to enter a team in the Leinster Senior Cup competition for the 1991/92 season.

The biggest disappointment of the season was the defeat by Limerick City in the semi-final of the Bord Gais League Cup. The game took place at Tolka Park on Wednesday, 12 December. Only ten days before that Rovers had recorded an impressive 4-1 victory in the League at home to Limerick with goals from Derek Swan (2), Vinny Arkins and Mick Byrne.

Before a small crowd at Tolka Park the Hoops slumped to a humiliating defeat at the hands of the Shannonsiders in the semi-final. From the outset Limerick took the Hoops by surprise with a determined performance that soon brought them dividends. After 25 minutes had elapsed Limerick forward Barry Ryan beat Paul Kavanagh in the Rovers' goal. Despite all the pressure which the Hoops exerted after that they could not get back on level terms and it was the Limerick side which went through to the final where they were beaten by Derry City.

Although Shamrock Rovers had been tenants at Dalymount Park for two and a half seasons their tenure at the Phibsboro' venue was soon to come to an end. John McNamara had been looking around for a suitable southside venue and considered taking Rovers to Shelbourne Park, Harold's Cross or the RDS. Having weighed all the possibilities McNamara pulled off one of the greatest deals involving a League of Ireland side when he successfully negotiated a deal with the Royal Dublin Society whereby Shamrock Rovers would play all their games at the showjumping arena.

Many were taken by surprise when the announcement came and this included Rovers' supporters. The decision to bring Rovers to the RDS had been taken twelve months earlier but it was a well-hidden secret by McNamara and the handful of people in the know. In all, it took eighteen months to get Rovers to the RDS due to the legalities involved and the preparation of the ground. While the Hoops were playing at Dalymount the management went quietly about the business of preparing the RDS for soccer. McNamara had given a commitment to bring Rovers back to the south side of the city and his promise was about to come through.

The 1989/90 season at Dalymount Park had seen a decrease in gate receipts on the previous season, most likely due to the fact that the Hoops were never in the running for any honours. The rent of £50,000 per annum at the RDS was staggering. The rent at Dalymount Park was £12,500 per annum and in the time that Rovers spent as tenants there Bohs benefited to the tune of £27,500. It was a mutual arrangement; Rovers needed a ground other than Tolka Park and Bohs badly needed the money.

Before deciding to take Rovers to the RDS McNamara sought the advice of leading businessmen in the city of Dublin. It was in the aftermath of Euro '88 and before Italia '90 where the exploits of the Irish international team brought new confidence to the game at home. The Rovers supremo got a positive response.

The first season at Ballsbridge cost Rovers quite a considerable sum. A lot had to be spent in preparing the pitch, buying goalposts, erecting signs, putting in entry points and fitting out executive boxes. There were also high costs incurred on match days in areas such as stewarding. But as time went on such costs became more manageable.

The Hoops played their last home game at Dalymount on Sunday, 16 September when they beat Sligo Rovers 2-1. The opening game at the RDS took place on Sunday, 30 September 1990 when Shamrock Rovers and premier division champions St Patrick's Athletic met in a League game. It was a beautiful sunny day and a crowd of 22,000 attended the game. It turned out to be a good day for the family, which was important in the eyes of the club management who felt that there was room in the game for more family groups. The Tallaght Festival Band provided excellent entertainment for the huge crowd and the atmosphere was generally carnival like.

Unfortunately the teams seemed to freeze on the big occasion and the scoresheet remained blank. It was generally accepted that this was a poor performance by both sides, especially in the second half, and that an excellent opportunity to promote the game of home soccer had been missed. Still when the crowd had gone and the sun started to go down there was a feeling that Rovers' stay at the RDS would be a long and successful one.

There was now the recognised need for League of Ireland clubs to provide better facilities in order to attract the crowds back to the game. Major improvements had been carried out at grounds around the country including the Brandywell (Derry City), Oriel Park (Dundalk) and Tolka Park (Shelbourne). In securing the RDS, Shamrock Rovers were not only returning as close as possible to their old home at Milltown but were also providing facilities on a par never witnessed before in the League of Ireland.

All eyes were on the next home game at the venue when Derry City, champions of 1988/89, provided the opposition. A crowd of 10,000 witnessed an enthralling affair. Rovers took the lead in the first half through a superb drive from Vinny Arkins. Derry got back on level terms late in the second half when Stuart Gauld scored from a penalty. Rovers should have been awarded a penalty of their own after that when Mick Byrne was impeded in the box by full back Kevin Brady. The referee blew his whistle and then awarded a free to Rovers outside the box much to the roaring disapproval of the Rovers' fans.

Rovers failed to set the scene alight in the League and were inconsistent up to the Christmas period during which time Bohemians broke their run of 23 games against Rovers without a victory.

With Cork City still leading the way at the top of the table and Rovers themselves having apparently got over their bad run, the scene was set for another intriguing clash between the sides at the RDS on 20 January. Cork, who came to the RDS with an unbeaten record in the League, seemed to be on their way to their first League of Ireland title. Rovers had, in the meantime, signed David Campbell on loan from Bradford City and he was to make his first appearance in this game. Mick Byrne was to leave soon after for Sligo Rovers as the Hoops had an abundance of strikers on their books including Liam Buckley who was struggling to overcome a severe knee injury that had kept him out of the game from the previous season.

Vinny Arkins was missing for the game against Cork and was replaced by Barry O'Connor. It turned out to be a memorable day for the lad from Ballyfermot as he scored twice in Rovers' impressive 4-0 defeat of Cork.

The Leesiders had started well and threatened the Rovers' goal several times but their heads went down after the Hoops scored through Derek Swan after 12 minutes and O'Connor had added another before half time. The duo scored one each again in the second half to add to Cork's misery and further disappointment came their way when midfielder Dave Barry missed a penalty late in the game, Paul Kavanagh diving to prevent a consolation score.

Cork slipped to second place following this defeat but only lost the chance of winning the premier division title when they lost to eventual champions Dundalk at Turner's Cross on 12 April. Rovers were in sixth place after they had played Cork City, a position they were to occupy when the season finished in late April.

The season ended with a 4-1 defeat by Everton at the RDS five days after the Cup final defeat by Galway. When Manchester City visited the RDS on 18 March a crowd in excess of 12,000 witnessed a thrilling encounter which ended 2-2. The 'Shamrock Trophy' was won by the visitors 4-3 on penalties after ninety minutes had elapsed. Manchester City had surged to a 2-0 lead at the interval thanks to goals from Irish international striker Niall Quinn and Michael Hughes. The Hoops blasted their way back in the second half with two very good goals from Swan and earned a very creditable draw. Both goals were like something out of a 'Roy of the Rovers' story.

A number of attractive friendlies were arranged for the start of the 1991/92 season. Rovers beat Scottish Premier Division side St Johnstone 2-1 at the RDS on 24 July. Four days later a crowd of 14,500 attended the game against Glasgow Celtic with victory going to the visitors. New signing Tony Cascarino gave the Scottish premier division side their first goal after nine minutes, Charlie Nicholas got their second in the second half and Celtic won by 2-0.

The Hoops were impressive, though, in their 1-0 win against English third division side Port Vale at Belfield Park on 4 August. Mick Moody scored for Rovers in the first half. The RDS was not available to Rovers for three weeks due to the staging of the annual Dublin Horse Show and the game against Port Vale plus the League Cup qualifying game against Shelbourne were held at UCD's ground with the home League Cup game against Bray Wanderers being held at the Carlisle Grounds.

During the close season there was a lot of comings and goings at the club. John Mannion had departed to Sligo Rovers during 1990/91 along with Jimmy Donnelly (to Drogheda) and now they were followed by long-serving Harry Kenny (also to Drogheda), Barry Murphy (to Kilkenny City), Pat Dolan (to St Pat's) and Ricky McEvoy (to Dundalk).

Into the squad came the St Pats' trio of Dave Henderson, John McDonnell (both former Hoops players) and Mick Moody.

The season got underway in earnest with the League Cup competition. John McDonnell had a memorable competitive debut against Shelbourne at Belfield. He was sent off early in the game. Still, Rovers held the initiative and the ten men should have beaten Shels. They did beat Home Farm and drew again with Bray Wanderers but only narrowly failed on goal difference to qualify for the quarter-finals.

The Hoops got off to an excellent start in the League campaign and remained unbeaten in the first series. They had, however, drawn six of the eleven games and this gave rise for concern. Derry City were visitors to the RDS on 10 November and Jonathan Speak scored before half time to give the Northerners a 1-0 victory and Rovers their first defeat of the season. The Hoops should have taken something out of this game with the amount of possession that they had. They went to Dundalk the following week and featured in a scoreless game. For this game Rovers welcomed back Paul Doolin from Portadown, the Irish League champions. Doolin started out as a midfielder on the Bohemians side of 1981/82 and came to Rovers from there in 1985/86 where he went on to win two League and two Cup medals. After Rovers, Doolin followed Jim McLaughlin to Derry City where he again won the 'double' before joining up with Portadown for a transfer fee of £20,000 sterling. He became the only player to win a League and Cup 'double' both north and south of the border but he became unsettled at Shamrock Park and was glad when Rovers came in with a record offer of £20,000 for his services.

The League game against Athlone Town at the RDS took place on Saturday, 5 October as Ireland were playing against Zimbabwe in the Rugby World Cup at Lansdowne Road. A crowd of around a thousand, the smallest for such a fixture, attended the RDS and the experiment was not repeated. Despite that defeat by Derry City Rovers remained in touch with the leaders. They had 16 points and were in fourth place with Derry on top with 19 points. In between were Dundalk and Shels on 17 points each. Had the Hoops won against Derry they would have been on top with 18 points, one ahead of the next three teams.

Luckily for the Hoops the top sides continued to take points off each other and they were still only three points off the top after they had been beaten by Cork City at the RDS on 1 December.

Much worse was to follow for the Hoops, they struggled to beat Sligo Rovers by 1-0 at the Showgrounds on 8 December and were on the wrong end of a 3-1 scoreline when Bohemians were the visitors to the RDS on 15 December. Rovers may just as well have given the points to Bohs; John McDonnell scored an own goal after thirty minutes then after the interval full back Martin

Lawlor's back pass to 'keeper Henderson was intercepted by Dave Tilson and finished off by Fran Hitchcock. After that Derek Tracey threw Rovers a lifeline with his 61st minute strike but with the Hoops committing everybody up front late in the game Joe Lawless made a superb run down the pitch and switched to Pat Fenlon who finished beautifully with a rocket of a shot that even had the home supporters applauding.

By now Rovers were five points behind the leaders Shelbourne and it was clear that they would continue to struggle after they were lucky to gain a 2-2 draw the following week in Athlone. Despite enjoying the lion's share of possession against Drogheda at the RDS on 29 December the Hoops were again beaten, a defeat which signalled the end of Noel King's reign at the club. Two days later King was asked to step down as manager and two days later again former Rovers' player Ray Treacy was appointed in his place.

Treacy, a former Irish international who had seen service in the English League with West Brom, Charlton Athletic, Swindon and Preston North End, was previously manager at Home Farm and before that at Drogheda United. Treacy's first game in charge was an away fixture against St Pat's when a 1-1 draw was recorded.

However, the bad run was to continue and the Hoops only picked up four points out of their next six games. Two successive victories at home, against Athlone Town and St. Patrick's Athletic, gave the Rovers' faithful something to cheer about but the season ended on a bad note when defeats against Shelbourne (2-1) and Derry City (3-1) were recorded in the final two games. Rovers finished sixth in the League table. Fortunately, they had amassed some points earlier on. Otherwise they could have faced the threat of relegation.

After the appointment of Ray Treacy as manager Garreth Kelly was signed from Home Farm and he was joined in midfield by Derek McGrath who was signed from Brighton. Irish youth international John Bacon was brought in on loan from Arsenal until the season ended.

During the 1991/92 season the chairman of Shamrock Rovers was Mr John McNamara and the other members of the board of directors were Brian Murphy, Jimmy Keane, Jack Wilson, John Breen, Gerard Black, Joe Colwell, Bill Tormey, Louise McNamara and Stuart Mullion. Ray Treacy's backroom team consisted of Tony Macken (assistant manager), Paddy Corbally ('B' team manager), Paddy O'Reilly and Dinny Lowry (trainers) and Charlie Walker (responsible for youth development and the FAS course).

There was a huge clearout of players during the weeks preceding the 1992/93 season. Out went 'keeper Dave Henderson (to Bohs), John Carroll and Neil Poutch (both of whom had been out on loan to Athlone and were now signed by Pat Devlin at Drogheda), David Campbell, Barry O'Connor (to Drogheda), Liam Buckley, Wayne Cooney (to Dundalk), Paul Doolin (to Shelbourne) and Martin Lawlor who returned to Dundalk as the season got under way.

There was also a huge influx of new faces. David Campbell, the ex-Bohs' and Huddersfield Town centre half, joined the club for a brief period but could not agree terms and departed to St Pat's in October. John Coady returned from Derry City, 'keeper Alan Kane came from St Pat's, Gary O'Sullivan and Paul Cullen signed from UCD, Paul Cashin (the ex-Waterford midfielder), John Toal and Stephen Geoghegan came from Drogheda. The other arrivals were Martin Bayly, Christian Bowes (an 18-year-old striker from Home Farm) and Seanan O'Duchon (a left full from junior side Wayside Celtic).

The new look Hoops' side gave a brilliant account of themselves in a pre-season friendly against Notts Forest at the RDS. Although the game ended scoreless the general consent was that Rovers should have easily won. The Rovers team which lined out on that occasion was as follows: Kane, Kelly, O'Sullivan, Eccles, Toal, Bowes, Brazil, Bayly, Geoghegan, Coady, McGrath. The subs were: Swan for Bowes, Hannigan for O'Sullivan, Kavanagh for Kane, Connell for Bayly and Treacy for Geoghegan.

In the League Cup competition Rovers lost their first game 1-0 to St Pat's at Harold's Cross, drew 0-0 with Bray Wanderers at the Carlisle Grounds and beat Home Farm by 1-0 at the RDS and did not qualify for the quarter-finals.

In the Leinster Senior Cup the Hoops went all the way to the final but a lacklustre performance against Bohemians at Dalymount Park on St Patrick's Day saw a golden opportunity of winning some silverware falter almost in shame. It was hard to believe that this was the famous Shamrock Rovers, a club that holds the record number of League championships and the record number of FAI Cups.

The road to the Leinster Cup final began with a 4-0 win against Newbridge Town at the RDS on Saturday, 8 August. Derek Swan notched up a hat trick that afternoon with Dave Connell scoring the other goal. That was followed up by another 4-0 win in the next round, this time against St Columba's Boys. One of the best performances of the season was given in the quarter-final tie against Shelbourne at Tolka Park when the Hoops emerged as 1-0 victors. The important goal came in the very first minute of the game when midfielder John Toal successfully got on to a through ball from Derek Tracey. Shels threw everything they could at Rovers in the second half but a brilliant performance in goal by Alan Kane enabled the Hoops to hold on to their narrow lead and qualify for the semi-finals.

The well-known and extremely successful Leinster Senior League side St Francis provided the opposition in the semi-final at Dalymount Park on Tuesday, 26 January. Rovers' reputation had suffered so badly in the weeks preceding that game that many of the previews suggested that the non-League side would go through to the final. An injury crisis at Rovers deprived them of some first choice players including 'keeper Paul Kavanagh, Willie Burke, Derek McGrath, Derek Tracey, Stephen Geoghegan and Eric Hogan. Still, there were some good youngsters on the team that evening. Christian Bowes had already made some first team appearances and he was joined by midfielders Gary Woodhead and Derek Hannigan. Woodhead was not a Rovers' player as such - he was a regular on the Stella Maris U-18 team - but as a participant on the Rovers/FAS scheme he was entitled to turn out with Rovers whenever called upon. Such was Rovers injury crisis then that all parties, including St Francis, agreed to his inclusion in the Rovers team that evening.

'The Saints' pushed the Hoops to the limit and the game went into extra time after a scoreless 90 minutes after which the non-Leaguers began to tire. Rovers scored twice during that period, firstly through Bowes and then through Paul Cullen. A place into the final had been earned and hopes were high. However, on the day the Hoops failed to perform and Bohs grabbed the only goal of the game when full back Paul Byrne floated in a free with 16 minutes to go, 'keeper Kane appeared to have it well covered but somehow lost the ball in a challenge with Bohs' prolific midfielder Pat Fenlon who headed into the net for the winning goal.

In the League campaign the Hoops made an inconspicuous start and had only two points to show after four games. It looked as though they had turned the corner, though, when they gave a truly brilliant display of pure football in a 6-1 win against Bray Wanderers at the RDS on 27 September. The scorers that day were Campbell, Cullen (2), Swan (2) and Cashin. The team lined out as follows: Kane, Kelly, Campbell, Brazil, Moody, McGrath, Bayly, O'Sullivan, Cullen, Swan, Cashin. *Subs*: Toal for Bayly (70 mins); McDonnell for Cashin (80 mins).

However, the Hoops went without a win in their next five outings, drawing against Limerick and Sligo and losing to Dundalk, Cork City and Bohs. The tide again seemed to turn when they beat Waterford twice in a back-to-back fixture. Stephen Geoghegan scored all four of Rovers' goals in the 4-0 defeat of the Blues at the RDS on 8 November. The team continued to blow hot and cold up to the break off point in the Premier Division on 17 January. The League of Ireland had decided at its AGM the previous summer that after the 22nd series of games had been played the top six teams in the Premier Division would break away from the bottom six and that the third last placed team in the bottom six would have to face the third team in the First Division to decide which of them would participate in the senior division in 1993/94. Although it had seemed highly unlikely that Shamrock Rovers would have any such worries it turned out to be the opposite as a nightmare season, reminiscent of 1975/76, began to unfold.

Although the team had been playing attractive football, their ability to beat teams above them was called into question and indeed when the 'split' came about in mid January the Hoops had failed to defeat any of these sides. Defensive errors cost Rovers dearly, particularly in goal where Alan Kane had a dreadful season. Points were dropped at home to Shelbourne (2-2), Bohs (0-1), St Pat's (1-1), Derry City (1-2), Limerick (1-4) and Dundalk (0-1). They were also unlucky to lose away to Derry City (0-1) and Dundalk (1-2). Of all the teams in the Premier Division that season only Cork City were emphatic winners against the Hoops at home and away although Rovers should never have found themselves down by 3-0 to Cork at the RDS on 10 January; the fact that the team had ability was proved when they came back to finish that game 3-2 with only time running out to prevent an almost certain share of the spoils. During the course of the season Dave Connell (to Ards), John McDonnell (to St Pat's) and Martin Bayly (to Linfield) were to follow David Campbell who was now with St Pat's.

Injuries took a high toll during the season too with both Derek McGrath and John Toal in and out of the team. Both midfielders were absent together for a short spell which did not help matters. Seanan O'Duchon and Garreth Kelly were also absent for considerable spells as well as full back Willie Burke and Midfielders Derek Tracey and Eric Hogan. Burke came into the team in early November and showed brilliant potential up to the time he picked up an injury in early January which ruled him out of action for the remainder of the season. The 20-year-old right full had signed for Rovers the previous season from St Joseph's Boys and made his debut in the very last game of the 1991/92 season against Utrecht. Eric Hogan signed for the Hoops in late October from Birmingham City having previously played with Cobh Ramblers. The flame haired left winger did not enjoy a good season either: injury ruled him out of the side as the new year began. The familiar name of Giles appeared in the Rovers' teamsheet once more, this time in the person of Christopher Giles, youngest son of the famous John. Christopher, or Christy as he was more often called at Rovers, slotted in at right full and proved to be no slouch when the going got tough.

When the breakaway in the Premier Division occurred in mid January Bohemians, Derry City, Dundalk, Cork City, Shelbourne and Limerick FC (formerly Limerick City) were the six clubs to form Group A. St Pat's, Rovers, Drogheda, Sligo, Waterford and Bray Wanderers made up Group B. Rovers started with a scoreless draw at home to Waterford on 24 January but the interest of supporters was aroused for the following League game against Drogheda at United Park when Rovers introduced their two new players, right winger David Byrne (31) and centre forward Joe Gallen (20) both of whom came on loan from Watford. That was an experiment which did not work out and as the injury crisis began to ease Gallen firstly and later Byrne went back to England.

As the season began to come to a close it looked as though Rovers might be relegated. Although they had picked up five points out of five games, defeat at the hands of fellow-strugglers Drogheda United at the RDS on 21 March set the alarm bells ringing. The 3-0 win for Drogheda allowed the Co Louth club to leapfrog above the Hoops into second place behind St Pat's. Rovers were stuck on 24 points, one ahead of Sligo and just two ahead of Waterford who were themselves three points clear of last placed Bray Wanderers.

Amazingly, the one game which everyone expected Rovers to lose was the one which they won and it was played in unusual circumstances. A strike by staff at the RDS saw the game against St Pat's on 4 April switched to Tolka Park. There was only a couple of minutes of the game remaining when Stephen Geoghegan scored the only goal of an encounter which looked as though it would end in stalemate. From a throw in by John Coady, Geoghegan hooked the ball over his head which caught 'keeper Tony O'Dowd by surprise and the slight breeze helped it over the line for a crucial two points. On the same afternoon Waterford beat Drogheda while Bray beat Sligo Rovers and all of this meant that just one point from the meeting of Waterford and Rovers at Kilcohan Park on Holy Thursday would ensure Rovers' survival in the Premier Division for 1993/94.

That game at Kilcohan ended 1-1 after Geoghegan again scored a vital goal for the Hoops. Although Vinny McCarthy cancelled out Rovers' early lead, the team held out against a Waterford onslaught in the second half to return home to Dublin in a joyous mood. The final game of the season was a scoreless draw away to Sligo Rovers. The most improved player of the season was centre half Gino Brazil (24). Brazil had played previously as right full under Noel King but formed a formidable central defensive partnership with Peter Eccles under Ray Treacy. At least his own good form was something for him to be cheerful about.

'At the start of the 1992/93 season everything looked good for us', he recalled. 'We were to be unlucky in a lot of games which could have gone either way such as Bohs on the Bank Holiday, Shels at home, Shels away, Derry at home amongst some others but unfortunately we just did not get the right breaks. After the split we did not play the way we had been and although the injuries did not help our cause it was always going to be very difficult once we went down to the bottom six.'

Defeat by an understrength Bohs side in the Leinster Senior Cup final did not help matters either for a win here would surely have been a major boost for a team lacking confidence. 'We were shattered in the dressing room after that match because we did not play well on the day. It was so disappointing to lose that one for a win otherwise would have had us buzzing, instead that defeat did not help our relegation cause', he said.

Gino Brazil himself did not believe at any stage that Rovers would be relegated. They were too good a side and would pull out of it no matter how late. 'Certainly Stephen Geoghegan will never score two more important goals for anyone in his career than he did for Rovers in the games against St Pat's and Waterford and that's for sure. After the game against Waterford there was a great relief. It was so great to experience something nice again after all that pressure and the bad luck we had endured during the season.'

THE PATH OF THE CUP

Under new ownership and under the guidance of player/manager Noel King the Hoops got as far as the semi-final of the FAI Cup in 1989.

In the first round they travelled to Donegal to take on Culdaff United and won 3-0 with second half goals from Larry Murray, Jimmy Donnelly and Harry Kenny. They then beat UCD in the second round at Belfield. Home Farm provided the opposition at Tolka Park in the quarter-final where Rovers were lucky to get out with a 1-1 draw. The replay at Dalymount Park was won by Rovers with Mumby scoring the only goal of the game.

Rovers were drawn against Derry City in the semi-final which was played on a two-leg basis. The first leg was staged at the Brandywell where Rovers had beaten Derry in the League a week before but this time Derry won by 3-0 in a game they always seemed to control. Jonathan Speak, who had returned to the Derry side following an absence of several weeks through injury, scored twice in a four minute spell before half-time and Liam Coyle added to the Derry score seven minutes from the end. The second leg at Dalymount Park was a cracking game. Rovers took the lead after 41 minutes when Peter Mumby scored but Noel King was sent off in the 71st minute and Derry equalised after that through Speak.

'The fact that the semi-final was a two-legged affair did not help us', recalled Noel King. 'We were slaughtered in the first leg in Derry when we were beaten 3-0. In the return leg I got sent off. We had managed to get one goal back in the first half of that game. In the second half Tommy McDermott beat the 'keeper, took a shot, it was heading across the line but Mick Neville kicked it out, only for that it would have been 3-2 on aggregate at that stage with about 40 minutes to go and I felt that if we had scored then we could have gone on and won the tie and we would have been in the final. It was a great game. Here was Shamrock Rovers right back in the limelight once again.'

In the first round of the 1990 competition Rovers beat

Drogheda 2-1 at Dalymount Park. A controversial penalty was awarded to Rovers by referee Pat Kelly after Vinny Arkins was seen to fall in the box. Harry Kenny converted from the spot. Denis Cunningham had given Drogheda the lead much to the delight of the sizeable visiting contingent but Rovers won the game after Barry O'Connor secured the winner.

In the second round the Hoops travelled to Turner's Cross to take on Cork City before a crowd of 6,000. After six minutes John Caulfield scored for the home side but the game ended level after Peter Eccles got the equaliser for the visitors in the 62nd minute.

Cork did enough in the first half of the replay at Dalymount Park to secure victory. After 33 minutes Kieron Nagle rounded Rovers' full back Wayne Cooney and sent over a beautiful cross which was met by Philip Long and the latter went on to score the only goal of the game. Try hard as they did in the second half Rovers could not get back on level terms. It was the first time since February 1953 that a Cork side had beaten Rovers in the FAI Cup, when Evergreen had beaten the Hoops 4-2 in a first round replay.

The draw for the first round of the 1991 competition presented Rovers with their first ever FAI Cup tie at the RDS when they were given a home draw against first division side Finn Harps. Although Finn Harps came into the League of Ireland in 1969 the two sides had met only once before in the Cup, in 1978 when Rovers won 3-2 after a scoreless draw. The Hoops went on to win the Cup that year. Would this be a good omen for 1991?

The first round took place on 10 March at the RDS and although the highlight of the game was a marvellous hat trick by Rovers' striker Derek Swan the Hoops had to battle all the way before overcoming the challenge of Harps and eventually win the game 4-3.

Rovers travelled to Sligo for the second round game in the belief that if they could come away from the Showgrounds with a win they could go all the way to lifting the Cup. This was probably the most difficult tie in the whole competition with Sligo nearly impossible to beat at home and with very little difference between the two sides throughout the season.

The Hoops were shocked early in the game when Sligo took the lead through midfielder John Byrne but as the game progressed they reversed the roles by equalising from the penalty spot through Campbell and then taking the lead through Arkins. Striker Fran Hitchcock equalised for Sligo with ten minutes to go and 30 minutes of extra time failed to separate the teams.

The replay at the RDS saw no goals despite the fact that both sides had chances and again extra time failed to resolve the issue. After 240 minutes of play had elapsed it was all down to a penalty shoot-out to decide who would provide the opposition to Athlone Town in the quarter-finals. Shamrock Rovers won the penalty shoot out by 4-2 when 'keeper Paul Kavanagh managed to save the spot kicks of former Hoops' players Paul McGee and Mick Byrne.

Again, in the quarter-final tie at St Mel's Park, 120 minutes of play saw no goals despite the almost complete domination by Rovers. It looked as though the Hoops might have lost their chance though, when full back John Devine was sent off for throwing the ball at Athlone striker Michael O'Connor having received the yellow card a minute earlier for a punch on the same player.

Devine played in the replay three days later and the former Arsenal, Norwich and Irish international extracted his own form of retribution when he scored the only goal of the game shortly after the second half had begun. Devine's goal was certainly one to remember as he must have been about 30 yards out when he sent in a powerful shot which gave Athlone 'keeper Jim Grace no chance.

The semi-final saw Rovers travel to Buckley Park in Kilkenny where a crowd of 6,000 crammed into the tiny ground to witness history being made. Kilkenny City's team were a very young side but did enough on the day to confine Rovers to a narrow victory. In fact, it was a dreadful game livened up for the Rovers following of 1,500 in the crowd by Derek Swan's headed goal in the second half. In the meantime Galway United had beaten St James's Gate by 3-1 at Tolka Park and a repeat of the 1985 final was about to take place.

A crowd of 15,257 attended the final at Lansdowne Road. It

was a close affair although Galway almost took the lead through Tommy Keane but his chipped in shot was cleared off the line by Rovers' midfielder, Dave Connell.

The Rovers strikers, Vinny Arkins and Derek Swan, were guilty of missing a 'sitter' apiece in the second half and with the score at 0-0 as the game drew to a close people began to think about the replay which would have been held at Tolka Park the following Sunday. However, Galway had other ideas and a superb run down along the right wing by Keane resulted in that player getting in a crisp low shot across the face of the Rovers' goal where Galway captain John Glynn was waiting to bang it into the back of the net.

When the draw for the 1992 FAI Cup first round was made Rovers were drawn away to St Patrick's Athletic. The 'Saints' were still playing all their home games at Harold's Cross while awaiting a return to their traditional home at Richmond Park.

Both sides were fearful of one another. Neither had any hope of winning the League title or qualifying for a UEFA Cup place so the Cup represented their last chance this season of winning a major trophy and, of course, qualifying for a place in Europe.

The game took place on Sunday, 16 February and a crowd which paid £5,824 in gate receipts were treated to a pretty one-sided affair.

St Pat's took the lead after 10 minutes through midfielder Paul Osam and he was also involved in their second goal 18 minutes later in a move which saw the ball finally tapped into the net by Morrys Scott. Rovers never looked part of the fray in the first half and although they came out fighting in the second half, and had St Pat's on the rack, desperate defending saw striker Mark Ennis left unmarked and he grabbed the 'Saints' third goal with just nine minutes of the half having been played. John McDonnell got one back for Rovers with 20 minutes to go but that third goal by Ennis had effectively killed off the Hoops and many Rovers' fans had already left the ground in disgust by then.

On the day the team did not perform; they did not live up to Rovers' Cup fighting traditions and the whole event left new manager Ray Treacy with very tough decisions to make for the future shaping of the team.

Although the team was struggling in the League during 1992/93 they seemed to reserve their best performances for the FAI Cup. The first round of 1993 saw the Hoops take on non-League side College Corinthians from the Munster Senior League. Although it appeared an easy task on paper the challenge of the Corkmen could not be taken lightly, especially with the success that other non-League sides had enjoyed in the Cup in recent years. There was also the added factor that Rovers were still the number one side for anybody to knock out of the Cup, even though it had been a poor season for them.

The result was a 3-0 victory for the Hoops. A big contingent had travelled from Cork to the RDS but they were to be disappointed when Rovers took the initiative in the second half to score a comprehensive win. The first half had been dour but almost immediately after the break Derek McGrath scored through a crowded goalmouth. Two minutes later Gary O'Sullivan fired in a cross from the right for Joe Gallen to head into the net. Incredibly, Rovers had all the time in the world to score their third goal. From a free kick by David Byrne, Derek Swan sent Derek Tracey on his way and he was virtually unchallenged as he walked the ball into the net.

The second round saw the Hoops at home to Waterford, a side they had beaten twice already in the League but still there was fear at the prospect of meeting the Blues for the sides had played a scoreless draw in the League at the RDS only weeks earlier. On that occasion Waterford gave a competent display but in the Cup game the breaks went in Rovers' favour. Again a 3-0 win was recorded. The Hoops took a 2-0 lead before half-time with goals from Stephen Geoghegan and Gino Brazil. The score from Brazil was particularly pleasing for Rovers' fans for, having run through the Waterford offside trap, he found himself all alone forty yards out with no support and a clear gap with only Blues 'keeper Martin Quinlivan to beat; urged on by the crowd the Rovers' centre half ran on all the way until he drew the 'keeper out and then slotted the ball into the net. Brazil's performance on the Hoops' team that day earned him the Harp Lager man of the match award. Derek McGrath made it 3-0 for the Hoops in the second half and a place into the quarter-finals was secured.

The draw for the quarter-finals gave Rovers an away task against Derry City. A large contingent of Hoops' supporters travelled to the Brandywell to chant on the team but it was not Rovers' day. They started brightly enough, Paul Cullen curbing the threat of Derry's flying winger Paul Carlyle to great effect. It was Cullen who opened the scoring after Derry 'keeper Dermot O'Neill found it necessary to come running off his line, the Rovers' midfielder, from about 35 yards out looped the ball over O'Neill's head for a spectacular goal.

Twelve minutes later Derry equalised after Paul Kavanagh had saved from Carlyle's effort but when the Rovers' custodian palmed the ball off the left upright it rebounded back across the face of the goal where Mark Ennis was on hand to head it into the net. Tragedy struck for Rovers when captain Peter Eccles was forced to leave the pitch after 40 minutes following an earlier incident in which he sustained a dislocated elbow. Then midfielder Paul Cashin was forced to depart too after he took a knock in the second half.

Derry brought on substitute midfielder Paul Trainor late in the second half and he earned the tag of super sub when he scored the winning goal with just one minute of normal time remaining. Right winger Martin McGinley was given acres of room by Rovers' substitute left full Seanan O'Duchon and the Derryman got a nice cross in to the goalmouth where Trainor was first to blast the ball into the net. Although injuries had played their part in this defeat there was a general feeling that Rovers' inadequacies had been shown up once again.

Spotlight on Peter Eccles

The longest serving players at Shamrock Rovers in recent times were Peter Eccles and Harry Kenny. The two became good friends during their time at the club yet, ironically, it was Kenny's 'big break' that gave Peter his 'big break', so to speak.

It was after Harry Kenny received a broken leg during the League game against Sligo Rovers on 11 October 1981, that Peter Eccles came onto the first team on a regular basis. Peter filled in as right full then although he signed for the Hoops as a centre half.

Peter played as a centre forward from the age of twelve up to sixteen when he was with St Brendan's in Cabra. Strangely enough, it was as a result of an injury to the regular centre half there that Peter came about to perform the role of a defender.

He was spotted playing in the centre of the St Brendan's defence and signed by Johnny Giles in 1981. During the Giles/Campbell era Peter alternated between the centre half and right full positions and this caused him some upset.

'I hated playing as a right full', recalled Peter. 'At one stage I contemplated leaving the club if they wanted me to continue there but then Jim McLaughlin took over team affairs and he put me in as a centre half.'

Of course, Peter was a regular on the team during the 'four in a row' era and only departed from Rovers at the end of the 1987/88 season. 'I scored a lot of goals during that time but having said that the team were playing well overall and I had more chances to score. I was really lucky to have been a part of that era. I didn't like playing at Tolka Park and I did not like the way Rovers were going so when Michael O'Connor told me that there was a club in Australia interested in me I jumped at the chance. On my return to Ireland I signed for Dundalk and I was only there a week when I was signed by Leicester City. It was stipulated that if I returned home again I would have to go back to Dundalk but my first love, as everybody knew, was Shamrock Rovers. I had an unhappy spell with Dundalk and eventually I got my wish to come back to Rovers', said Peter.

Peter won League and FAI Cup honours with Rovers during that successful era of the 'eighties and everything seemed to go right for him as he was selected to represent Ireland at Inter League and Olympic level. His Career reached a peak when he was selected by manager Jack Charlton to play for the Republic of Ireland in a friendly against Uruguay at Lansdowne Road in April 1986.

'Looking back at it now I would have to say that the highlight of it all was being capped for Ireland against Uruguay but at that time everything was happening for me. I was supposed to be going here or going there. It all happened so quickly then, I felt that I got the recognition I deserved when I was selected to play for Ireland.'

So, after a brief sojourn with Kingsway Olympic in Australia, Leicester City and Dundalk Peter returned to the Hoops in October 1989 to continue where he left off. His best goal, he says, was the one he scored against Shelbourne in a 6-1 rout at Milltown in January 1983. 'The one I enjoyed most, though, was the one I scored against Linfield in the European Cup at Milltown', said Peter.

At 6'2" in height, Peter was equally effective in stopping goals as he was in scoring them and was a stumbling block for many a good striker in the League of Ireland who feared coming up against him - and still do today.

When the 1992/93 season ended, Peter was awarded the Joint Supporters Club Senior Player of the Year award, and was presented with the inaugural Paddy Coad Memorial Award as a consequence. This was presented to the club by Paddy's daughter, Suzanne Cooney, who told the gathering at Lansdowne RFC that her father had often spoken highly of Peter Eccles.

Roll of Honour

LEAGUE CHAMPIONS: 1922/23, 1924/25, 1926/27, 1931/32,
1937/38, 1938/39, 1953/54, 1956/57,
1958/59, 1963/64, 1983/84, 1984/85,
1985/86, 1986/87

LEAGUE RUNNERS-UP: 1925/26, 1932/33, 1939/40, 1941/42,
1955/56, 1957/58, 1964/65, 1965/66,
1968/69, 1969/70, 1970/71, 1981/82

FAI CUP WINNERS: 1925, 1929, 1930, 1931, 1932, 1933,
1936, 1940, 1944, 1945, 1948, 1955,
1956, 1962, 1964, 1965, 1966, 1967,
1968, 1969, 1978, 1985, 1986, 1987

FAI CUP RUNNERS-UP: 1922, 1926, 1946, 1957, 1958,
1984, 1991

LEAGUE OF IRELAND: 1924/25, 1926/27, 1931/32, 1932/33,
SHIELD WINNERS 1934/35, 1937/38, 1941/42, 1949/50,
1951/52, 1954/55, 1955/56, 1956/57,
1957/58, 1962/63, 1963/64, 1964/65,
1965/66, 1967/68

SHIELD RUNNERS-UP: 1925/26, 1927/28, 1928/29, 1929/30,
1933/34, 1943/44, 1947/48, 1958/59,
1972/73

LEINSTER SENIOR: 1923, 1927, 1929, 1930, 1933, 1938,
CUP WINNERS 1953, 1955, 1956, 1957, 1958, 1964,
1969, 1982, 1985

LEINSTER SENIOR:
CUP RUNNERS-UP
1940, 1944, 1946, 1949, 1963, 1973,
1975, 1979, 1993

DUBLIN CITY CUP:
WINNERS
1944/45, 1947/48, 1952/53, 1954/55,
1956/57, 1957/58, 1959/60, 1963/64,
1966/67, 1983/84

DUBLIN CITY CUP:
RUNNERS-UP
1941/42, 1948/49, 1967/68, 1968/69

TOP FOUR WINNERS: 1955/56, 1957/58, 1965/66

TOP FOUR RUNNERS-UP: 1958/59, 1964/65, 1967/68, 1968/69

INTER-CITY CUP WINNERS: 1942/43, 1945/46, 1946/47, 1948/49

INTER-CITY CUP RUNNERS-UP: 1941/42

PRESIDENT'S CUP WINNERS: 1929/30, 1932/33, 1940/41,
1941/42, 1943/44, 1944/45, 1945/46,
1948/49, 1954/55, 1956/57, 1957/58,
1959/60, 1962/63, 1968/69, 1969/70,
1970/71, 1972/73, 1984/85, 1985/86,
1986/87, 1987/88

PRESIDENT'S CUP :
RUNNERS-UP
1930/31, 1939/40, 1946/47, 1955/56,
1960/61, 1964/65, 1965/66, 1966/67,
1978/79

LEAGUE CUP WINNERS: 1976/77

LEAGUE CUP RUNNERS-UP: 1978/79, 1981/82,
1986/87, 1987/88

TYLER ALL-IRELAND:
CUP WINNERS
1978

BLAXNIT ALL-IRELAND: 1967/68
CUP WINNERS

BLAXNIT ALL-IRELAND: 1968/69
CUP RUNNERS-UP

IFA JUNIOR CUP WINNERS: 1915

Co. DUBLIN LEAGUE: 1904/05
WINNERS

LEINSTER JUNIOR LEAGUE: 1905/06, 1914/15
WINNERS

LEINSTER JUNIOR CUP: 1905, 1906
WINNERS

LEINSTER YOUTHS CUP: 1959/60, 1979/80

LEINSTER SENIOR LEAGUE WINNERS: Rovers did win the Leinster Senior League on a number of occasions but this information is not readily to hand at present.

LFA METROPOLITAN CUP: 1924/25, 1927/28, 1934/35, 1939/40,
WINNERS   1946/47, 1947/48, 1948/49, 1949/50

LEAGUE OF IRELAND: 1984/85, 1986/87
'B' WINNERS

RECORD WIN: 11 - 0 v Bray Unknowns, League,
                        28 October 1928

RECORD DEFEAT:*   0 - 7 v St James's Gate, League,
                        22 April 1937
                        0 - 7 v Cork City, Dublin City Cup,
                        31 August 1938
                        * = domestic competition

(In 1961 Rovers were beaten 10-0 by Dulka Prague on a tour of the US.)

SHAMROCK ROVERS' PLAYERS CAPPED FOR IRELAND (FULL INTERNATIONAL)

Paddy Ambrose	5	(1954 - 1964)
Eddie Bailham	1	(1964)
Tom Breen	3	(1946 - 1947)
John Burke	1	(1929)
Liam Buckley	1	(1984)
David Byrne	1	(1931)
Pat Byrne	8	(1984 - 1986)
Mattie Clarke	1	(1950)
Paddy Coad	11	(1946 - 1952)
Jimmy Daly	2	(1932 - 1935)
Paddy Daly	1	(1949)
Tommy Donnelly	1	(1938)
Dinny Doyle	1	(1926)
Bob Duffy	1	(1950)
Jimmy Dunne	9	(1937 - 1939)
Peter Eccles	1	(1986)
Tommy Eglington	2	(1946)
Eamon Fagan	1	(1973)
John 'Kruger' Fagan	1	(1926)
Peter Farrell	2	(1946)
John Joe Flood	5	(1926 - 1931)
Tommy Foy	2	(1937 - 1939)
Bob Fullam	2	(1926 - 1927)
Johnny Fullam	10	(1964 - 1969)
Peader Gaskins	5	(1934 - 1935)
John Giles	9	(1978 - 1979)
William 'Sacky' Glen	8	(1927 - 1936)
Bobby Gilbert	1	(1966)
Tommy Godwin	5	(1949)
Joseph 'Lye' Golding	2	(1928 - 1930)
Tommy Hamilton	2	(1959)
John Herrick	1	(1973)

Mick Kearin	1	(1971)
John Keogh	1	(1966)
Shay Keogh	1	(1958)
Freddie Kiernan	2	(1951)
Owen Kinsella	2	(1932 - 1937)
Alec Kirkland	1	(1927)
Mick Lawlor	5	(1970 - 1973)
Mick Leech	8	(1969 - 1972)
Gerry Mackey	3	(1956 - 1957)
Jim Maguire	1	(1929)
Jimmy 'Maxie' McCann	1	(1956)
Mick McCarthy	1	(1932)
Jackie Mooney	2	(1964 - 1965)
Jacko McDonagh	3	(1983 - 1984)
Paddy Moore	5	(1931 - 1936)
Paddy Mulligan	10	(1969 - 1979)
Liam Munroe	1	(1953)
Ronnie Nolan	10	(1956 - 1962)
Liam O'Brien	1	(1986)
Lar O'Byrne	1	(1949)
Tommy O'Connor	4	(1949)
Pierce O'Leary	7	(1979 - 1980)
Frank O'Neill	20	(1961 - 1971)
Noel Peyton	1	(1956)
Damien Richardson	1	(1971)
Mick Smyth	1	(1968)
Noel Synnott	3	(1978)
Ray Treacy	3	(1978 - 1979)
Liam Tuohy	6	(1955 - 1965)
Joe Williams	1	(1937)

INTERNATIONAL GOALSCORERS

Paddy Ambrose	1
Paddy Coad	3
Tommy Donnelly	1
Bob Duffy	1

Jimmy Dunne	5
John Joe Flood	4
Bob Fullam	1
Johnny Giles	1
Mick Leech	2
Jimmy 'Maxie' McCann	1
Jackie Mooney	1
Paddy Moore	7
Frank O'Neill	1
Ray Treacy	2
Liam Tuohy	1

ROVERS' PLAYERS CAPPED FOR THE REPUBLIC OF IRELAND AT UNDER-21 LEVEL

Vincent Arkins	8	(1990 - 1991)
John Bacon	1	(1991)
Richie Bayly	4	(1979)
Liam Buckley	1	(1981)
Robbie Gaffney	1	(1979)
David Henderson	2	(1978 - 1979)
Jacko McDonagh	3	(1983)
Derek McGrath	6	(1992)
Mark Meagan	8	(1978 - 1979)
Larry Murray	4	(1978)
Barry O'Connor	2	(1991 - 1992)
Pierce O'Leary	5	(1979)
Alan O'Neill	2	(1978 - 1979)
Neil Poutch	1	(1990)

ROVERS' PLAYERS CAPPED FOR THE REPUBLIC OF IRELAND AT UNDER-23 LEVEL

Eamon Fagan	2	(1972 - 1973)
Mick Lawlor	1	(1972)
Paddy Mulligan	1	(1966)

ROVERS' PLAYERS CAPPED FOR THE REPUBLIC OF IRELAND AT 'B' LEVEL

Paddy Ambrose	2	(1958)
Eamonn Darcy	1	(1960)
Tommy Farrell	1	(1960)
Tommy Hamilton	1	(1960)
Shay Keogh	2	(1957 - 1958)
'Maxie' McCann	2	(1958)
Gerry Mackey	1	(1958)
Ronnie Nolan	3	(1958 - 1960)
Noel Peyton	1	(1957)
Liam Tuohy	3	(1957 - 1958)

PLAYERS CAPPED AT INTER-LEAGUE LEVEL
(NOT INCLUDING 'B' OR U-21 GAMES)

Paddy Ambrose	7	(1954 - 1958)
Vinny Arkins	1	(1991)
Tom Breen	3	(1947)
John Burke	1	(1929)
Bobby Bryson	1	(1941)
Mickey Burke	12	(1953 - 1957)
Eddie Bailham	4	(1962 - 1964)
Liam Buckley	2	(1979 - 1980)
Jody Byrne	1	(1987)
Pat Byrne	3	(1984 - 1987)
David Campbell	1	(1991)
Tom Caulfield	1	(1930)
Paddy Coad	26	(1943 - 1955)
Jackie Coyle	1	(1945)
Jimmy Collins	3	(1946 - 1948)
Davy Cochrane	4	(1942 - 1946)
Mattie Clarke	9	(1948 - 1951)
Dermot Cross	1	(1960)
Pat Courtney	4	(1962 - 1967)
John Coady	2	(1984 - 1986)
Matt Doherty	3	(1943 - 1944)

Paddy Daly	3	(1949 - 1952)
Bob Duffy	2	(1950)
Jimmy Dunne	6	(1939 - 1942)
Eamonn Darcy	2	(1960)
Billy Dixon	1	(1966)
Paul Doolin	1	(1986)
Peter Eccles	1	(1986)
John 'Kruger' Fagan	5	(1924 - 1927)
John Joe Flood	8	(1925 - 1932)
Billy 'Juicy' Farrell	3	(1925 - 1926)
Peter Farrell	7	(1943 - 1946)
Bob Fullam	6	(1925 - 1930)
Johnny Fullam	11	(1961 - 1968)
Eamonn Farrell	1	(1962)
Tommy Farrell	2	(1959 - 1960)
William 'Sacky' Glen	2	(1930)
Peader Gaskins	1	(1935)
Joseph 'Lye' Golding	2	(1928 - 1929)
Tommy Godwin	1	(1948)
Podge Gregg	1	(1948)
Jimmy Gaynor	1	(1949)
Bobby Gilbert	1	(1967)
Liam Hennessy	5	(1954 - 1959)
Tommy Hamilton	20	(1955 - 1962)
Alec Kirkland	5	(1925 - 1928)
Freddie Kiernan	1	(1951)
Shay Keogh	9	(1955 - 1959)
John Keogh	4	(1963 - 1966)
Mick Kearin	4	(1967 - 1971)
Harry Kenny	1	(1989)
Dermot Keely	1	(1987)
Noel King	1	(1984)
James 'Hooky' Leonard	3	(1927 - 1928)
Mick Leech	4	(1969 - 1972)
Martin Lawlor	1	(1991)
Mick Lawlor	1	(1970)

Noel Larkin	1	(1987)
Paddy Moore	1	(1932)
Ned Marlowe	5	(1925 - 1929)
John McDonnell	1	(1991)
Mick McCarthy	1	(1941)
Jimmy McAlinden	1	(1946)
Paddy Mullen	1	(1949)
Liam Munroe	3	(1953 - 1954)
Jimmy 'Maxie' McCann	4	(1956 - 1958)
Gerry Mackey	10	(1955 - 1958)
Jackie Mooney	6	(1962 - 1965)
Paddy Mulligan	6	(1965 - 1979)
Tom McConville	1	(1974)
Jacko McDonagh	2	(1983 - 1984)
John Mannion	1	(1989)
Ossie Nash	1	(1948)
Ronnie Nolan	32	(1954 - 1964)
Mick Neville	2	(1986 - 1987)
Paddy O'Reilly	2	(1928)
Lar O'Byrne	4	(1949)
Tommy O'Connor	1	(1951)
Christy O'Callaghan	2	(1956)
Danny O'Callaghan	1	(1952)
Frank O'Neill	15	(1961 - 1969)
Tony O'Connell	3	(1963 - 1964)
Alan O'Neill	2	(1979 - 1980)
Liam O'Brien	1	(1986)
Noel Peyton	5	(1956 - 1957)
Frank Radford	1	(1950)
Damien Richardson	1	(1968)
Jim Smith	1	(1932)
John Staines	2	(1947)
Mick Smyth	1	(1968)
Noel Synnott	1	(1979)
Liam Tuohy	24	(1954 - 1965)

INTER-LEAGUE GOALSCORERS

Paddy Ambrose	1
Eddie Bailham	4
Pat Byrne	1
Paddy Coad	2
Dermot Cross	1
Jimmy Dunne	2
John Joe Flood	3
Bob Fullam	2
Johnny Fullam	1
Billy 'Juicy' Farrell	1
Tommy Hamilton	1
Mick Leech	1
James 'Hooky' Leonard	1
Noel Larkin	1
'Maxie' McCann	3
Paddy Moore	2
Jackie Mooney	1
John Mannion	1
Ronnie Nolan	2
Frank O'Neill	1
Noel Peyton	1
Frank Radford	1
Liam Tuohy	7

THE TOP LEAGUE SCORERS

Paddy Ambrose	109
Paddy Coad	104
Bob Fullam	92
Frank O'Neill	87
Liam Tuohy	87
David 'Babby' Byrne	85
Mick Leech	84
Alan Campbell	71
Liam Buckley	67
John Joe Flood	61

Joe Ward	60
Billy 'Juicy' Farrell	58
Jimmy Dunne	52
Eddie Bailham	49
Mick Byrne	46
Jimmy 'Maxie' McCann	46
Tommy Hamilton	44
Ronnie Nolan	42
Mick Lawlor	41
Damien Richardson	41
Liam Hennessy	39
Jackie Mooney	38
Ray Treacy	35
Noel Larkin	34
William 'Sacky' Glen	32
John 'Kruger' Fagan	31
Paddy Moore	31
Tommy Foy	29
Vinny Arkins	28
Peter Eccles	26
Derek Swan	25
Johnny Fullam	24
Noel Peyton	24
Podge Gregg	23
Tony O'Connell	22
Bobby Gilbert	21
Liam O'Brien	21
Charlie Reid	21
Joseph 'Lye' Golding	20
Paul Doolin	20
Bob Duffy	19

LEADING LEAGUE GOALSCORERS PER SEASON

1922/23	Bob Fullam	27
1924/25	Billy 'Juicy' Farrell	25
1925/26	Billy 'Juicy' Farrell	24
1926/27	David 'Babby' Byrne	17
(shared with 'Jock' McMillan, Shelbourne)		
1946/47	Paddy Coad	11
(shared with Alf Hanson, Shelbourne)		
1956/57	Tommy Hamilton	15
(shared with Donal Leahy, Evergreen United)		
1961/62	Eddie Bailham	21
1963/64	Eddie Bailham	18
(shared with Jimmy Hasty, Dundalk and Johnny Kingston, Cork Hibs)		
1964/65	Jackie Mooney	16
1968/69	Mick Leech	19
1979/80	Alan Campbell	22
1983/84	Alan Campbell	24
1986/87	Mick Byrne	12

TOP SCORERS IN THE FAI CUP

Paddy Coad	37
Liam Tuohy	20
John Joe Flood	18
Mick Leech	18
Paddy Moore	18
'Podge' Gregg	14
David 'Babby' Byrne	13
Frank O'Neill	13
Eddie Bailham	12
Noel Larkin	12
Joe Ward	12
Mick Byrne	10
Jackie Mooney	11
Paddy Ambrose	10
Jimmy Dunne	10
Bob Fullam	9

Liam Hennessy   9
Tommy Hamilton   9
Mick Lawlor   8
Jimmy 'Maxie' McCann   7
Liam O'Brien (1984 - 1985)   7

SHAMROCK ROVERS' LEAGUE RECORD

Season	P	W	D	L	F	A	Pts.	Position
1922/23	22	18	3	1	77	19	39	1
1923/24	18	7	3	8	35	32	17	7
1924/25	18	13	5	0	67	12	31	1
1925/26	18	13	3	2	62	21	29	2
1926/27	18	14	4	0	60	20	32	1
1927/28	18	9	7	2	41	18	25	3
1928/29	18	10	4	4	58	28	24	3
1929/30	18	12	2	4	44	22	26	3
1930/31	22	9	5	8	54	49	23	7
1931/32	22	13	6	3	70	34	32	1
1932/33	18	11	2	5	48	32	24	2
1933/34	18	9	4	5	28	23	22	3
1934/35	18	5	6	7	27	33	16	6
1935/36	22	10	2	10	61	58	22	6
1936/37	22	8	3	11	46	55	19	9
1937/38	22	14	4	4	71	47	32	1
1938/39	22	16	4	2	60	32	36	1
1939/40	22	13	4	5	51	39	30	2
1940/41	20	9	3	8	48	43	21	4
1941/42	18	12	4	2	52	23	28	2
1942/43	18	8	4	6	36	28	20	4
1943/44	14	5	5	4	38	27	15	3
1944/45	14	6	5	3	20	20	17	3
1945/46	14	6	2	6	40	31	14	4
1946/47	14	7	3	4	34	21	17	3
1947/48	14	4	6	4	26	24	14	4
1948/49	18	6	8	4	33	25	20	4

1949/50	18	7	4	7	39	30	18	7
1950/51	18	7	3	8	33	30	17	6
1951/52	22	12	5	5	43	18	29	3
1952/53	22	12	3	7	40	27	27	3
1953/54	22	11	8	3	44	20	30	1
1954/55	22	12	4	6	63	37	28	3
1955/56	22	15	1	6	54	30	31	2
1956/57	22	15	6	1	68	24	36	1
1957/58	22	15	1	6	55	26	31	2
1958/59	22	15	4	3	58	29	34	1
1959/60	22	12	3	7	54	31	27	4
1960/61	22	9	7	6	40	29	25	6
1961/62	22	14	3	5	51	32	31	3
1962/63	18	7	5	6	36	25	19	5
1963/64	22	14	7	1	68	27	35	1
1964/65	22	14	3	5	40	22	31	2
1965/66	22	15	4	3	59	23	34	2
1966/67	22	8	4	10	31	31	20	7
1967/68	22	11	5	6	44	26	27	4
1968/69	22	14	3	5	56	28	31	2
1969/70	26	14	8	4	55	29	36	2
1970/71	26	14	7	5	49	38	35	2
1971/72	26	12	4	10	52	41	28	5
1972/73	26	12	6	8	45	32	30	5
1973/74	26	11	5	10	31	33	27	5
1974/75	26	10	5	11	40	38	25	8
1975/76	26	4	7	15	27	49	15	last
1976/77	26	7	3	16	26	46	17	11
1977/78	30	14	12	4	45	22	40	4
1978/79	30	17	3	10	45	25	37	5
1979/80	30	14	10	6	61	29	38	4
1980/81	30	14	8	8	37	29	36	5
1981/82	30	21	3	6	50	23	76	2
1982/83	26	10	8	8	39	25	38	6
1983/84	26	19	4	3	64	15	42	1
1984/85	30	22	5	3	63	21	49	1

1985/86	22	15	3	4	44	17	33	1
1986/87	22	18	3	1	51	16	39	1
1987/88	33	16	9	8	53	30	41	4
1988/89	33	8	13	12	34	42	29	7
1989/90	33	16	8	9	45	37	40	4
1990/91	33	14	9	10	51	37	37	6
1991/92	33	9	15	9	33	30	33	6
1992/93	32	8	12	12	39	35	28	8
Total:	1609	825	364	420	3342	2100	2055	

NOTES

(1) Shamrock Rovers and Cork Hibernians were level on points at the end of the 1970/71 season. Cork Hibs won the resultant play-off for the title. The statistics above do not include that play-off.

(2) An experimental points system was operated for the 1981/82 season whereby a team was awarded four points for an away win, three points for a home win, two points for an away draw and one point for a home draw.

(3) In 1982/83 three points were awarded for a win and one point for a draw. The system reverted the following season to the pre-1981/82 system, i.e. two points for a win and one point for a draw.

(4) From 1985/86, league figures apply to the Premier Division.

(5) In 1992/93 the Premier Division 'split' into two sections of six after the 22nd series of games had been played on 17 January. Rovers did not qualify for the top six and finished in second place of the bottom six (Group 'B') or eighth place overall.

ROVERS IN EUROPE

Summary of games

Season	Opponents	Competition
1957/58	Manchester United (England)	European Cup
1959/60	OGC Nice (France)	European Cup
1962/63	Botev Plovdiv (Bulgaria)	Cup Winners' Cup
1963/64	Valencia (Spain)	Fairs Cup
1964/65	Rapid Vienna (Austria)	European Cup
1965/66	Real Zaragosa (Spain)	Fairs Cup
1966/67	Spora Luxembourg (Luxembourg)	Cup Winners' Cup
1966/67	Bayern Munich (West Germany)	Cup Winners' Cup
1967/68	Cardiff City (Wales)	Cup Winners' Cup
1968/69	Randers Freja (Denmark)	Cup Winners' Cup
1969/70	Schalke 04 (West Germany)	Cup Winners' Cup
1978/79	Apoel Nicosia (Cyprus)	Cup Winners' Cup
1978/79	Banik Ostrava (Czechslovakia)	Cup Winners' Cup
1982/83	Fram Reykjavik (Iceland)	UEFA Cup
1982/83	Universitatea Craiova (Romania)	UEFA Cup
1984/85	Linfield (Northern Ireland)	European Cup
1985/86	BP Honved (Hungary)	European Cup
1986/87	Glasgow Celtic (Scotland)	European Cup
1987/88	Omonia Nicosia (Cyprus)	European Cup

SHAMROCK ROVERS' RECORD IN EUROPE:

	P	W	D	L	F	A
European Cup	14	0	4	10	7	28
Fairs Cup	4	0	2	2	4	6
UEFA Cup	4	2	0	2	7	5
Cup Winners' Cup	16	5	2	9	19	27
Total	38	7	8	23	37	66

SUMMARY OF GOALSCORERS

EUROPEAN CUP

John Coady	1
Peter Eccles	1
Tommy Hamilton	2
Liam Hennessy	1
Maxie McCann	1
Liam Tuohy	1

UEFA CUP

Jim Beglin	1
Liam Buckley	1
Alan Campbell	1
Tommy Gaynor	2
Ronnie Murphy	1
Gay O'Carroll	1

EUROPEAN CUP WINNERS' CUP

Eric Barber	2
Billy Dixon	4
Johnny Fullam	2
Bobby Gilbert	2
Johnny Giles	2
Nick Kearin	2
Steve Lynex	2
Frank O'Neill	2
Liam Tuohy	1

*For the 1972/73 season the League runners-up were nominated for the UEFA Cup place. Before that the winners of the Shield, or runners-up if the winners went on to win the League or FAI Cup, were nominated for the Fairs Cup which was organised independently from UEFA by the Fairs Cup Committee.

FAIRS CUP*

Johnny Fullam	1
Jackie Mooney	1
Liam Tuohy	2

FAI CUP FINAL TEAMS, RESULTS, SCORERS
(All games at Dalymount Park unless otherwise stated)

17 MARCH 1922

St James's Gate	1 (Kelly)
Shamrock Rovers	1 (Campbell)

'Gate': Paddy Coleman, Tom Murphy, 'Fatty' Kavanagh, Ernie McKay, Frank Hearney, Bob Carter, Johnny Carey, Jack Kelly, Paddy Duncan, Charlie Dowdall, Johnny Gargan.
Rovers: Bill Nagle, Jim Kelly, Peter Warren, William 'Sacky' Glen,

Joe 'Buller' Byrne, Harry Birdthistle, Charlie Campbell, Bob
Cowzer, John Joe Flood, Bob Fullam, Dinny Doyle.
Attendance: 15,000 (£636). Referee: Mr Broderick (Athlone)

8 APRIL 1922, FINAL REPLAY
St James's Gate   1 (Kelly)
Shamrock Rovers   0
Changes: 'Gate', Bill O'Shea for Carter; Rovers, unchanged
Attendance: 10,000 (£407).

17 MARCH 1925
Shamrock Rovers   2 (Fullam, Flood)
Shelbourne   1 (Glen o.g.)
Rovers: Paddy O'Reilly, Alec Kirkland, John Malone, William
'Sacky' Glen, Dinny Doyle, Ned Marlowe, Charlie Jordan, Bob
Fullam, Billy 'Juicy' Farrell, John Joe Flood, John 'Kruger' Fagan.
Shelbourne: Paddy Walsh, Frank Daly, Paddy Kavanagh,—Kelly,
Val Harris, Mick Foley, Bob Laxton, Bob Cowzer, John Doran,
Terry Mulvanny, Sammy Wilson.
Attendance: 23,000 (£1,235). Referee: W. J. Howcroft (England)

17 MARCH 1926
Fordsons   3 (Barry 2, Roberts)
Shamrock Rovers   2 (Farrell, Fagan)
Fordsons: Bill O'Hagan, Jack Baylor, Jimmy Corabine, James
Connolly, Jack O'Sullivan, Barney Collins, Malachy McKinney,
Paddy Kelly, Dave Roberts, Harry Buckle, Paddy Barry.
Rovers: Paddy O'Reilly, John Malone, Alec Kirkland, William
'Sacky' Glen, Dinny Doyle, Ned Marlowe, Charlie 'Spid' Jordan,
John Joe Flood, Billy 'Juicy' Farrell, Bob Fullam, John 'Kruger'
Fagan.
Attendance: 25,000 (£1,528). Referee: A. E. Fogg (Bolton)

18 MARCH 1929
Shamrock Rovers   0
Bohemians   0
Rovers: Paddy O'Reilly, Jim Maguire, John Burke, William 'Sacky'
Glen, Tom Caulfield, Ned Marlowe, John 'Lye' Golding, John Joe

Flood, Jack Sloan, Bob Fullam, 'Emmer' Sherwin.

Bohemians: Harry Cannon, Mick O'Kane, Jack McCarthy, Paddy O'Kane, Johnny McMahon, Alec Morton, Jimmy Birmingham, Billy Dennis, Jimmy White, Fred Horlacher, Peter Kavanagh. Attendance: 22,000 (£1,500). Referee: R. H. Bull (Burnley)

6 APRIL 1929, FINAL REPLAY (AT SHELBOURNE PARK)

Shamrock Rovers	3 (Flood 2, Fullam)
Bohemians	0

Changes: Rovers, Charlie Campbell for Sherwin; Bohemians, unchanged. Attendance: 15,000 (£713).

17 MARCH 1930

Shamrock Rovers	1 (Byrne)
Brideville	0

Rovers: Paddy O'Reilly, Francis Cervi, John Burke, William 'Sacky' Glen, Tom Caulfield, Ned Marlowe, John Joe Flood, Jack Sloan, David 'Babby' Byrne, John 'Lye' Golding, Bob Fullam. Brideville: Charlie O'Callaghan, Paddy Kenny, Paddy Bermingham, Joe O'Reilly, Bill Charles, Johnny Fox, Jack Smith, Peader Gaskins, Davy Blair, Charlie Reid, Paul O'Brien. Attendance: 17,000 (£1,160).

18 APRIL 1931

Shamrock Rovers	1 (Moore)
Dundalk	1 (McCourt)

Rovers: Billy Behan, Francis Cervi, John Burke, William 'Sacky' Glen, Tom Caulfield, Owen Kinsella, 'Diller' Delaney, Paddy Moore, David 'Babby' Byrne, John Joe Flood, John 'Lye' Golding. Dundalk: Sam McMullen, Tommy McKeon, Clancey McDiarmuid, Jack Slowey, Ted Reid, Dicky Johnstone, Gerry McCourt, Owen McCahill, Ledger Firth, Harry Hirst, Joey Donnelly.
Attendance: 20,000 (£1,122). Referee: H. N. Mee (Nottingham)

9 MAY 1931, FINAL REPLAY

Shamrock Rovers   1 (Moore)

Dundalk   0

Changes: Rovers, Paddy O'Reilly for Behan, Bob Fullam for
Delaney; Dundalk, unchanged

Attendance: 10,000 (£806).

17 APRIL 1932

Shamrock Rovers   1 (Moore)

Dolphin   0

Rovers: Mick McCarthy, Jimmy Daly, John Burke, William 'Sacky'
Glen, Vincent Matthews, Owen Kinsella, David 'Babby' Byrne,
John Joe Flood, Paddy Moore, Jock McMillan, Jimmy Smith.

Dolphin: Jimmy Power, Bobby Nisbet, Larry Doyle, Joe 'Sam'
Robinson, Gerry Kelly, Jimmy Watt, Jimmy Smith, Alec
Stevenson, Jimmy Shields, Johnny Somers, Danny Patterson.

Attendance: 32,000 (£1,710). Referee: Mr Cresswell (England)

17 MARCH 1933

Shamrock Rovers   3 (Byrne, Buchanan, Matthews pen.)

Dolphin   3 (Lennox 2 pens, Fallon)

Rovers: Mick McCarthy, Peader Gaskins, John Burke, William
'Sacky' Glen, Vincent Matthews, Owen Kinsella, Jimmy Daly,
John Joe Flood, David 'Babby' Byrne, Jimmy 'Scot' Buchanan,
Jimmy Smith.

Dolphin: Slater, George Lennox, Larry Doyle, Jimmy Watt, Gerry
Kelly, Joe Hendrick, Jimmy Bermingham, Jimmy Weldon, Owen
McCarney, Johnny Somers, Willie Fallon.

Attendance: 22,000 (£1,522). Referee: W. F. Bunnell (Preston)

26 MARCH 1933, FINAL REPLAY

Shamrock Rovers   3 (Daly 2, Byrne)

Dolphin   0

Changes: Dolphin, Charlie Reid for Jimmy Bermingham; Rovers,
unchanged

Attendance: 18,000 (£1,410).

19 APRIL 1936

Shamrock Rovers   2 (Moore, Reid)

Cork   1 (Turnbull)

Rovers: Billy Behan, Joe Williams, Peader Gaskins, William 'Sacky' Glen, Jim Blake, Owen Kinsella, Mick Byrne, Paddy Moore, Charlie Reid, Joe Ward, Denis 'Dinger' Dunne.

Cork: Bill Harrington, Hugh Foy, Charlie Wade, Bill Williams, Billy Little, Hugh Connolly, Jack O'Reilly, Bernie King, Jimmy Turnbull, Owen Madden, Andy Percy.

Attendance: 30,946 (£1,899).

21 APRIL 1940

Shamrock Rovers   3 (Ward, Fallon, Dunne)

Sligo Rovers   0

Rovers: Mick McCarthy, Mattie Clarke, Shay Healy, Harry Finnegan, Bobby Bryson, Joe Creevy, Joe Ward, Jimmy Dunne, Jimmy Clark, Bill Cameron, Billy Fallon.

Sligo: Jimmy Twomey, Denis Thompson, Bill Powell, Jim McCann, Alf Peachey, Tom Arrigan, Matt Began, Bob Gregg, Joe McAleer, Jimmy Connor, Sam Prout.

Attendance: 38,509 (£2,225). Referee: H. Mattrass (Sunderland)

16 APRIL 1944

Shamrock Rovers   3 (Rogers, Gannon o.g., Crowe)

Shelbourne   2 (Fallon, McCluskey)

Rovers: Larry Palmer, Joe Nolan, Mattie Clarke, Matt Doherty, Charlie Byrne, Peter Farrell, Mickey Delaney, Paddy Coad, Liam Crowe, Bobby Rogers, Tommy Eglington.

Shelbourne: Fred Kiernan, Arthur Whelan, Johnny Olphert, Eddie Gannon, Paddy Kinsella, Charlie Mullally, Billy Kennedy, Joe Cassidy, Mick McCluskey, Sid Walsh, Willie Fallon.

Attendance: 34,000 (£2,048).

22 APRIL 1945

Shamrock Rovers   1 (Gregg)

Bohemians   0

Rovers: Larry Palmer, Mattie Clarke, Jackie Coyle, Matt Doherty, Charlie Byrne, Peter Farrell, Mickey Delaney, Paddy Coad, Podge Gregg, Bobby Rogers, Tommy Eglington.

Bohemians: Jimmy Collins, Frank Glennon, Billy Richardson, Ossie Nash, Peter Molloy, Pat Waters, Kevin O'Flanagan, Noel Kelly, Mattie Burns, Frank Morris, Mick O'Flanagan.

Attendance: 41,238 (£2,441).

21 APRIL 1946

Drumcondra	2 (McCormack, Henderson)
Shamrock Rovers	1 (Coad)

Drumcondra: Peter Keogh, Con Martin, Joe Barnwell, Joseph 'Robin' Lawlor, Kevin Clarke, Jim O'Mara, Benny 'Rosie' Henderson, Dermot Delaney, Tommy McCormack, Jimmy Lawlor, Leo Ward.

Rovers: Jimmy Collins, Mattie Clarke, Frank Glennon, Noel Kelly, Charlie Byrne, Peter Farrell, Davy Cochrane, Paddy Coad, Mickey Delaney, Jimmy McAlinden, Tommy Eglington.

Attendance: 34,248 (£2,856). Referee: W. Keane (Limerick)

11 APRIL 1948

Shamrock Rovers	2 (Coad, Kirby)
Drumcondra	1 (Henderson)

Rovers: Jimmy Collins, Mattie Clarke, Jackie Coyle, Ossie Nash, Bobby Rogers, Tommy Dunne, Frank Glennon, Paddy Coad, Podge Gregg, Des Treacy, Eugene Kirby.

Drumcondra: Peter Keogh, Jimmy Robinson, Joe Barnwell, Tommy Kinsella, Kevin Clarke, Billy Mulville, Christy Giles, John 'Kit' Lawlor, Dermot Delaney, Paddy Daly, Benny 'Rosie' Henderson.

Attendance: 33,812 (£3,615). Referee: E. Whelan

24 APRIL 1955

Shamrock Rovers	1 (Tuohy)
Drumcondra	0

Rovers: Christy O'Callaghan, Mickey Burke, Gerry Mackey, Ronnie Nolan, Shay Keogh, Liam Hennessy, Jimmy 'Maxie'

McCann, Noel Peyton, Paddy Ambrose, Hughie Gannon, Liam Tuohy.

Drumcondra: Paddy Neville, Shay Noonan, Pat Lynch, Tommy Kinsella, Johnny Robinson, Dessie Glynn, Benny 'Rosie' Henderson, Tommy Rowe, Eddie O'Hara, Stan Pownall, Bob Duffy.

Attendance: 33,041 (£4,467). Referee: A. Ellis (Halifax)

29 APRIL 1956

| Shamrock Rovers | 3 (Hamilton, Hennessy pen., Nolan) |
| Cork Athletic | 2 (Delaney, Murphy) |

Rovers: Christy O'Callaghan, Mickey Burke, Ronnie Nolan, Paddy Coad, Gerry Mackey, Liam Hennessy, Jimmy 'Maxie' McCann, Noel Peyton, Paddy Ambrose, Tommy Hamilton, Liam Tuohy.

Cork: Pascal O'Toole, Paddy Noonan, Dave Noonan, Johnny Moloney, John Coughlan, Tim Daly, John Horgan, Tommy Collins, Jimmy Delaney, Jimmy Murphy, Donie Wallace.

Attendance: 35,017 (£4,657). Referee: Mr Bond (London)

28 APRIL 1957

| Drumcondra | 2 (Fullam pen., Coleman) |
| Shamrock Rovers | 0 |

Drumcondra: Alan Kelly, Christy 'Bunny' Fullam, George McDonnell, Brendan Healy, John 'Sonny' O'Neill, Tommy Rowe, Stan Pownall, John 'Kit' Lawlor, Mickey Gorman, Jackie McCourt, Willie Coleman.

Rovers: Eamonn 'Sheila' Darcy, Mickey Burke, Shay Keogh, Ronnie Nolan, Gerry Mackey, Liam Hennessy, Jimmy 'Maxie' McCann, Noel Peyton, Paddy Ambrose, Paddy Coad, Liam Tuohy.

Attendance: 30,000 (£4,000).

20 APRIL 1958

| Dundalk | 1 (Gannon) |
| Shamrock Rovers | 0 |

Dundalk: Ted McNeill, Joe Ralph, Ken Finn, Leo McDonagh, Johnny Robinson, Shay Noonan, Niall McGahon, Hughie

Gannon, Vincent Gilmore, George Toner, Tommy Kerr.
Rovers: Christy O'Callaghan, Mickey Burke, Gerry Mackey,
Ronnie Nolan, Tommy Farrell, Liam Hennessy, Jimmy 'Maxie'
McCann, Sean Carroll, Paddy Ambrose, Paddy Coad, Liam Tuohy.
Attendance: 27,000. Referee: B. H. Howell (Birmingham)

28 APRIL 1962

Shamrock Rovers	4 (Ambrose 2, Hamilton 2)
Shelbourne	1 (Barber)

Rovers: Paddy Henderson, John Keogh, Pat Courtney, Ronnie
Nolan, Tommy Farrell, Eamonn Farrell, Frank O'Neill, Tommy
Hamilton, Eddie Bailham, Paddy Ambrose, Tony O'Connell.
Shelbourne: John Heavey, Tommy Carroll, Brendan O'Brien,
Paddy Bonham, Freddie Strahan, Paddy Roberts, Joey Wilson, Ben
Hannigan, Eric Barber, Jackie Hennessy, Ollie Conroy.
Attendance: 32,000 (£4,600). Referee: S. Spillane (Cork)

26 APRIL 1964

Shamrock Rovers	1 (Mooney)
Cork Celtic	1 (Leahy)

Rovers: Pat Dunne, John Keogh, Pat Courtney, Ronnie Nolan,
Tommy Farrell, Johnny Fullam, Frank O'Neill, Jackie Mooney,
Eddie Bailham, Paddy Ambrose, Liam Tuohy.
Cork Celtic: Kevin Blount, Liam O'Flynn, Pat O'Mahony, Ray
Cowhie, John Coughlan, Mick Millington, Paul O'Donovan,
Austin Noonan, Donal Leahy, Al Casey, Frank McCarthy.
Attendance: 35,500 (£5,500). Referee: D. A. Corbett
(Wolverhampton)

29 APRIL 1964, FINAL REPLAY

Shamrock Rovers	2 (Bailham 2, 1 pen.)
Cork Celtic	1 (Casey)

Changes: Rovers, Tony Byrne for O'Neill. Sub: Sean Smyth for
Tommy Farrell (injured), 20 mins; Cork, George Lynam for
Coughlan
Attendance: 23,600 (£3,600).

25 APRIL 1965

Shamrock Rovers   1 (Dunne)

Limerick   1 (Mulvey)

Rovers: Mick Smyth, John Keogh, Pat Courtney, Ronnie Nolan, Tommy Farrell, Paddy Mulligan, Frank O'Neill, Jackie Mooney, Noel Dunne, Johnny Fullam, Liam Tuohy.

Limerick: Kevin Fitzpatrick, Vinny Quinn, Joe Casey, Al Finucane, Ewan Fenton, Dessie McNamara, Dick O'Connor, Eddie Mulvey, Peter Mitchell, Paddy 'Ginger' O'Rourke, Mick Doyle. Sub: Denis Linnane for Doyle, 41 mins.

Attendance: 22,000

28 APRIL 1965, FINAL REPLAY

Shamrock Rovers   1 (Fullam)

Limerick   0

Changes: Rovers, Tony O'Connell for Tuohy; Limerick, Denis Linnane for Doyle

Attendance: 19,436

24 APRIL 1966

Shamrock Rovers   2 (O'Connell, O'Neill)

Limerick   0

Rovers: Mick Smyth, John Keogh, Pat Courtney, Paddy Mulligan, Ronnie Nolan, Johnny Fullam, Frank O'Neill, Brian Tyrrell, Bobby Gilbert, Tony O'Connell, Noel Hayes.

Limerick: Kevin Fitzpatrick, Vinny Quinn, Joe Casey, Al Finucane, Ewan Fenton, Dessie McNamara, Dick O'Connor, Tommy Hamilton, Eddie Mulvey, Joe O'Brien, Pascal Curtin.

Attendance: 26,898 (£5,636). Referee: P. Graham (Dublin)

23 APRIL 1967

Shamrock Rovers   3 (O'Neill pen., Leech, Dixon)

St Patrick's Ath.   2 (Dunne, Bates)

Rovers: Mick Smyth, John Keogh, Pat Courtney, Johnny Fullam, Paddy Mulligan, Mick Kearin, Frank O'Neill, Billy Dixon, Bobby Gilbert, Mick Leech, Tommy Kinsella.

St Patrick's: Dinny Lowry, Paddy Dowling, Vinny O'Reilly, Willie
Roche, Doug Boucher, Jackie Hennessy, Gerry Monaghan, Noel
Dunne, Noel Bates, Johnny Campbell, Willie Peyton.
Attendance: 12,000. Referee: Mr Coates

21 APRIL 1968

Shamrock Rovers   3 (Leech 2, Lawlor)
Waterford   0
Rovers: Mick Smyth, Jimmy Gregg, Pat Courtney, Mick Kearin,
Frank Brady, Johnny Fullam, Frank O'Neill, Mick Lawlor, Bobby
Gilbert, Mick Leech, Damien Richardson.
Waterford: Peter Thomas, Peter Bryan, Paul Morrissey, Vinny
Maguire, Jackie Morley, Jimmy McGeough, John O'Neill, Alfie
Hale, Mick Lynch, Shamie Coad, Johnny Matthews.
Attendance: 39,128 (£8,500). Referee: Owen McCarthy (Cork)

20 APRIL 1969

Shamrock Rovers   1 (Keogh o.g.)
Cork Celtic   1 (Carroll)
Rovers: Mick Smyth, Christy Canavan, Pat Courtney, Paddy
Mulligan, David Pugh, Mick Kearin, Frank O'Neill, Ben
Hannigan, Mick Leech, Mick Lawlor, Tom Kinsella. Sub: Hugh
Brophy for Leech, 79 mins.
Cork Celtic: Tommy Taylor, John Keogh, Pat O'Mahony, Liam
Ronayne, Eamonn Heffernan, Billy McCullough, Paddy Shortt,
John Carroll, Donal Leahy, Les Wilson, Frank McCarthy.
Attendance: 28,000 (£6,900). Referee: J. Carpenter (Dublin)

23 APRIL 1969, FINAL REPLAY

Shamrock Rovers   4 (Leech 2, Kearin, Richardson)
Cork Celtic   1 (McCarthy)
Changes: Rovers, Damien Richardson for Hannigan, Hugh Brophy
for Kinsella; Cork, unchanged.
Attendance: 18,000 (£5,000).

30 APRIL 1978

Shamrock Rovers   1 (Treacy pen.)

Sligo Rovers   0

Shamrock Rovers: Alan O'Neill, Mick Gannon, Pierce O'Leary, Noel Synnott, Johnny Fullam, Eamonn Dunphy, Johnny Giles, Mark Meagan, Larry Murray, Ray Treacy, Steve Lynex. Sub: Eddie O'Sullivan for Gannon, 63 mins.

Sligo Rovers: Alan Patterson, Paul Fielding, Chris Rutherford, Tony Stenson, Graham Fox, John Gilligan, Tony Fagan, Don Tobin, Tony Cavanagh, Gary Hulmes, John Delamere. Sub: Harry McLoughlin for Delamere, 77 mins.

Attendance: 12,500 (£17,500). Referee: J. Carpenter (Dublin)

29 APRIL 1984

University College

Dublin   0

Shamrock Rovers   0

UCD: Alan O'Neill, Robbie Lawlor, Ken O'Doherty, Paddy Dunning, Martin Moran, Robbie Gaffney, Keith Dignam, John Cullen, Aidan Reynolds, Frank Devlin, Joe Hanrahan.
Sub: Brendan Murphy for Reynolds, 78 mins.

Rovers: Jody Byrne, Anto Whelan, Jacko McDonagh, Dermot Keely, John Coady, Neville Steedman, Noel King, Pat Byrne, Mick Neville, Alan Campbell, Liam Buckley. Sub: Terry Eviston for Whelan, 78 mins.

Attendance: 8,000. Referee: J. Carpenter (Dublin)

4 MAY 1984, FINAL REPLAY (AT TOLKA PARK)

University College

Dublin   2 (Hanrahan, O'Doherty)

Shamrock Rovers   1 (McDonagh, pen.)

Changes: UCD, Brendan Murphy for Reynolds; Rovers, unchanged.

Attendance: 6,500.

28 April 1985

Shamrock Rovers   1 (Larkin)

Galway United   0

Rovers: Jody Byrne, Mick Neville, Dermot Keely, Jacko McDonagh, Kevin Brady, Liam O'Brien, Pat Byrne, Noel King, John Coady, Noel Larkin, Mick Byrne.

Galway: Tom Lally, Gerry Daly, Brian Gardiner, Denis Bonner, Jimmy Nolan, Eamonn Deacy, John Mannion, Martin McDonnell, Paul Murphy, Kevin Cassidy, John Glynn. Sub: Noel Mernagh for Glynn, 76 mins.

Attendance: 7,000. Referee: Wilifred Wallace (Donegal)

27 April 1986

Shamrock Rovers   2 (Brady, Synnott o.g.)

Waterford United   0

Rovers: Jody Byrne, Harry Kenny, Mick Neville, Peter Eccles, Kevin Brady, Paul Doolin, Pat Byrne, Liam O'Brien, John Coady, Mick Byrne, Noel Larkin.

Waterford: David Flavin, Derek Grace, Kevin Power, Noel Synnott, Duncan Burns, Jimmy Donnelly, Tony Macken, Kieron McCabe, Terry Kearns, Mick Bennett, Martin Reid. Subs: Vinny McCarthy for McCabe h.t.; Noel Bollard for Grace, 64 mins.

Attendance: 11,500. Referee: E. Farrell (Dublin)

26 April 1987

Shamrock Rovers   3 (Kenny pen., Byrne, Larkin)

Dundalk   0

Rovers: Jody Byrne, Harry Kenny, Mick Neville, Peter Eccles, Kevin Brady, Paul Doolin, Pat Byrne, Keith Dignam, Brendan Murphy, Mick Byrne, Noel Larkin.

Dundalk: Alan O'Neill, Gino Lawless, Joey Malone, Harry McCue, Martin Lawlor, Larry Wyse, Martin Murray, Barry Kehoe, Terry Eviston, Dessie Gorman, Tom McNulty.

Attendance: 8,569. Referee: P. Kelly (Cork)

12 MAY 1991

Galway United   1 (Glynn)

Shamrock Rovers   0

Galway: Declan McIntyré, Johnny Morris-Burke, Derek Rodgers, John Cleary, Jimmy Nolan, Paul Campbell, Larry Wyse, Peter Carpenter, Tommy Keane, Noel Mernagh, John Glynn. Subs: Stephen Lally for Morris-Burke, 60 mins; Kevin Cassidy for Wyse, 87 mins.

Rovers: Paul Kavanagh, John Devine, Peter Eccles, Barry Murphy, Wayne Cooney, Dave Connell, Neil Poutch, David Campbell, Derek Treacy, Vinny Arkins, Derek Swan. Subs: Sean Byrne for Devine and Barry O'Connor for Poutch, 87 mins.

Attendance: 15,257. Referee: John Purcell (Dublin)

INDEX